Word 2000 VBA Programmer's Reference

Duncan Mackenzie
Felipe Martins

Wrox Press Ltd. ®

Word 2000 VBA Programmer's Reference

© 1999 Wrox Press

Published by Wrox Press Ltd. Arden House, 1102 Warwick Road, Acocks Green, Birmingham, B27 6BH.

Printed in USA

ISBN 1-861002-5-56

Trademark Acknowledgements

Wrox has endeavored to provide trademark information about all the companies and products mentioned in this book by the appropriate use of capitals. However, Wrox cannot guarantee the accuracy of this information.

Credits

Author
Duncan Mackenzie
Felipe Martins

Development Editor
Dominic Shakeshaft

Editors
Sarah Bowers
Kate Hall

Technical Reviewers
Mark Bell
Max Dahl
Chris Devrell
Erick Nelson
Elizabeth Seifert
Joe Sutphin
Richard Ward
Sakhr Youness

Cover
Andrew Guillaume
Image by Rita Ruban

Design/Layout
Noel Donnelly

Index
Andrew Criddle

About the Authors

Duncan Mackenzie

Duncan Mackenzie provides consulting and training in Visual Basic and Visual Basic for Applications through Scribe Technologies, based out of Winnipeg, Manitoba. He can be reached at duncan@scribe.mb.ca, or through his web site at http://www.scribe.mb.ca

Although this is his first complete book, Duncan's writing has appeared in five books on Visual Basic and Visual InterDev, and he has been a technical editor for numerous published works.

During the few minutes each day when he is not writing, coding, training, or sleeping, he spends quality time with his wife Laura and their two cats.

Felipe Martins

Felipe Martins is an MCSD and MCT who has been programming with Office products and VB for many years, building applications in the manufacturing, healthcare, and aerospace industries. He currently works for ImagiNET Resources Corp. as a Senior Solutions Developer. ImagiNET Resources Corp supplies clients with leading edge business solutions by employing highly skilled and experienced people who are experts at using Microsoft technologies.

Currently Felipe can be found somewhere in a Starbucks in Winnipeg, Canada.

Felipe Martins can be reached at fmartins@imaginets.com

Acknowlegements

Above all else, I'd like to thank my wife Laura; I don't think I could have written this book without her support and understanding. I would also like to extend my gratitude to my friend, Felipe Martins, who provided this book with a wonderfully complete and detailed reference section. Finally, I am also grateful to everyone at Wrox who was involved with this book including Dominic Shakeshaft, Kate Hall, Sarah Bowers, and many others. I am extremely thankful that they asked me to write this book, and even more thankful for their support when I decided to do so. *Duncan Mackenzie*

To my beautiful wife, Angie, and to my daughter, Marissa. *Felipe Martins*

Table of Contents

Introduction

Word 2000 is the most recent edition of Microsoft's popular word processing product. Since Word 97, Visual Basic for Applications (VBA) has been included with Word allowing users to control the way they work with Word. We can now automate procedures so that we can work quicker and more efficiently. We can create VBA applications that use Word 2000. We can even take advantage of the integration of Office 2000 to create Word documents from information contained in Access, Excel and Outlook.

Who This Book Is For?

This book is aimed at power users who just want to know how to do useful things more quickly, administrative and support staff who need to create template libraries and other internal applications, and developers who want to build an application that uses Word 2000, either through VBA or from another language (usually Visual Basic itself) or Office application.

What This Book Contains

The first part of this book provides a general introduction to VBA programming and the features of Word 2000. It is designed to be read as a whole and in sequence. The first part includes:

- ❏ Chapter 1, Macros. This chapter provides an introduction to macros and the Visual Basic for Applications environment.

- ❏ Chapter2, VBA Fundamentals. This chapter introduces objects, properties, variables and arrays. These are the backbone of VBA and you will be using these throughout your projects.

- ❏ Chapter 3, Conditionals and Loops. To get your code to do anything really useful you need to give it decision-making capabilities and the ability to repeat blocks of code if necessary. This chapter deals with the various different methods of controlling the flow of your program using conditionals and loops.

- ❏ Chapter 4, Forms and Controls. Your program may need input from the user to operate; alternatively you may want to show the results of program to the user through a dialog box or window. This chapter introduces the forms and controls available to you so that you can provide an interface for your users.

- ❏ Chapter 5, Word 2000 Development. This chapter provides guidelines for Word development as well as a brief introduction to the Word 2000 object model.

In the second part of the book, standalone projects show various techniques used in Word development. Each chapter includes one or more projects and, although a project may touch on a topic covered in another chapter, the chapters can be read individually and out of sequence. The chapters in the second part are:

- ❑ Chapter 6, Creating Documents. The projects in this chapter will show you how to create a fax coversheet for the current document, ask the user for information and use Outlook information from Word 2000.

- ❑ Chapter 7, Document Management. In this chapter, the projects will show you how to create a summary of a group of documents, batch process files and work with custom document properties.

- ❑ Chapter 8, Databases. This chapter shows you how to connect your VBA projects to databases and create documents from the information retrieved.

- ❑ Chapter 9, More Databases. Following on from the previous chapter, this one will show you to create and control tables, to format the information from your database into an easily readable form. There are two example projects: a product price list and an order invoice.

- ❑ Chapter 10, External Applications. This chapter will show you how to use VBA to access other Office applications. Useful functions of Outlook and Excel are covered as well as how to control Word from another Visual Basic or VBA application.

Part 3 of this book will include a detailed description of the Word 2000 object model, a VBA reference section (covering the objects, properties and methods, as well as functions and statements), a summary of the ADO (ActiveX Data Objects) object model and a brief introduction to programming the Office Assistant.

What Do I Need to Use this Book?

The most important thing you'll need to use this book is Word 2000. However, an important advantage to programming in Word VBA is that it allows you to access the functionality of the other Office 2000 applications. For that reason, included in this book are example projects using Outlook 2000, Excel 2000 and Access 2000.

Conventions

We have used a number of different styles of text and layout in the book to help differentiate between the different kinds of information. Here are examples of the styles we use and an explanation of what they mean:

Advice, hints and background information comes in this type of font.

Important pieces of information come in boxes like this.

Bullets appear indented, with each new bullet marked as follows:

❑   **Important Words** are in a bold type font

❑   Words that appear on the screen, in menus like the File or Window, are in a similar font to that which you see on screen

❑   Keys that you press on the keyboard, like *Ctrl* and *Enter*, are in italics

Code has several fonts. If it's a word that we're talking about in the text – for example, when discussing the For...Next loop – it's in this font. If it's a block of code that you can type in as a program and run, then it's also in a gray box:

```
Documents.Add
```

Sometimes you'll see code in a mixture of styles, like this:

```
Selection.Font.Bold = True

If ActiveDocument.Bookmarks.Exists("InvoiceNumber") Then
    ActiveDoument.Bookmarks("InvoiceNumber") = iInvoiceNumber
End If
```

The code with a white background is code we've already looked at and that we don't wish to examine further.

Source Code

You'll find all the code from the projects, the templates used and the Java Jitters database on the Wrox Press web site:

http://www.wrox.com

You'll also find information on forthcoming books, sample chapters and interviews with authors. You can even order your next Wrox Press book.

Tell Us What You Think

We've worked hard on this book to make it useful. We've tried to understand what you're willing to exchange your hard-earned money for, and we've tried to make the book live up to your expectations.

Please let us know what you think about this book. Tell us what we did wrong, and what we did right. We take your feedback seriously – if you don't believe us, then send us a note. We'll answer, and we'll take on board whatever you say for future editions. The easiest way is to use email:

http://feedback@wrox.com

1

Macros

Introduction

The intention of computers has always been to simplify our work, freeing us from the mindless repetitive tasks and allowing us to concentrate on the portions of our jobs that actually require our attention, creativity and intelligence. Despite this goal, much of our time on the computer is still spent doing the same things over and over again. We are essentially wasting our time, performing tasks that only required thought the first few times they were done.

Macros were invented to deal with this problem. By enabling a user to encapsulate several distinct actions into a single command, macros can eliminate an entire sequence of button clicks, key presses and menu selections. Word, and the rest of Office 2000 has the ability to create and use very advanced macros and this chapter will introduce you to this feature. Before moving on to creating projects, this chapter will show you how to:

- ❑ Record and playback a series of actions
- ❑ Make your macro easier to use by placing it on a toolbar button
- ❑ Examine the code created by your recording
- ❑ Modify that code to do something a little different

Once you have been introduced to macros in Word and are familiar with creating and using them, you will ready to move on to more advanced topics.

Repeating Yourself

Since macros were invented, their primary purpose has always been to replace a sequence of user actions. To make this as easy as possible, a tool called a **macro recorder** is provided for you. This tool allows you to start selectively recording your actions inside Word into a new macro, tracking every command you execute until you stop recording. The new macro you have created can be played back at any time, and Word will execute each of your actions again.

Recording a Macro

Word 2000 provides you with two different ways to start recording a macro, through the Tools menu or through a toolbar button. The toolbar button is part of the Visual Basic toolbar. This toolbar contains a few buttons that will be particularly useful to developers, so we will be referring to it from time to time:

Word 2000 has many different toolbars so you may quickly find yourself with a very cluttered screen. Remember that you can show or hide any toolbar by right-clicking in the toolbar area and toggling that toolbar on or off from the list that appears:

Another way to control which toolbars are visible is through the Toolbars tab of the Customize dialog box (accessible via Tools | Customize), simply check those items that you wish to have displayed, and uncheck any that you want hidden. The Customize dialog box also gives you the ability to remove or add buttons from any existing toolbars or to create a completely new toolbar containing whichever buttons you wish.

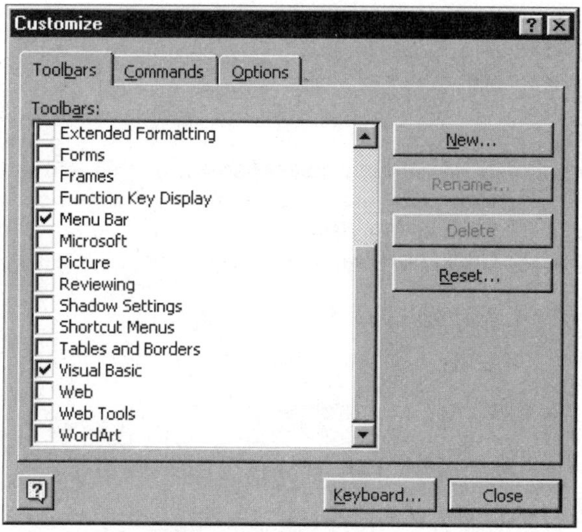

The small circle button on the Visual Basic toolbar is the Record Macro button, clicking on it starts recording a new macro. The Record Macro dialog box will appear, allowing you to specify some information about the macro you are about to record. The name you assign to the macro can be changed later, but should still always be something distinctive (not Macro1), so that you can find it again. The description is not required, but is a useful place to put comments about the purpose and use of your macro. We will look at the other values later, each of them is important and needed to accomplish certain things. Once you click the OK button on this dialog, the actual recording will begin:

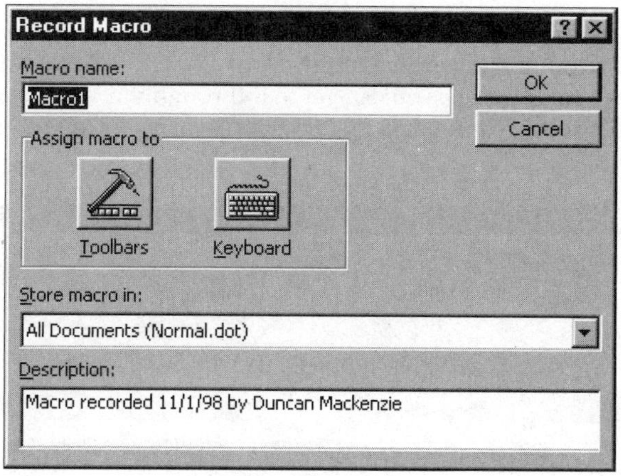

From this moment on (until you stop recording by clicking the Record Macro button on the Visual Basic toolbar again) all of your actions will be recorded and added to this new macro.

In addition to clicking the **Record Macro** button again to stop recording, there is a toolbar (the **Stop Recording** toolbar), which is only available when a macro is being recorded:

This toolbar has two buttons on it, a **Stop Recording** button that will stop the recording and save the macro, and a **Pause Recording** button that will stop the recording until you press it again. If this toolbar is not visible (if you had closed it, for instance), you can turn it on through the **Customize** dialog or by right-clicking on the toolbar area:

The macro itself is really VBA code, which you can look at and edit directly. We will look at the VBA development environment in more detail later, but if you wish to look at the code for a particular macro, you can get to it through the **Macros** dialog. This dialog is accessible through the keyboard shortcut *Alt+F8*, or through the <u>T</u>ools | <u>M</u>acro | <u>M</u>acros... menu option:

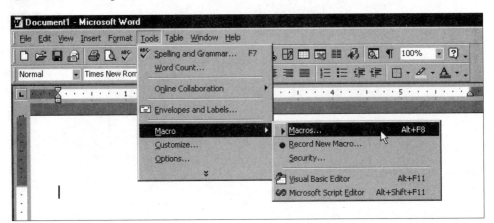

The Macros dialog box itself looks like this:

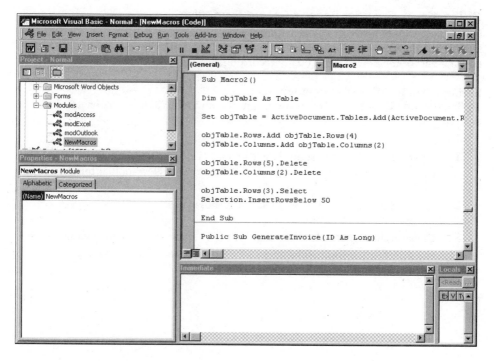

The Macros dialog contains a list that shows all the macros that are currently available to you, and you can run, delete or edit whichever macro you have selected. Clicking the <u>E</u>dit button will bring you into the VBA development environment, and display the code for the macro you selected.

For example, clicking <u>E</u>dit on Macro2 on my machine will display the code for that macro:

To exit the development environment and return to Word 2000, you can select Close from the File menu (or click the close button in the upper right corner of the window).

> You can switch from the Visual Basic Editor back to Word without closing the Editor down through one of several methods: *Alt+F11*, the **View Microsoft Word** toolbar button (standard Microsoft Word Application icon), or by using *Alt+Tab* to switch between the two windows.

Things to Remember about Macro Recording

Although macro recording is a straightforward process, there are a few things to keep in mind.

1. You Can't Use the Mouse to Select Text

When you are recording a macro, your pointer will change into an arrow with a cassette tape attached to it:

When this cursor is present, you cannot click on anything. If you move your mouse around the screen, you will note that this special pointer goes away when you are over menus and toolbars. During the recording of a macro, you can click on any toolbar button or menu option, just like normal, but you cannot use your mouse to work with the document itself. This means that selecting text and repositioning your cursor will have to be done with keyboard commands.

2. The Macro Recorder Doesn't Record Everything

Only actions taken in Word will be recorded into a macro, so if you spend some time looking through menus, or even switch to another application, none of that will become part of the new macro you are recording.

Seeing What the Macro Recorder Ignores

To demonstrate what the macro recorder ignores, and what it does not, try this little exercise yourself.

1. Open Word 2000, you should have an empty document already open by default, if you do not, create one by clicking on the New toolbar button.

2. Ensure that the Visual Basic toolbar is visible.

3. Click on the Record Macro toolbar button to start recording a new macro. The Record Macro button will stay pressed down to indicate that you are recording:

> ▼ Visual Basic   ✕
> ▶ ● Security... 🗁 🛠 📐 🔗
>
> Record Macro

4. The Record Macro dialog will be displayed, with all the options already filled in with default information. Give it a name of `TestMacro`, and just leave the rest of the options as they are.

5. Click OK. Your mouse pointer will change to the arrow with the cassette attached to indicate that you are now recording.

6. Move the mouse around, click on the File menu (but don't select anything), hover over a few toolbar buttons, look at the ToolTips that are displayed. Click on the Windows Start button (on your taskbar) and launch another program, like WordPad, or Calculator. Switch back to Word 2000.

7. Click on the Bold toolbar button:

8. Unless you had text selected at this point, the only change on your screen will be to the appearance of the Bold button, which is now depressed.

9. Click on the Record Macro button on the Visual Basic toolbar to stop recording your macro. Your cursor and the Record Macro button will return to normal.

10. Select the menu option Tools I Macro I Macros... to bring up the Macros dialog. Find `TestMacro` in the list of macros displayed. Click the Edit button to bring up the code for this macro.

At this point, the VBA development environment will be displayed. Approximately in the center of the screen will be a window containing various color-coded text. That center window is the where you will find your code and right now, there will be code similar to the following:

```
Sub TestMacro()
'
' TestMacro Macro
' Macro recorded 10/29/98 by Duncan Mackenzie
'
    Selection.Font.Bold = wdToggle
End Sub
```

Lines with the single quote in front of them are **comment lines**; they are there just for information and, in the case of recorded macros, are placed there automatically. Comments are usually used to store information about what the purpose of this macro is and who created it. You will see more examples of comments in the macros we create in later chapters.

There is only one real line of code in this macro, `Selection.Font.Bold =` `wdToggle`, which is the recorded version of your click on the **Bold** toolbar button. The macro recorder recorded nothing else you did. This means that time does not matter, do not worry about executing all the steps of your macro quickly when you are recording it. All the actions will be played back almost instantly, one after another; regardless of how much time you took to execute them the first time.

> `Selection.Font.Bold` is VBA's way of saying "The bold (`.Bold`) state of the font (`.Font`) of the currently selected text (`Selection`)". Seem confusing? It is, until you get the hang of it. This style of programming works with objects and properties and we will discuss it in detail in the next chapter.

3. The Macro Recorder Can Record More than You Expect

Some actions that you take in Word 2000 can involve the use of dialog boxes, such as the **Page Setup** dialog, in which you can set a number of values at one time. When using the Macro Recorder, it always records all of the settings from any dialog box that you use, regardless of which ones you actually changed. This can result in a macro that does more than you want.

Recording the Use of Dialog Boxes

Sometimes you need to use Word's dialog boxes, instead of the equivalent toolbar buttons, to ensure you get the desired effect when you run your macro. Consider the macro you recorded in the last exercise, perhaps your purpose was to create a macro that would bold the selected text whenever it was run. Follow the steps below to see if that is what your macro really does.

1. With your empty document still open from the previous exercise, make sure that the **Bold** toolbar button is not selected (it should not be indented) and type some text. Select a portion of that text and then click the **Run Macro** button on the **Visual Basic** toolbar.

    This will bring up the list of available macros, select `TestMacro` (the one created in the last exercise) and click on the Run button. Notice that the text you had selected is now bold. Perfect.

2. Now, with that same text still selected, run the same macro again. The text will no longer be bold, which is not good considering that you wanted this macro to always bold the selected text. Regardless of the state of the text before running the macro, you want it to be bold afterwards, and that is not what this macro does.

The reason for this result can be found in the code that was recorded for `TestMacro`, which you can take a look at by selecting that macro in the **Macros** dialog box and clicking **E**dit.

```
Sub TestMacro()
'
' TestMacro Macro
' Macro recorded 10/29/98 by Duncan Mackenzie
'
    Selection.Font.Bold = wdToggle
End Sub
```

The line `Selection.Font.Bold = wdToggle`, is the problem. It means that the bold state of the currently selected text should be toggled, which would bold text that is not bolded already and vice versa. To explicitly make the selected text bold, regardless of whether it currently is or not, you need to use the **F**ormat | **F**ont menu option, and the dialog box that it brings up. The steps below take you through recording a macro that does exactly that.

1. Return to Word 2000 and select some non-bold text.

2. Click on the **Record Macro** toolbar button. Name the new macro `DialogTest` in the **Record Macro** dialog box, leave the other values the same.

3. Click **OK** to start recording your macro.

4. Select **F**ont from the **F**ormat menu.

5. The **Font** dialog will be displayed:

6. In the **Font style** list, choose **Bold**, and then click **OK**.

7. Stop the recording using the **Record Macro** button on the **Visual Basic** toolbar.

8. To look at the results of your recording, edit the new `DialogTest` macro (through the **Macros** dialog). The following code will be displayed:

```
Sub DialogTest()
'
' DialogTest Macro
' Macro recorded 10/29/98 by Duncan Mackenzie
'
    With Selection.Font
        .Name = "Times New Roman"
        .Size = 9
        .Bold = True
        .Italic = False
        .Underline = wdUnderlineNone
        .UnderlineColor = wdColorAutomatic
        .StrikeThrough = False
        .DoubleStrikeThrough = False
        .Outline = False
        .Emboss = False
        .Shadow = False
        .Hidden = False
        .SmallCaps = False
        .AllCaps = False
        .Color = wdColorAutomatic
        .Engrave = False
        .Superscript = False
        .Subscript = False
        .Spacing = 0.3
        .Scaling = 100
        .Position = 0
        .Kerning = 0
        .Animation = wdAnimationNone
    End With

End Sub
```

9. Although you did not set all of these values in the dialog box, the code generated by the macro recorder is setting them all. This occurs due to the way in which it handles dialog boxes. Instead of tracking what you do while you are using a dialog, it simply records the value of every single setting in the dialog box when you close it. Simpler for the developer of the macro recorder certainly, but it can cause you some problems. If you tried to run this macro on some 14 pt, Arial text that you want to have in bold, you will be quite annoyed to see it change into 9pt Times New Roman. Fortunately, the fix is easy. Simply delete all the code for values other than the ones you want set (in this case, everything except the line setting bold to true). Once you are finished, your macro should look like this:

```
Sub DialogTest()
'
' DialogTest Macro
' Macro recorded 10/29/98 by Duncan Mackenzie
'
    With Selection.Font

        .Bold = True

    End With

End Sub
```

This code uses something new, the With ... End With statements. Placing With Selection.Font at the top of this macro means that any code between that statement and the End With that starts with a "." is considered the same as starting with Selection.Font. The result is much clearer code (and less typing for you), but the effect is the same. This means that the code that was recorded by the macro recorder was the equivalent of:

```
Selection.Font.Name = "Times New Roman"
Selection.Font.Size = 9
Selection.Font.Bold = True
Selection.Font.Italic = False
Selection.Font.Underline = wdUnderlineNone
...
...
```

In addition to providing your fingers with a break, the With ... End With structure also has the positive effect of improving the performance of your code. The code shown directly above may be the equivalent of what the macro recorder created, but it would not be as fast.

You could also have removed the With ... End With statements and made the entire macro even simpler, the single remaining line of code would then become Selection.Font.Bold = True. The With ... End With structure is usually only used when you are setting many values at one time, when used with only one line it might even cause a loss of performance.

4. You Should only Record Actions You Want to Repeat

This is a problem that everyone runs into. When you are recording a macro, you need to keep in mind that every step that you record will repeat again when the macro runs. What this means is that if you want a macro that works on the currently selected text, have some text selected before you record it. If you start recording, then select the text, the act of selecting will be part of your macro. The same thing applies to mistakes, if you perform some action accidentally during the recording, even if you reverse it, it will be a part of your finished macro. For instance, if you mistakenly cut (*Ctrl+X*) some text out of your document, when you meant to copy it (*Ctrl+C*), you can easily put the text back by pasting it in (*Ctrl+V*). The end result in your macro will reflect all of these actions like so:

```
Selection.Cut
Selection.Paste
```

The two commands cancel each other out, but they are still in the code and will run every time your macro executes. As you saw in the previous exercise, it is not difficult to go into your recorded macro and modify it, but it is sometimes easier just to record it again until you do it correctly, once all the way through.

> The **Undo** command (menu option, toolbar button, or shortcut key) is not available during the recording of a macro; so do not work with anything irreplaceable.

Understanding the Limits of Macro Recording

Although the macro recorder is an amazing feature, it is not capable of doing everything necessary for the creation of complex macros. You will need to write most of your macros yourself if you want to build anything beyond a simple repetition of some user actions. To go beyond the macro recorder, you have to edit and write your own VBA code, which will be covered in more detail later in this chapter and the rest of the book.

> *Despite the fact that you cannot build complex macros using only the macro recorder, you will find yourself recording macros almost continually during the process of developing in Word. Recording a complex action is often the quickest way to determine how it would be coded.*

Determining Where to Place Your Macros

When you looked at the Record Macro dialog earlier, you just entered a name for your macro, but there is another option in that dialog that you need to understand. The Store macro in: setting allows you to choose where your macro is placed:

The choices available in this list depend on the current document you have open in Word, but there are really only three possibilities available to you:

All Documents (Normal.dot)

<Current Document Name> (document)

Documents based on <template name>

The first option, which is the default if you have never selected anything else, is a little misleading. The macro will not be placed into all of your documents; it will be stored into a template file called Normal.dot. This template is available to all Word documents and placing a macro into it will make that macro **available** from any Word document that you open or create.

The next option is fairly clear, it will place the macro into the current document, the one that was open and selected when you clicked on the Record Macro button on the toolbar. This option will not be available if you do not have a document open when you click on the Record Macro button (in fact, only the first option will be available in this situation). If you place macros into the current document then you will only be able to play back those macros from that document.

The third type of option that may be available to you involves templates. Above, it was mentioned that all Word documents have the `Normal.dot` template available, but they may also be based on other templates, such as ones for Memos and other purposes. Choosing this third option stores the macro into the template file you have picked, after which the macro is available to any document that is based on that template.

The concept of a macro's location effecting where you can use it is known as **scope**. A macro is considered to have a certain scope, which means the area in which it can be seen and used. If you were to store a macro into the current document, for instance, then its scope is limited to that document. At the other extreme, a macro that is in the `Normal.dot` template has a scope that covers every Word document.

> **Always think about where you will need to use your macro when choosing where to save it. If it will only work with certain templates, then save it with those templates. If it is to be used at anytime, in any file, then you should probably save it into the `Normal.dot` template. It is also possible to designate particular templates to be loaded at all times by placing them into Word's startup folder (discussed later in the chapter) which means that code in those templates are available at all times. The only time that saving it to the current document is likely is when the current document is an actual template (`.dot` file) itself, or if you need the macro to be transported with the document.**

Wherever you choose to place your macro, remember that it must be saved along with that document. If you choose to store your macros in the current document, they are now part of that file. When you close that file, you may be prompted to save changes, and if you do not, any macros you have created or modified since opening that file will be lost:

This is especially true when you are doing a lot of development. It is relatively easy to accidentally start saving your macros into a new blank document (good old `Document1`), which you then close without saving. As far as you were aware, (at the time), and as far as you could see, it was a completely empty document. Losing all of an afternoon's work can make you into a saving fanatic.

To see firsthand how a macro's location can effect its scope, try out the exercise below.

Macro Scope
Open a new document in Word. It will be named `Document1` or 2 or 3, the actual number displayed depends on how many other new documents you have opened since you started Word 2000. Now record a new empty macro and make sure it is placed into the current document. The steps for doing this are listed below:

1. Click on the Record Macro toolbar button.

2. In the Record Macro dialog, enter a name of `Document1Macro` and then select the current document name from the Store macro in: dropdown.

3. Click OK. Your mouse pointer should change to indicate that you are now recording. Click on the Record Macro toolbar button again to stop recording. This will record an empty macro into the current document, named `Document1Macro`.

4. Now create another new document, which will have a name that is numbered one higher than the last one you created. Repeat steps one to three from above, making sure to use the most recently created document's name in place of "`Document1`".

5. Create a third new macro, but store this one in `Normal.dot`, and call it `NormalMacro`. When you have stopped recording the third macro, use the Windo menu to activate the first new document you created.

6. Now, with that document active, click on the Run Macro toolbar button. You will be presented with a list of all the macros that are currently available, those whose scope allows them to be visible to the current document:

Which macros you actually see is dependent on what is selected in the Macros in: dropdown list. If you have All active templates and documents selected then you will see every macro that is visible to the current document. You can limit this to only those macros in a specific document or template simply by selecting that particular option from the list.

Notice that NormalMacro is in the list, Document1Macro (the first macro you created) should also be visible. Close the dialog; you do not need to run anything. Use the Window menu to select the second new document you created. Click on the Run Macro toolbar button again, displaying the same dialog. Now, Document1Macro is not in the list anywhere, Document2Macro should be visible and NormalMacro, as one might expect, is also still visible:

Placing all your macros into individual documents would severely limit their usefulness, but placing them all into the Normal.dot file would quickly become confusing, as every macro would be listed in the Macros dialog. The best solution to this, and the one that will be used throughout the projects in this book, is to place your macros into template files designed for that purpose, where they will be available only when needed.

More about Comments

Another option of the Record Macro dialog box is the Description field. This allows you to specify some information about the macro, such as what it does and who created it. Word 2000 automatically places your name (or whatever name has been entered into the User Information tab of Word's Options dialog, see below) along with the date on which you started recording the macro:

This is not a very useful comment, unless the name of the macro alone is sufficiently descriptive. When you are building macros that will be used either by other developers or directly by users, you should always provide a detailed description of what the macro does.

Playing Back Macros

Recording a macro would not be much use if you could not easily play it back. By this point in the chapter, you have already seen a couple of ways to run a macro, using the Macros dialog box or the Run Macro toolbar button, but there are others. Both of the ways mentioned involve selecting the macro from a list, but there are ways to make it even easier for your end user. Most users are used to performing actions through one of three ways: a toolbar button, a menu selection, or a keyboard shortcut. It is possible to provide any or all of these methods to access any macro you have created, making it very easy and familiar for your users to run.

Setting up Toolbar Buttons and Keyboard Shortcuts

You can create a toolbar button that will run a macro and place that button onto any of the existing toolbars or even create a new toolbar just for this purpose. All of these options can be accessed through the Tools | Customize... menu option, or by right-clicking on an empty portion of the toolbar area and selecting Customize... from the menu. Both of these methods bring up the Customize dialog box:

The Customize dialog contains three tabs that allow you to modify the appearance and content of Word's toolbars and menus.

The first tab, Toolbars, is where you can choose which toolbars should be visible, and can create a new toolbar through the New... button.

The Commands tab is more complicated, allowing you to drag individual items from the list of commands on the dialog onto any toolbar or menu, and through dragging, rearrange the existing items on the visible toolbars and menus. This tab is where you can create a menu item or toolbar button that runs a macro. Simply select Macros from the Categories list on the left as shown and then drag the specific macro from the Commands list into position on whichever toolbar or menu you wish:

If you have created a new toolbar, and it is visible at this time, you can drag items on to it in the same manner.

Throughout this section, we have been discussing toolbars and menus as if they were separate items. Starting in Office 97, this is not the case. Both interfaces merged into one and have become Command Bars - even the menu bar is a Command Bar. This means that you can dock and undock it, or control its visibility just like one of the toolbars.

Note the Save in drop-down at the bottom of the Customize dialog's Commands tab. Similar to Macros, you can control where your toolbar and keystroke modifications are stored and available by what document or template is selected in this drop down. Ensure that you have the right location selected or you may find that all your changes are only available in the current document.

Once you have placed your macro onto a toolbar or menu then you can customize its appearance by right-clicking on it and selecting from the various options:

> You can only edit a button or menu item's properties by right clicking on it when you have the **Customize** dialog box open. Right-clicking a toolbar at any other time brings up a menu that allows you to selectively display or hide toolbars and gives you the option to **Customize**, which would open the **Customize** dialog box.

You can even create a button image for the new button by selecting Edit Button Image, which brings up the Button Editor dialog. As you can see, the author is an accomplished icon artist:

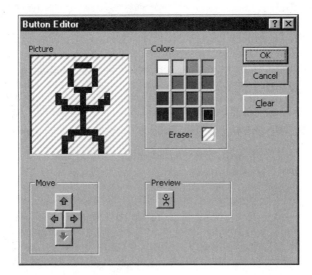

After creating, a button image, you can display it by selecting Default Style or Image and Text from the right-click menu. You can also copy an image from another toolbar button, say one of Word's own, by doing a right-click on the desired button and selecting Copy Button Image. Then you just right-click on the target button and select Paste Button Image. Select Begin a Group if you want to add a separator bar between this button and the one to its left.

In addition to associating a macro with a menu or toolbar item, you can use the Customize dialog to associate a keyboard shortcut with a particular macro. At the bottom of the Customize dialog, below all the tabs, is a button labeled Keyboard. This button will bring up the Customize Keyboard dialog, in which you can choose any Word command, including any macro, and then enter in a keyboard shortcut to associate with that command. This makes it easy to assign *Alt+* or other keystroke to instantly run your macro:

Many keyboard shortcuts are already assigned; Word 2000 has many commands. When you enter in the desired shortcut, any existing assignment will be displayed directly below the shortcut field. You do not need to worry about multiple macros being assigned to a single keyboard shortcut though; any existing assignment is broken when you associate it with a different command. It is possible to assign more than one shortcut key to a single command, and all of the currently assigned shortcuts are displayed in the Current Keys list box:

All three of the methods discussed above for making your macros easily accessible are also available from the Record Macro dialog box. The two buttons in the Assign macro to frame of this dialog, will bring up either a limited version of the Customize Keyboard dialog or the standard Customize dialog:

The dialogs that come up when you click these buttons are different from the regular versions in that they only show one command, the new macro. This filtering makes it very easy to setup menu options, keyboard shortcuts or toolbar buttons for that single item.

Consider the possibilities of customizing your users' interface with the ability to modify their menus, toolbars and keyboard shortcuts. For instance, you could replace the File I Print... menu option, the Print toolbar icon, and the *Ctrl* + *P* keyboard shortcut with your own. This allows you complete control over a standard Word action, perhaps so you can standardize certain information, or limit the user's choices in some way. You shouldn't change the purpose of a standard Word shortcut though, regardless of your customization, *Ctrl* + *P* should always print, even if you are changing how that printing occurs.

> Remember that, unless you take more complex steps, a user can always go into the **Customize** dialog and undo the changes you have made. Replacing a command will work for 95% of your users, but you cannot count on them never using the original. Word provides a better way to accomplish the same goal. If you create a macro with one of several specific names, such as `FilePrint` for the print function, Word will automatically (without any toolbar or menu customization) call that code instead of its normal behavior.

Playing Back Multiple Macros

It is often the case, especially with recorded macros, that you want more than one individual macro to run when the user clicks a button, or performs some other action. It is not possible to associate a single toolbar button directly with multiple macros (run macro 1, then macro 2, then macro 3), but there is an indirect way. You can accomplish the same effect by creating a macro that runs all the other desired macros, then associating a toolbar button with that new macro. How do you do this? Simply record a macro of you running some macros, clicking on the Run Macro toolbar button for each one in order. This finished macro's code would appear similar to the code below (if you switched to the Visual Basic Editor).

```
Application.Run MacroName:="Macro1"
Application.Run MacroName:="Macro3"
Application.Run MacroName:="MyPrint"
```

You will learn other, simpler, ways to accomplish the same thing in future chapters, but this code does exactly what you want. This allows you to create individual macros that each perform small tasks and use them, in combination with other macros, to perform a large, complex task.

Naming Your Macros

The need to refer to other macros in your code brings up the concept of naming your macros. Every time you record or create a macro, you are asked to supply a name for it, unfortunately Microsoft goes ahead and provides one for you (when you are recording), the default of Macro1, Macro2, and so on. Maybe if it were not so easy to use that default name we would not do it so often. Regardless, you may find yourself with a large number of macros floating around with descriptive names such as Macro9 or maybe the completely different and much more meaningful Macro6. Macros with names like this are not easy to work with. You should always pick a descriptive name, even if it is just TestMacro (at least you will know it is safe to delete when you find it a year later).

That is one reason to pay attention to what you call your macros, the other has to do with the concept of scope that was discussed earlier. If two macros have the same name and are both in scope (available to the current user) then there is a conflict. Rather than just having an error, Word 2000 handles this conflict by requiring you to refer to the macros using a fully qualified name consisting of the Project Name, Module Name and Macro Name, such as Document1.Module1.Macro5. This is not a big issue if you are selecting the proper macro manually from the Macros dialog, you can just choose which one to use. It is a different matter if you have created code that runs macros by name, like the code shown above in "Playing Back Multiple Macros". That kind of code will fail when it tries to run a macro name that is not fully qualified.

Overall, everything is easier if you choose a name for your macro that is descriptive and unique. The Macro Recorder's default names are the same for every Word developer making duplication extremely likely.

> It is very likely that someone else will use the descriptive macro names you choose. You are not the only developer who thinks EmailDocument is a good name for a macro that sends the current document through electronic mail. To further reduce the risk of conflict with another developer's macros, use an identifying prefix on your macro names, such as dmc (for Duncan Mackenzie Consulting). EmailDocument may be common, but the chance of running into another dmcEmailDocument is low. Of course, if neither you nor your users ever use any other macros, conflicts may not be a concern.

Getting into the Code

As you record your actions in Word, the macro recorder is creating Visual Basic for Applications code that corresponds to each action. As you saw earlier in this chapter, you can view that code by selecting the macro in the Macros dialog and clicking the Edit button. You can also use the Visual Basic Editor button from the Visual Basic toolbar:

Either one takes you into the Visual Basic for Applications Development Environment:

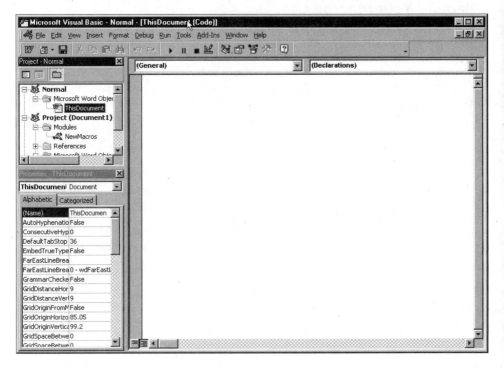

The Visual Basic for Applications Development Environment

This Visual Basic Editor is like another complete application that allows you to view, edit, and create VBA code. It contains many separate windows (called tool windows) that assist you in finding and working with your code. Similar to toolbars in many ways, these windows can be hidden or shown as desired, and can even be docked and undocked against the sides of the main window. Two of these windows are shown below with an explanation of their use:

The Project Explorer Window

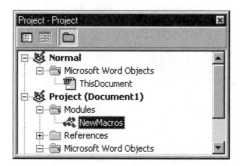

Earlier in this chapter, you learned about scope and how the placement of macros effects their visibility. When you chose where to place a particular macro, you were just controlling where the code for that macro would be created. Every document that is open in Word appears in this window as a Project, and each of those projects can have Modules associated with them. A module is simply an area where you can create and place code, and a single project can have many modules in it.

Although each module may seem like a separate file, especially to programmers used to Visual Basic (where each module is a separate file), they are not. All the modules in a VBA project are stored in the document (or template) itself.

Office documents are stored on disk using a technology known as OLE compound documents, which allows them to contain the equivalent of many different files as discrete portions of their single file.

When you come into the Visual Basic development environment, it is through this window that you can find and open modules. You may need to open some modules before you will see any code, unless they are already open for you (as they are when you select Edit from the Macros dialog). A document does not have any modules by default, but Word will automatically add one if you choose to store a macro into that document, and that new module will be used to store future macros as well.

In addition to projects for the obvious open documents in Word, there will be at least one other project visible in the Project Explorer, the Normal project. This project represents the Normal.dot template and contains the code that is stored into that particular item. In most respects, a template project is no different from a project for a regular document. The main exception to this being that a template's project is loaded whenever a document based on it is loaded. More details on templates and Normal.dot are provided in the section on templates later in this chapter.

The Properties Window

In VBA, every object has properties, which are attributes that describe that object, such as its name, height, and width. Properties will be described in greater detail in the next chapter. If the Properties window isn't visible, select Properties Window from the View menu to show it. When you have an object selected, the Properties window displays, and allows you to modify, the attributes of that object. For projects, modules and document objects, there are few properties displayed in this window. When we move on to form objects and controls in the upcoming chapters, this window will become much more useful as they have many important properties.

The Normal.dot File and Other Templates

A **template** is a type of document that you can base other documents on, and the new document will inherit content, styles and other features from the template. Whenever you choose a document type from the New dialog, you are really choosing which template to base your new document on. Word determines which templates to display in that dialog by looking in the `Templates` folder, and making each subfolder from there into a separate tab. Each `.dot` file becomes an icon, under the appropriate tab.

> By default, this folder is named `Templates` and is located under the root Office installation directory (such as `C:\Program Files\Microsoft Office\Templates`), but you can make Word look anywhere you want. The File Locations tab in the **Tools | Options** dialog allows you to change this or any of the paths used by Word. There is also another location available for storing templates, which is described a little later under "Workgroup Templates".

Templates for Developers

When you create a document based on a template, the auto-text entries, styles, toolbars, keystroke assignments, menus and macros from the template are available to the new document. This means that by placing macros that you write into a template, those macros can be available to any document based on that template. These features make templates a better way to manage macros than by simply placing every macro you create into the `Normal.dot` file on each user's machine.

The Template Family Tree

New templates can be based on pre-existing templates, creating a form of "Family Tree" of documents. In such a case, the new template will "inherit" all the features of the template it is based on. Documents created from these "second generation" templates will have access to the resources of all their "ancestors". Unfortunately there is no actual link between the new template and the one from which it was created. Changes made to the original template will not have any effect on templates that have been created from it.

> *We call them "second generation" templates above, but there is no real limit to how many successive templates can be used. As the number of generations increases though, so does the complexity of the final document. One or two levels of templates are generally as far as this concept is taken.*

Working with templates in this fashion can be confusing, but can be useful in many different situations, consider the following example:

Java Jitters Inc., a coffee company, has created a company wide memo template, which includes several special macros:

- ❏ SendMemo, which emails your memo
- ❏ SendMemoToEveryone, which emails your memo to everyone in the company

The Accounting Department decides to create their own memo template, but they do not want to redo anything that has already been done. They create a new template, based on the company-wide memo template, and then make two changes to the new file:

- ❏ Fill in the department field on the memo template with "Accounting"
- ❏ Add a macro called SendMemoToAccounting, which emails everyone in the accounting department

When users in the Accounting department use the finished template to create a new Accounting Memo they end up with a document that contains the SendMemo, SendMemoToEveryone, and SendMemoToAccounting macros. By basing a template on a template, they have managed to build their own version of that template, without losing or changing any of the original template's functionality.

> Note that, as mentioned earlier, there is no link between the new Accounting Memo template and the original Java Jitters Memo template. If the code for SendMemo is modified in the Java Jitters Memo template, it will not effect the copy of this function that exists in the Accounting Memo template.

Don't Lose the Template

Unfortunately, macros from the template remain there; they are not transferred to the
new document, which means that they are only available if the template is available.
Normally, this is not a problem unless you move or delete the template file, or the user
emails the document to someone who does not have your template. In either such case,
the document would remain intact, but no macros would be available. You should
decide on a final location for your template before it is put into active use. If a template
file does move, is lost or for any other reason you need to change the template a
document is associated with, you can use the Templates and Add-ins dialog, available
through the menu option Tools | Templates and Add-Ins. The Document template
shows the template that this document is currently associated with, you can change
this value manually (by typing over the existing template name) or through the nearby
Attach   button.

Once you have changed the template attached to a document, you should have the
Automatically update document styles option checked if you want the document's
current styles to be modified. By default, the document is left as it is, regardless of
which template you attach.

The upside to this behavior is that when you update your macros, you only need to
update the template and every new or existing file will use the latest version of your
code.

Workgroup Templates

To allow for shared templates, Word provides the Workgroup Templates file location.
Whatever path is assigned to this option will be used in combination with the User
Templates value to find .dot files.

It is common for the Workgroup path to be a network share containing various
company-wide templates. You should make sure that Workgroup templates cannot be
modified by users, to protect them from intentional or unintentional changes, by
marking them read-only or (if they are on a server) modifying permissions for non-
developers.

Reduce the Workload on Your Macros

Another benefit of templates, for developers, is that they can act as form letters for
your code. By creating a template of a corporate fax sheet, for instance, your code only
has to fill in a few areas on the page to make a finished document. If you did not have
that template, you would have to provide code to build every element of the page,
even those portions that never change. This reason alone would make templates
invaluable to you, and there are many other wonderful things you can do with these
features.

Normal.dot, Lord of the Templates

When you choose Blank Document from the New dialog, or simply click on the New
toolbar button, you are really creating a document based on the Normal.dot
template. In fact, every document is, essentially, linked to Normal.dot. This unique
relationship is what causes anything placed into Normal.dot (macros, auto-text
entries) to be available to all documents. This file is responsible for holding a great deal
of information and can quickly become cluttered. Avoid the temptation to place code
and other information into this file, the fewer developers that use it as their main
development environment, the better off we will all be. If the concept of better code
organization isn't sufficient to dissuade you from using the Normal.dot template to
store your code then here are two other reasons to avoid it:

- ❑ If the Normal.dot template becomes corrupted or deleted, Word will
  spontaneously create a new version of the file that contains none of your
  code or customizations.

- ❑ The more information (styles, code, toolbar customizations, etc...) you
  store into this file, the larger it will become and the longer it will take to
  load. As it is loaded by default whenever you start Word, a longer load
  time for Normal.dot will result in a noticeable delay every time you
  load Word.

Global Templates

Despite the power of templates, sometimes you are creating macros that need to be
loaded in Word at all times, and the Normal.dot file seems like the only way. There
is a better way, through global templates. These files are .dot or .doc files that are
loaded into Word itself, independent of any particular document. The code and other
resources stored in these files are available to any document, and are even available
when nothing else is open (good for macros that create documents). This is the
preferred method of creating and maintaining any code that seems destined for the
Normal.dot template. You can load and unload global templates through the list box
of the Templates and Add-ins dialog. Click the Add button to choose a .dot or .doc
file to load as a global template.

> Global templates, other than how they are loaded, are not any different
> from a regular template and can be created just as easily.

The Startup Folder

Ok, so the global templates are the way to go, you should not use `Normal.dot`, but how do you make sure your global template is always loaded when Word 2000 runs? The `Startup` folder is provided for just this reason, any templates that are located in this folder when Word runs will be loaded in as global templates. The default location of the `Startup` folder is usually under the `Microsoft Office` root and under the `Office` folder, but you can change this location through the Tools | Options | File Locations menu option.

> Note that users cannot change the global templates in any way - another real plus for using them over `Normal.dot`.

Macro Viruses

It seems to always happen, once a new technology comes out, the virus creators find a way to use it. The same thing happened with Java, ActiveX Controls, HTML Email, and macros are no exception. Macro viruses are Word macros that are self-replicating (they transfer themselves to every document they come in contact with) and usually harmful in some way to your documents or computer. These macros transfer themselves through the Word documents, infecting your `Normal.dot` file when you open the document and then infecting every document that you create or open after that point. At the moment though, you can be almost 100% safe from these macros by making your `Normal.dot` file read-only and through the following dialog:

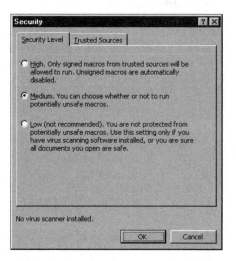

Office 2000 has added new features to deal with the problem of macro viruses. Based on the Internet Explorer model, Office allows you to control your level of security. This dialog, which you can get to through clicking on Security... on the Visual Basic toolbar or through Tools | Macro | Security, has three possible settings for macro security; High, Medium, and Low.

High is pretty intense security, it only allows **signed macros** to run, and everything else is disabled. Signed macros are pieces of code that have been certified by some special corporation, not as being safe, but as having been written by a particular company (such as Microsoft). By knowing, for certain, who has written each macro, you are able to choose to selectively trust certain companies (Trusted Sources). Code from those companies will be allowed to run, other code will not.

We won't be covering code signing in any more detail as it is not usually used for personal or internal business development, our focus in this book.

> *For more information on code signing and how it applies to the security of code, check out Microsoft's web site at* http://www.microsoft.com *and Verisign at* http://www.verisign.com *(the leading code signing authority).*

The second level of security, and the one that we would recommend, is Medium. This level still provides you the ability to disable any document's macros, but doesn't just disable them for you. With this security level set, when you open a document that contains macros (regardless of the code in those macros), you are presented with the following dialog:

Selecting Disable Macros will prevent the macros in this document from running automatically or being used at all, which should (as far as we know) protect you from any potential macro virus. Selecting Enable Macros has the exact opposite result; the macros are left completely free to run however and whenever they wish. With the Security Level at Medium, you would be fairly safe if you selected Disable Macros for any file that you didn't expect to contain macros, or whose source is unknown or distrusted (such as a downloaded file from an web site). This is not a complete guarantee, a macro virus may have infected a document that you trust and is supposed to contain macros already (such as your company wide memo template), but it allows for more flexibility than High security. These viruses are another key argument for making any templates (especially shared ones) read-only.

Selecting Low is not recommended, all macros from any source will be allowed to run, and you won't even receive a warning. Use this setting at your own risk.

Summary

Word 2000 has an advanced macro language, one that is made easier to use through the macro recorder. This tool can simply and quickly record almost any action you take inside Word, saving it for playback later. Recording alone is not sufficient to develop complex tools in Word, but you are able to edit existing macro code and create your own through the Visual Basic for Applications development environment built into Office 2000. Together, the macro recorder and straight VBA code will allow you to build almost anything in Word.

In the next few chapters, we will be looking at the VBA programming language itself, and building a few routines completely without the macro recorder. Before moving on to VBA and the projects that are coming up in a few chapters, make sure you are familiar with the concept of recording and playing back macros. Create some sample macros of your own and experiment with assigning them to toolbars.

On to Chapter 2 !!

VBA Fundamentals

Introduction

In the previous chapter, you learned about creating macros with the macro recorder, and took a brief look at the code generated by this tool. That code was written in a language called Visual Basic for Applications (VBA), which is the language that you will be using to do all of your Microsoft Word development. VBA is the language used in several other applications as well, including the rest of Office 2000, Visio, and the latest version of AutoCAD. This chapter is a quick introduction, or review, of the VBA language, designed to prepare you for creating (not recording) your own macros. Only by working directly in the code, and not relying on the macro recorder can you build truly useful Word applications.

In this chapter, we will cover a large amount of material, including:

- ❑ Objects and properties
- ❑ Declaring and working with variables
- ❑ Using both static and dynamic arrays
- ❑ Procedures
- ❑ Scope

Along the way, we will learn about several useful functions and techniques from both VBA and Word, just to keep it interesting.

Object Properties and Methods

In the previous chapter, we looked at several examples of code produced by the macro recorder, such as the lines below:

```
Sub TestMacro()
'
' TestMacro Macro
' Macro recorded 10/29/98 by Duncan Mackenzie
'
    Selection.Font.Bold = wdToggle

End Sub
```

This section of code is a good example of how VBA works with Word, through objects. The highlighted line above is setting the `Bold` property of the `Font` object, which in turn is a property of the `Selection` object. It is a little complicated, so let's take a step back and define some terms.

Introducing Objects

An **object** in VBA represents an item, something that you can describe and manipulate. In VBA these objects present interfaces to the outside world that we can access through our code. An object has attributes that describe it, known as **properties**. An object can also perform actions, known as **methods**. An object is defined by a **class**. A class is a template from which an object is created. We can create many different objects from a single class and those objects are said to be **instances** of the class.

Here is an example using objects that are more familiar to us, to help explain the concept:

- John is an object of class Human
- Name, Age, Height and Weight are some of the properties of Humans
- For John these properties might equal John Smith, 43, 5' 11", and 190lbs respectively
- Walk, Sit and Blink would be methods for all Humans

Given the above statements, you could write VBA code to manipulate John, which would look something like this:

```
Sub SetUpPerson()

    John.Height = 71
    John.Weight = 190
    John.Age = 43

    John.Walk

End Sub
```

This style of programming provides VBA (and Visual Basic, which behaves in the same way) with a great deal of flexibility. With objects, properties and methods VBA can be used to do almost anything, as long as it has the right objects.

VBA itself has only a few objects, but Word has hundreds, and it is through these objects that you can manipulate Word to do exactly what you want. In our original snippet of code, `Selection.Font.Bold = wdToggle`, the `Selection` object is provided by Word and represents whatever portion of the active document is currently selected. This `Selection` object has a `Font` property, which is itself another object, representing various font-related formatting information about the document contents represented by the `Selection` object. Finally, that `Font` object has a property, `Bold`, which determines whether or not the font is bold.

Depending on what result you wanted, you could set the `Bold` property accordingly. Setting it to `True` would mean that the selected portion of the document would be bolded (regardless of whether it currently is or is not bold), setting it to `False` would accomplish the reverse. In this case, the code above sets the property equal to `wdToggle`, which causes the property to become the reverse of its current value.

In addition to setting property values, you can also retrieve them, and use that information however you wish. For example, the following code retrieves information about the currently selected portion of the active document and displays it to the user:

```
Sub DisplaySelectionInfo()

    MsgBox Selection.Text
    MsgBox Selection.Font.Name
    MsgBox Selection.Font.Size

End Sub
```

This code would produce a series of dialogs, showing the currently selected text itself, the name of the font in use, and the font size. You can retrieve the value of almost any property, and use that information as part of your macro.

> `MsgBox` is a VBA function that displays text to the user in a dialog box, and is very useful for warnings, questions and alerts. It is often used in sample code especially, as a quick and easy way to display a variable's value or to indicate that you have reached a certain point in a macro. We will use this function often and you will see more of its features in later chapters, but for now it is sufficient to realize this function will display a message to the user.

The following macro both retrieves and sets a property on the same line, with the effect of doubling the size of the selected text:

```
Sub MakeTwiceAsBig()

    Selection.Font.Size = Selection.Font.Size * 2

End Sub
```

Almost all your code in VBA will involve working with objects, so it is important to understand a few general rules:

- ❑ Objects are items to be manipulated
- ❑ They have properties and methods
- ❑ Properties are attributes of the object; they describe it
- ❑ Methods are actions that the object can perform; they do something

These rules are not always true, sometimes properties cause the object to do something and sometimes methods merely change attributes, but these are usually valid. To do anything that is very useful in VBA, we need the ability to keep values around, not just in object properties, but also in some form of storage. This is where variables come in, a way to store data, and the next section will explain what they are and how to use them.

Variables and Data Types

Variables are a concept of most programming languages, places to store information. These variables are then used throughout the program in place of the values they represent, allowing the same program to work with many different possible values. The use of variables usually takes one of only a few forms:

❑   Declaring the variable with the `Dim` keyword, which prepares it for use (`Dim X`)

❑   Storing values into the variable (`X=3`)

❑   Retrieving previously stored values out of the variable (`MsgBox X` or `Y = X + 3`)

That is it, three ways to work with variables, making it one of the simplest programming concepts, but yet it is something that you will be doing repeatedly throughout every program you write.

Declaring Variables

Before you can store values into a variable, VBA must know that the variable exists. Somewhere in our code we have to state that we are going to be using this certain name to refer to a variable. This is usually done right at the beginning of our code, and uses the `Dim` statement. The code below declares the variables X, Y, and Z:

```
Sub WorkingWithVariables()

    Dim X
    Dim Y
    Dim Z

    ...

End Sub
```

Once the variable is declared, VBA understands that it is a variable and allocates memory for you to store information. From that point on, anytime you use this variable's name in your code, VBA knows what it is and can treat it accordingly, as in this code:

```
Sub WorkingWithVariables()

    Dim X
    Dim Y
    Dim Z

    Z = 3
    Y = 4
    X = 1

    Z = Y / X
    X = Y + Z

End Sub
```

In the code above, numbers are being stored into the three variables, but you could store almost any type of information into them if you wished. In our programs we usually create our variables to hold specific types of information and VBA allows us to specify what type of information when we first create the variable. This is known as the **data type** of the variable and the next section covers what types are available and how to determine which one to use.

Data Types

When we declare a variable, we can tell VBA what type of information that variable will contain by providing a data type. If we don't specifically tell VBA the data type for a variable, it assumes that the variable should be declared as a **variant**, which can hold any type of information but is very inefficient. More information on variants is given at the end of this section on data types. We specify a data type for a variable by adding As <Data Type> after the variable's declaration. For instance, in the code below, we are declaring X, Y, and Z as variables that will be used for **integers**:

```
Sub WorkingWithVariables()

    Dim X As Integer
    Dim Y As Integer
    Dim Z As Integer

    Z = 3
    Y = 4
    X = 1

    Z = Y / X
    X = Y + Z

End Sub
```

It is tempting, especially to those used to other programming languages, to simplify the variable declarations shown above to: Dim X, Y, Z As Integer. Although this would not result in an error, it does not achieve the desired result. In VBA, it is possible to place multiple variable declarations onto one place, but each variable requires its data type to be specified separately. This makes the correct way to simplify those three variable declarations: Dim X As Integer, Y As Integer, Z As Integer. The first version of this line would have declared X and Y as variants and only Z as an integer.

There are many different data types available in VBA, and it is difficult to be exactly sure which data type to use for what situation. The types can be grouped into:

❑ Numeric variables, designed to hold various forms of numbers

❑ String variables, designed to hold text

❑ Date variables, actually for storing both date and time information

❑ Boolean variables, for storing information that is binary (True/False, Yes/No)

❑ Object variables, used to represent objects

❑ Variants, generic variables, capable of holding almost any data

The definition and usage of these data types is covered below, in individual sections for each group.

Numeric Data Types

Since there are so many different types of applications that require numbers, and the accuracy, precision and size of numbers can vary so widely, there are several distinct data types in this category.

Integer	The most familiar of data types, this can store whole numbers from -32,768 to 32,767 (the standard range for a 16 bit, or two byte, number).
Long	The big brother of the Integer, this data type is referred to as a Long integer, being made up of 32 bits (four bytes). It is therefore capable of holding a much wider range of whole (non-decimal) values than the Integer data type. You can store values between -2,147,483,648 and 2,147,483,647 into variables of this type.
Single	This is a Single-Precision Floating-Point value, using 4 bytes to store real numbers, which are limited more in precision than range. You can store positive numbers between 1.401298E-45 and 3.402823E38, and the opposite range of negative numbers.
Double	This is the same type of information as for Single, but using twice as many bytes to store the information (8 bytes). As with Single, it is the precision of this data type that is of primary concern. Both the Single and Double data types will be discussed in more detail after this table. A Double can hold values from 4.94065645841247E-324 to 1.79769313486232E308.
Currency	As the name implies, this data type is designed to hold monetary values and, as such, is limited to a fixed number of decimals places (4). By fixing the decimal point and using 8 bytes for storage, this data type can accurately store values between -922,337,203,685,477.5808 and +922,337,203,685,477.5807, making it the best choice for financial transactions.
Byte	Using one byte to store integer values, variables of this type can store numbers between 0 and 255.
Decimal*	This is the largest available numeric data type, capable of holding negative or positive numbers using up to 29 digits (the decimal point can be positioned anywhere within those 29 digits). This provides the Decimal data type with the ability to store a number as large as 79,228,162,514,264,337,593,543,950,335 negative or positive.

* You cannot declare a variable of type Decimal. This will be covered later, under the section on Variants.

Each data type is well suited for certain applications, such as the `Currency` data type, which should be used for monetary values.

Integer Values (Long Integer, Integer and Byte)

Integers are used in any situation that requires non-decimal values, such as for counters, although the `Byte` data type would actually be sufficient in most situations. `Long` **integers** are used in any situation that requires whole numbers that cover a wide range. This is often the data type used for ID values in databases, uniquely identifying some specific item such as a Customer, Product, or an Invoice.

Floating-Point Values (Single and Double)

`Single` and `Double` data types are floating-point numbers, meaning that they have a certain degree of precision (number of significant digits). They manage to represent a wide range of values through manipulation of the decimal point. This is not really the place to go into an in-depth explanation of significant digits and scientific notation, but a quick overview will show you how these data types work.

The number 0.001 has 4 digits in it, and the decimal point is positioned after the first digit. This number could be expressed as 1 times 10^3; they are the same. There is only one significant digit in this value, the 1. The number 2,322,000 is a seven digit number, but is equivalent to 2.322 times 10^6, so there are only 4 significant digits. Now, consider the number 2,322,000.001, how many significant digits are there? In this case, there are 10, the zeroes are all significant because they separate non-zero values. Thinking of this another way, you could not display this number (accurately) without using all 10 digits.

The `Single` data type supports values with up to 7 significant digits. This means that, although it could easily handle 2,322,000 or 0.001, it could not hold the value 2,322,000.001. This data type is useful for many things, but you must consider precision in its use. Use variables of type `Single` to store values that require low precision, such as interest rates (generally one or two digits of precision, 0.05 %, 6.9 %, etc) or values where it is acceptable to sacrifice some accuracy.

The `Double` data type supports values with up to 15 significant digits, which raises it to a level capable of handling most floating point information with acceptable accuracy. `Doubles` are often used as part of statistical or scientific calculations.

Monetary Values (Currency)

Many programs have used doubles to store monetary values, such as bank balances, payroll information, etc… but this is not a good idea. When dealing with money, you cannot lose any information, every cent is important. Floating-point values deal only with a certain number of significant digits, and they are continually rounding values down to maintain that number. In the case of money, you should always work with a fixed-point data type, such as `Integer`, `Long` and the **Currency** data type.

43

> One successful method of storing monetary information, before the
> Currency data type was available, was to use Long integers and just
> assume two decimal places at the end. In reality, the Currency data type
> is doing almost the same thing, but with four decimal places.

The Decimal Data Type

The Decimal data type is an oddity, you cannot declare a variable of type Decimal,
but it is possible to use it through a Variant (more information in the section on
variants). This data type is really just a 12 byte integer value (capable of producing 29
digit numbers) that can have a decimal point anywhere within it. It is not a floating-
point number, it does not round information to fit based on significant digits. This data
type should only be necessary in unusual circumstances (such as complex scientific or
statistical calculations) and should otherwise be ignored.

String Data Types

Strings are used to store any textual information, any combination of ASCII characters.
There are only two types of strings:

Variable Length Strings (Regular)

When you declare a variable as String, you can store almost any amount of text into
that variable (up to 2 billion characters). The realistic limit on how much you place into
the String is dependent on your available memory, which would likely be exceeded
before you reached 2 billion characters.

Fixed Length Strings

The variable declaration of a string can contain an additional piece of information, the
string length, making the string fixed in size. A fixed length string can hold only that
number of characters, and cannot grow beyond that length. The length information is
added to your declaration by placing *<length> after the As String. The following
code declares a fixed length string of 20 characters:

```
Dim FirstName As String * 20
```

Fixed length strings are used to save memory, but, in most cases, the small amount of
space you could save is not worth the extra effort. The major exception to this would
be situations where you are using a large number (hundreds or thousands) of these
strings. Remember that you could end up using more space than you need if you
create a fixed length string that is longer than your data.

Date

Date variables can be used to store date values, time values or a combined date/time
value. Assigning a value to a Date variable is the only trick to using them. You have to
use a special method of letting VBA know that you are dealing with dates, the #
character. The code below demonstrates how to assign a specific date to a Date
variable:

```
ExpiryDate = #08/12/98#
```

You have to do the same thing with time values, and when using both time and date values. An example of each method is listed below:

```
ExpiryDate = #4:00:00 PM#
ExpiryDate = #08/12/98 4:00:00 PM#
```

> Note that VBA uses your regional settings to determine what date/time formats to use. The statement above, using the date 8/12/98, could mean different things depending on whether your date format is set to Month/Day/Year or Day/Month/Year.

Boolean Variables

Often you need to store data that is binary (having only two possible values). **Boolean** variables are provided for this purpose, capable of storing only True or False. VBA provides two **constants** (special values represented by names, allowing you to use those names instead of the actual information), True and False, which make it easier to assign values to this type of variable. The code below shows several examples of setting Boolean variables:

```
Dim SendAsEmail As Boolean
Dim CollateCopies As Boolean
Dim ProductIsAvailable As Boolean

SendAsEmail = True
CollateCopies = False
ProductIsAvailable = Not ProductIsAvailable
```

The last line of code shows an example of using logic statements to manipulate Boolean values, in this case making `ProductIsAvailable` the opposite of its current value. You can also use the logical operators AND, OR, and XOR (which stands for Exclusive OR, which returns `True` if only one of the two values is `True`) with these variables as well. The tables below are provided as a quick reference to the common logic operators and their results:

Expression		Result
True	**NOT**	False
False	**NOT**	True

The NOT expression reverses the Boolean value.

Expression			Result
True	**OR**	True	True
True	**OR**	False	True
False	**OR**	False	False

OR is true when one or both values are true.

Expression			Result
True	AND	True	True
True	AND	False	False
False	AND	False	False

AND is true when both values are true.

Expression			Result
True	XOR	True	False
True	XOR	False	True
False	XOR	False	False

XOR is only true when the two values are different.

You will learn more about both **Boolean** variables and Boolean logic when the If statement is covered in the next chapter.

Object Variables

Certain types of variables are capable of storing objects. These variables can be either generic variables that can hold any object, or variables that hold a single specific object type. These variables are declared like regular variables, using As Object to signify a generic object variable, and As <Object Type> to declare it as a specific type of object.

Once you have declared the variable though, you work with it a little differently. You must use the Set keyword when assigning a value to an object variable. The code below shows the declaration of both types of object variables and the use of the Set keyword:

```
Sub WorkingWithObjects()

    Dim objGeneric As Object
    Dim objSelection As Selection

    Set objSelection = Application.Selection
    Set objGeneric = objSelection

    objSelection.Font.Size = 18
    objGeneric.Font.Bold = True

End Sub
```

You can see from the example that you can use the generic object in the exact same manner as the specific one, with the same effects. You will not get the wonderful code completion features of VBA when you are working with the generic object though, VBA doesn't pop up the list of object properties and methods for you automatically. Object variables will be used in many of the projects in this book, but they are usually of a specific type.

Variants

When we originally started this discussion of variables, the example showed declaring variables without a data type. When that occurs, VBA automatically makes the variable a `Variant`, the default data type in both VBA and VB itself. `Variant`s are variables that can hold any data type, performing automatic conversions as necessary, allowing you to assign any value to them without error. It is possible to determine the current data type stored in a `Variant` through the `VarType` function. This function returns a number that indicates which of the many different possible data types is currently being stored. VBA provides a series of **constants** (which, as mentioned earlier, are special named values provided so that you can use the name instead of the actual value in your code), listed below, that you can use in place of the various numeric values returned by this function:

Constant	Value
vbEmpty	0
vbNull	1
vbInteger	2
vbLong	3
vbSingle	4
vbDouble	5
vbCurrency	6
vbDate	7
vbString	8
vbObject	9
vbError	10
vbBoolean	11
vbVariant	12
vbDataObject	13
vbDecimal	14
vbByte	17
vbArray	8192

Despite their flexibility, or perhaps because of it, you should not use `Variant` variables unless you need to. If you know what you will be placing into the variable, then declare it as that type. This will avoid any problems of unwanted variable conversion, etc. There will be a few situations where you truly need a variable that can hold any data type, at which time a `Variant` will become essential, but these situations are not common.

Conversion between Data Types

For each type, only specific information can be stored, but there is some overlap and it is possible to convert data from one type to another. VBA will perform automatic conversions in most situations, such as in the code below:

```
Sub WorkingWithVariables()

    Dim X As Double
    Dim Y As Integer

    X = "3.5"
    Y = 32.2122

    MsgBox X
    MsgBox Y

End Sub
```

The code above would display a value of 3.5 for X, and 32 for Y. VBA converted the information appropriately in each case, even rounding the second value before placing it into an Integer variable. Despite this automatic conversion, it is sometimes helpful to have a method of forcing a conversion into a specific data type, allowing you to control exactly what happens to your information. VBA provides a large group of conversion functions for this purpose, each designed to convert values into one specific data type:

Cint	Converts values into Integers, rounding if necessary.
CLng	Converts values into Long integers, rounding if necessary.
Cdate	Converts values into Dates, especially useful for converting Strings into Date variables. Capable of accepting a wide variety of date formats.
CDbl	Converts values into Doubles, potentially reducing their number of significant digits.
Ccur	Converts values into Currency.
Cdec	Useful only when assigning the result to a Variant, this converts values into Decimal data types.
Cbool	Converts into Boolean
CStr	Converts anything into a String. For instance, Boolean variables become "True" or "False".

Arrays

An **array** is a series of values of the same data type, such as 10 integers, or 100 strings. Each value can be set or retrieved using its index or position in the arra. You can visualize an arra as a row of values, each capable of holding an individual value.

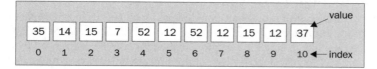

In VBA, you declare an array just like a variable with the addition of the size of the array; this is shown below for several different sizes and types of arrays:

```
Sub WorkingWithArrays()

    Dim Numbers(10) As Integer
    Dim Names(30) As String
    Dim Stuff(100)

    Numbers(1) = 5
    Numbers(2) = Numbers(1) + 5

    Names(5) = "Duncan"
    Names(7) = "Fred"
    Names(23) = "Laura"

    MsgBox Names(5)

    Stuff(5) = "Duncan"
    Stuff(6) = 32

End Sub
```

Determining Array Bounds

When you specify the array size with a single number, it just specifies the upper bound of the array, the lower bound is assumed. VBA, by default, places the lower bound of arrays at zero, so `Dim Names(30) As String` is creating an array with 31 positions in it. You can avoid this default behavior by including both the lower and upper bounds in your declaration, like this:

```
Dim Numbers(1 To 10) As Integer
```

Alternatively, you can change the default behavior of VBA through the `Option Base` statement. At the beginning of any VBA module (before any procedures), you can place a line of code that reads `Option Base 1` or `Option Base 0`. This line tells VBA what to use as the default lower bound for arrays in that module. Whatever lower bound you choose, you should be consistent and use the same value for all your arrays.

> 1 and 0 are not your only options for the lower bound of an array, you can just as easily create an array that starts at 10, 20, or even 5000. Just declare the array appropriately, `Dim X(5 to 342) As Integer`, for instance. You can only make VBA default to 1 or 0 though, the `Option Base` statement will not accept any other values.

Multi-Dimensional Arrays

You can create arrays with more than one dimension by specifying **multiple index sizes**, which can be very suitable to certain applications. The result is a set of variables (all of the same type, just like in single dimension arrays) that can be referenced by their "co-ordinates". The code below declares two **multi-dimensional arrays**, which are illustrated immediately following:

```
Sub WorkingWithArrays()

    Dim Grid(1 To 8, 1 To 8) As Integer
    Dim Cube(1 To 8, 1 To 8, 1 To 8) As Single

    'Code to fill arrays with values would go here….

    Grid(3, 5) = 23
    Grid(5, 1) = Grid(2, 1) + Grid(3, 2)

    Cube(3, 3, 3) = Cube(2, 1, 5)
    Cube(8, 1, 5) = 53.3232

End Sub
```

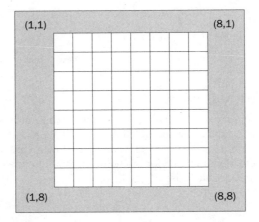

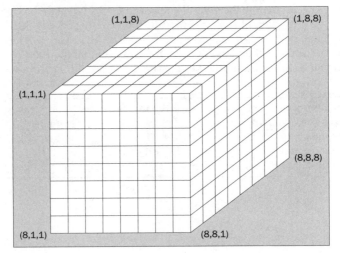

`Multi-Dimensional` arrays take up a large amount of memory (the size of the data type * dimension 1 * dimension 2 * dimension 3 and so on...) so you should use them sparingly, and not make them any bigger than you need.

Dynamic Arrays

Often you are unsure of how large to make your array, perhaps you are using it to store certain words as you find them in a document. When you are writing your code you have no way of knowing how many words you might find, so you can't determine how to declare the array. You could declare the array an arbitrarily large value, such as 1000, but that would cause two problems:

- ❑ What if there happened to be more than 1000 items? Your code could not handle it.
- ❑ What if there was less (and there usually would be)? You would be wasting memory.

Neither one of these problems can be ignored; you do not want to write code like that. Fortunately, VBA provides us with a way to deal with these issues, **dynamic arrays**. These arrays are declared without specifying their size, and then they can have their size set or adjusted at anytime.

The array is declared with empty parentheses to indicate that it is a dynamic array:

```
Dim Names() As String
```

Then the `ReDim` statement is used to set the size of the array:

```
ReDim Names(34)
```

> The ReDim statement will erase any existing data in the array unless the Preserve keyword is added:
>
> `ReDim Preserve Names(68)`
>
> Of course, data would still be lost if the array was reduced in size, even if the Preserve keyword is used.

Multi-dimensional dynamic arrays are also possible, although this is slightly limited. With multi-dimensional arrays, you can only adjust the size of the last dimension if you are using the `Preserve` keyword. However, if you are just calling `ReDim` (such as the first time you set the size of the array), you can set the number of dimensions and their size however you wish.

Collections

Arrays are designed to hold information in a very structured, linear fashion, and, despite the existence of dynamic arrays, they are designed to be fixed in size. That type of storage is well suited for information that follows the same pattern, seats on a plane, positions on a chess board etc, but there are other types of information that are not as suitable. Some information is not organized by position but instead by some other key value, such as an ID value, or a name. **Collections** are designed to store that type of information, the storage and retrieval of items is not based on position, but is instead based on unique key values provided for each item. You can add or remove items from a collection at any time, it doesn't require you to do any resizing or shuffling of items.

> Under the surface, items in a collection do have positions. You can use those positions to retrieve values just like from an array, but an item's position can change whenever other items are added or removed, making it rather difficult. This is not the way that collections are designed to be used, so use an array if you need position-based storage. In an array, once you put information into position 3, for instance, it will stay in that position regardless of the values you put into other positions. In a collection, position 3 could become position 4 if a new item was inserted, or become position 2 if an item was deleted.

Creating a New Collection

A collection is a type of object variable, which you can declare and use in your programs using the New keyword, something that is only used with objects. The code below declares and (due to the New keyword) creates an empty collection for use:

```
Dim Passengers As New Collection
```

Common Properties and Methods

Once you have created a collection, you will want to be able to add, remove and retrieve items from it. All of these tasks are accomplished through a collection's properties and methods.

Add Method

The Add method is used to insert items into a collection, it has the following syntax (the optional parts are held between [and]):

```
<Collection Name>.Add <Item>, [<Key>], [<Before>], [<After>]
```

Item is what is being added to the collection and it can be an expression of any type (string, numeric, object, etc). The items do not need to be of the same data type (unlike an array) but they usually are.

Key is a string value (such as "Document1"), which can be used to reference this item in the collection. It must be unique and it is used to retrieve the item from the collection. If a key is not specified, then you will not be able to directly retrieve this object from the collection; it will only be available through its position (which is not fixed).

Before and After are used to specify where this item should be inserted into the collection. As mentioned earlier, there is an underlying position for items in a collection, and these arguments are used to control that positioning. For both of these values you can either specify a string representing another item's key, or an integer representing an item's position. These arguments are optional and are often left blank.

This code shows creating a new collection and adding an item. In this example, only the item and its key are specified, which is the most common usage:

```
Sub WorkingWithCollections()

    Dim Passengers As New Collection

    Passengers.Add "John Smith", "641032934"

End Sub
```

Remove Method

As its name suggests, this method allows you to remove an item from a collection. Its syntax is specified below, showing its one argument:

<Collection Name>.Remove <Index>

An argument is a value passed to a method or procedure that is used to tell it what to do. There can be multiple arguments, or none, and arguments may be optional.

Index is a required argument, used to specify which member of the collection should be removed. This can be the item's key value (which is a string), or a numeric value representing the item's position. An error will be generated if no such item exists.

This code demonstrates removing an item by specifying its key:

```
Sub WorkingWithCollections()

    Dim Passengers As New Collection

    Passengers.Add "John Smith", "641032934"

    Passengers.Remove "641032934"

End Sub
```

Count Property

This property returns the current number of items in the collection. When referencing items by position, the range of possible values is from 0 to Count - 1. There are Count items and the first item is at position 0.

Item Method

This method returns a specific item from the collection and is how you retrieve and set the values of items that are already part of the collection. It uses the following syntax:

```
<Collection Name>.Item <Index>
```

Index is the only argument to this method, and it can be either a numeric positional value, or a string value representing an item's key.

This method is the default method of the collection object. This means that if you do not specify a property or method, VBA assumes you mean Item. The two lines highlighted below refer to the exact same item:

```
Sub WorkingWithCollections()

    Dim Passengers As New Collection

    Passengers.Add "John Smith", "641032934"

    MsgBox Passengers.Item("641032934")
    Passengers("641032934") = "Jane Smith"

    Passengers.Remove "641032934"

End Sub
```

Using Existing Collections

As mentioned earlier, there are many collections available from Word and from VBA itself, collections that you can use as you wish. These collections are not usually Collection variables, they are each a specific type of collection designed to hold and manipulate a certain type of item. For instance, one collection that you will be using on a regular basis in Word 2000 is the Documents collection. This collection represents all the currently open documents in Word and is useful for many different reasons. It is an object of type Documents, not Collection. As these collections are not exactly the same as the ones described earlier (which are generic VBA collections), they can have varied properties and methods; ones that are better suited to dealing with the particular type of information being stored. The Documents collection, for instance, has an Add method for creating new documents, but it takes different parameters than the one described above, has an Open method for opening Word documents from disk, and doesn't have a Remove method at all. Each of these collection variables needs to be treated differently, but they are the same in certain ways, all of them having certain characteristics such as the Count property.

The Documents collection itself will be covered later when we discuss the Word Object Model, in Chapter 5, and full details on its properties and methods will be provided at that time.

User-Defined Types

All of the data types we have been discussing, even arrays and collections, are part of the VBA language, generic ways to classify information. It is possible to create new data types though; data types that hold combinations of information that are specific to your needs. These **user-defined types**, as they are known, are a way to combine multiple variables into one structure that can be treated as a single variable.

Consider a program that tracks information about customers, each one has multiple pieces of information that need to be stored. For this example, we will be tracking an ID number (long integer), a Name (string), and a Phone Number (a fixed size string, 10 characters) for each customer.

We could create three variables for this purpose:

```
Sub CustomerInfo()

    Dim lCustomerID As Long
    Dim sCustomerName As String
    Dim sPhoneNumber As String * 10

    lCustomerID = 350
    sCustomerName = "Duncan Mackenzie"
    sPhoneNumber = "2045552321"

End Sub
```

The problem with this is that we have to work with three separate variables to work with a single customer, which complicates our code and makes it difficult to work with. A **user-defined type** allows us to take these three separate values and create one variable that can store them all. To be able to use a `Customer` variable type, it must be created. The code below accomplishes this, but must be placed in the General Declarations part of your code (the area at the very top of the code window, before any macro code):

```
Type Customer
    ID As Long
    Name As String
    Phone As String * 10
End Type
```

> You can use any data-type you wish as part of your type declaration, including objects, arrays, collections and even other user-defined types. Although, there is no limit to the number of variables that can be grouped together into a single type, it can be confusing to have too many. If there are a large number, you should divide them into sub-groups (using individual types for each sub-group) and then combine them into a single data type.

The new user-defined type allows us to rewrite the previous code sample as:

```
Sub CustomerInfo()

    Dim NewCustomer As Customer

    NewCustomer.ID = 350
    NewCustomer.Name = "Duncan Mackenzie"
    NewCustomer.Phone = "2045552321"

End Sub
```

This has not saved any lines of code, yet. The real benefit of combining these variables comes when you start working with multiple variables of the same type.

You can copy all of the information for a customer to a new variable with one line:

```
Sub CustomerInfo()

    Dim NewCustomer As Customer
    Dim OtherCustomer As Customer

    NewCustomer.ID = 350
    NewCustomer.Name = "Duncan Mackenzie"
    NewCustomer.Phone = "2045552321"

    OtherCustomer = NewCustomer

End Sub
```

You can also create arrays of a user-defined type just like any other data type:

```
Sub CustomerInfo()

    Dim Customers(100) As Customer

    Customers(34).ID = 350
    Customers(34).Name = "Duncan Mackenzie"
    Customers(34).Phone = "2045552323"

    Customers(35) = Customers(34)

End Sub
```

You can even store these variables into collections, and retrieve them in the same manner as any other value. User-defined types allow you to store a group of related information just like any single variable, making them powerful tools to simplify your code.

Constants

The last type of "variable" covered in this section is not really a variable at all. **Constants** cannot be changed through code, the very thing that defines variables. Like variables though, constants are used to associate a name with a value, allowing you to use that name in your code in place of the value itself. The difference is that the value is set as part of the constant's declaration, and cannot be changed (you can, of course, change its value by editing the declaration). The syntax for declaring a constant is shown below, with optional arguments shown enclosed between [and]:

[Public|Private] Const <Constant Name> [As <Data Type>] = <Value>

The optional Public or Private at the beginning of the declaration is used to control the constant's **scope**, and is covered in the section on scope later in this chapter. If you do not specify either Public or Private, then it is assumed that the constant is Private. The other optional portion of this declaration is the data type - as with variables, the constant will be declared as a Variant if you do not specify otherwise. Several example constant declarations are shown below:

```
Const MaxLength = 20
Const CompanyName As String = "Java Jitters Inc."
Const YearEnd As Date = #08/12/99#
```

Using a **constant** in place of a particular value has several benefits, not the least of which is improving the readability of your code, the name `MaxLength` carries a great deal more meaning than the number 20. The other main benefit of using a constant becomes apparent when the value changes. If you have a program that uses a certain value (the name of your company, for example) in hundreds of different places in the code, you should use a constant and not the value itself. Then, if the company name were changed, however slightly, at some point, you would only have to make one change to your program, not search through all your code trying to find every place that name was used.

Procedures

When a new macro is created, it becomes code in a **module**, located in the document or template of your choosing. This code takes the following form:

```
Sub <MacroName>()

    Macro Code

End Sub
```

What has actually been created is a procedure, a block of code that can be executed on its own. You can create your own procedures simply by typing in a new block of code (but not within an existing procedure) and supplying a unique name. Macros are just another name for these blocks of code, you do not need the **macro** recorder to create them, and that is not the only reason they are used.

Why Use Procedures?

Procedures exist for two main reasons:

- ❏ Code organization
- ❏ Code reuse

Code Organization

By breaking a large amount of code up into smaller pieces, it is easier to understand the code and to work with it. Conceptually, most large tasks can be broken up into several smaller tasks; procedures allow you to do the same thing with your code. By dividing a large program into smaller **subroutines** (the term that is implied by the keyword `Sub` at the beginning of our procedures), we can approach each of those smaller sections individually. This reduces the large problem, which appeared overwhelmingly complex, into a sequence of smaller tasks that are definitely manageable.

Consider the sequence of events involved in driving to the store to get some coffee. It is actually quite a large undertaking, to explain the complete task to someone new to the area could be difficult. By breaking it down into a series of small steps, it becomes easier to understand and explain:

- ❑ Leave the house
- ❑ Get in the car
- ❑ Start the car
- ❑ Back out of driveway
- ❑ Turn left
- ❑ Drive 2 blocks
- ❑ Turn right
- ❑ Park car in parking lot
- ❑ Turn car off
- ❑ Get out of car
- ❑ Get coffee
- ❑ Get in the car
- ❑ Start the car
- ❑ Leave parking lot
- ❑ Turn left
- ❑ Drive 2 blocks
- ❑ Turn right
- ❑ Park car in driveway
- ❑ Turn car off
- ❑ Get out of car
- ❑ Go into house

Explaining how to start the car is a manageable task, much more so than just explaining everything. Problems in programming work in the same way, it is possible to code large complex systems as one big pile of code, but by breaking it down you can tackle each item individually. You will really appreciate having your code separated when something goes wrong and you have to figure out why. Just having procedures in place allows you to quickly narrow down a problem to one particular part of your code, which can greatly reduce the time required to solve that problem.

You'll notice that a lot of the individual tasks listed in the example above are used more than once, that is very common, and a complex task usually involves the repetition of at least some actions. This repetition is where the concept of code reuse comes in.

Code Reuse

In the list of tasks that make up a trip to the store, there were several items that were present more than once, such as "Start the car". When you explained these steps to someone, you would only explain how to start the car once, and after that you would just tell them to do what they did before. If you were coding a similar task you would not want to repeat yourself either, and with procedures, you do not have to.

In addition to being able to be run from the Macros dialog, procedures can be called from other procedures. The code below shows three procedures Sub GoToTheStore, Sub GetInTheCar, and Sub StartTheCar, with GoToTheStore running the other two procedures as needed:

```
Sub GoToTheStore()

    GetInTheCar
    StartTheCar

    . . .

    GetInTheCar
    StartTheCar

    . . .

End Sub
```

```
Sub GetInTheCar()

    MsgBox "Getting In The Car"

End Sub
```

```
Sub StartTheCar()

    MsgBox "Starting The Car"

End Sub
```

As you can see, **calling** (which means running) a procedure is not complicated. You can place the code for a commonly used task into a procedure, and then call that procedure from anywhere it is needed. Regardless of how many other programs need to call your StartTheCar procedure, or how many times they call it, **you have only written the code once**.

Reusing code provides several benefits, in addition to the reduced typing time for the programmer:

Simplify Other Programs

From the time that you create it, you should never have to write that code again, and neither should any one else who is programming with you. Other programs can use it without having to know anything about how it works.

Ease of Maintenance

If there needs to be something changed about how that particular task is accomplished, how you start the car for example, you can change the code in that single location and every other program that uses it will automatically be using the new code.

Creating Procedures

Procedures can be created by simply typing `Sub` followed by the procedure name and hitting *Enter*. Remember to make sure you are not inside another procedure and that the procedure name is unique. The syntax for a basic procedure is straightforward:

```
Sub <ProcedureName>()

    Code

End Sub
```

> If you type in the `Sub` and `ProcedureName` portions, and hit *Return*, the brackets and the `End Sub` will all be added for you. The code, unfortunately, will not. It is also possible to use the menu option, **Insert | Procedure**, which will bring up a dialog box prompting you for a procedure name and other information which it will then insert into a new procedure.

Arguments

Some procedures require information to be passed to them to be able to run, information that you supply when you call them. The pieces of information required are called the **arguments** or **parameters** of the procedure, and are specified in the procedure declaration. Specify parameters in the brackets after the procedure name, by typing in a comma-separated list of variable names and data types, which look very similar to standard variable declarations:

```
Sub DisplayMessage(Message As String, Title As String)

    Message = "This is the Message: " & Message
    MsgBox Message, vbOKOnly, Title

End Sub
```

> There is that pesky `MsgBox` statement again, this time using more than one argument. The additional arguments, `vbOKOnly` and `Title`, specify what type of buttons should appear with the displayed message and what title the display window should have, respectively.
>
> Also note the use of the & character between `"This is the Message: "` and our `Message` parameter. This character is the concatenation operator; it is used to join two strings together.

In the code above, the procedure has two arguments, `Message` and `Title`. Inside the procedure itself, these arguments are treated just like variables; their values having been set to whatever values were passed when the procedure was called. The syntax for calling a procedure with parameters is to provide them as a list of values after the procedure name:

```
DisplayMessage "Disk Full", "Error Saving File"
```

ByRef and ByVal

You can pass any expression of the correct data type into a procedure, just like setting a variable of the same type, but when you pass an actual variable, procedures treat them differently. In this procedure, for instance, MyMessage is modified by the DisplayMessage procedure, changing its value from "Test" to "This is the Message: Test". When we run this code we see two text boxes, both announcing, This is the Message: Test:

```
Public Sub DisplaySelectionInfo()

    Dim MyMessage As String

    MyMessage = "Test"
    DisplayMessage MyMessage, "Error"

    MsgBox MyMessage

End Sub
```

This behavior occurs because variables can be passed into procedures in one of two ways, **by value** or **by reference**.

When a variable is passed by reference, the procedure is working with that actual variable when it modifies the parameter.

When you pass a variable by value, only a copy of its contents are given to the procedure.

You can control how each parameter is passed to a procedure by modifying the procedure declaration. The keywords ByRef or ByVal can be placed in front of a parameter, making all variables passed to this parameter explicitly by reference or by value. These keywords effect each parameter individually, and any parameter that doesn't have a keyword in front of it is considered ByRef by default.

Redefining the procedure declaration for DisplayMessage to ensure that neither of its parameters is inadvertently modified results in the following:

```
Sub DisplayMessage(ByVal Message As String, ByVal Title As String)

    Message = "This is the Message: " & Message
    MsgBox Message, vbOKOnly, Title

End Sub
```

Now when we run the code, the value in MyMessage will be passed to DisplayMessage and converted, but the value of MyMessage in DisplaySelectionInfo will be unaffected by the conversion. Two message boxes appear, one displaying This is the Message: Test and one displaying Test.

Optional Arguments

Many of the procedures that are supplied by Word or by VBA contain **optional arguments**, parameters that we can supply if needed but can also be skipped. The MsgBox function is good example of this, accepting five parameters, only one of which is required. Optional parameters allow us to make procedures easy to use; the user of the procedure need only supply the information that fits their current needs. To make a parameter optional in a procedure declaration that parameter must:

❑ Be after any required parameters, all optional parameters must fall at the end of the parameter list

❑ Have the Optional keyword before this parameter, and any that follow it in the parameter list

> **Parameters without a specific data type, (nothing after the parameter name), are automatically considered to be Variant.**

Optional parameters can have a default value specified; a value that the parameter will be assigned if none is supplied. Default values are added to the procedure declaration as an equal sign and value. The procedure declaration below illustrates the various parts of declaring an optional parameter:

```
Sub DisplayMessage(ByVal Message As String, Optional ByVal Title = "My
Message")
```

ParamArray

The last parameter in a procedure declaration can have the ParamArray keyword in front of it, signifying that it will accept an optional array of values as arguments. If a ParamArray argument is present in an argument list, there can be no Optional parameters for the same procedure and you can't use the ByVal or ByRef keywords. Use of this keyword allows you to create procedures like the following example, one that can take a varying number of values and then work with those values to solve a problem:

```
Sub ParamArrayTest()

    SalaryAverage 32000, 34200, 50000

    SalaryAverage 34200, 34500, 50000

End Sub
```

```
Sub SalaryAverage(ParamArray Values())

    '...

End Sub
```

> **This type of function is useful, and it is extremely important to know that such abilities exist, but it is slightly unusual and we will not need to use it anywhere in this book.**

Functions

In addition to taking values into a procedure, it is possible to return information as well. Procedures that return a value are known as **functions** and they are declared a little differently. The keyword Sub is replaced with Function and the data type of the return value is indicated at the end of the declaration:

```
Function Squared(Number As Long) As Long

    Squared = Number * Number

End Function
```

> **Like a variable, if you do not specify the data type returned by a function then it is considered to be a Variant.**

In the code of the function, you return a value by a statement of the form <Function Name> = <Value>. That value is then returned to the code that called the function. From the calling end, there are two differences when working with functions, first you have to do something with that returned value, and second you place brackets around the arguments you are sending to the function. The code below shows an example of calling a function.

```
X = Squared(34)
```

After this line of code executes, X would be equal to the return value of Squared, or X * X.

> **You do not have to return a value from a function, but then it is just like a standard procedure and should be just defined using the Sub keyword.**

General Tips and Guidelines

When it comes to creating procedures, it isn't just a matter of placing some code between a Sub and an End Sub statement, that isn't enough. Procedures are most useful when they are reusable, not just in the same project, but in any project. To provide this usability a procedure should be:

- ❑ Independent
- ❑ Complete
- ❑ Flexible

Procedure Independence

In the context of procedures, being independent means that the code inside the procedure doesn't rely on any feature of its position, being in a certain project, or having access to certain global variables. If you can manage it, the procedure should be able to work perfectly with only what is passed into it through its parameters and with its own internal code. This will allow it to be called by another project without any worry about loss of functionality.

Procedure Completeness

A procedure should completely encapsulate the task it is designed to perform. It should be possible to call just that procedure and have a complete, distinct task performed without being required to call any other code. If each procedure is designed in this fashion, they can be reused easily without complicated instructions being required.

Flexibility

Always design your procedures to deal with more than you have to. If you are writing a procedure that emails the current document and you always need to send the email to the same address, a common approach would be to hardcode that email address in the procedure. This makes it useless to anyone who needs to email the current document to a different address, or perhaps needs to email a different document. If you created the procedure with parameters for `ToAddress`, `DocumentName`, etc, you would be able to use that procedure in almost any situation. Consider situations beyond your current needs, even though you currently send just one document to just one address you should design your code to handle multiple of both or either of these items.

> Reality often prevents us from building our code as well as is discussed above, but if you at least consider the future uses of your code, you will produce procedures that are better suited to reuse.

Scope

Everything in Visual Basic has a certain **scope**, including variables and procedures. We looked at this topic earlier when dealing with where macros were stored, but we need to cover it again with our increased knowledge of creating procedures and variables. The scope of a procedure effects where it can be called from; if it is not visible to another procedure then it cannot be used. For variables it is the same concept, their scope determines where they (and therefore the information they carry) can be accessed. If you need a certain value to be visible to every piece of code in your project, that variable has to have the correct scope.

There are three distinct levels of scope possible in VBA:

- ❑ Global. Visible from any code in the same project.
- ❑ Module-Level.. Visible from any code in the same module.
- ❑ Local. Visible only in the procedure it was declared in. (Does not apply to procedures, they always have a scope of at least module-level.)

Variable Declarations

To create a variable with global scope, it must be declared in the `General Declarations` section of a module. This is the area at the top of the module, before the start of any procedures in that file. It must also be declared with the **Public** keyword, as shown in this example:

```
Public sUserName As String
```

A variable declared in this fashion is visible to every procedure in the project.

> To place module-level declarations into a module that already contains procedures, you may have to make space at the top of the module by inserting several blank lines (using the *Return* key).

To make a variable that has module-level scope, it must also be declared in the `General Declarations` area of the module, but it should be declared without using the `Public` keyword. Instead, it should either use no keyword and be declared with `Dim` or `Const` (for variable and constants respectively), or have the keyword `Private` in front of it. The sample code below shows how the first option would appear:

```
Dim sUserName As String
Const MaxNameLength = 20
```

and using the `Private` keyword;

```
Private sUserName As String
Private Const MaxNameLength = 20
```

> Note that the `Private` keyword replaces `Dim`, but is used together with `Const`. This is true of the `Public` keyword as well.

Variables and constants declared inside a procedure always have local scope, regardless of how they are declared, in fact you cannot declare them as `Public` (this will cause an error).

Procedures

When declaring a procedure, you have only two choices; a procedure can only have global or module-level scope. Your use, or omission of, one of the keywords `Public` or `Private` determines the level of scope.

`Sub` and `Function` declarations that do not specify their scope are `Public` by default, and therefore visible to all the code in the project. The same effect results if you place `Public` in front of the declaration, as in the code below:

```
Public Sub StartTheCar()

End Sub
```

To make a procedure have module-level scope, visible only to code in that module, place the `Private` keyword in front of the declaration:

```
Private Sub StartTheCar()

End Sub
```

Only procedures with global (`Public`) scope are visible in the **Macros** dialog box, making a procedur `Private` will remove it from the list. In addition to `Private` procedures, any procedure (`Public` or not) that takes parameters is not available through the **Macros** dialog box, as it couldn't be run without supplying those arguments.

Scope allows you to create many different procedures, with only a select few being made visible to the user. This creates a layer between the user and your code, restricting them to using only those procedures that you want available.

Cross Project Considerations

In Word 2000 VBA, it is possible for code in one project to work with variables, procedures, and objects from other projects. You can make the `Public` portions (those with global scope) of a project visible to another project by setting a **reference**. References that exist in a project are visible under a separate folder in the Project Explorer, as visible here:

One or more references will already exist for projects that are based on a template (including `Normal.dot`), but all others have to be added through the **References** dialog. This dialog, opened by selecting **References** from the **T**ools menu, displays a large list of available objects:

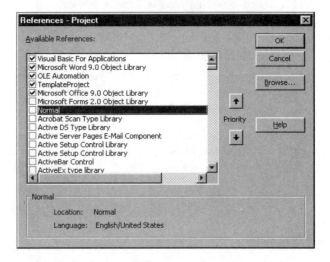

These objects are, for the most part, COM libraries installed onto your machine (an explanation of what COM is, and why it is important is provided in Chapter 10 of this book), but some are just Word documents and templates (.doc and .dot files). Any Word files that are currently loaded, but not referenced yet, will be shown in the list directly below those that are selected, making it easy to add them to the current project's references. The <u>B</u>rowse button on this dialog allows you to go and select additional COM libraries and Word documents to appear in the list.

Once you have created a reference to a project, you can use that project's public members directly in your code just like procedures and variables from your own project. You can use these items on their own with nothing distinguishing them as being from an external reference, or you can preface them with <project name>. An example of code using the project name Normal is shown below:

```
Normal.CustomerInfo
Normal.sUserName = "Duncanm"
MsgBox Normal.X
```

Or without the project name (which is only available if there are no local variables or procedures with conflicting names):

```
CustomerInfo
sUserName = "Duncanm"
MsgBox X
```

The power to reference code and variables stored in another project opens up the ability to use a project as a **code library**, a shared location containing procedures used by many different projects. This can greatly add to your productivity and organization as a Word developer, helping to prevent the rewriting of code that has already been created.

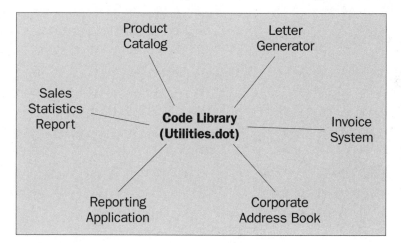

Summary

VBA is a powerful programming language with all of the features you will need to build complete applications in Word 2000. This chapter has provided you with the general information you will need to start directly coding macros, without being limited to what the macro recorder is capable of generating. From this point on, the recorder will become primarily a learning tool only, showing you how to code a particular action, and producing code that you will cut and paste into your own procedures.

Chapter 3 continues to explore the features of Word 2000 VBA, moving on to controlling the flow of your program and working with forms and dialogs.

Conditionals and Loops

Introduction

In the last chapter, we looked at some basic VBA concepts to prepare you to write your own procedures from scratch. This chapter continues that topic, introducing you to **conditionals** and **loops**. These two VBA features enable you to control the flow of your programs. We'll also take a more in-depth look at Boolean expressions and we'll see how to use comparison operators and Boolean values to add decision-making capability to our programs. We'll wrap up the chapter with a discussion of loops, which allow a section of code to be repeated. We'll look at two types of loop, one that repeats a certain number of times and another that executes while or until a condition is met.

To sum up we'll look at:

- ❑ Decision-making with conditionals
- ❑ Boolean expressions
- ❑ Repeating code with loops

By the end of this chapter, you will have complete control of the flow of your programs. So let's get started!

Conditionals

Macros are linear, they record a series of actions in order, and then playback those actions in the exact order that they were recorded. Most processes in life and business are not like that, one step always followed by the next. Instead, things change according to the situation. Processes have **decision points**; places where there is a determination made about what should be done next. **Conditionals** provide a way to code those decision points, without which you would be limited to code that always behaves the same.

If Statements

The most common way to control the flow of your program is through the `If` statement. This statement evaluates a Boolean expression, an expression that can only be resolved into a true or false value. If the result of that expression is true, a block of code is executed, if the expression is false, that block of code is skipped and not executed. The general format of an `If` statement can be illustrated as:

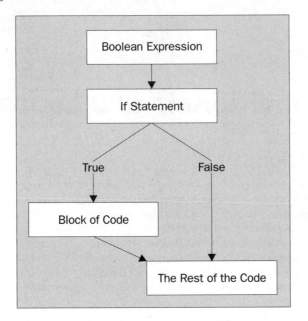

In actual VBA code, this translates into the following syntax:

```
If <Boolean Expression> Then

    <Actions>

End If
```

There is no limit on how many lines of code can fall between the `If` and `End If` statements. You can **nest** (place one statement inside another) `If` statements, but there must always be a corresponding `End If` statement for every `If`. To facilitate matching all the `If` statements with their `End If`, indenting is often used, moving all the code inside an If statement several spaces to the right. The code below shows an example of nested `If` statements without indents:

> Note the operators in the code below, those symbols such as > (greater than), < (less than), = (equal to), and <> (not equal to) that are placed in between two parts of an expression to create a comparison. These operators will be used throughout VBA to compare two expressions and obtain a true or false result. These operators are covered further on, under the heading "Comparisons".

```
If X > 3 Then
X = X - 2
If Y < 21 Then
Y = Y + X
If Y >= 21 Then
X = Y * 2
End If
J = J + X * Y
End If
If X > Y Then
X = Y
End If
End If
```

The same code is repeated below with the addition of indenting. Notice the increased readability and how easily pairs of If ... End If can be matched:

```
If X > 3 Then
    X = X - 2
    If Y < 21 Then
        Y = Y + X
        If Y >= 21 Then
            X = Y * 2
        End If
        J = J + X * Y
    End If
    If X > Y Then
        X = Y
    End If
End If
```

There are many different variations on the standard If statement, each of which are covered individually in the following sections.

Single Line

The standard If statement takes at least three lines of code to implement, assuming that there is at least one line of code between the If and the End If. Having only a single piece of code inside an If statement is a common occurrence so, to reduce the number of lines of code needed, a variation on the If statement is available that places all the code onto a single line. The syntax for this type of If statement is:

```
If <Boolean Expression> Then <Action>
```

Only one line of code can follow the Then keyword, restricting the use of this statement to only those situations where that is enough. The end result looks similar to this example:

```
If X > 3 Then X = X + 34
```

Note that in VBA you can split a single logical line of code across multiple physical lines using the code continuation character "_". This can make for clearer code and easier reading:

```
If (X > 3) Or (X < 0) Then MsgBox "This is a really big problem, " & _
"X has gone wild!!", vbCritical, "Error in X"
```

> **The code continuation character cannot be placed within quotes or it will be treated as a part of the string.**

If...Then...Else...End If

After the standard If ... End If, this is the most common format for an If statement. This type of If statement adds some functionality to the If ... End If statement; allowing it to run one of two blocks of code, based on the value of the expression. The statement has the following syntax:

```
If <Boolean Expression> Then

    <Code Block 1>

Else

    <Code Block 2>

    End If
```

If the expression evaluates to True, the first block of code is run, otherwise the second block executes. One and one only, will execute; the two are mutually exclusive.

If...Then...ElseIf...End If

Another enhancement or variation on the If statement involves the addition of a new line of code, the ElseIf statement. This new statement takes the form:

```
If <Boolean Expression 1> Then

    <Action 1>

Else

If <Boolean Expression 2> Then
```

```
      <Action 2>

   End If

End If
```

and simplifies it to:

```
If <Boolean Expression 1> Then

      <Action 1>

ElseIf <Boolean Expression 2> Then

      <Action 2>

End If
```

The `ElseIf` clause can have its own `Else` or `ElseIf` sections as well, which can make for confusing code when proper indentation is not used.

Boolean Expressions

`If` statements and other conditionals depend on Boolean expressions to do their work, it is these expressions that really determine which blocks of code are skipped and which are executed. A Boolean expression is anything that results in a `True` or `False` value and can cover a wide range. This usually consists of one of four types of expressions:

- ❑   Comparisons
- ❑   Boolean values
- ❑   Boolean logic
- ❑   Function calls

Comparisons

The first type of expression that is commonly found in conditionals is the **comparison**. A comparison is a statement about the relative value of two objects, the result of which is either true or false. Some examples of comparisons include:

```
X > 3
Y < 5 - X
X = Y
```

In general, a comparison consists of two values with a **comparison operator** between them. The two values may actually be expressions in themselves, such as `(X + 5) > (Y - 2 * X)`, that need to be evaluated before the results can be compared. The operator can be any one of the following **binary operators** (operators that work on two values):

Name	Operator
Equals	=
Greater than	>
Less than	<
Greater than or equal to	>=
Less than or equal to	<=
Not equal	<>

> Note the order of the symbols in the "Less than or equal to" (<=) and the "Greater than or equal to" (>=) operators. They will only work in the order shown (=> will not work, for instance), but VBA happily changes them for you if you happen to type them in reverse.

Boolean Values

It is possible for a conditional to have a single Boolean value as its expression, generally using a variable, but it could also use an actual value. Placing True or False into an expression is a good way to see what will happen if the block of code never runs or if it runs every time. The code below demonstrates the use of a Boolean value in an expression:

```
If PrintDocument Then
    'Print It
End If

If False Then
    'Erase Document
End If
```

Boolean Logic

Using logical operators in your expressions allows you to combine multiple Boolean values in various ways to get a single true or false result. The various operators and their effects are covered back in Chapter 2 under "Boolean Variables". Here are a few examples of how these operators can be used:

```
If PrintDocument And PrinterAvailable Then

If Not PrinterAvailable Or Not PrintDocument Then

If ((X > 4) AND (Y > 4)) OR (Y + X > 20) Then
```

The first example shown would result in True only if both PrintDocument and PrinterAvailable were equal to True.

The second case, is a little more difficult since we are using the Not operator which has the effect of switching the value of a Boolean variable. The complete expression would return True if either PrinterAvailable or PrintDocument was equal to False.

The final example is quite complex as it involves multiple comparisons. It returns
True if either X and Y are both greater than 4, or if the sum of X and Y is greater than
20.

Functions

You can use function calls as part of, or the entire Boolean expression for your
conditionals, allowing you to move complex calculations into separate pieces of code.
When building the expression, simply treat the function call as if it were the return
value from that procedure, placing it wherever it is required. This results in code like
the following:

```
If PrinterAvailable("INVOICE PRINTER") Then

If Tax(OrderTotal) > 20 Then

If PrinterAvailable("INVOICE PRINTER") And PrintDocument(ThisDocument) Then

If DefaultPrinter() <> CurrentPrinter() Then
```

When VBA evaluates the expression, it will call the functions to retrieve their results,
and then use those results to continue evaluating the expression. In an expression like
PrinterAvailable("INVOICE PRINTER") And
PrintDocument(ThisDocument), if the first function returns False then the entire
expression is False, regardless of the second result. A similar situation applies with
the Or operator, if the first expression is True, there is no need to go to the effort of
evaluating the second.

Unfortunately, VB is not that smart, it will always evaluate both sides of the expression
(calling any functions necessary) before comparing their values. If you have a routine
on the right-hand side of an expression that contains a call to a time-consuming
function, you can increase the performance of your application by breaking the
expression into two separate If statements. An example of this is shown below:

The Slow Way

```
If (X > 20) And (Calculated_YTD_Orders(1999) > 3400) Then

   ' Do Something

End If
```

The function will be evaluated every time, regardless of X's value.

The Fast Way

```
If X > 20 Then

   If Calculated_YTD_Order(1999) > 3400 Then

      'Do Something

   End If

End If
```

> What do you do if your time consuming function is on the left hand side
> of the expression? Move it; rewrite the expression to place it on the other
> side of the operator.

Select Case

Some situations demand that you check the same variable or expression against
multiple values. This can be done with If and ElseIf statements, but it involves a
fair bit of code. The code below shows an example of this, checking the variable
OrderAmount against many different numeric values:

```
If OrderAmount < 0 Then
    MsgBox "Customer Receives A Credit"
    Shipping = 0
ElseIf OrderAmount = 0 Then
    MsgBox "Empty Order"
    Shipping = 0
ElseIf OrderAmount < 100 Then
    MsgBox "Small Order"
    Shipping = 4
ElseIf OrderAmount <= 200 Then
    MsgBox "Medium Order"
    Shipping = 6.75
Else
    MsgBox "Large Order"
    Shipping = 15
End If
```

There is a special type of conditional statement intended to handle exactly this type of
situation - Select Case. Select Case tests a value against multiple possible values
and executes a block of code corresponding to the matching result. Select Case has
the following general syntax:

```
Select Case <Expression>

    Case <Value>

        <Actions>

    Case <Value>

        <Actions>

        repeated as needed

    Case Else

        <Actions>

End Select
```

The last `Case` block (the `Case Else`) executes if the expression does not match any of the others and is useful as a place to handle unexpected data or data outside the range being tested for. The values for each `Case` block can be specified using any comparison operator with a special operator, `Is`. Equals is the default when no operator is specified.

The code sample given earlier could be programmed using the `Select Case` statement like this:

```
Select Case OrderAmount

    Case Is < 0

        MsgBox "Customer Receives A Credit"
        Shipping = 0

    Case 0

        MsgBox "Empty Order"
        Shipping = 0

    Case Is < 100

        MsgBox "Small Order"
        Shipping = 4

    Case Is <= 200

        MsgBox "Medium Order"
        Shipping = 6.75

    Case Else

        MsgBox "Large Order"
        Shipping = 15

End Select
```

Looping

Conditionals, which we just covered, allow you to determine if a block of code should be executed. The next way to control your program's flow is very similar. **Loops** determine how many times a certain block of code should be executed, sometimes using Boolean expressions almost identical to those used in conditionals. VBA include several different types of loops and each works a little differently.

For...Next

This is the standard `For` loop. It exists in many different programming languages and it is designed to simply repeat a block of code a certain number of times. In its most basic form, a `For` loop is written like this:

```
For <Counter Variable> = <Lower Bound> To <Upper Bound>

    <Actions>

Next <Counter Variable>
```

The counter variable isn't a special type of variable; it is just an integer or long integer variable which is used by the loop. This variable is set equal to the **lower bound** at the start of the loop and is incremented by one each time the loop executes. The best way to understand the For loop is to show it in use. The code below shows a For loop that is designed to execute 10 times:

```
For i = 1 to 10
    MsgBox i
Next i
```

> In the example above, the Next statement is followed by the loop's counter variable (as in Next i). This is optional and is sometimes done to make your code easier to follow, associating the Next statement clearly with a particular For loop.

This code sample would simply display the numbers from 1 to 10 as dialogs to the user, as it executed the line MsgBox i ten times. The value of the counter variable, in this case i, is often used inside the loop as an array index or in other locations that require an increasing value.

It is possible to customize the amount of the increment as well as the boundaries of it. This is an additional, optional part of the For loop: the Step keyword. By placing the Step keyword, followed by the value you wish to use as the increment, at the end of the loop's starting line, the counter variable will be incremented by that value:

```
For i = 1 to 10 Step 5
    MsgBox I
Next i
```

This modified code would display the number 1 the first time through, then the number 6 (1 + the Step value of 5). The loop would end at this point, as the next value would exceed its boundaries. Using this Step keyword, you can create For loops that move backwards, simply by setting the lower and upper bounds appropriately and using a negative Step value. The code below will count backwards (in messages to the user) from 10 to 1:

```
For i = 10 to 1 Step -1
    MsgBox i
Next i
```

When a For loop ends, the counter variable will have a value that is greater than the upper boundary of the loop, the exact value depends on the increment being used.

> You can modify the value of the counter variable inside the For loop, but this is not recommended. This can result in unexpected behavior such as an infinite loop, a loop that never ends.

For Each...Next

This is a variation on the `For` loop that is designed to work with collections and arrays. A collection is composed of a number of items and this loop allows you to iterate through all of those items, regardless of how many there are. A counter variable is also used, like in the regular `For` loop, but it has a slightly different purpose. Once again, a code example is the best way to represent how this loop works:

```
Sub PrintAllDocuments()

    Dim CurrentDocument As Document

    For Each CurrentDocument In Documents

        MsgBox CurrentDocument.Name

    Next CurrentDocument

End Sub
```

The `For Each` loop above executes once for each `Document` in the `Documents` collection and sets `CurrentDocument` equal to the current collection item with each iteration of the loop. This loop displays the names of all open documents.

Do Loops

Another type of loop, the `Do` loop, behaves differently than `For` loops. The `Do` loop is designed to execute a block of code placed between a `Do` statement and a `Loop` statement either while or until a certain Boolean expression returns `True`. This loop comes in five different varieties but they are all similar.

The first type of `Do Loop` is one without any end condition, it will continue to execute the block of code indefinitely, or until an `Exit Do` statement is executed (more information on the `Exit Do` statement will be provided shortly):

```
Do

    X = 1

Loop
```

Anything between the two statements will be repeated until the loop is exited. This type of loop, one with no exit condition, is not very useful and it will in fact hang your application. There are two clauses that can be added to this loop to make it more useful - `Until` or `While`. Each of the clauses allows you to specify a Boolean expression that will cause the loop to exit, but they differ in that the `Until` clause will exit the loop if the Boolean expression returns `True`, and the `While` clause is the reverse, exiting on a `False` value. The two clauses can also be used at either end of the loop, their position determining when the exit condition is checked, at the beginning or end of the loop. Altogether, this allows four different types of loops (five when you include the one from above), illustrated here:

```
Do While <Boolean Expression>

    'Actions
```

```
Loop

    Do Until <Boolean Expression>

        'Actions

    Loop

    Do

        'Actions

    Loop While <Boolean Expression>

    Do

        'Actions

    Loop Until <Boolean Expression>
```

Each type and arrangement of exit condition has its advantages and purpose. Either `Until` or `While` will work for any situation, simply change the Boolean expression to suit the clause, but the position is more important. When deciding where to place your exit condition, at the beginning or end of the loop, consider whether or not you want the code to execute at least once regardless of the Boolean expression. In the case of placing the condition at the end of the loop, that is what will always happen, the code inside the loop will execute once before the exit condition is ever checked. In the opposite situation, where the exit condition is at the start of the loop, the code will be skipped entirely if that condition is met when the loop is entered. In most cases, placing the condition at the start of the loop will be the most useful and the easiest to understand. Finally, if you have code that should always run, regardless of the exit condition, place it outside the loop.

> This is an appropriate time to explain how to deal with an infinite loop. If your code has entered a loop that has no exit condition, it will stay inside that loop forever, or until you stop its execution. During an infinite loop, it is usually not possible to click on the **Reset** button on the Visual Basic editor's toolbar. If you can, do so, as this will stop the code execution immediately. The next best thing is to press the key combination *Ctrl + Break*, which will accomplish the same goal.

Exiting a Loop in Code

The exit condition of a loop is the preferred way to leave that loop; that is why it is there. However there are also commands provided that will force immediate exit of an executing loop. These commands are specific to the loop type, so there are two of them, `Exit Do` and `Exit For`. The execution of the appropriate command will result in the immediate continuation of your code on the line immediately following the end of the loop. Once again, it is important to note that, while there is nothing incorrect with these commands, it produces better, easier to follow code if you do not use them.

Summary

A program isn't all that useful if it always does the same thing, which is all that a recorded macro is capable of. To really accomplish something, your programs have to be able to make decisions and execute code based on various conditions.

In this chapter, we've seen several different ways to control the execution of your program. With all of these techniques, you will be able to create programs that behave differently under almost any condition. We've seen:

- `If...Then`
- `If...Then...End If`
- `If...ElseIf...End If`
- The comparison operators =, >, <, >=, <= and <>
- `Select Case`
- `For...Next`
- `For Each...Next`
- `Do` loops
- Extending `Do` loops with `While` and `Until`

In the next chapter, we'll learn about forms and controls. See you there!

Forms and Controls

Introduction

In this chapter we will learn about **forms** (dialogs and windows that we can create) and **controls** (objects that can be placed onto forms to enhance them). These are the building blocks of a custom interface and it is through this custom interface that users of your VBA project will be able to interact with the program itself.

We will cover:

- ❑ The main properties, methods and events of forms
- ❑ The controls intrinsic to VBA
- ❑ Setting the properties of a control
- ❑ Event procedures
- ❑ ActiveX controls

Forms

For various reasons, your code often requires input from users, requiring them to supply information or to select one out of several choices. To allow this, you need to provide those users with an interface; a visual means to provide their input. Windows-based programs usually do this with a dialog, window, or form, three names that all effectively mean the same thing. Whatever it is called, it is a screen of information displayed to the user with buttons, text entry fields and other objects on it, allowing the user to interact with it and then click a button or otherwise tell you that they are done. This image shows a sample screen, highlighting and defining various items of interest on that form:

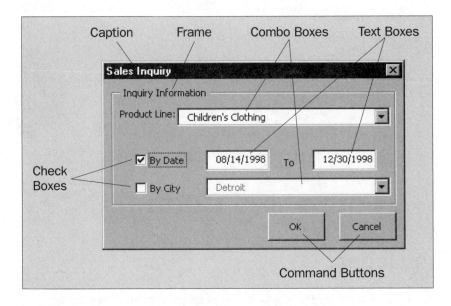

In Word 2000 VBA, you can create and use your own forms and then control them from within your programs. With a complex Word application you may wish to create a custom interface for your users, providing them with an easier way to enter information or select options. From within VBA code, you can display forms that you have created and then retrieve information from them about what text the user entered, what buttons they clicked and use that data to control how your program behaves. These forms are added to your project through the Insert menu and can be removed through the File | Remove menu option. When you insert a new form into your project, it starts out blank with no controls on it at all, as shown here:

Forms are objects. This means they have properties, methods, and events (described below in the section "Events"). Together, all three of those attributes allow you to use forms in your programs.

Properties

The form itself has many different properties, as shown in the Properties window, giving you the ability to change the form's appearance and behavior as needed. Although there are many different properties available, we will list and explain some of the more commonly used ones.

Name

The Name property is common to many different objects including modules, forms and even projects. This property controls how you refer to the form in code, and also how it appears inside your project. When you first create a new form, it has a Name property of UserForm1, the default name given to it by Word. If you wanted to write some code that worked with this form, the code would look something like this:

```
UserForm1.Caption = "Testing"
UserForm1.Show
```

Unless you change the form's name, you must refer to it by this name. This can make your code very difficult to understand and relatively meaningless to anyone else, especially when your VBA programs become more complex and have a number of different forms. You should always assign a new name to your form, one that represents its purpose, such as frmSalesInquiry.

BackColor, BorderColor and ForeColor

These three properties control the appearance of the form, each corresponding to the color of specific elements.

BackColor sets the background color of the whole form. BorderColor sets the color of the form's border, although you'll need to have the BorderStyle property set to frmBorderStyleSingle to see this. ForeColor sets the foreground color of the form. This determines the color of the grid of small dots that cover the form. The ForeColor is also used for the text of some of the controls placed on the form. The label, check box, option button, frame, tab strip and multi-page controls (we'll discuss all of these later in the chapter) all take the ForeColor of the form as their default ForeColor value.

When you set these properties, you are presented with a list of colors with names like Button Text and Desktop. These correspond to settings from the Display control panel in Windows, settings chosen by the user to apply across all applications. If you choose a color from this list, Desktop for instance, then your form will use whatever color is currently set as the user's desktop color. Choosing elements from this list will ensure that your application changes its colors when the user modifies the settings in the Display control panel. If you wish to set one of these properties to be a specific color, click on the Palette tab and you will be able to select any color you wish. Colors chosen from the Palette tab are specific and so will not change automatically with the system settings.

Caption

This property controls the text displayed at the top of the form. It defaults to the name of the form, and is likely to be set to UserForm1 or something similar at this point. As with the Name of the form, the Caption property should be changed to reflect the purpose of the form.

Height and Width

These two properties control the size of the form. You can change both of these properties interactively by resizing the form directly using the mouse.

Picture, PictureAlignment, PictureSizeMode and PictureTiling

These properties allow you to place an image onto your form and control its scaling and positioning. When the Picture property is selected, it displays a small button with three dots on it. Clicking on that button will bring up a browse window to select an image for display. Once you have an image loaded, PictureAlignment controls where that picture is placed on the form, and can be set to put the picture in the TopLeft, TopRight, Center, BottomLeft or BottomRight.

PictureSizeMode controls how the picture is scaled to fit into the form. If this property is set to frmPictureSizeModeClip then the picture is not scaled at all, if it is smaller than the form, then some of the form is left blank, if the picture is larger than the form, the picture is just clipped to fit. The frmPictureSizeModeStretch setting makes the picture's dimensions the same as the form's, potentially causing distortion to the picture in the process. The final setting, frmPictureSizeModeZoom, enlarges the image without distorting its aspect ratio (i.e. maintaining the image's proportions) until it hits a vertical or horizontal edge.

All three PictureSizeMode settings are demonstrated below using a single picture (100 pixels square) of three concentric circles. The effect of each setting is shown on a form that is 50 x 100 and one that is 200 x 100:

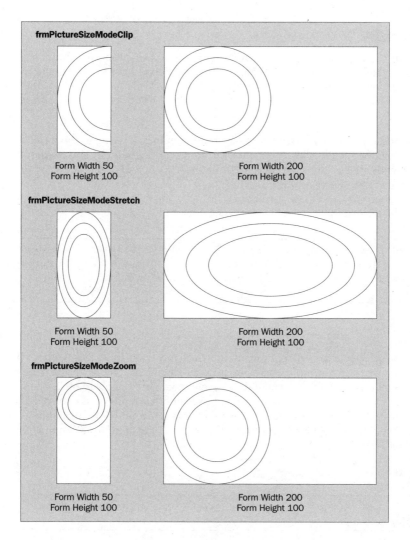

frmPictureSizeModeClip

Form Width 50
Form Height 100

Form Width 200
Form Height 100

frmPictureSizeModeStretch

Form Width 50
Form Height 100

Form Width 200
Form Height 100

frmPictureSizeModeZoom

Form Width 50
Form Height 100

Form Width 200
Form Height 100

The final picture-related property is PictureTiling. This property controls whether or not the form's picture (set through the Picture property above) is repeated over the entire area of the form. If it is set to True, the PictureSizeMode must be set to frmPictureSizeModeClip to achieve the proper effect.

The ability to tile a picture across a form can be used to create an interface with an appearance similar to a web page. Look in the Microsoft Office Clip Art directory under Backgrounds for some good images to tile, but be aware that using a large image will significantly increase the size of your template (or whatever Word file contains the form).

Methods

From your code, you will interact with forms through their properties, but it is through their methods that you can cause things to happen. Forms have several methods, but we'll just cover the most useful ones at this point.

Show

This method is one that you will use every time with forms, it causes the form to be displayed on the screen, allowing the user to start working with it. This method takes one argument, `Modal`, which determines if the form is modal or modeless (by passing in the constant `vbModal` or `vbModeless`).

```
UserForm1.Show vbModal
```

> Modal forms prevent the user from interacting with any other part of the application until the form is closed. Modeless forms are the opposite; they do not restrict the user from using any other window while they are open.

Hide

When the user wants to close your form, there are few ways to do this, you can hide it or you can get rid of it completely (using another statement, `Unload`, which we will cover in a moment). If you get rid of it completely, you are unable to retrieve any information that has been entered into text boxes or other fields on the form, which is not very useful if the form's purpose was to retrieve information. By using the `Hide` method instead, you remove it from view, but can still get at information that was entered into the form:

```
UserForm1.Hide
```

> Note that if you just hide the form, as opposed to unloading it, it is still taking up memory.

Events

In the previous chapter, we defined objects and said that objects had properties and methods, but they also have one more thing that we did not mention, **events**. Events are particular occurrences in the lifetime of the object that VBA is aware of, occurrences such as the loading and unloading of a form. For every event like this, events that we refer to as being **trapped**, you can write code that will run whenever that event occurs. This code is known as an **event procedure**, and it allows you to perform actions at these specific moments without having to know exactly when the event will occur. Each event procedure receives certain parameters when it is called, information about the event that has occurred. This information can be used in determining how to respond to the event.

You can place code in one of the form's event procedures by following these steps:

Open the form's code module (this is a module that is considered to be part of the form), which you can get to by double-clicking on the form. Select UserForm from the Object drop-down list (the left dropdown at the top of the module editing window). Then select a particular event from the Procedure drop-down list (that's the one to the right):

Forms have several events, and each of these events occurs at specific points in its life. The most useful events supported by forms are listed below with an explanation of when each event occurs and why it can be useful to place code into the corresponding event procedure.

Initialize

The Initialize event occurs when the form is first referenced in code, which is usually when you call the Show method in your code, but can also occur if you manipulate a property of the form or a property of an object on the form (for example a text box or check box) before that form has been loaded.

You can always count on this event **firing** (the term used for when an event occurs and its event procedure is called) before the form is visible. This makes it a good place to put code for setting up the items on your form, the caption of the window, and other general setup duties such as initializing drop-down lists.

Click and DblClick

These events fire when the user clicks or double-clicks on the form itself. They do not fire when the user clicks on items that are on the form, such as command buttons and text boxes as these controls have their own Click and DblClick events.

MouseDown and MouseUp

These events fire when the mouse button is pressed down and when it is released, respectively. These events have parameters that specify information about the mouse at the time its button is pressed. The parameters and their significance are described below:

Parameter	Description
Button	This parameter is an integer that indicates which of the mouse's buttons was pressed or released. The value is equal to 1 (left button), 2 (right button) or 4 (middle button).

Shift	This integer value indicates the state of the three keyboard keys *Shift*, *Ctrl*, and *Alt* at the time the mouse button was pressed or released. This parameter has a value of 1 for *Shift*, 2 for *Ctrl*, and 4 for *Alt*. Since it is possible that multiple keys were pressed simultaneously, you need to use the bitwise operator And to check for the presence of each specific value. For example, Shift And 4 will be equal to True if the *Alt* key was pressed, regardless of the state of the other keys. For instance, the following code would display a message box if and only if the *Ctrl* key was held down when the user clicked the mouse button:
	
	`If Shift And 2 Then`
	
	`    MsgBox "Ctrl Key Pressed"`
	
	`End If`

X, Y	These two values contain the current position of the mouse pointer on the screen when the mouse button was pressed down or released.

> Note that you receive information in these two events that you do not get from the Click or DblClick events, you may need to use the two sets of events together to create certain effects.

MouseMove

This event fires often, every few moments while the mouse is moved anywhere over the form, which can often be several times a second. The event procedure receives all the same parameters as the MouseUp and MouseDown events, described above, allowing you to respond to both the current position and button state of the mouse as it moves.

> Whatever you do in this event, do not do anything too annoying. A beeping noise or a message box occurring several times a second will quickly result in the death of the offending programmer.

KeyPress

This event fires whenever the form has focus (an active form) and the user presses a regular keyboard character. This event does not fire for every type of key, ignoring in particular, the function keys and navigation keys. KeyPress only supports the **ANSI character set** (standard characters such as letters and numbers, as well as other regular keys such as *Enter* and *Delete*). To recognize any of those other keys, such as *F1* you must use the KeyDown and KeyUp events.

KeyDown and KeyUp

Similar to the Mouse events above, these events fire when the user presses or releases a key on the keyboard. The event procedure for these events receives two pieces of information - the keyboard code of the key that was pressed or released and a value that indicates which, if any, modifier keys (*Shift, Ctrl* or *Alt*) were held down. You can check for specific modifier keys using the method described in the MouseDown and MouseUp events. To help determine which keyboard key was pressed, VBA supplies a set of constants, all of which start with vbKey. To get a complete list, type vbKey into the VBA editor and then press *Ctrl + Spa*   and you will see a drop-down list of all the constants.

Resize and Layout

These two events serve similar purposes, the adjustment of your form to fit changes in size. The Resize event fires whenever the size of the form itself is changed (if the user resizes or maximizes your form, for instance), while the Layout event fires when the size of one or more controls change, such as the label control which can grow to fit its current contents.

In either case, you can place code into these event procedures to modify the size and position of the controls on your form as the new form or control dimensions dictate.

> The Resize event is called once when the form is first made visible, as well as at any time the user changes the form's size, to allow you to set up the form before it is seen by your users.

QueryClose

This event fires when the form is asked to close, but before it actually closes. The timing of this event is useful; it allows your code to determine if you should let the user close the form. Word 2000 itself uses this event to ask you if you wish to save changes to your document before closing. If you click on the Cancel button of Word's dialog box, Word will not close. This same functionality is available to you in your applications through the Cancel parameter of this event, setting it equal to True will cancel the closing of your form.

In addition to the Cancel parameter of this event, it also receives a value that lets it know why the form was being asked to close. This parameter, CloseMode, can have one of four values, each of which has a corresponding VBA constant. The four values and their meaning are described below:

`vbFormControlMenu`	0	This value indicates that the user clicked the close (**X**) button of your form, pressed *Alt + F4*, or selected C<u>l</u>ose from the menu that appears if you right-click the title bar of a form.
`vbFormCode`	1	This indicates that the form is closing because your code asked it to close by using the `Unload` statement: `Unload UserForm1`
`vbAppWindows`	2	Your form is closing down because Windows is shutting down and has requested that all applications exit.
`vbAppTaskManager`	3	Your form has been asked to close by the Windows Task Manager, the dialog that appears when you press *Ctrl + Alt + Delete* once. The user has brought up this dialog, selected your application from the list that appears, and clicked on <u>E</u>nd Task. If you receive this message, end gracefully and quickly.

Terminate

The opposite of the `Initialize` event, this event fires when the form is unloaded. Consider this the place to put any code that you wish to run at the last moment of this form's existence, but do not use any code that works with the visual appearance of the form, as it will no longer be visible by the time this event occurs. Note that this event occurs only when the form is actually unloaded, and will not occur when the form is hidden.

Controls

For all their features, forms are not much use without anything on them. The various elements that you can place on a form, such as text boxes, labels and check boxes, are known as controls, and it is through these controls that you add functionality to your form.

The VBA environment has certain controls that are available all the time, known as **intrinsic** controls. Other controls, known as **ActiveX** controls, are also available and will be discussed briefly after covering the ones provided with VBA.

VBA Intrinsic Controls

These controls are available through the toolbox, a small window that is visible only when you have a form open and selected. If this window is closed it can be viewed again by selecting <u>V</u>iew I Toolbo<u>x</u> from the menu bar, or by clicking on the Toolbox button on the toolbar:

Placing controls onto your form is simply a matter of selecting the appropriate icon from the toolbox, and then clicking and dragging on the form to position a new copy of the control. You can place as many copies of each control as you like onto your form, as many as you need to create the proper interface.

Label

The label control allows the placement of static text on your form, text that cannot be edited. These controls are useful as captions for other controls and also for displaying information to your users.

Text Box

This is the standard control to allow the user to select and enter text. It can be single or multiple lines and has built-in support for cut, copy, and paste commands.

Combo Box

This is a drop-down list, allowing the user to select a value from a provided list, or to type a value directly in.

List Box

This control displays a list of items, with a scroll bar if necessary, allowing the user to select one or more items.

Check Box

This control displays a small square that the user can check or uncheck by clicking on it. Multiple check boxes are used when you want the user to be able to select any number of items in a group.

Option Button

This control is also known as a radio button and is similar to the check box in that it allows the user to select or unselect it by clicking. Groups of this control allow only one item to be selected at a time, which is better suited to some situations.

Command Button

This control is the regular Windows button, it has a caption and can be clicked on by the user. One of these buttons on the form can be made the **Default** button (using the `Default` property of the control), which will cause it to be clicked whenever the user presses the *Return* key. Similarly, one button can be made the **Cancel** button (through the `Cancel` property of the control), which will cause it to be clicked whenever the user presses the *Esc* key.

Toggle Button

Toggle buttons can be used to make choices. Unlike a regular command button, the toggle button is changed from a "down" state to an "up" state or back again when clicked. This allows the button to indicate the state of something, similar to a checkbox.

Frame

This control is for appearance purposes only, allowing you to draw a 3D-styled box on your form for the purpose of grouping controls.

Tab Strip

This control simulates the row of tabs commonly found in Windows option dialogs. You can write code to respond to changes in which tab is selected, but it does not allow for the automatic display and hiding of portions of your form.

Multi-Page

This control is similar to the previous one, tab strip, but it actually supports multiple pages of controls, and will show and hide those pages automatically as the user switches tabs.

Scroll Bar

Functioning just like a regular Windows scroll bar, this control can be used for anything where you want the user to set a value within a range.

Spin Button

This control is usually used to increment or decrement a numeric value. It has two arrows on it that can be individually clicked by the user, giving them a visual method to increase or decrease a value. The associated value is often displayed in a text box or label control next to the spin button.

Image

The last of the intrinsic controls, this allows the display of a picture file on your form. The picture file can be selected from bitmaps (`*.bmp`), gifs (`*.gif`), jpegs (`*.jpg`), metafiles (`*.wmf` or `*.emf`) or icon files.

Setting Properties

Each control on your form has certain properties that define its appearance and behavior. For instance, a label control has a `Caption` property that sets the text shown on the control. You can set the properties of these controls in two ways, at design-time through the Properties window or at execution time through code. The Properties window will display information for whichever object is currently selected. To work with the properties of a specific control, simply select that item and then edit the values shown in the Properties window.

To change or view the properties of a control through code, you can just use the standard object property syntax, referring to the control by its name (set through the `Name` property). An example of setting one of these properties is shown here:

```
Label1.Caption = "Enter First Name:"
```

It is important to give your controls relevant names, to prevent code like the example above. If a control is a text box, you should reflect that in the name by assigning the same prefix to every control of the same type. For instance, text boxes could all start with `txt` or `tb`, check boxes could be `chk` or `cb`, etc. By using these common prefixes, along with relevant names you will end up with code that is easily understood, as shown below:

```
txtFirstName.Text = "Duncan"
```

When you look at this code in the future, you will be able to tell that it is a text box and that it is intended to hold a person's first name, just by looking at the name.

Control Events

Controls, like forms, have events for which you can write code. These event procedures are available through the form's code module. Simply double-click on a control or the form itself to bring up the code module and then use the left-hand dropdown list at the top of the module to select the specific control you want. Once you have selected the control, all the control's events will be listed in the right-hand dropdown list, select the one you want and you will be ready to create your event procedure. To see this in action, follow the steps below:

- ❑ Use the Insert menu to create a new form
- ❑ Select the CommandButton control from the toolbox
- ❑ Click and drag on the form to place a new command button
- ❑ Select the menu option View I Code or press F7 to switch to the form's code

❑ Now use the left drop-down list to select your new command button (CommandButton1)

❑ Once you have the command button selected, the right hand list should contain all of the appropriate events, pick DblClick from that list

❑ A new empty event procedure will be created as shown below:

```
Private Sub CommandButton1_DblClick(ByVal Cancel As MSForms.ReturnBoolean)

End Sub
```

ActiveX Controls

In addition to the controls shown when you first create a form, there are other controls that you can make available for use. These other controls (any that are not on the toolbox by default) are known as **ActiveX controls** and these were created by Microsoft or another development company and installed onto your machine. To select which of these ActiveX controls you wish to have on your toolbox, select the menu option Tools I Additional Controls (which is only available when you have a form open and selected), or right-click on the Controls tab of the toolbox and select Additional Controls from the popup menu. This will bring up a dialog containing a list of all the ActiveX controls available on your machine.

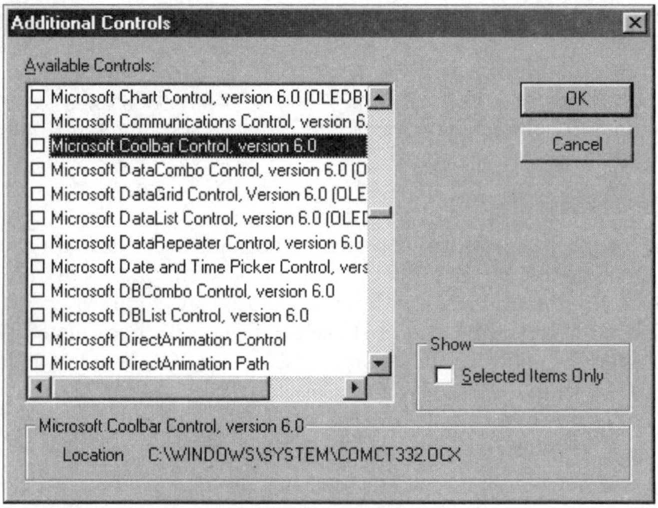

Check off any controls that you want to use and they will be added to the toolbox. Once it is there, you can select and position it on your form in the same manner as a text box or other intrinsic control:

Summary

In this chapter we've seen how to create a visual interface through forms and controls. Specifically, we've looked at:

❑   The properties controlling the color of the form

❑   The properties that allow you to place an image on a form and control its appearance

❑   The `Show` method of the form

❑   The `Hide` method of the form

❑   The most commonly used form events

❑   The intrinsic and ActiveX controls

While many VBA techniques will be discussed throughout the rest of this book, this was the last chapter that focused directly on this subject. From this point on, the chapters will be discussing Word 2000 specific information.

The next chapter will prepare you for this type of programming, by introducing the general techniques used for creating applications inside Word. After that information has been covered, we will move on to the project chapters, each one covering a large number of specific implementation details for Word 2000 developers.

Word 2000 Development

Introduction

The previous chapters have covered the basics of programming in Visual Basic for Applications, but they haven't been focused on Word itself. Although all the Office components use VBA, you do not program them all in the same way. Word 2000 is a word processor, and programming for a word processor creates certain issues, issues that may not exist when you are working with other applications. This chapter is focused on the general guidelines and techniques that apply to working in Word, important things to remember as you move on to the specific projects and technologies covered by the rest of the book. Some of the information in this chapter will apply to the other Office applications as well, Word is not that different than Excel, but they will be discussed in terms of Word alone.

Four Guidelines for Word Development

These could be labeled many things, but 'rules' or 'commandments' seem too harsh, and 'suggestions' is a little weak. Consider them to be useful advice that should be kept in mind, but if they don't fit with your work or your company then feel free to modify them to suit yourself. These 'guidelines' are not in any particular order, but they are all important.

Let the Users Control the Document's Appearance

The appearance of documents produced by your program is as important as their content (some people would say it is more important, but that depends on the content). The best way to ensure that everyone is happy with your work is to base your documents on templates and on styles, and then let your users change those styles and templates in whatever way they wish. You will save yourself a lot of extra work by doing this, if someone wants to change the font used for the address field of your automatically generated invoices, they can do it themselves or get anyone with some Word experience to do it for them.

If you create your programs using templates and bookmarks, then almost any change to your documents should be possible without modifying your code. The two invoices shown here can be generated with the exact same code just by using two different templates:

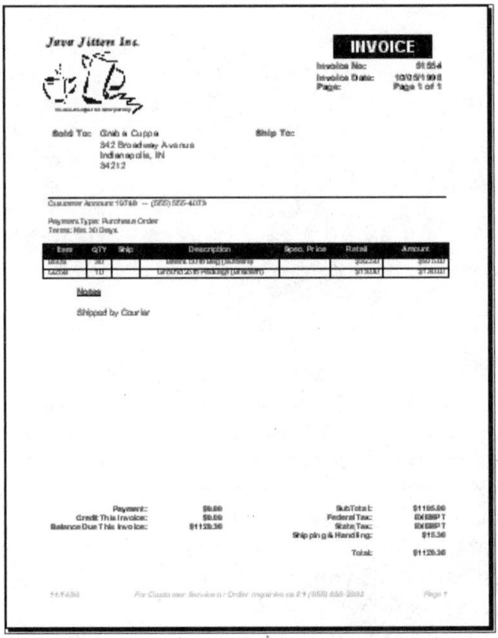

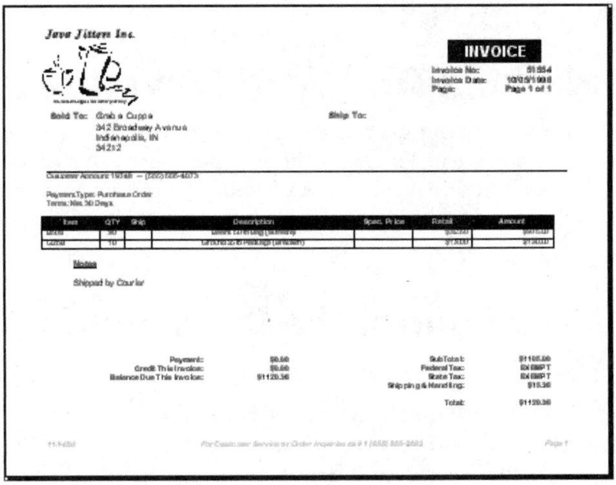

Programming in this manner is especially important in companies where a person or department is responsible for the look of corporate documents. You will avoid conflict if you can let those people create the templates for your documents, or at least modify them as desired. Even if you are one of, or the only, person responsible for your company's printed material (as many of you are), working in this manner will still save you time. The more you can avoid changing your code, the better, which means that the more things that can be changed without touching your code, the better off you will be. This leads well into the next guideline, which deals with that same topic.

Allow for Change

Everything changes, and it usually changes faster than we expect. Regardless of how unlikely something is to change, you should expect it to (keep this one to yourself or you'll be known as 'The Paranoid Programmer'). This means that you shouldn't hardcode things into your programs:

- ❑ Don't use specific font names and sizes
- ❑ Don't use specific path names, not even `"C:\"`
- ❑ Don't use specific template names, even when they exist only for this program
- ❑ Don't use your company name, specific employee names or specific email addresses
- ❑ And so on...

This might seem too restrictive, or even impossible, but it doesn't really involve much more work to program in this manner. The items mentioned above were only examples, you have to apply this guideline to everything that can change, you might need to worry about information that most programmers don't.

Specifically, the items listed above could all be dealt with in one of two ways, through the template that holds your code, or through the Windows Registry (the Windows 95/98/NT method of storing application settings). Using your template means supplying font and size information through styles, and using document properties and AutoText entries for everything else. The Registry is capable of storing any information you need, but is limited to a single user or a single machine, if a setting is to be common across all users then you need to store it in a shared database or other location where every user can access it.

If something is likely to change on a regular basis, such as the email address to send a sales report to, or the printer to output a piece of letterhead on, you shouldn't code it into your program at all, simply use a system or custom dialog to request that information from the user. Certain types of information are even available directly from the operating system, (such as the path to the Windows directory, which isn't always `C:\Windows\`), and can be obtained using the Win32 API.

The Win32 API is a set of functions that Windows makes available to programmers to allow them to access many of the Operating System's special features. For more information on the Win32 API, and how to use them in VB/VBA, check out the Wrox book "VB6 Win32 API Tutorial" This book is aimed at Visual Basic users, but most of its content applies equally well to the VBA programmer.

Take Advantage of Word's Features.

There is only one reason why you are developing programs in Word 2000, to use its features. There is no real argument about that statement, but we all have to remind ourselves of this from time to time. If you need the user to pick a filename, use Word's open file dialog, if you need to apply the same formatting to several parts of a document, use styles. In short, don't build code to do things that Word can already do, and don't do something the slow, complicated way if Word has another, better way. For instance, if you needed to take five documents and make them into one; don't open each file and cut and paste it into a new one, use the insert file or master document feature. There is an extension to this guideline if you have other parts of the Office 2000 suite available - Take Advantage of Office 2000's Features. For instance, if you need to perform some statistical analysis, use Excel, or if you are making a calendar, check out what Outlook has to offer. Like the Microsoft ad says, "Genius is 1% inspiration and 99% existing application" (borrowing a little from Edison), don't waste your time building something that has already been done.

Of course, every guideline has exceptions, and this one is no different. Sometimes when you are programming an application using Word, you need to perform a particular action that Word can do, but not quite the way you need. Perhaps you want to display a list of email addresses, which Word can do (see Chapter 6, Project 6C), but you want to filter that list, which Word can't do. In these cases, you will have to do it yourself, duplicating at least some of Word's functionality. Fortunately, situations like this are becoming less common with every version of Word, as new features are added and existing ones are improved.

If You Can't Use It, You Can't Program It

This is one of the most important things to remember when programming in Word, you have to know how to use the application before you can really be effective. The previous guideline runs right into this one, but they are different. This goes beyond just knowing that Word has a feature, like Style, this means knowing how styles work, what a base style is, how styles are updated when you attach a different template, etc. Word can do some amazing things, but you have to spend some time playing around with the features as a user before you can program them properly. One good way to accomplish this is to always manually perform the task before trying to build it into a program. Build a sample Sales Summary, figure out how that email routing thing works, and try inserting an Excel chart, all through the Word interface. Once you get it to work successfully as a user, your coding will go much smoother.

Introduction to the Word 2000 Object Model

Back in Chapter 2, we introduced the concept of objects, something that may or may not have been new to you, but they are an integral part of understanding VBA regardless. At that point, we mentioned that the objects you will be working with are mostly from Word, not from VBA, a distinction that is a key part of how VBA works.

Visual Basic for Applications is a generic programming language; it is not designed to work with just Word 2000, but with any application that has it built in. VBA works with a particular application through one or more exposed objects from that application:

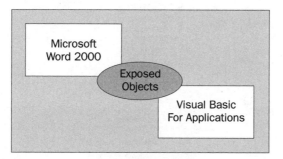

Those objects, and any objects available through them, are known as the **application's object model**. It is with this set of objects that VBA can work with the application, and every VBA-enabled application has its own object model. The language itself is not changing as you move from Excel to Word to Outlook; it is the available objects that are different in each case.

Word has a large and complex object model, starting with the `Application` object and with objects representing everything, right down to individual cells in a table, individual paragraphs in a document and individual characters in a word. The complete set of objects forms a **hierarchy** that moves from the top-level objects (such as `Application`) to the more detailed ones (such as `Paragraph`). Word 2000's object model is documented completely later in the book, but the sections that follow will give you a quick overview of the main objects and their purpose.

The Application Object

The top-level object (from which all others are available) is the `Application` object, which represents Microsoft Word 2000 itself. This object has properties and methods that are independent of any one document, such as Word's toolbars and menu bars (collectively known as command bars), the currently active printer, the Office Assistant, etc. Many of the objects that we will be using in our projects are actually properties of this object, such as the `ActiveDocument` (representing the open Word document that currently has the focus), `Selection` (the currently selected area of the `ActiveDocument`), and the `Documents` collection (the collection of all currently open files in Word).

The diagram shown here displays a subset of the properties associated with the `Application` object:

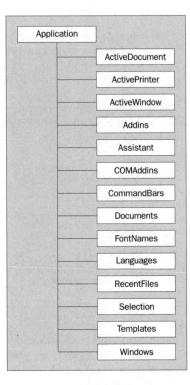

Code that refers to this object isn't always obvious, it may not refer to the `Application` object at all, and that portion of the code is assumed by VBA. Due to this helpful behavior, the two code fragments (which show the setting of a bookmark, and changing the current printer) below are equivalent.

With the `Application` object:

```
Application.Selection.Font.Bold = True

If Application.ActiveDocument.Bookmarks.Exists("InvoiceNumber") Then
  Application.ActiveDocument.Bookmarks("InvoiceNumber") = iInvoiceNumber
End If

Application.ActivePrinter = "INVOICEPRINTER"    'Fails if no such printer
      'exists
Application.ActiveDocument.PrintOut
```

Without the `Application` object:

```
Selection.Font.Bold = True

If ActiveDocument.Bookmarks.Exists("InvoiceNumber") Then
  ActiveDocument.Bookmarks("InvoiceNumber") = iInvoiceNumber
End If

ActivePrinter = "INVOICEPRINTER"    'Fails if no such printer exists
ActiveDocument.PrintOut
```

As the topmost object of the Word 2000 object model, it is this object that any external programming languages use to work with Word. Any other objects that you use from Word, are all available through the `Application` object, regardless of how far down in the object hierarchy they are.

The two sections below cover some of the more useful properties and methods of the `Application` object.

Application Properties

Property	Description
ActiveDocument	Returns a `Document` object representing whichever document is currently selected. Useful when you need to work with the current document, not a specific one that you created or opened.
ActivePrinter	This property allows you to set or retrieve the name of the selected printer, the printer used by default when you print a document.
ActiveWindow	Returns a `Window` object representing the currently active document window. A single document can have more than one window, but each window's settings (multiple panes, window size, etc) are independent of the others. The `Window` object has a `Document` property that returns the document that corresponds to that window.
AddIns	A collection of all the templates and add-ins available from <u>T</u>ools I Templates and Add-<u>I</u>ns. Add-ins are utility programs that are constructed so that they can work within Word.
Application	This property contains a reference to the `Application` object itself, unnecessary in this case, but it is a property common to almost every Word object. Through this property (in other objects) you can get at the topmost object (`Application`) through the object you have.
Assistant	Returns an `Assistant` object, representing the Office Assistant. This is actually part of the Office object model and is covered at the end of the book.
Background_ PrintingStatus	Returns the number of documents that are still printing in the background. You should always wait for this, and the next property, to be zero before closing Word, or else you will receive errors.

Table Continued on Following Page

Property	Description
Background_ SavingStatus	Similar to the previous property, this returns a value indicating how many documents (and templates) are currently in the process of saving.
COMAddIns	A collection of all the COM add-ins available. These are not the same as the other add-ins, having a file extension of .exe or .dll.
CommandBars	This property contains the collection of all the command bars (toolbars and menu bars) available in Word. You can add or remove items through these objects, and control the visibility of individual command bars.
Documents	Returns the Documents collection, which contains all the currently open documents and allows you to create new documents, open existing ones, or close documents that are already in the collection.
FontNames	A collection of all the fonts available on the current machine.
MAPIAvailable	This property tells you if MAPI, the standard Windows Messaging technology, is installed. If it returns false it means that Word doesn't support messaging functions on this machine, and you will not be able to use any of the built-in email related functions. You could always create your own functions that did not rely on MAPI, if it was not available.
MouseAvailable	Returns True or False depending on whether or not there is a mouse installed. Can be used to customize interfaces appropriately, but it is rarely False; most keyboard users have a mouse; they just don't want to use it.
Path	Returns the path to the Word 2000 executable file (by default this path is C:\Program Files\Microsoft Office\Office\winword.exe).
RecentFiles	This property contains a collection of the files recently opened in Word, the same files that are displayed at the bottom of the File menu. In addition to the files themselves, this collection has two useful properties: DisplayRecentFiles and Maximum, which control whether or not the files are listed on the File menu and how many of them are shown, respectively. These properties are also available through the Options collection (another property of the Application object).

Property	Description
ScreenUpdating	Can be set to a `True` or `False` value to control whether or not Word updates its visual display. If it is `False`, then changes that you make in your code will not be visible to the user until you set it equal to `True`. Can be used to get rid of screen flashing problems and can potentially speed up your code, but make sure you set it back to `True` when finished or you will have a great deal of trouble using Word.
Selection	This property is used all the time because it refers to the currently selected portion of the active document.
StatusBar	This property has a misleading name; it does not refer to the status bar itself, merely to the text displayed on the status bar. You can only set this property; you cannot look at its value. Set it equal to a string to display that string on Word's status bar. Useful for progress statements during long operations.
UserAddress, UserInitials, UserName	These three properties return or set the values from the User Information tab of the Options dialog. Usually you only retrieve values from here and leave setting them to the user:

Application Methods

Method	Description
Activate	Make Word the currently active task in Windows.
CentimetersTo_ Points	One of a series of conversion methods which include: CentimetersToPoints InchesToPoints LinesToPoints MillimetersToPoints PicasToPoints PixelsToPoints PointsToCentimeters PointsToInches PointsToLines PointsToMillimeters PointsToPicas PointsToPixels All of these methods convert values from one form of measurement to another. These methods exist because most Word functions and properties are set using **points** (there are 72 points per inch) and most people, including programmers, work in other forms of measurement such as inches or centimeters. All the methods can be used in the same manner: `Application.Width = InchesToPoints(2.5)`
ChangeFile_ OpenDirectory	When the user, or your code, goes to open a file, a specific folder is displayed, such as `"C:\My Documents"`, usually whichever folder was last used for opening or saving a file. This method allows you to change that folder to a different one, `"F:\NetworkDocs"` for instance, which will then be used the next time the user brings up the File Open dialog. This setting is reset to a default every time Word is started, but you can change that default through the `DefaultFilePath` property of the `Application` object.

Method	Description
CheckGrammar	This method checks a particular string for grammar errors, it returns True if none are found.
CheckSpelling	Used to check a string for spelling mistakes. You can specify various settings, controlling whether Word suggests alternate spellings, whether it is case sensitive and specifying up to 10 custom dictionaries to use. This method returns True if no mistakes are found in the string. The same method exists for both the Range and Document objects, but checks the contents of those objects instead of a string.
GetAddress	Used to get information from the Outlook/Exchange address lists, see details on how to use this function in Chapter 6.
Help	Displays the Word Help information, either through the Office Assistant or through regular Windows Help, depending on what options have been set by the user. Takes one argument, which is required to define what type of help should be displayed. The following line of code shows how to bring up the Help dialog displaying the standard topics window: `Application.Help wdHelp`
PrintOut	Used to print a Word document. Has a filename argument that specifies which document to print, or, if that argument is omitted, it prints the active document. This method is also available from the Document object.
Quit	This method shuts down Word 2000, taking arguments to specify how to deal with any loaded documents. The options for saving are: ❑ Don't save (wdDoNotSaveChanges) ❑ Prompt the user (wdPromptToSaveChanges) ❑ Save without prompting (wdSaveChanges) You should always specify either the first or the last of these choices if you are designing a program that will run unattended, as a prompt would hold up the execution of your program until a user was present to click Yes or No. There are also arguments to specify what format to save any non-Word documents as, and for dealing with **routed documents**. (A routed document is a type of document that is sent to a list of people for comments, and can be sent on to the next person in the list when it is closed.)

Table Continued on Following Page

Method	Description
Run	Runs a macro by name, taking a string argument for that value. This function is relatively unnecessary in most situations. Macros are simply procedures and can be called without this method. There is one benefit to this method though, the ability to call a macro based on the value of a variable, which might be useful in certain advanced programs.
ScreenRefresh	Causes Word to redraw its display. Although this method can be useful to ensure that user is seeing the proper display after a series of modifications it is generally not needed.
ShowClipboard	This is one of the few commands in Word that is available only on one platform (Macintosh, in this case), not in both Windows and Macintosh. Such commands can be used in your code, and will appear in the Object Browser (visible by pressing *F2*), but will cause an error when run:

Microsoft Visual Basic

Run-time error '4605':

The ShowClipboard method or property is not available because the command is not available on this platform.

| Continue | End | Debug | Help |

This command, by the way, is designed to put up a window displaying the current contents of the clipboard, which may be text, a picture, or some other type of information.

The Documents Collection

Word uses a lot of collections, representing groups of related objects, including documents, styles, tables, even paragraphs in a document. The Documents collection is one of the most important of these groups, as it not only represents all the open files in Word (documents), it is the object through which other files can be opened.

The Add method of this collection is equivalent to the New command in Word's interface, it creates a new document. This new document can be based on a template, or start out as a completely blank file, whatever is needed for your purposes. There is also an Open method, which adds documents to the collection by opening them from a supplied path and file name. Between these two methods, you have the only way to create a new document, or to edit any document that isn't already open.

All the members of this collection, whether created using the Add method, opened with the Open method, or already loaded when your code is executed, are represented as Document objects.

> Note that the lists below do not include every property or method of the
> Documents collection, but they do provide the most useful ones.

Documents Properties

Property	Description
Count	Returns the current number of documents open in this particular instance of Word (since more than one copy of Word can be open at one time, this Documents collection only refers to a specific instance).
Parent	This property, which is common to most objects in Word, returns the object that is the creator or predecessor of this one. In the case of the Documents collection, this property would return the Application object.

Documents Methods

Method	Description
Add	Creates a new document, which can be based on a particular template, and adds it to the collection. This method returns a Document object corresponding to the new document.

Close	Closes all documents in the Documents collection (all open documents) and takes the same three arguments as Application.Quit. Note that since the Quit method calls this method before closing Word, there is no benefit to calling Close first, as in the code below (the Application.Quit call on its own would accomplish the same thing):
	
	`Application.Documents.Close wdSaveChanges, _`
	`    wdWordDocument, True`
	
	`Application.Quit wdSaveChanges,_`
	`    wdWordDocument, True`
	
	To close a single document you would use the Close method of the individual Document object.

Table Continued on Following Page

Method	Description
Item	The default method of the Documents collection, Item takes an index value (either a number indicating the document's position in the collection, or a string referencing its name) and returns the corresponding Document object. The string index value does not refer to the document's complete path, only its filename ("Document1.doc").

	As the default method, you can use this method without specifying it. The two lines of code below both produce the same result:
	
	`Set MyDoc = Application.Documents("Ch 4")`
	
	`Set MyDoc = Application.Documents.Item("Ch 4")`

Open	Opens an existing document and adds it to the collection, takes many different arguments, including a filename.
Save	Saves all the documents in the collection. Great method when working with many different files. Takes two arguments:
	The first, NoPrompt, can be True (save all documents without any prompting, although if the document has never been saved then a dialog will appear regardless of this argument's value) or False (prompt the user for each unsaved document).
	The second, OriginalFormat, can be set to one of three values: wdOrginalDocumentFormat (which saves the files in whatever format they were opened from), wdPromptUser (which asks the user for each non-Word format document whether it should use the original or save as a Word document), and wdWordDocument (which saves all documents as Word 2000 style documents).

The Document Object

This object represents a Word 2000 document (a single document, as opposed to the Documents collection which represents all the open documents) and provides an interface to that document's settings and content. This is a complex object, there are so many different properties and methods, and many of the properties return objects or collections themselves. The following diagram shows the most commonly used objects and collections that are part of the Document object:

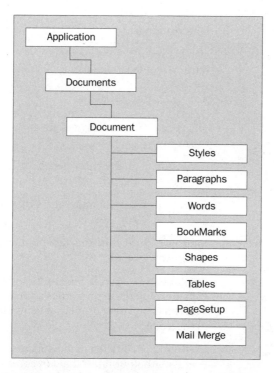

A complete reference to this object, and the rest of the Word 2000 object model, is provided in Appendix A at the end of the book, and various parts are explained within each project.

Only a small number of the Document object's collections, properties and methods are covered here - the most useful ones.

Collection Document Properties

The Document object has so many properties that return collections of objects that they deserved to be grouped separately.

Property	Description
Bookmarks	Collection of all the bookmarks (special areas that have been named through the interface or through code) in the document. The Bookmarks collection has a method Exists, which should be used to check if a certain bookmark is defined before attempting to set its value. Bookmarks are covered in more detail in the next chapter.

Property	Description
BuiltInDocument_ Properties	Using a set of pre-defined index values, you can retrieve/set the value of various document properties, such as Author, Comments, Company, Keywords, Notes, Title, etc. Some BuiltInDocumentProperties are read-only, while others can be modified (as long as the document is not read-only).
Characters	Collection of all the characters in the document. Allows you to get to a specific character by position.
CommandBars	Represents those command bars that are a part of this document, if any exist.
Comments	Returns all the comments (annotations) in the document.
CustomDocument_ Properties	Similar to BuiltInDocumentProperties, but contains only those properties added to the document. You can create new properties using the Add method of this collection.
Fields	Collection of all fields in the document. Has a very useful method Update that forces all document fields to be updated.
Footnotes	Collection of all footnotes in the document.
GrammaticalErrors	Returns a ProofreadingErrors collection, which contains a ProofreadingError object for each error found in the document by a grammar check.
Hyperlinks	Provides a collection of all hyperlinks in the document. Could be used with a HTML document to iterate through all links and corresponding linked documents.
Paragraphs	Collection of all paragraphs in the document, defined as text that is terminated by a hard return.
Sections	Collection of all sections in the document, defined by the use of section breaks.
Sentences	Collection of all sentences in the document.
Shapes	Collection of Shape objects contained in document.
SpellingErrors	Just like the GrammaticalErrors collection, is used for the results of a spelling check.

Property	Description
Styles	Returns a collection of all styles defined (not necessarily used) in the document. For instance, `objDocument.Styles.Count` would likely return over a hundred, even from an empty document.
SubDocuments	If the document is a master document, this is a collection of all subdocuments.
Tables	Collection of all `Table` objects in document, indexed only by position.
Windows	A single document may have multiple windows; this is the collection of those windows. Returns a `Window` object for any item.
Words	Collection of all words in the document.

Document Properties

Property	Description
AttachedTemplate	Returns a `Template` object representing the document's base template. This property can also be set to a `Template` object, or to the name of a template, to set the document's base template.
AutoHyphenation	`True` or `False` value controlling whether or not Word performs automatic hyphenation on the document. This property is `False` by default.
Content	Returns a `Range` object representing the document's main content. Note that headers, footers, footnotes, etc are not returned by this property.
FullName	This is the full path and filename of the document.
GrammarChecked	`True` or `False` depending on whether the grammar has been checked.
MailMerge	Returns a `MailMerge` object, which can setup and execute a mail merge.
Name	Filename of the document, not including path information.
PageSetup	Returns an object representing all the objects from the **Page Setup** dialog (margins, page sizes, etc).

Table Continued on Following Page

Property	Description
Path	Complete path (not including the file name, but including the trailing directory separator) to the document.
Saved	True or False value indicating if the document has been saved. Can be set to False to make Word think that the document doesn't have any unsaved information.
ShowGrammaticalErrors	Controls whether or not grammar errors are visible (green squiggly lines under each error). For this document only.
ShowSpellingErrors	Controls display of spelling errors (red squiggly lines). For this document only.
SpellingChecked	True or False value indicating whether or not the spelling has been checked.

Document Methods

Method	Description
CheckSpelling	Checks the spelling in the specified document. If the document contains errors, the Spelling and Grammar dialog box appears with the Check grammar check box removed.
Close	Closes the specified document. Contains three parameters: SaveChanges, OriginalFormat and RouteDocument. SaveChanges specifies the save action. OriginalFormat specifies the save format. For more details on these two parameters, see the Save method for the Documents collection. RouteDocument is a Boolean value that, if set to True for a document that contains a routing slip, indicates that it should be routed to the next recipient.
Compare	Takes a path and filename of another Word document as a parameter and compares the two documents. Any differences are shown in the document using revision marks.
FollowHyperlink	Navigates to the address specified by a hyperlink and displays the linked document.

Method	Description
Merge	This method takes another document's filename as an argument and merges revisions (changes marked with revision marks) from that document with any revisions in this document.
PrintOut	Prints the document. This method has several arguments, corresponding to the options in the Print dialog.
PrintPreview	Puts up a preview of the current document.
Protect	Allows you to restrict what type of modifications can be made to the document and specify a document password. Modifications can be restricted to allow only comments, revisions, or form field changes.
Repaginate	Forces a complete repagination of the document.
Save	Saves the document using the current filename. If the file has never been saved before, this method causes the Save As dialog to appear.
SaveAs	Saves the document, with arguments specifying all the details including filename and format.

Each collection contains another group of objects, Style objects in the Styles collection, Table objects in the Tables collection, and so on. Each of these objects has their own properties and methods, and many contain more collections and objects as well.

General Techniques

In addition to the many specific implementation details covered by the projects, discussed later on in this chapter, there are many common techniques that run throughout all the projects. Here are some of those techniques with a brief explanation of what they are and why they are being used.

Templates and Bookmarks

The first technique that will be discussed is the use of templates for document creation. You could create any document completely in code, building every element from scratch, but that isn't the simplest method. At least some portion of every document you create is usually static, parts of the document that will be the same for every one you create. By building a template, those portions can be pre-built through Word, simplifying your code. Even a blank template provides a place to store document styles, AutoText entries and other information that you can use from your programs.

As we said earlier, the template provides the static portion of the document, the parts that aren't generated by your program, but you still have to deal with that information. The key is being able to easily place information into your template, and still keep the flexibility that the template provided. The technique that we use to accomplish this is usually **bookmarks**, a feature of Word that lets you associate a name with a specific part of a document or template. Names are defined for pieces of information that we intend to place into our document (such as Company Name, Year To Date Sales, etc), and then bookmarks are created in the template using those names. Not every bookmark has to be present; if one is not there it isn't used. This method allows the users to modify the templates in potentially extreme ways, but nothing matters except the bookmarks.

> A complete example of creating a template in this manner will be covered in Chapter 6, including creating the bookmarks.

Code Reuse

Although the projects are independent of each other, we will be identifying useful code routines as we build each project and those code routines will be reused in other projects. These routines will be added into a single template, a template that each project will reference - ensuring that every project has access to this code. This is the best way to share code between projects or between developers as the code is located in only one place. If each project contained its own copy of these routines, then problems would quickly arise as many different versions would exist, and updates to these common procedures would be difficult.

In some cases, making these routines available for general use will increase their development time as we attempt to make them completely generic. This is unavoidable, but well worth it for the end result, a library of code that will save hours of programming time in the future.

Separating Business Logic from Interface Code

In most programs we build, there will be a certain amount of code that is determining the content, and a certain amount that is actually displaying that content. The projects in this book will be designed to keep those two types of code separated in some way. Although both types of code are prone to modification, most changes are applied to only one or the other, not both. By separating the content-generation code out, that code is ready if you need to reuse it with another type of interface altogether, such as in a regular Visual Basic application.

Proof of Concept

This is a term that is often used in the world of application development, so you may have heard of it before. Either way, here is a quick definition. Whenever you set out to accomplish a task, there are certain ideas and techniques required to do so. Instead of attempting to build the complete solution and then discovering that those particular techniques are not possible, a 'proof of concept' is done first. This is a quick and dirty bit of programming that serves only one purpose, to show that the ideas, techniques, and technology can be used to do what you need it to do. Once you have finished this proof of concept, you discard it and start building the true program confident that you can complete it.

For example, if you are to build a document containing a series of pie charts, each detailing the sales results for a particular city, you have two main concepts that should be put through a proof of concept: Can I make a pie chart? And, can I get the sales figure for a particular city? To prove the first, you could create a pie chart on a new document using some fake data. If you can do that, then creating a series of them at a particular position with a particular appearance isn't a problem. For the second, pick a single city and work out the code to get the sales figures for that city. Just displaying the information to the screen would be sufficient to show that you can get that information. In the rest of this book, some techniques will be covered through quick programs like those described above, but once you have done this with a technique, you will not need to do it again.

> This technique is similar to building a prototype, but isn't the same. In a prototype, you attempt to create something that is an unfinished version of the finished product. This technique, on the other hand, produces much smaller programs that are useless to anyone but the programmer.

The Projects

Part 2, chapters 6 through 10, covers specific implementation details for Word 2000 VBA. Each chapter does this through a series of projects, projects that cover many of the most common Word development tasks. Every chapter is designed to be independent of the others, allowing you to focus on the information you need, but certain elements from a chapter may be reused in later projects.

> All of the code and template files for the projects can be downloaded from the Wrox Press web site at http://www.wrox.com/

The projects covered by each chapter, along with the topics demonstrated by each project, are described below.

Chapter 6 Creating Documents

This chapter covers the basics of creating a document from VBA. The projects covered all involve the creation of fax coversheets, in three separate stages:

- ❑ Creating a Fax Coversheet for the current document
- ❑ Asking the user for information
- ❑ Using Outlook information from Word 2000

There is a wide range of topics covered by these projects, including:

- ❑ Creating Templates
- ❑ Bookmarks
- ❑ Creating New Documents
- ❑ Using Document Properties
- ❑ The Range Object
- ❑ Address Functions

An advanced project is also included for this chapter. This interesting project involves controlling Word from another application, namely from Outlook 2000, and will explore a number of issues surrounding that type of development.

Chapter 7 Document Management

The projects in Chapter 7 deal primarily with documents that already exist, although there will be some documents created as well. The three projects all work with a group of existing documents, but with different purposes, performing each of the following tasks:

- ❑ Creating a summary of a group of documents
- ❑ Custom Document Properties
- ❑ Batch Processing Files

A number of important topics are covered by these projects, including:

- ❑ Working with Files and Directories
- ❑ Dynamic Arrays
- ❑ Document Properties
- ❑ Procedures and Code Reuse
- ❑ Converting Documents
- ❑ HTML Documents
- ❑ Web Folders

Chapter 8 Databases

As databases are likely to be a large part of any company information system, your VBA programs will need to use them frequently. With that in mind, Chapter 8 covers the creation of documents from information stored in databases. There is a great deal of information in this chapter as it covers the use of both ActiveX Data Objects (ADO) and tables through a single sample project that creates a simple Product Price List.

Chapter 9 More Databases

This chapter continues the database concepts from Chapter 8, moving into more complex topics including the creation and control of tables. Chapter 9's projects include producing a professionally formatted version of the product price list and a new project that takes you through the building of a complete order invoice.

Chapter 10 External Applications

This chapter introduces you to an exciting ability of VBA, the control of other applications from within you code. Common functions of both Outlook and Excel are covered as well as details on how to control Word from another VB or VBA application.

Java Jitters Inc.

All of the projects in section 2 will be designed for the fictional company, Java Jitters, a coffee company that sells a wide range of coffee beans and ground coffee. A sample company is necessary to provide our projects with product information for the price lists, invoices and sales reports. It is also useful to see how a company can create a corporate appearance through the use of consistent styles and templates.

Despite using a particular company for all of our examples, there is not a single project that couldn't be applied easily to any company. In fact, for many of these projects, their code may even be suitable for you to use without any modifications; merely needing changes to the template.

Summary

This chapter has briefly covered the Word object-model and given you an overview of the projects coming up in Part 2 of this book. From this point you can read through the various projects in order, or skip to the ones that are the most interesting to you, progress through the material however you wish. Remember that the appendices are available and provide a complete reference to the Word 2000 object model, VBA functions, ADO, and more, they can be a great source of further information while you are reading through the projects.

Creating Documents

Introduction

There are really two types of programs created using Word, those that create documents and those that work with existing documents. This chapter is about the first type of program, making a new document and filling it with the appropriate information.

To do this we will start with building a template designed to be used by our program, and then move on to working with bookmarks.

Project 6A Creating a Corporate Template

Java Jitters Inc. sends a lot of faxes, and for each one the employees, fills out a paper cover sheet to send with whatever documents they are faxing. The company has decided that this isn't acceptable and has decided to build a program using Word to improve the process. This program will be developed in stages, the first of which will be to create a corporate fax template and make it available for everyone's use.

Since the long-term goal is to automate this process even further, the template is to be created with the needs of a program in mind. This means that for every piece of information on the coversheet, there should be an associated bookmark, which will facilitate the automatic replacement of those elements later.

Determining Information Requirements

The first step when creating a template for use in Word development is to determine what information has to exist in the document. For our fax coversheet, we can come up with the following list, assigning each element a unique name for use later:

- ❑ Who the fax is going to (To) and their fax number (ToFax)
- ❑ Who the fax is from (From), their voice (FromPhone) and fax (FromFax) numbers

- ❏ Java Jitters Company Information (CompanyAddress, CompanyPhone, CompanyFax)
- ❏ Number of Pages Sent (Pages)
- ❏ Subject of the Fax (Subject)
- ❏ Date Fax sent (Date)
- ❏ Notes or Comments (Comments)

Once you have this information, you can start creating your coversheet. The coversheet should contain all the information listed above, or have space left for that information. Any information that will likely be left unchanged for every use of the document, such as the company information in this case, should be provided completely.

Building the Template

It doesn't matter what your coversheet looks like, at least not from a technical standpoint, which is the whole point of using templates and bookmarks in this fashion. You can create it any way you wish, even adding additional information. The coversheet we created is shown below, and is also available for download from the Internet at `http://www.wrox.com/`:

> When you have to create a template, consider starting with one of the many provided for you by Microsoft. There is nothing wrong with modifying one of those documents, and it can save you some time.

Java Jitters Inc.

32 Coffee Bean Rd.
Winnipeg, Manitoba
Canada
204.241.3423 v
204.293.3422 f

FAX

We make the coffee that makes your day

To:	To	From:	From
Fax Number:	ToFax	Voice:	FromPhone
		Fax:	FromFax

| Pages: | Pages | Date: | Date |
| Subject: | Subject | | |

Notes: Comments

You can see that in our first version of the template, we just placed the name of each element into the appropriate space, except for the company information, which we filled in completely. You could place sample data into each of the spaces instead (real phone numbers, for instance), and that is recommended if you need to show the coversheet to other people at this stage (users prefer to see sample data, it is less confusing).

Styles

Another tip mentioned back in Chapter 5 was to use **styles** in the documents you create, to make it easier to be consistent and to make it easier to make changes. The best method is to have a single template (that contains all the defined styles) available to everyone, and base any other templates (such as this Fax Coversheet) on that master template. That way, all the company's documents can be designed using the same styles and will have a common appearance.

Even if the master template concept is not feasible, you should still implement styles in your templates. The template we have created (available from http://www.wrox.com/) gives a good example of how to accomplish this.

MACROBUTTON Fields

To make the template easier to use, we'll borrow a little trick from the Microsoft templates and put special field codes in the place of each of our elements. There is a field code called MACROBUTTON, which can be found under the Document Automation category in the Field dialog (accessible via Insert | Field). This particular field is used to turn a piece of text into an element that can be clicked, like a button. The intended purpose of this feature is to run a macro whenever it is clicked, but that isn't how we are going to use it. If you do not tell the field what macro to run, nothing will happen when it is clicked, but it will select the entire field. Because of this feature, the user will be able to simply click once on the area and then start typing and whatever they type will replace the selected text.

Adding Fields to Your Template

Placing one of these fields into your document will make it clear how it all works. To add a field code in place of our elements, follow these steps:

1. Select the sample data or element name that you have placed into your document for one of the coversheet elements, such as To. (Remember to select the area that should contain the user-supplied information, not the header, as shown):

To:	To
Fax Number:	ToFax

2. With the text selected, select the menu option Insert I Field…

3. Choose Document Automation from the left hand list box, and MacroButton from the right hand list. Type the following text after MACROBUTTON: `NoMacro (Click to enter To)` (ensure that there is a space between MACROBUTTON and NoMacro and a space before the rest of the text).

4. Click the OK button, your coversheet element should look like this:

To:	(Click to enter To)
Fax Number:	ToFax

5. The field code is now in place, try clicking on it and typing to see how it will work for your users (undo your actions afterwards using Edit I Undo or *Ctrl +
Z*).

If you want to edit the display text after inserting the field, or change its formatting (for instance, it might look good to bold the To portion of the text), you have to toggle the field first. To do this simply right click the field and select Toggle Field Codes from the right-click menu. This will display the underlying field codes and allow you to select or edit any portion of it. Simply right click again and toggle the field codes back when you are finished.

	{ MACROBUTTON
To:	NoMacro (Click to enter To)
	}
Fax Number:	ToFax

> If we were always going to fill this document out from VBA, there would
> be no need for this, but to create the most flexible and useful tools for
> your users, you should allow for either possibility.

You should continue through the rest of your elements applying these field codes to all
those that are not already filled out. It wouldn't be useful to replace the company
information with these types of codes, unless the company name you are sending faxes
from is changing all the time. Don't forget to set up the MACROBUTTON field code on
the Comments section of the fax cover sheet, people will like having an easy way to
select and replace that area as well.

> If desired, you can use a different field code for the Date element, such as
> the PRINTDATE, CREATEDATE, or SAVEDATE field. These field
> codes cause the display of the date the document was last printed, the
> date the document was created, or the date the document was last
> changed respectively. The finished template on the web has done this,
> but you may not want to, depending on the needs of your users.·

At this point, the template is ready for use by people, but not for a program. We need
to add bookmarks to make it easy to find and replace each of the elements in this
document.

Bookmarks

It would be possible to work with the template the way it is at this point, without
bookmarks. VBA code could be written that would replace the contents of specific
lines, cells, and paragraphs of text, but that code would have a problem; it would not
allow for almost any modification of the template's content by the users. If they were to
change the position of any key section of the document (by adding a paragraph to the
top of the document, for instance) then code that was based purely on position would
no longer work. By using bookmarks to identify the areas of a document to a program,
you allow for changes to be made. Bookmarks can be added to the template, regardless
of formatting, and (as long as all the required bookmarks were present and named
correctly) your program will still work.

Adding Bookmarks

Creating bookmarks is a quick two-step process in Word:

1. Select the area that will be assigned to the bookmark. This can be any selection
    in Word, which means it could cover a large area if desired. In this case, you
    would click to select one of the field codes we used to represent the elements
    of our template.

2. Select Bookmark… from the Insert menu. A dialog box will be displayed, enter
    a name for the bookmark and click Add. The name you use here is important,
    as it will be the name used in your code to refer to this location. Make a note
    of each element and the name of the corresponding bookmark, this will make
    the coding easier.

For our template, the bookmarks are named as follows:

Element Description	Bookmark Name
Who is the fax going to:	To
What fax number is the fax being sent to:	ToFax
Who is the fax from:	From
Phone Number for sender:	FromPhone
Fax Number for sender:	FromFax
Company Address (Street, City, Postal, etc.):	CompanyAddress
General Company Phone:	CompanyPhone
General Company Fax:	CompanyFax
Number of Pages:	Pages
Subject of the Fax:	Subject
Date Fax Sent:	Date
Comments	Comments

Proceed through all the elements of the template, creating bookmarks for each.

Tip: Adding bookmarks would be a lot faster if the Insert Bookmark command was available as a button on a toolbar, shown below, or as a keyboard shortcut.

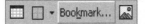

You can add this option to your toolbar, and make any other toolbar or menu modifications, through the Tools | Customize menu option. Make sure that you have Normal.dot selected at the bottom of the dialog or your changes will only effect the current document. Once you have the Customize dialog open, find the Insert | Bookmark... command, as shown in the image, and drag it into an appropriate location on one of your toolbars.

There are two important things to remember here:

1. You can create bookmarks that your program won't use.

If you were creating your own version of this fax coversheet, you might have a space left for the user to enter in their department, or (as is necessary in some companies) a billing or project code for this fax. The program we will cover in this chapter doesn't ever set the value of a department bookmark, but if there is one it will just be ignored. So, if you are adding additional information to the template, providing bookmarks for that information will make it easy to add that functionality to your program later.

2. Not all the elements that the program uses need to be book marked.

Always keep those guidelines from Chapter 5 in mind, we want to make our programs in such a way that the users can modify their templates as much as they want. If we forced them to always have every one of these elements on their coversheets that would be a pretty big restriction. If someone decides that they do not need to put a phone or fax number for the sender on their coversheets, fine, just remove that portion of the document. The corresponding bookmarks will be deleted as well, which could present a problem for some programs, but not the way that we'll show you. In the code that we'll demonstrate, we always check if a bookmark exists before trying to set it, avoiding the error that would result. If a particular bookmark isn't there, we just ignore it and it doesn't get set.

> This method of designing our program so that it can handle even unexpected changes is known in the IT Industry as "Defensive Coding".

Examining, Deleting and Replacing Bookmarks

Once you start creating bookmarks you will sooner or later need to:

- ❑ Check the bookmarks you created
- ❑ Remove a bookmark that you created accidentally
- ❑ Change a bookmark to point at a different location

All of these things are easy to do using Word's built-in features.

First, to check the bookmarks you have set (to see what each is set to, and to see exactly which ones have been set), you'll use the Go To... menu option from the Edit menu. This command, which is also available through the keyboard shortcut *Ctrl + G* or *F5*, brings up the Find and Replace dialog, with its third tab selected:

Clicking the Go To button once you have a particular bookmark selected will highlight the corresponding portion of the document and scroll the document to ensure that text is visible. You can use this dialog to check the value and existence of any bookmark.

Removing an existing bookmark can be accomplished through the Bookmark dialog, which you can display by selecting Bookmark from the Insert menu. Once this dialog is visible, select an existing bookmark from the displayed list and click the Delete button to remove it.

Repositioning could of course be done by deleting a bookmark and then recreating it, but it is even easier than that. Follow the regular steps for creating a bookmark, and enter the name of the existing bookmark that you wish to replace. When you click the Add button, Word will replace it with your new location automatically. It is important to note that bookmark names are unique; you cannot have two with the same name in the same document.

Before moving on to the coding section (Project 6B), if you have created the template and set its bookmarks, save the template to disk. When you save it, Word will default to your personal template location (usually `C:\Windows\Application Data\Microsoft\Templates`, but it may be different on your machine). Files saved at this location will appear in the first tab (General) of the new document dialog, which can quickly become full:

Instead of just accepting the default location, create a new folder called `Java Jitters` (using the **Create New Folder** icon in the **Save As** dialog) under your personal template location and save the template into there. If you want a preview image to show for your coversheet (as in the image above) you have to remember to check **Save Preview** when you save it. Now, when you bring up the new document dialog, there will be a new tab labeled Java Jitters and containing this one template. If you had already saved the template somewhere else you can leave it there or do a **Save As** into the location described.

Ensure that the template is saved and closed before trying any of the techniques described in the following section.

Project 6B Fax Coversheet for the Current Document

Java Jitters Inc. now has a template for its fax coversheets, one that is available fro every single machine that has it installed, and everyone has been very happy with it. Of course, as usually happens, after a short while people start wanting something more. Often, the fax coversheet is being created to send with an actual Word document, and it has been decided that it would be helpful if the coversheet could automatically fill in some of its fields with information from that document. The coversheet will pull only two things from the document, the title, which will become the subject line of the fax, and the number of pages, which will be incremented by one to account for the cover itself. The entire process should be automated and linked to a button on everyone's toolbar.

For this project, we will approach the problem in two stages, developing code that is capable of doing what we want (creating the document and filling in certain fields) and then we'll worry about the toolbar button and other elements later.

Developing with a Template

The template we have created is now set up for both regular use (just pick it from the new document dialog), and for use by developers (thanks to all those bookmarks we set up). This is perfect, a single template that serves both purposes. By doing it this way only one document will require modification when something changes.

The next step is to actually start using it from your code, which, at its most basic level, involves two things:

- ❑ Creating a new document based on the template (from code)
- ❑ Filling in those bookmarks.

Creating a New Document

Using code to create a new document is accomplished through the `Documents` collection's `Add` method. The following line of code will open a new, blank document:

```
Documents.Add
```

This is the equivalent of clicking on the **New Blank Document** toolbar button, basing the document only on the `Normal.dot` template. To create our new fax coversheet, we want a bit more than that; we want it to create a new document from our template.

The `Documents.Add` method takes a few different arguments, the first of which (`Template Name`) allows us to specify the filename of a template for the new document. Using this option with the filename of our Fax Coversheet template will open up a new document containing the information from our template:

```
Documents.Add "C:\Windows\Application Data" & _
    "\Microsoft\Templates\Java Jitters\Fax Coversheet.dot"
```

This code relies on knowing where the template file is located, which could be different on each machine. The code above would fail (resulting in the error shown) on a machine with user profiles enabled, for instance, or if the Windows folder on the machine was named something other than `C:\Windows`:

If we could assume that the Java Jitters folder was located under the user or workgroup template folders for Word, then there is a better way to code this. This would seem to be a logical assumption; if it isn't in one of those locations it won't appear in the New dialog either.

> Word can automatically look in two different locations for template files, one for the user's personal templates, and one for shared templates that are often located on a network server. These locations are known as the User Templates and Workgroup Templates folders and are set through the **File Locations** tab of the **Options** dialog (available under the **Tools** menu). As this is a company-wide template, it would likely be located under the **Workgroup Templates** folder, but for examples we will be using the **User Templates** location.

Word has some built-in ways to find either one of those two folders, methods that return the appropriate value from the Options dialog box. By using these methods in our program, any changes in that dialog will automatically be used by our code. Most of the settings from the Options dialog are available through the `Options` object, which can be used on its own in code but is really a property of the `Application` object (just like the `Documents` collection).

This object has a huge number of properties and methods, but the one that represents the File Locations tab is `DefaultFilePath`. This is a property that takes a special index value and returns the corresponding file path. The various index values don't need to be memorized, they will be displayed to you when you get to the appropriate point in your code, but the meaning of several particularly useful entries are described here:

```
= Options.DefaultFilePath(
```

```
wdTempFilePath
wdTextConvertersPath
wdToolsPath
wdTutorialPath
wdUserOptionsPath
wdUserTemplatesPath
wdWorkgroupTemplatesPath
```

Index Item	Description
WdCurrentFolderPath	This entry represents the path Word is currently using to look for files. If you selected Open from the File menu, this is the folder that would be displayed.
WdDocumentsPath	The path where you store your Word documents, Word uses this as the default value for opening and saving files, from when you open Word until you save or open in a different folder.
WdPicturesPath	Default path for the Insert I Picture command, used from when you start Word until you insert a picture from another location.
WdProgramPath	Path to `winword.exe`, equivalent to `Application.Path`
WdUserTemplatesPath	As discussed, this points to the folder containing the user's local templates.
wdWorkgroupTemplatesPath	This value represents the path to a shared templates folder, usually located on a network share.

Any of the `DefaultFilePath` values that have not been set (such as the `Workgroup Templates` location) will return the `wdProgramPath` value, not a blank string as you might expect. This actually works in your benefit, you can freely use any of these paths, and they will always work, even if you do not find the template or other file in that location. A blank string, on the other hand, would likely cause errors in your program. If you use these paths though, do not be surprised if you end up saving files into the same directory as `winword.exe`.

The two indexes that apply to our current situation are `wdUserTemplatesPath` and `wdWorkgroupTemplatesPath`, which together represent the possible locations for our special templates. In the case of our example, we are going to use the `User Templates` location, but using the other would require only changing the index value. In the code below, we add an additional step and retrieve the path into a variable first. This isn't required but it makes the code clearer and that is always desirable as it makes it easier to maintain by other programmers:

```
Dim sUserTemplates As String

    sUserTemplates = Options.DefaultFilePath(wdUserTemplatesPath)

    Documents.Add sUserTemplates & "\Java Jitters\Fax Coversheet.dot"
```

Setting Bookmark Values

If we were to take the code above and run it (after placing it into a new procedure) we would accomplish at least our first goal, creating a new document based on our template. Now we have to add some more functionality by setting a few of those bookmark values.

Getting a Document Object

To set the value of our bookmarks we need access to the `Bookmarks` collection, which is a property of the `Document` object. This means, that we need the `Document` object that represents our new document, which is available in one of two ways:

❑ Through the `Application` object's `ActiveDocument` property, which returns a `Document` object corresponding to whichever document is currently selected

❑ Directly from the `Add` method

The first way is always available, but it isn't a very elegant solution, it takes advantage of the fact that immediately after adding a new document to Word, that document should be the `ActiveDocument`. It will work, but lets look at a better way.

> If you are an engineer, or the person who pays the bills, you might be wondering why do we care if it is elegant, as long as it works? Well, in this case, the rationale behind our search for the elegant solution is to code our system so that it is not dependent on the happy coincidences in Word. If we were to depend on such a thing and then, while our code was running (and at exactly the right moment) a user were to innocently click on another document, then the `ActiveDocument` would change and our code would fail. If we had done it the "right way" or the "elegant way" then we could safely ignore the user's actions, because our code would work anyway.

When we called `Documents.Add` to create our document we didn't worry about any return value from that method, but there is one. The `Add` method returns a document object representing the document that was added, which will be our new document. We can modify our code a little to get that return value:

```
Dim objNewDoc As Document
Dim sUserTemplates As String

    sUserTemplates = Options.DefaultFilePath(wdUserTemplatesPath)

    Set objNewDoc = Documents.Add(sUserTemplates & "\Java Jitters\Fax
Coversheet.dot")
```

There are several changes being made here, each of which is required and important:

❑   We declare our document variable, `objNewDoc`; this will be used to represent the new document in the rest of our code.

❑   We add the variable and the keyword `Set` to the front of our method call. `Set` is required because we are dealing with an object.

❑   We put parentheses around the argument(s) of our method call. You have to do this if you are going to use the return code from a function.

Now we have our `Document` object, which has the `Bookmarks` collection that we will need.

Setting Bookmarks

At this point in coding, it is important that we remember the names of our bookmarks, and what each of them meant, which is why we created a list of these values earlier. To illustrate how to set a bookmark, we just need to pick one; we'll choose `Subject` (for no particular reason). The code below will set that bookmark to the text `"This is my subject!"`:

```
Dim objNewDoc As Document
Dim sUserTemplates As String
Dim objBookmark As Bookmark
Dim objRange As Range

    sUserTemplates = Options.DefaultFilePath(wdUserTemplatesPath)

    Set objNewDoc = Documents.Add(sUserTemplates & _
"\Java Jitters\Fax Coversheet.dot")

    Set objBookmark = objNewDoc.Bookmarks("Subject")

    Set objRange = objBookmark.Range

    objRange.Text = "This is my subject!"
```

This code uses the `Bookmarks` collection to return a particular bookmark object, the one named `"Subject"` and then gets a `Range` object from that bookmark. To understand this code fully, we need to take a look at the `Range` object and how it works.

The Range Object

A range represents any portion of document information, anything from nothing to pages and pages of text. This makes the `Range` object one of the powerful and common objects in Word development; everything can be represented as a range. Many different objects have a `Range` property, which returns a range representing that object, and it is a common way to work with its information. The examples below show some of the ways we can use `Range` objects:

```
MsgBox Selection.Range.Text
```

Displays the text that is currently selected.

```
Selection.Range.Text = "The Quick Brown Fox Jumped Over The Moon"
```

Replaces the entire current selection with the assigned text.

```
MsgBox Selection.Range.Paragraphs(1).Range.Words(5).Range.Characters(1).Text
```

Displays the first letter of the fifth word of the first paragraph of the current selection.

```
MsgBox ActiveDocument.Paragraphs(5).Range.Words.Count
```

Displays the number of words in the fifth paragraph of the active document.

Sub-objects of Ranges

A range can represent any portion of a document, and can contain any of the elements that a document can. Because of this, the Range object has many of the same collections within it as the Document object. These collections (Tables, Words, Paragraphs, etc) represent only those objects contained with the Range and are numbered accordingly. If a document had ten tables in it, then those tables could be referred to through the Document object like this:

```
ActiveDocument.Tables(1)....
ActiveDocument.Tables(2)....

and so on....
```

If, in that same document, you had selected an area containing tables 5 through 8, then those tables would be become the Selection.Range's tables 1 through 4. All the collections within the Range deal only with the Range and nothing outside of it.

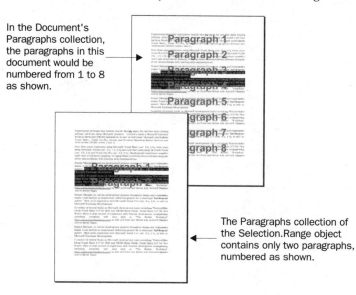

In the Document's Paragraphs collection, the paragraphs in this document would be numbered from 1 to 8 as shown.

The Paragraphs collection of the Selection.Range object contains only two paragraphs, numbered as shown.

We won't cover all the Range object's properties and method at this point, but we'll provide a description of the ones we will be using frequently.

Collections

As was discussed above, the Range object contains several collections, some of which it has in common with the Document object:

❑ Bookmarks represents all the document's bookmarks that exist within the Range

❑ Cells, Rows, and Columns all apply only if any tables are contained within the Range, and if so they represent a collection of the appropriate type of object

❑ SpellingErrors and GrammaticalErrors are collections of errors found when either the Document or Range's CheckSpelling or CheckGrammar methods were used

❑ Paragraphs, Words, Sentences, and Characters are the same collections as for the Document object, but refer only to the information within the Range

Properties

The Range object has many different properties all of which can be used to manipulate the properties of all the included text and other document elements:

❑ Bold can be used to set or retrieve the bold state for all the text in the Range

❑ Style controls which style is applied to the entire Range

❑ Text returns or sets the Range's contents

❑ GrammarChecked and SpellingChecked both return a True/False (Boolean) value to indicate if the Range's contents have been checked for spelling or grammar errors

Methods

There are several methods that can be used to act on the contents of the Range:

❑ Cut, Copy, and Paste will perform the standard Edit menu functions on the contents of the Range.

❑ CheckSpelling and CheckGrammar perform a complete grammar or spelling check on the words and sentences inside the Range.

❑ InsertParagraph replaces the entire range with a blank line. Useful for inserting blank lines when the Range is at the end of the document.

❑ InsertParagraphAfter types a blank line at the end of the Range, does not replace or alter the contents of the Range.

Overall, the Range object is one of the most useful objects present in Word, and we will be using it extensively throughout the book. Now, having completed our detour through the Range object, we will return to the project and the setting of bookmarks.

Checking if a Bookmark Exists

```
Dim objNewDoc As Document
Dim sUserTemplates As String
Dim objBookmark As Bookmark
Dim objRange As Range

    sUserTemplates = Options.DefaultFilePath(wdUserTemplatesPath)

    Set objNewDoc = Documents.Add(sUserTemplates & _
"\Java Jitters\Fax Coversheet.dot")

    Set objBookmark = objNewDoc.Bookmarks("Subject")

    Set objRange = objBookmark.Range

    objRange.Text = "This is my subject!"
```

The code above works fine to set a bookmark, but it doesn't do any checking. If the bookmark didn't exist, an error would occur when we tried to set objBookmark. There is a way to avoid a situation like that; the Bookmarks collection has a method that can be used to check if a bookmark is there, before you set it. The method is Exists, and we can modify the code to only set the bookmark if that method returns True:

```
Dim objNewDoc As Document
Dim sUserTemplates As String

    sUserTemplates = Options.DefaultFilePath(wdUserTemplatesPath)

    Set objNewDoc = Documents.Add(sUserTemplates & _
"\Java Jitters\Fax Coversheet.dot")

    If objNewDoc.Bookmarks.Exists("Subject") Then

        objNewDoc.Bookmarks("Subject").Range.Text = "This is my Subject!"

    End If
```

At the same time, we also simplified the code into a single line for setting the bookmark. The two different pieces of code accomplish the same thing, but you can always choose between a single long line of code or multiple variable assignments. The multiple variable assignment method is a little slower (both to type and to execute), but it is also very clear. Use whichever style you prefer, but always remember to code defensively, protecting from all eventualities.

Now the code works well, it creates a new document (based on our template) and then, if the bookmark exists, replaces a bookmark portion of the document with a new value. We can continue on in this fashion to set all the bookmarks in the document. Setting the next bookmark is simply a matter of copying those last three lines of code and changing the bookmark's name and the value we are setting. Anytime you find yourself doing this (copying code and just changing some values), stop and consider what is happening. In this case, we have realized that those three lines will work well to set any bookmark, and if that is true, we shouldn't just be copying them. This is the point in our code when we decide to make a procedure.

A procedure will encapsulate the functionality of those three lines into a single location, and then we will call that procedure every time we set a bookmark in the future. To properly build this procedure we need to determine what portions of the code will stay the same and what portions will change every time it runs:

```
If objNewDoc.Bookmarks.Exists("Subject") Then

    objNewDoc.Bookmarks("Subject").Range.Text = "This is my Subject!"

End If
```

In this code above, the information that changes is shown in bold, so is the information we need to replace with parameters to our new procedure. Although there are five different areas in bold, there are only three pieces of unique information, which we will create parameters for: the document containing the bookmark, the bookmark's name, and the value we want to set the bookmark to. The finished procedure should look like this:

```
Public Sub SetBookmark(objDoc As Document, sBookmark As String, _
sValue As String)

    If objDoc.Bookmarks.Exists(sBookmark) Then

        objDoc.Bookmarks(sBookmark).Range.Text = sValue

    End If

End Sub
```

With the new procedure available, we would recode the original section as:

```
Dim objNewDoc As Document
Dim sUserTemplates As String

    sUserTemplates = Options.DefaultFilePath(wdUserTemplatesPath)

    Set objNewDoc = Documents.Add(sUserTemplates & "\Java Jitters\Fax
Coversheet.dot")

    SetBookmark objNewDoc, "Subject", "This is my Subject!"
```

Setting each of the remaining bookmarks can now be done with a single line for each, not to mention the setting of bookmarks in future projects.

Document Properties

Now, after figuring exactly how to create a blank coversheet, and how to set the value of bookmarks, we need to move on to determining how to get some information about the current document. The original purpose of this project was to create a button that would create a fax coversheet, pre-filled with information about the current document, so we need to get that information. The exact pieces of information we need are:

- ❏ The fax's sender (From)
- ❏ The document's name
- ❏ The number of pages in the document

Without worrying about all the code to create the document and set bookmarks, we'll just figure out some code to get these values, then we can put it all together.

User Information

Word keeps track of certain information about the user, information that is accessible through the Options dialog's User Information tab. Under this tab, there are fields for the user name, user address, and user initials, and all three of those pieces of information are available through code as well.

Although this information is a part of the Options dialog, it is not available through the Options object, but instead all three types of user information are properties of the Application object. The code below would display the user name, user address, and user initials in three dialog boxes (one after another):

```
MsgBox Application.UserName

MsgBox Application.UserAddress

MsgBox Application.UserInitials
```

To retrieve the piece of information we need, the user's name, we will just need to use the code Application.UserName.

Document Name

The name of a document can be easily retrieved from the Name property of the corresponding document object.

```
MsgBox ActiveDocument.Name
```

For instance, the line of code above would display the name of the active document. This is not quite what we want for our purposes, as then name returned will have an extension on it, .doc for example.

If there was another property available that returned the name without this extension, we would use it, but this is the only one available, so we need to figure out a way to get only the part of the name that we need. Fortunately, VBA contains a large number of functions designed to manipulate strings, and with the help of a few of those we will be able to chop off those unneeded characters easily. We'll cover each of the most useful string functions below, and then use several of them together in solving our problem.

Left, Right

These two functions allow you to take a certain number of characters off the right or the left side of a string. Each function takes two arguments: a string and a number indicating how many characters are to be selected. If the number of characters specified exceeds the length of the string, the entire string is returned:

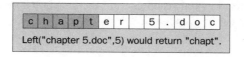
Left("chapter 5.doc",5) would return "chapt".

Right("chapter 5.doc",7) would return "r 5.doc".

Mid

Mid is a function that performs a similar, but more powerful task than Left or Right. This function takes three separate arguments: a string, a starting position, and a length (*n*) that indicates how many characters to return.

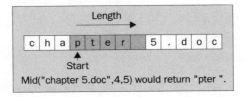

Mid("chapter 5.doc",4,5) would return "pter ".

Note: Using Mid with a starting point of 1 makes it behave exactly like Left.

Len

A simple, but extremely valuable function, Len takes a single string as an argument and returns that string's length as a result. For example, Len("chapter 5.doc") would return a value of 13.

InStr, InStrRev

These functions, whose names are abbreviations for In String and In String Reverse, return the location of one string within another.

Each of these functions take 4 arguments: the string to be found, the string to be searched, the position within the string to start searching, and what method of comparison to use for determining a match. The order of the arguments is slightly different for the two functions, and is often difficult to determine which of the two strings is being searched and which is being sought. For both functions, though, the string being searched is always listed first. The location of the starting position argument is different for both functions though, coming first in InStr and third in InStrRev.

The main difference between the two functions is in how they search; InStr starts at the starting position and searches every character from that point on, while InStrRev starts at the starting position and searches from that position back to the beginning of the string. If the sought string is not found, both InStr and InStrRev will return a zero.

The comparison method argument is not usually used, and it defaults to a binary comparison. You may need to use this argument if you want a case-insensitive search, which could be done by specifying vbTextCompare for this argument.

```
Match
 ▼
┌─┬─┬─┬─┬─┬─┬─┬─┬─┬─┬─┬─┐
│c│h│a│p│t│e│r│ │5│.│d│o│c│
└─┴─┴─┴─┴─┴─┴─┴─┴─┴─┴─┴─┘
InStr("chapter 5.doc","c") would return 1.
```

```
                              Match
                               ▼
┌─┬─┬─┬─┬─┬─┬─┬─┬─┬─┬─┬─┐
│c│h│a│p│t│e│r│ │5│.│d│o│c│
└─┴─┴─┴─┴─┴─┴─┴─┴─┴─┴─┴─┘
 ▲
Start
InStr(2,"chapter 5.doc","c") would return 13.
```

```
            Match
             ▼
┌─┬─┬─┬─┬─┬─┬─┬─┬─┬─┬─┬─┐
│c│h│a│p│t│e│r│ │5│.│d│o│c│
└─┴─┴─┴─┴─┴─┴─┴─┴─┴─┴─┴─┘
 ▲
Start
InStr("chapter 5.doc","ter") would return 5.
```

```
                              Match
                               ▼
┌─┬─┬─┬─┬─┬─┬─┬─┬─┬─┬─┬─┐
│c│h│a│p│t│e│r│ │5│.│d│o│c│
└─┴─┴─┴─┴─┴─┴─┴─┴─┴─┴─┴─┘
InStrRev("chapter 5.doc", "c") would return 13.
```

```
Match
 ▼
┌─┬─┬─┬─┬─┬─┬─┬─┬─┬─┬─┬─┐
│c│h│a│p│t│e│r│ │5│.│d│o│c│
└─┴─┴─┴─┴─┴─┴─┴─┴─┴─┴─┴─┘
                         ▲
                        Start
InStr("chapter 5.doc","c",12) would return 1.
```

Replace

This function takes a string and replaces every instance of one substring with another, returning the modified result. The supplied string is not modified, unless it is used to store the function's result.

This function takes, in addition to the two substrings and the original string, a starting position argument that defines where it should start working.

Using this function with an empty string as the replacement value (" ") results in the removal of every instance of the substring found within the original. This is often used to remove unwanted characters, like spaces, from a string.

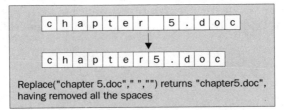

Replace("chapter 5.doc"," ","") returns "chapter5.doc",
having removed all the spaces

Split

This function accepts a string and a delimiter as arguments and creates an array by
dividing the string wherever it contains the delimiter. This can be used to turn a string
containing several values separated by commas into an array, where each of those
values becomes an individual array element.

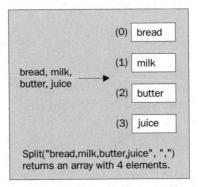

Split("bread,milk,butter,juice", ",")
returns an array with 4 elements.

The return value is a variant that contains an array, so declare your variable
appropriately. The code below gives an example of how to call this function.

```
Dim X
X = Split("bread,milk,butter,juice", ",")
MsgBox X(2)      'Displays "butter"
```

There are several other, less used arguments to this function; Limit or Count, which
can be used to restrict how many individual elements are returned, and Compare
which specifies the how VBA searches the delimiter character.

Join

Basically the reverse of Split, this function creates a string from an array, separating the
elements using a specific delimiter.

This is a very useful function when you are dealing with arrays, and especially if you
have to import and export information to text files.

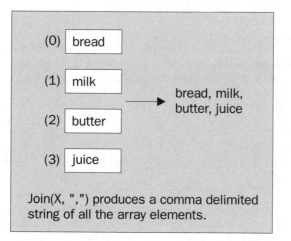

Join(X, ",") produces a comma delimited string of all the array elements.

If no delimiter is specified, then a space is assumed (the same applies to Split).

These string functions are very useful for a variety of situations. To solve our particular problem, there are a few different ways to go about it. We could use a combination of Len (to determine the total length of the string) and Left to grab all the characters except the four at the end. This would be coded as follows:

```
Dim sTitle As String
    sTitle = ActiveDocument.Name
    sTitle = Left(sTitle, Len(sTitle) - 4)
```

The problem with this solution is that it assumes that the document's extension is 3 characters long (like doc), but it could possibly be more or less. This code wouldn't produce the correct result if the document happened to have an extension of .html. So, a more complicated solution is required. If we didn't assume a certain length for the extension, then we have to determine that length with code. The best way to do that would be to determine the position of the " . " within the name, and then take only characters up to that point. The InStr function will provide us with the position of one string within another, so we can use it to determine where " . " is and then use Left to select only characters up to that point:

```
Dim sTitle As String
    sTitle = ActiveDocument.Name
    sTitle = Left(sTitle, InStr(sTitle, ".") - 1)
```

This will work regardless of the length of the extension, but (this is starting to seem more complicated than it should be) it would have a problem with a filename that contains more than one " . ". This is not a common situation, and would often be ignored, resulting in code that usually works, but will sometimes produce odd results.

You are trying to create code that can be used from now on, without requiring any changes, so you should do it right the first time and try to handle every known issue. Regardless of how many "."s are present in a filename, the last one will be the one that we care about, so we can use InStrRev to find out the position of that character. The only other issue that requires handling is a name without any "."s. This can be dealt with by a quick If statement, modifying the code to:

```
Dim sTitle As String

    sTitle = ActiveDocument.Name

    If InStr(sTitle, ".") <> 0 Then

        sTitle = Left(sTitle, InStrRev(sTitle, ".") - 1)

    End If
```

It is conceivable that we will need to perform these steps again, so we will turn them into a little function with a few additions. The final result, the code that we will use in our project, is shown below:

```
Public Function NameWithoutExtension(sFileName As String) As String

    If InStr(sFileName, ".") <> 0 Then

        NameWithoutExtension = Mid(sFileName, 1, InStrRev(sFileName, _
".") - 1)

    Else

        NameWithoutExtension = sFileName

    End If

End Function
```

> Note that we made the function Public instead of Private. This is to ensure that this function is visible to anyone who references this code module. When creating sub procedures (not functions), remember that if they are Public they will be visible to the user in the **Macros** dialog.

Document Statistics

The final piece of information we need is the number of pages in the document, a value that can actually be retrieved in two different ways. The number of pages in a document is considered to be both a statistic and a document property, allowing us to retrieve it through the ComputeStatistics method of the Document object, or through the BuiltInDocumentProperties collection. An explanation of both methods is provided below.

ComputeStatistics

This method of the Document object is also available from Range objects, in which case it calculates the appropriate statistic for only the contents of the Range. There are seven different statistics that this method can calculate and return:

- Characters
- Characters (with spaces)
- Far East characters
- Lines
- Pages
- Paragraphs
- Words

For each of the seven statistic types, there is a corresponding Word constant for use in your code (wdStatisticCharacters, wdStatisticCharactersWithSpaces, etc). You must supply one of these values as the first parameter to ComputeStatistics to tell it which one to return.

There is also a second parameter to this method, an optional one that takes a Boolean value (True/False) to indicate whether or not footnotes and endnotes should be included in the calculation. The default for this value is False, which corresponds to the common convention when counting words for essays and articles. In certain cases, though, you need to know the exact number of words, pages, or other elements in the document, regardless of whether they are footnotes or not. In such a situation, you should specify a True value for the second parameter.

BuiltInDocumentProperties

Every Word document has a set of properties stored with it, some of which are automatically generated, such as the number of pages, and others that are supplied by the user (or by code). All of these properties are accessible through the Properties dialog (opened through the File | Properties menu option):

Chapter 6.doc Properties

General | Summary | Statistics | Contents | Custom

Title: Chapter Six

Subject: Creating Documents

Author: Duncan Mackenzie

Manager:

Company: Wrox Press

Category:

Keywords:

Comments:

Hyperlink base:

Template: ProgRefTemplate.dot

☑ Save preview picture

OK   Cancel

The `BuiltInDocumentProperties` collection contains all the values shown, along with those values from other tabs. Each of these values is accessed using a different Word constant as an index into the collection. Several of the values, and their corresponding constant are listed below:

Value	Constant
Author	`wdPropertyAuthor`
Comments	`wdPropertyComments`
Category	`WdPropertyCategory`
Title	`WdPropertyTitle`
Subject	`WdPropertySubject`

As you can see by the few examples above, it is not difficult to determine which constant applies to which property value. For our current project, we could have chosen to use the Title or Subject properties instead of the document's name, but most users do not set any of these properties and the name is guaranteed to exist.

There is another collection of property values, the `CustomDocumentProperties`, which represent those properties that have been added to the document by the user or by code. We will cover more about document properties in Chapter 7.

As was mentioned before, it doesn't matter which of these two methods you use since they will both work. For our project, we will go with the `ComputeStatistics` call, which would be written as:

```
iNumberOfPages = ActiveDocument.ComputeStatistics(wdStatisticPages, True)
```

Putting It All together

We now know how to create a new document, using a specific template, set a series of bookmarks, and retrieve certain information about the current user and document. This is all we need to finish our project, so we can start putting it together into a single procedure. Before we actually writing any more code, it is a good idea to plan out the series of steps that will be performed by the procedure. Referring back to our original goal, here are the steps for our procedure:

❑ Create a new, blank document based on our Fax Coversheet template

❑ Fill in the Subject, From, and Pages bookmarks of that new document with information from the current document (the active document when our program is run)

We have done each of these things individually, but when we put them together we have to make sure we do a few things:

❑ Check if there is any documents open, and do nothing if there isn't

❑ Ensure that we get a hold of the current document *before* we create our new document, because it will no longer be the active document after

The end result is shown in the following procedure:

```
Public Sub CreateFaxCoversheet()

Dim objCurrentDoc As Document
Dim objNewDoc As Document

Dim sUserTemplates As String

Dim sTitle As String
Dim iNumberofPages As Integer
Dim sUserName As String
    'First check if there are any open documents, code would fail if there
wasn't.
    If Documents.Count > 0 Then

        Set objCurrentDoc = ActiveDocument

        'Get information for fax coversheet
        sTitle = NameWithoutExtension(objCurrentDoc.Name)
    'Number of Pages equals the number of pages in the document
    'plus one for the cover page

        iNumberofPages = objCurrentDoc.ComputeStatistics(wdStatisticPages) _
+ 1

        sUserName = Application.UserName

        'Path for User Templates
        sUserTemplates = Options.DefaultFilePath(wdUserTemplatesPath)

        'Create Fax Coversheet
        Set objNewDoc = Documents.Add(sUserTemplates _
            & "\Java Jitters\Fax Coversheet.dot")

        SetBookmark objNewDoc, "Subject", sTitle
        SetBookmark objNewDoc, "Pages", CStr(iNumberofPages)
        SetBookmark objNewDoc, "From", sUserName

        objNewDoc.Bookmarks("To").Select

    Else

        'There were no open documents
        MsgBox "No Open Documents!",vbCritical,"Error In Macro"

    End If

End Sub
```

The last section of the procedure, `objNewDoc.Bookmarks("To").Select`, is added for esthetic reasons. Without this line, the cursor would be sitting at the top of the document when the code completes. That wouldn't be very convenient for the user, and it looks silly, so this line ensures that the "To" field is highlighted and ready to accept the user's input.

For now, to demonstrate how this project works, place the code above, the `SetBookmark` function and the `NameWithoutExtension` function into a module in your `Normal.dot` file and then link a toolbar button to the macro `CreateFaxCoversheet`. Open a document and click this new toolbar button and you will get an appropriately filled out Fax Coversheet:

The next project continues with the Fax Coversheet, but adds some interaction with the user.

Project 6C Asking the User for Information

Basking in the glory of a successful and useful project, you roam the halls of Java Jitters Inc. and everywhere you see people using your fax coversheet. Stopping at one desk though, you notice all these scribbled paper notes with people's names and fax numbers. To use your coversheet, the employees are first switching to their contact list in Outlook, writing down the name and fax number they need, and then switching back to Word and typing it in. The glory is fading, your program is good, but it isn't quite the time saver you may have hoped. As Java Jitters Inc. makes extensive use of contact lists (through Outlook 2000 and Microsoft Exchange Server), it would be very useful if your fax coversheet could be integrated with that information.

For this project, we are going to explore the functions in Word that allow you to work with Outlook's contact information, and then use those functions to improve our Fax Coversheet program.

Windows Contact Management

We have been repeatedly referring to this as integration with Outlook and Exchange, but it actually works with the Windows default contact management program, which may not be Outlook. Regardless of which program it works with, Word is capable of bringing up a list of contacts from that source and allowing the user to pick which one they want. The code in this project (although not in the Advanced Project, which is covered directly after this one) will work with any contact list provider that is compatible with Microsoft Office.

`GetAddress`, or any function that works with Outlook 2000, has to start Outlook to work. Depending on the setup of your system, this may cause logon dialogs, Internet connections or other events to occur. These events are associated with Outlook, not VBA, and are not documented in the sections below.

GetAddress

The `Application` object has a method designed to integrate directly with the contact management software on your machine. This method is `GetAddress`, and it allows the user to select a name directly from the standard contact dialogs, and returns specific portions of the address for the selected name. It takes eight different arguments, but they are all optional. We will cover each parameter individually, but the complete syntax for this command is shown below:

```
GetAddress(Name, AddressProperties, UseAutoText, DisplaySelectDialog,
SelectDialog, CheckNamesDialog, RecentAddressesChoice, UpdateRecentAddresses)
```

To get a quick idea of how this function works, you can call it with no parameters (it will use the defaults for each one) and take a look at what happens:

```
Application.GetAddress
```

When this code is run it will put up a dialog box containing a list of contacts, and a dropdown list to select between the various available contact lists. You can choose any contact you want and click **OK** to select it:

When you click **OK** on the **Select Name** dialog, nothing will seem to happen if your code is the same as shown above. The `GetAddress` method is a function; it returns the address information as its result. Without a variable or something other way of dealing with that result, it is simply ignored. Modify the code by placing `MsgBox` in front of the call to `GetAddress` and run it again:

```
MsgBox Application.GetAddress
```

This time, in addition to the **Select Name** dialog, you will receive a dialog displaying certain pieces of address information for the contact you chose:

The exact pieces of information returned by the GetAddress method defaults to those shown above, but can be set to whatever you want using the AddressProperties parameter.

AddressProperties

This parameter controls which individual parts of a contact's address are returned from GetAddress. The address portions are specified with special property names enclosed in angle brackets ("<" and ">"). These properties can be any of the following values:

Name Properties

Property Name	Description
<PR_DISPLAY_NAME>	The complete name for this contact, the same displayed in Outlook's name field.
<PR_COURTESY_TITLE>	The contact's title, if they have one assigned, such as "Mr.", "Ms.", "Dr.", etc... Not be confused with their job title, which is available as <PR_TITLE>.
<PR_GIVEN_NAME>	First name (as specified in the contact information)
<PR_SURNAME>	Last name
<PR_COMPANY_NAME>	Company name
<PR_DEPARTMENT_NAME>	Department name
<PR_OFFICE_LOCATION>	Office location
<PR_TITLE>	Job title

Address Information

Property Name	Description
<PR_STREET_ADDRESS>	Entered street address, including any apartment number, etc
<PR_LOCALITY>	City
<PR_STATE_OR_PROVINCE>	State or province, could be either the two letter code (for the US and Canada) or the complete name, it is whatever was entered when the contact was created.
<PR_POSTAL_CODE>	Postal or zip code
<PR_COUNTRY>	Country

Most contact management programs, including Outlook, support the entry of multiple addresses (Home, Office, etc) but this method will only return a single address. An option in the **Select Name** dialog box allows you to choose which address is used for those that have multiple entries:

Phone/Fax Information

Property Name	Description
<PR_PRIMARY_TELEPHONE_NUMBER>	Supposedly, the main telephone number for a contact, regardless of whether it is their business, home, cellular, or other number. It is not usually set, and doesn't automatically attempt to determine which number to use, often returning nothing even when there is only one phone number.
<PR_PRIMARY_FAX_NUMBER>	Supposedly, the main fax number; see the previous item for comments.
<PR_OFFICE_TELEPHONE_NUMBER>	Business phone
<PR_OFFICE2_TELEPHONE_NUMBER>	Second business number, if one is present.

Table Continued on Following Page

Property Name	Description
`<PR_BUSINESS_FAX_NUMBER>`	Business fax, usually the one used instead of the Primary Fax Number.
`<PR_HOME_TELEPHONE_NUMBER>`	Home/Personal number
`<PR_HOME_FAX_NUMBER>`	Number of a fax machine at home.
`<PR_CELLULAR_TELEPHONE_NUMBER>`	Also known as Mobile number, could also be entered as `<PR_CAR_TELEPHONE_NUMBER>`.
`<PR_BEEPER_TELEPHONE_NUMBER>`	More commonly labeled as a Pager number.
`<PR_OTHER_TELEPHONE_NUMBER>`	Any number entered as something other than those above.
`<PR_CAR_TELEPHONE_NUMBER>`	Usually used for a cellular number.
`<PR_RADIO_TELEPHONE_NUMBER>`	Although we don't know what this is, if someone had one, this should be where its number is stored.

Other Information

Property Name	Description
`<PR_COMMENT>`	The text portion of any notes for this contact. In Outlook, the notes field can contain pictures and OLE objects (such as Word Documents) in addition to text, but those other items will not be returned.
`<PR_EMAIL_ADDRESS>`	The user's main or default email address. Although most contact programs allow the entry of multiple email addresses, only one is returned. Unlike the primary fax and primary phone fields, this property works correctly and returns the proper value.
`<PR_ADDRTYPE>`	This property represents what type of Email address is being returned by the previous item, such as SMTP (a standard internet style email address).
`<PR_INITIALS>`	Returns the contact's initials.
`<PR_LOCATION>`	Primarily used for internal (staff) employee lists, this is a combination of the contact's building and room location. This may not apply to most contacts.

As you can gather from many of the descriptions above, the contents of these fields are very dependent on what was entered into the contact, if the wrong information was placed into a field then that is what you will get from this function. Any properties that do not apply to the contact, or were never filled in, will be returned as blank. To help you understand exactly which values apply in terms in Outlook 2000, here is a diagram of the standard Outlook contact form with all the properties labeled:

For example, based on the values listed above, if we wanted to retrieve the fax number for whichever contact was selected, we would use the following code:

```
MsgBox Application.GetAddress(AddressProperties:="<PR_BUSINESS_FAX_NUMBER>")
```

> Note that the code sample uses named arguments, a way of specifying procedure parameters that is explained immediately following the coverage of this parameter.

The various properties can be combined, to create a string that is formatted however you need, and `GetAddress` will simply replace the property names with their values. For example, calling `GetAddress` with an `AddressProperties` parameter of `"<PR_GIVEN_NAME> <PR_SURNAME>, <PR_BUSINESS_FAX_NUMBER>"` would return a result like "Duncan Mackenzie, (555) 123-4567".

How this argument is interpreted is dependent on the `UseAutoText` parameter, discussed later.

Named Arguments

The `GetAddress` method takes many arguments, but all of them are optional. This would make for confusing code if you had to include a series of commas with nothing between them, so as to set a single argument and skip a series of optional ones. This makes this a perfect situation to introduce a special way to specify arguments to a procedure, a method called **named arguments**. Using this method allows you to specify any argument in any order when calling a procedure; by stating which argument you are setting. An example is given below with the `MsgBox` function, which has the following syntax:

```
MsgBox Prompt,[Buttons],[Title],[HelpFile],[Context]
```

Only the `Prompt` argument is required, everything else is optional. To call this function and only set `Prompt`, `Title` and `Context` would require the following code using normal methods:

```
MsgBox "This is the Prompt",,"This is the Title",,34
```

Named arguments would allow the following code:

```
MsgBox Context:=34, Prompt:= "This is the Prompt", _
    Title:= "This is the Title"
```

Each argument is separated by commas, but each is also specified by name and uses the ":=" symbol to signify assignment. The arguments ignore position, and any argument not clearly mentioned is considered missing. Not every procedure can be called this way, but most can, and this can make your code much easier to read and maintain. Despite the flexibility this method provides, certain rules are still enforced; you can only set a particular argument once, and required arguments are still required although no commas have to be left for parameters that are being omitted.

UseAutoText

This parameter is `False` by default, but if it is set to `True`, it indicates that the `AddressProperties` parameter (discussed earlier) should be treated as the name of an AutoText entry. If an AutoText entry exists by the name supplied, its contents are used to specify the address information to return. In this case, the contents of the AutoText entry should comply with the same formatting and use the same property names as was described earlier for `AddressProperties`.

This is an interesting parameter, and it opens up the possibility of having the user provide the address properties for your program to use, by having them create the AutoText entry. For simplicity though, it is safer and easier to specify the information yourself and leave this argument as `False`.

Name

This argument allows you to specify a name to be searched for. This is useful to allow the `GetAddress` method to be used without any dialog being displayed at all (controlled by the `DisplaySelectDialog` parameter). If the name supplied is not specific enough for the address book to locate a matching entry, the Check Name dialog is displayed showing all the entries that are possible matches and allowing the user to pick one (or create a new one):

This dialog is displayed as a result of the code:

```
Application.GetAddress Name:="Mackenzie", DisplaySelectDialog:=0
```

DisplaySelectDialog

When working with the `GetAddress` method you often need to retrieve several distinct pieces of information about a contact, such as their name and fax number. You could do this by creating a combination of all the necessary properties and then calling `GetAddress` with that value for `AddressProperties`, as shown below:

```
Dim sAddress As String
Dim sProperties As String

    sProperties = "<PR_DISPLAY_NAME>, <PR_BUSINESS_FAX_NUMBER>"

    sAddress = Application.GetAddress(AddressProperties:=sProperties)
```

If you used this method, you would have to use some string manipulation functions to retrieve individual values from the result, which would contain both pieces of information together. Instead, there is another, better, way to accomplish this. You can specify a value for the `DisplaySelectDialog` parameter of 2, which tells `GetAddress` not to display any contact lists and to just use whichever contact was last retrieved. This can be used to call `GetAddress` as many times as you have separate pieces of information to retrieve.

```
Dim sFirstName As String
Dim sLastName As String
Dim sFaxNumber As String

    sFirstName = Application.GetAddress _
    (AddressProperties:="<PR_GIVEN_NAME>", _
    DisplaySelectDialog:=1)
    sLastName = Application.GetAddress _
    (AddressProperties:="<PR_SURNAME>", _
    DisplaySelectDialog:=2)
    sFaxNumber = Application.GetAddress _
    (AddressProperties:="<PR_BUSINESS_FAX_NUMBER>", _
    DisplaySelectDialog:=2)
```

> **If you use a value of 2 for this parameter without first using `GetAddress` once without it, you will receive a blank result.**

The three possible values for this parameter are:

- ❏ 0, which indicates the dialog shouldn't be displayed at all, only useful when you have specified the `Name` argument
- ❏ 1 (default), which displays the dialog
- ❏ 2, as discussed above, doesn't search for any additional contacts, uses the previously selected information

SelectDialog

This argument determines what type of Select Name dialog is displayed, the standard version (as shown earlier), which appears if this argument is omitted or set to zero, or one of two special **Compose** versions designed for picking names for the purpose of sending a message. The first Compose version (parameter value 1) displays a To box to hold selected names:

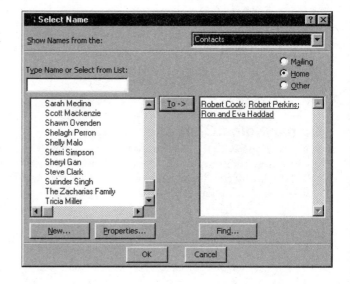

The other version (parameter value 2) has both a To box and a Cc box:

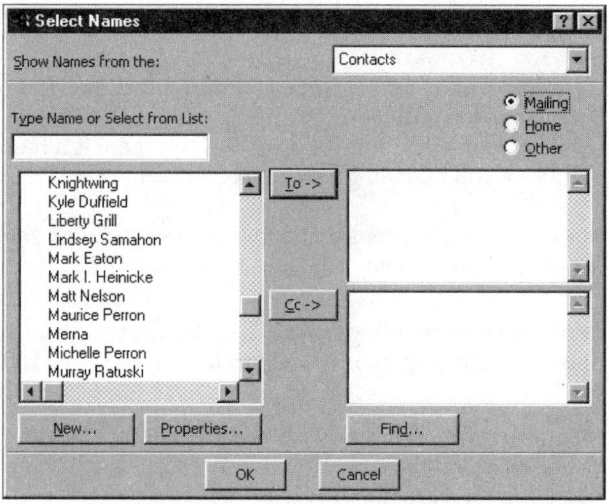

The two Compose versions of this dialog box support multiple selections, which can cause problems using the returned values. When more than one contact is selected, the requested properties of each contact are placed together into the result, with commas separating each contact's information.

For example, the code below is executed and the user selects the contacts displayed in the picture shown immediately afterwards:

```
sValue = Application.GetAddress(AddressProperties:="<PR_GIVEN_NAME> " _
    & "<PR_SURNAME>, <PR_BUSINESS_FAX_NUMBER>", selectdialog:=1, _
    displayselectdialog:=1)
```

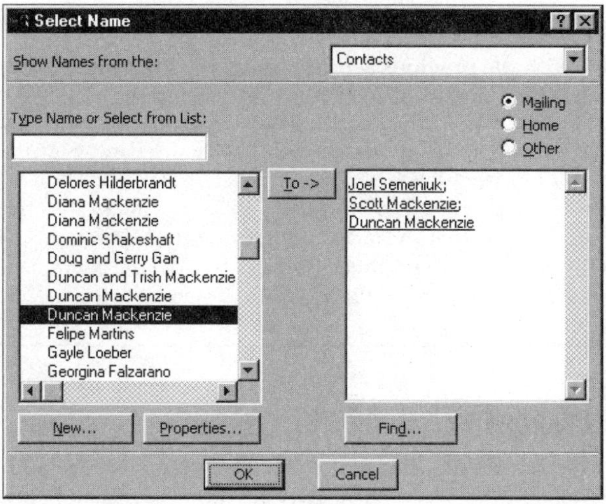

Returns the following result, all as a single string:

```
Joel Semeniuk, (554) 707-7531, Scott Mackenzie, (555) 212-0201, Duncan
Mackenzie, (555) 123-4569
```

To pull out just the fax numbers from this list would be difficult, although not impossible. When using the version with both <u>T</u>o and <u>C</u>c boxes available, the contacts are placed together and separated with commas, as above, but there is a return between the two lines to allow you to distinguish between them.

When using either of the dialog box versions that allow multi-select, you should follow these tips to make it easier to use your data:

❑ Never use commas as part of your `AddressProperties` string. This would make it nearly impossible to separate your data into individual elements.

❑ Don't attempt to retrieve multiple properties using a series of `GetAddress` calls and the `DisplaySelectDialog` parameter with a value of 2; it doesn't work if there are multiple selections.

❑ Use the `Split` function to convert the results into an array, allowing easier retrieval of information.

If you do not want the user to select more than one contact, then use only the standard version of the dialog (`SelectDialog:=0`).

UpdateRecentAddresses

Set to `True`, this parameter causes the selected contact to be added to a list of recently selected contacts.

RecentAddressesChoice

Working in conjunction with the previous setting, setting this parameter to `True` causes `GetAddress` to display the list of recently used addresses.

> Regardless of how we set the two arguments that deal with the supposed recent address list, in either Office 97 or 2000, we couldn't get the function to do anything different or special. This could mean that these arguments do not work, or that there are undocumented system requirements. The information on these options is still included, as it is possible that this is a problem that will not affect everyone, or will be fixed in the future.

Other Address-Related Methods

Word 2000 includes two other procedures that work with your system's address book, whether it is Outlook 2000 or otherwise. These two functions are listed below with brief descriptions of their purpose and how they are used.

AddAddress

Using the same property codes as `GetAddress`, this method adds a new address to your address book, if your address book supports new entries. It takes two string arrays as parameters, one that contains property codes, and one that contains the values associated with those properties. An example of setting up the arrays and calling this method is shown below:

```
Public Sub AddNameToAddressBook _
    (DisplayName As String, FirstName As String, LastName As String)

Dim Codes(0 To 2) As String
Dim Values(0 To 2) As String

    Codes(0) = "PR_DISPLAY_NAME"
    Codes(1) = "PR_GIVEN_NAME"
    Codes(2) = "PR_SURNAME"
    Values(0) = DisplayName
    Values(1) = FirstName
    Values(2) = LastName
    Application.AddAddress Codes(), Values()

End Sub
```

LookupNameProperties

This method attempts to find and display the properties of a particular contact in your address book, using a name that you supply. The name argument is supplied in one of two ways; if this function is called as a method of the `Application` object then you must supply the name, if it is called as a method of a `Range` object, then the current contents of the `Range` (text it represents) is used for the lookup. Examples of both methods of use are shown below:

```
Application.LookupNameProperties("Duncan Mackenzie")

Selection.Range.LookupNameProperties
```

Completing the Project

Now that we have seen how to retrieve address information from the Address Book on our computer, we can use that information to add functionality to our coversheet project. We'll start with the code we created in the previous project, and then add a bit of code to get a name and fax number for the recipient. To do this, we will have to check to make sure the user wants to retrieve the name, allowing them the ability to use the coversheet without this feature, and if they do, make sure they actually chose someone from the list. The code required is shown below (changed portions are highlighted):

```
Public Sub CreateFaxCoversheet()

Dim objCurrentDoc As Document
Dim objNewDoc As Document

Dim sUserTemplates As String

Dim sTitle As String
Dim iNumberofPages As Integer
Dim sUserName As String
```

```
Dim sToName As String
Dim sToFax As String

    If Documents.Count > 0 Then

        Set objCurrentDoc = ActiveDocument

        'Get information for fax coversheet
        sTitle = NameWithoutExtension(objCurrentDoc.Name)
        iNumberofPages = objCurrentDoc.ComputeStatistics(wdStatisticPages) _
+ 1
        sUserName = Application.UserName

            'Project 6C -- GetAddress Information
            If MsgBox("Retrieve Recipient Information from Address Book ?" _
            , vbQuestion Or vbYesNo, "Coversheet Generator") = vbYes Then

                Do
                        sToName = _
Application.GetAddress(AddressProperties:="<PR_DISPLAY_NAME>")

                Loop Until sToName <> "" 'Loop until user selects an Address

                sToFax = _

Application.GetAddress(AddressProperties:="<PR_BUSINESS_FAX_NUMBER>" _
                , DisplaySelectDialog:=2)

            End If

            'Path for User Templates
            sUserTemplates = Options.DefaultFilePath(wdUserTemplatesPath)

            'Create Fax Coversheet
            Set objNewDoc = Documents.Add(sUserTemplates & _
"\Java Jitters\Fax Coversheet.dot")

            SetBookmark objNewDoc, "Subject", sTitle
            SetBookmark objNewDoc, "Pages", CStr(iNumberofPages)
            SetBookmark objNewDoc, "From", sUserName

            If sToName <> "" Then

                SetBookmark objNewDoc, "To", sToName
                SetBookmark objNewDoc, "ToFax", sToFax
                objNewDoc.Bookmarks("Comments").Select

            Else

                objNewDoc.Bookmarks("To").Select

            End If
        Else

            'No Documents open
            MsgBox "No Open Documents!", vbCritical, "Error In Macro"

        End If

End Sub
```

Of course, there are many possible variations on this project; you could retrieve the company name as well, and put it in brackets behind the name, etc. You have the information to build whatever you need, and the projects in the rest of this book will provide you with more information that could apply to this application as well.

Advanced Project Working with Outlook 2000

When designing any integration between office components, you have to decide which program will be the main host of your solution. In the projects above, and in this entire book, Word 2000 will be that host, but this does not have to always be the case in your own work.

For this particular chapter, we have focused on building a fax coversheet, with its final version taking address information from the Outlook address book, but this project could be approached from a different direction. It is possible to create this exact same functionality from Outlook, generating a fax coversheet in Word.

All the steps and the techniques involved will not be covered here, the purpose of this Advanced Project is to give an idea of where you can go with Microsoft Office technology without providing all the details. Shown below is a screen shot of a custom Outlook contact form, showing you the additional tab that has been added to allow the generation of both fax coversheets and letters to that contact. In the same manner as the fax coversheet developed earlier in this chapter, the document created by this code contains the appropriate name and fax number for the contact selected. The code that runs behind this form is also shown below, illustrating how similar it is to the code developed in the rest of this chapter:

```
Sub cmdGenerateFax_Click()
Dim WordObj
Dim DocObj
Dim TemplateName

    TemplateName = CStr(Item.UserProperties("Document Name")) & ".dot"

    Set WordObj = CreateObject("Word.Application")
```

```
    Set DocObj = WordObj.Documents.Add(TemplateName)

    WordObj.Visible = True
    WordObj.WindowState = 1

    DocObj.Bookmarks("To").Range.Text = _
    CStr(Item.FirstName & " " & Item.LastName)

    DocObj.Bookmarks("Phone").Range.Text = _
    CStr(Item.BusinessTelephoneNumber)

    DocObj.Bookmarks("Fax").Range.Text = _
    CStr(Item.BusinessFaxNumber)

    DocObj.Bookmarks("CC").Range.Text = " "

    DocObj.Bookmarks("Subject").Range.Text = _
    CStr(Item.UserProperties("Subject Line"))

    DocObj.Bookmarks("Pages").Range.Text = _
    CStr(Item.UserProperties("NumberOfPages"))

    DocObj.Bookmarks("Comments").Select
Dim JournalObj

    Set JournalObj = Item.Application.CreateItem(4)

    JournalObj.Recipients.Add Item.FileAs

    JournalObj.Type = "Fax"

    JournalObj.Subject = Item.UserProperties("Subject Line")

    JournalObj.Close 0
End Sub
```

The similarity between programming in Outlook and programming in Word is true for working with any of the other Office components, and you should consider them possible tools to use in building solutions.

Summary

This chapter has covered a great deal of information: templates, bookmarks, user properties, ranges, and even how to use the Windows Address Book from VBA. The next chapter continues on into Word development with projects that work with existing documents, custom document properties, HTML documents, and web folders.

Document Management

Introduction

Chapter 6 focused on using VBA to create new documents in Word and the techniques of using bookmarks and templates to simplify your programming tasks, but that is not the only type of code you can create. In addition to creating new documents, a common application of VBA is to work with existing files, opening, editing, printing, or whatever else is required. This chapter will take you through two projects that deal with existing documents, including:

❑ Building a summary for a group of documents

❑ Batch processing a group of files, converting them into HTML

❑ An introduction to custom properties

Project 7A Summary of Multiple Documents

Our mythical company, Java Jitters Inc., has another little problem. They have thousands of documents scattered all over the company, with no real idea of whether a document is important, who created it, when was it last modified, etc. They would like an easy way to get a summary sheet describing all the documents in a certain directory. The particular information they would like isn't set in stone, but they are thinking of at least the following facts for each document:

❑ Who created it?

❑ When was it created?

❑ When was it last modified?

❑ Number of pages

While this isn't a common type of application, you won't find it in many real companies, the need for a method of document management is something that exists in every one of those companies. This project will give you an idea of how such a system could be built, through a small-scale example.

As with the projects in Chapter 6, and all the projects in this book, we will not jump right into a complete solution. Instead, we will tackle each of the major tasks from the project, determine the complete details of how to program each one, and then worry about combining them into a complete solution.

Working with Files and Directories

The first task for this project is to obtain a list of all the Word files in a directory, giving us the path of every document for later use. At this time, we will not worry about which directory or what to do with the files once we find them, all that matters is producing our list.

Listing Files

To accomplish this, we are going to use a VBA function called Dir. This function accepts a path as an argument, and returns the name of any file at that location, if no file is found Dir returns a blank (empty) string. The code below demonstrates calling Dir and displaying the results:

```
Sub FindFiles()

Dim sFileName As String

    sFileName = Dir("C:\")

    If sFileName <> "" Then

        MsgBox "File Found: " & sFileName

    End If

End Sub
```

Running this code produces, on one machine, a dialog stating that the file CONFIG.SYS was found. Although that file is likely present at the same path on your machine, you might get a different result when you run this code.

So far this is a good result, we specified a path, and Dir returned a filename from that path, but we need more than a single filename. If we run that exact same code again, without changing anything, we won't get the next file from that path, we will get the exact same result, CONFIG.SYS. This is actually by design; Dir returns the first file (based on a file system order, not alphabetical) from the path you specify. When we called it the second time, it still returned the first file. To get Dir to return the next file from the same location, we have to call it without specifying a path. Modifying the code slightly will demonstrate this behavior:

```
Sub FindFiles()

Dim sFileName As String

    sFileName = Dir("C:\")

    If sFileName <> "" Then

        MsgBox "File Found: " & sFileName

    'End If

    sFileName = Dir

    If sFileName <> "" Then

        MsgBox "File Found: " & sFileName

    End If

End Sub
```

Now, when the code is run, we get two dialog boxes coming up, one at a time:

Notice, when you run the code the second dialog doesn't appear until you click **OK** on the first one. This is because the MsgBox command is modal, nothing else (this effects Word only, other programs are not effected, unless you specify vbSystemModal as a value for the Button argument) happens until that command is finished executing. The code that follows the first MsgBox statement doesn't run until you click **OK**, the program is effectively stalled waiting for you to do something. Keep this behavior in mind when designing macros to run without user intervention, if you pop up a little MsgBox in the middle of a long running process, that process is paused until the user clicks **OK** (which might be difficult if they decided to go for lunch while your program was running).

As was mentioned earlier, you may get different filenames, but you will get two distinct files, which is the whole point. Now, the code above is not a very good way to code this procedure, for every additional file, we would need to copy and paste the same four lines of code. In an earlier chapter, we learned about loops, and that is what we need in this situation.

Anytime you have a loop, you need an **exit condition**. An exit condition is the reason for the loop to end, the Boolean expression you are going to use to check if you should continue looping. In this case, we want to loop until there aren't any more filenames to be retrieved, which will be indicated when `Dir` returns an empty, or blank, string. The diagram below details how the loop will work:

To get all the files from a certain path, we will follow these steps:

1. Retrieve the first file from that path.

2. If the filename isn't blank, display it and retrieve the next. Repeat this step until filename is blank.

3. Stop processing when a blank filename is returned.

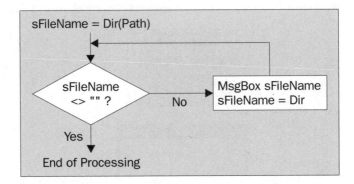

Turning these steps into code produces the following procedure:

```
Public Sub FindFiles(sPath As String)
Dim sFileName As String
    sFileName = Dir(sPath)
    Do While sFileName <> ""
        MsgBox sFileName
        sFileName = Dir
    Loop
End Sub
```

Calling this procedure with a path of `"C:\"`, (e.g. `FindFiles "C:\"`), causes the files from that directory to be displayed in message boxes, one by one.

Filling a Dynamic Array

Displaying the files as they were found was useful as part of our development, making it easy to see what the code was doing, but it doesn't work as part of our project. We need this code to return the files it finds, not just display them. Since there may be more than one file, a simple string wouldn't be suitable as a return value. Instead, we will use a dynamic array, an array that can change in size as needed (discussed in chapter 2). Instead of creating a new, empty array, filling it with filenames and then returning it as the result of our function, we will accept the array as a parameter. This allows the possibility of pre-existing content in the array (from before the function was called), and will give our code flexibility.

Modifying the code from above to accept and use a dynamic array (which has to have been ReDim'ed before this procedure is called) results in the following procedure:

```
Public Sub FindFiles(sPath As String, Files() As String)
Dim sFileName As String

    If Right(sPath, 1) <> Application.PathSeparator Then

        sPath = sPath & Application.PathSeparator

    End If

    sFileName = Dir(sPath)

    Do While sFileName <> ""

        'Add File to Array
        ReDim Preserve Files(UBound(Files) + 1)
        Files(UBound(Files)) = sPath & sFileName
        sFileName = Dir

    Loop

End Sub
```

> Code was also added to this procedure to deal with incorrect input. The path provided must end with a path separator character ("\" in Windows, ":" on the Macintosh), so code is added to check for one. The Application.PathSeparator property is used instead of an actual character because Macintosh and Windows machines use different characters for this purpose.

To test the function, here is another small routine:

```
Public Sub TestFindFiles()

Dim FileArray() As String
Dim i As Integer

    'Initialize our array
    ReDim FileArray(0)

    FindFiles "C:\", FileArray

    For i = 1 To UBound(FileArray)

        MsgBox FileArray(i)

    Next i

End Sub
```

Recursive Programming

The flexibility provided by using an array, and providing it as a parameter, allows you to call `FindFiles` several different times, with different paths, and end up with a single array filled with the contents of multiple directories. This ability also makes it easy to expand the functionality of our code.

The procedure `FindFiles`, as it is now, will return all the files from within a directory, but it doesn't do anything with sub-directories, and the files within those subdirectories. If we added that feature to our function, it would be much easier to process large numbers of files. Entire drives could be processed with a single call to this procedure, or any directory tree of documents.

To add this feature, we will need to use the `Dir` function again, but this time we will use its optional second parameter. This parameter allows you to specify special attributes to filter the filenames retrieved. By default, it is set equal to `vbNormal`, which tells it to return only regular files, but it can have any combination of the following values (although files with no attributes set are always returned):

Value	Meaning
vbAlias	Although a Windows shortcut (`*.lnk` file) is very similar to an Alias (which is the Macintosh equivalent), this attribute applies only on the Macintosh and will have no effect under Windows. Specifying this option causes Alias files to be returned.
vbArchive	Includes any files with their Archive attribute set, which is commonly used to indicate that file should be backed up.
vbDirectory	Specifies directories or folders.
vbHidden	Includes files that are hidden, meaning that they have their hidden attribute set.
vbNormal	The default, this includes files that do not have any attributes set.
vbReadOnly	Includes files that are marked as Read-Only.
vbSystem	Includes System files.
vbVolume	Includes files that represent volumes (drives).

Despite what the Word documentation says, when you specify only `vbNormal`, or nothing at all, for this parameter, files marked as Read-Only and/or Archive are still returned. Many of these values represent file attributes that can be viewed and/or set through the Windows Explorer. Right-clicking a file and selecting **Properties** brings up a dialog containing these settings:

The setting that we need to use is `vbDirectory`, which will cause both directories and regular files to be returned by `Dir`. All the file and directory names are returned together, so we will have to use another function, `GetAttr`, to determine which of the returned values are directories. `GetAttr` takes a filename as a parameter (which could represent any type of file, including a directory) and returns the combination of attributes (those same values from above) possessed by that file. To check if a file has a certain attribute you "AND" the two values together, which will return `True` or `False`. An example of this is shown below, checking if the file is hidden:

```
If GetAttr(sPath & sFileName) And vbHidden Then

    MsgBox "File is Hidden"

Else

    MsgBox "File is not Hidden"

End If
```

So, by using `Dir` with the `vbDirectory` option, and then using `GetAttr` we can rewrite our procedure so that it recognizes sub-directories:

```
Public Sub FindFiles(sPath As String, Files() As String)
 'The line below ensures that if an error occurs,
 'the code will continue with the next statement
 On Error Resume Next
 Dim sFileName As String

 If Right(sPath, 1) <> Application.PathSeparator Then
```

```
    sPath = sPath & Application.PathSeparator

End If

sFileName = Dir(sPath, vbDirectory)

Do While sFileName <> ""

   If Not (GetAttr(sPath & sFileName) And vbDirectory) Then

      'Add File to Array
      ReDim Preserve Files(UBound(Files) + 1)
      Files(UBound(Files)) = sPath & sFileName

   Else

      MsgBox "Directory: " & sFileName

   End If

   sFileName = Dir

Loop

End Sub
```

Once we have the path of one of the sub-directories, we need to retrieve all the filenames from within it. Fortunately we already have a procedure that (given a path) can do exactly that, FindFiles. So, we will call FindFiles from within FindFiles, creating a procedure that calls itself. Procedures that work in this fashion are known as **recursive** and allow a very elegant solution to a complex problem. By calling FindFiles with the path of the sub-directory, it will process all the files in that sub-directory and call FindFiles for each of the directories it finds, and the cycle will continue... FindFiles may end up being called hundreds, or thousands of times before you get your result, but your main program only had to call it once. This would work great, and is almost exactly what we will do, except for one thing. We can't call Dir with a different path, until we have found all the files for the first path. Due to the manner in which Dir works, if we call it with a path value, it will start working with the files under that path, and, when we return to the first procedure, will no longer be working with the proper directory.

To get around this, we loop through the files returned by Dir once for the files, storing every directory we find into a temporary array, and then loop through the directories. A diagram of how this will work is shown below, followed by the completed code:

```
FindFiles("C:\",Files())

    autoexec.bat
    config.sys
    DOS
    command.com
    msdos.sys
    WINDOWS
    autoexec.bak
    win386.swp
    no more files in c:\
    process DOS
        FindFiles("C:\DOS\",Files())

            xcopy32.exe
            delete.exe
            fdisk.exe
            .
            .
            no more files in C:\DOS\

    process WINDOWS
        FindFiles("C:\WINDOWS\",Files())

            mystify.scr
            sol.exe
            background.bmp
            SYSTEM
            moricons.dll
            mouse.com
            pbrush.exe
            no more files in C:\WINDOWS\
            process SYSTEM
                FindFiles("C:\WINDOWS\SYSTEM\",Files())

                    user32.exe
                    actmovie.exe
                    cmmon32.exe
                    kernel386.exe
                    .
                    .
                    no more files in C:\WINDOWS\SYSTEM\
```

```vb
Public Sub FindFiles(sPath As String, Files() As String)

    Dim sFileName As String
    Dim Directories() As String
    Dim i As Integer

    ReDim Directories(0)

    If Right(sPath, 1) <> Application.PathSeparator Then

        sPath = sPath & Application.PathSeparator

    End If

    sFileName = Dir(sPath, vbDirectory)

    Do While sFileName <> ""

        If GetAttr(sPath & sFileName) And vbDirectory Then

            If sFileName <> "." And sFileName <> ".." Then
```

```
        ReDim Preserve Directories(UBound(Directories) + 1)
        Directories(UBound(Directories)) = sPath & sFileName

    End If

  Else

    'Add File to Array
    ReDim Preserve Files(UBound(Files) + 1)
    Files(UBound(Files)) = sPath & sFileName

  End If

  sFileName = Dir

Loop

'Process Directories

For i = 1 To UBound(Directories)

  FindFiles Directories(i), Files()

Next i

End Sub
```

> No changes are required to `TestFindFiles()`, our procedure designed
> to test the retrieval of files. If you don't change the parameters required,
> your client code shouldn't require any modification, which is part of the
> benefit gained from using modular code. All the programs that are
> written to use a certain procedure can be instantly updated, simply by
> improving that single piece of code.

There is a line of code in the procedure above that we didn't discuss, a check for the
values "." and "..":

```
If sFileName <> "." And sFileName <> ".." Then
```

This is required because of the way Windows returns directories. Every directory
contains two special sub-directories, one that represents the current directory (".") and
one that represents the parent of the current directory (".."). This is why, in DOS, the
command cd .. takes you up one directory level, and the command cd . appears to
do nothing. If we didn't skip these two special sub-directories, we would end up in an
endless loop, processing the same files over and over again.

Filtering the Files

The FindFiles procedure works perfectly now, but we are going to add another
feature. As it is, it will return all the files in the given directory (except the hidden
ones), but we probably only want files of a certain type (likely .doc files). We'll start
by adding a Filter argument to our procedure, which we will then use to pass in the
format of files we want, returned (such as "*.doc"). Although we haven't used this
procedure in any programs yet, we will add the argument as an optional one, which
would allow any existing programs to continue working without any changes. The
new procedure declaration is shown below, with the new optional argument and a
default value for that argument all added in:

```
Public Sub FindFiles(sPath As String, Files() As String, _
        Optional Filter = "*.*")
```

Remember that optional arguments must:

- ❑ Be after any non-optional arguments; you have to place all your optional arguments at the end.

- ❑ Be checked with `IsMissing`(argument name) in case the optional argument was not supplied. This is not required if you specify a default value, if the argument isn't supplied it will just use the default value. You can only use `IsMissing` if you didn't specify a data type for the optional argument, or you specified Variant as the type.

By making this an optional argument, and one with a default value, we can maintain compatibility with programs that used the old version. For true compatibility, the procedure should behave exactly as it did before, when it is called without the new argument. You do not want to change the functionality of existing programs that use this code.

Modifying our code to check for the filter value involves placing an additional piece of conditional code before we add a filename to our list:

```
Public Sub FindFiles(sPath As String, Files() As String, _
        Optional Filter = "*.*")
Dim sFileName As String
Dim Directories() As String
Dim i As Integer

ReDim Directories(0)

If Right(sPath, 1) <> Application.PathSeparator Then

   sPath = sPath & Application.PathSeparator

End If

sFileName = Dir(sPath, vbDirectory)

Do While sFileName <> ""

   If GetAttr(sPath & sFileName) And vbDirectory Then

      If sFileName <> "." And sFileName <> ".." Then

         ReDim Preserve Directories(UBound(Directories) + 1)
         Directories(UBound(Directories)) = sPath & sFileName

      End If

   ElseIf sFileName Like Filter Then

      'Add File to Array
      ReDim Preserve Files(UBound(Files) + 1)
      Files(UBound(Files)) = sPath & sFileName

   End If

   sFileName = Dir
```

```
Loop

'Process Directories

For i = 1 To UBound(Directories)

    FindFiles Directories(i), Files(), Filter

Next i

End Sub
```

Notice that we only check the files, not the directories. If we checked every value returned from `Dir` with a filter like `"*.doc"` no directories would make it through. The Boolean expression we use to check for our filter value is a special one for use with wildcard values, `Like`. This operator compares the strings in a flexible way, ignoring case and paying attention to wildcards, returning that `"Document1.doc"`, `"Chapter 5.doc"` and `"Cats.and.dogs.doc"` are all `Like "*.doc"`. If no filter is specified, then it will use the default value provided in the declaration (*.*) which will match all files.

To test our new filter argument, we need to modify a single line of our test procedure, making it find only files with a `doc` extension:

```
FindFiles "C:\", FileArray, "*.doc"
```

Determining Which Path to Search

Now that we have a final version of the `FindFiles` procedure, we need a way for the user to choose a folder to be scanned for files. The simplest way is to use a VBA function similar to `MsgBox`, called `InputBox`. This function displays a simple text box and returns whatever the user types in. It takes several key arguments; `Prompt` which determines the message shown, `Title` which controls the caption of the displayed dialog box and `Default` which sets the original value displayed in the text box. The code below shows an example of calling this function, and the picture directly below it shows the results:

```
sFolder = InputBox("Enter Directory to Summarize", _
        "Document Summary", "C:\")
```

If the user selects **Cancel**, a blank string is returned. Due to that possibility, and the fact that the user could simply delete the default value of "C:\" and then click **OK**, we need to check the value returned before attempting to use it. With these checks in place, the `InputBox` can be added to our `TestFindFiles` routine like this:

```
Public Sub TestFindFiles()
 Dim FileArray() As String
 Dim i As Integer
 Dim sFolder As String

 Do

   sFolder = Trim(InputBox("Enter Directory to Summarize", _
     "Document Summary", "C:\"))

   If sFolder = "" Then

     If MsgBox("Abort Scan?", vbYesNo Or vbQuestion, _
       "No Folder Entered") = vbYes Then

     Exit Sub

     End If

   End If

 Loop Until sFolder <> ""

 'Initialize our array
 ReDim FileArray(0)

 FindFiles sFolder, FileArray(), "*.doc"

 For i = 1 To UBound(FileArray)

   'Do Something With Returned Filename (open it, copy it etc..)

 Next i

End Sub
```

> Notice that the **MsgBox** command has been removed from within the **For** loop. This is intentional, it was just there for testing, and clicking **OK** for every single .doc file on your C drive can take a long time.

The code added to the procedure contains a reference to a string function we haven't discussed before, `Trim`. This function strips any spaces off the beginning and end of a string, ignoring any that are in between other characters.

This works all right, but it is dependent on the user entering a valid path. If you can avoid it, you should never provide a way for the user to enter data directly like this. In Chapter 6, we needed a name and address from the user so we displayed the **Select Name** dialog and let them choose one, so that mistakes in typing are not a problem. For selecting a folder we would like to do the same thing, but neither Word nor VBA provide an easy way to do this.

There is another way though, but it involves the use of the **Windows API**, a set of functions provided as an interface into the features of Windows. Calling Windows API functions isn't simple, but all the code for performing this particular feature will be provided for you.

Calling API Functions

API (Application Programming Interface) functions are procedures built into Windows (95/98/NT), and available to our programs to allow us to take advantage of some of Windows's features. These procedures are the ones responsible for many of the common elements of Windows applications, including the appearance of dialogs; even the MsgBox routine is actually calling a Windows API function (MessageBox). We won't be covering the full details of how to call these routines, but if you add the code below to the very top of a module (so that the Type declarations are in the General Declarations area) you will be able to call the ChooseFolder function just like any other VBA procedure. All the complexities of calling a Windows API call, in this case SHBrowseForFolder, is taken care of by this code, simply call ChooseFolder and use the value it returns as your folder path:

```
Private Type SHITEMID
  cb As Long
  abID As Byte
End Type

Private Type ITEMIDLIST
  mkid As SHITEMID
End Type

Private Type BROWSEINFO
  hOwner As Long
  pidlRoot As Long
  pszDisplayName As String
  lpszTitle As String
  ulFlags As Long
  lpfn As Long
  lParam As Long
  iImage As Long
End Type

Private Declare Function SHGetPathFromIDList Lib _
    "shell32.dll" Alias "SHGetPathFromIDListA" _
    (ByVal pIDL As Long, ByVal pszPath As String) As Long
Private Declare Function SHBrowseForFolder Lib _
    "shell32.dll" Alias "SHBrowseForFolderA" _
    (lpBrowseInfo As BROWSEINFO) As Long

Private Const BIF_RETURNONLYFSDIRS = &H1

Public Function ChooseFolder(sTitle As String)
  On Error GoTo ChooseFolder_Err

  Dim BI As BROWSEINFO
  Dim IDL As ITEMIDLIST
  Dim pIDL As Long
  Dim lResult As Long
  Dim ipos As Integer
  Dim sPath As String

  BI.hOwner = 0
  BI.pidlRoot = 0&
  BI.lpszTitle = sTitle
  BI.ulFlags = BIF_RETURNONLYFSDIRS

  pIDL& = SHBrowseForFolder(BI)

  sPath = Space(1024)

  lResult = SHGetPathFromIDList(ByVal pIDL, ByVal sPath)

  If lResult = 1 Then       'a return value of 1
                            ' indicates success
    ipos = InStr(sPath, Chr(0)) 'Trim string
                            'before last null char
```

```
    ChooseFolder = Left(sPath, ipos - 1)
  Else
    ChooseFolder = ""
  End If
ChooseFolder_Err:

  Exit Function

End Function
```

When you have replaced the `InputBox` function with a call to `ChooseFolder`:

```
sFolder = ChooseFolder("Choose Directory to Summarize")
```

Your folder selection dialog will look like this:

Building the Document Summary

We have already seen, in Chapter 6, how to retrieve various properties from a document, including the number of pages, from the `ComputeStatistics` method and the `BuiltInDocumentProperties` collection. Both of those items are part of the `Document` object, so the only thing we need to do is get a hold of a `Document` object for each of the documents we find. This unfortunately requires opening each file, which can be done through the `Documents` collection's `Open` method. Processing these documents therefore involves four separate pieces of code; creating a new document to contain the summary information, opening each document in turn, retrieving the appropriate document properties, inserting those values into our summary document and closing the document.

Although all the code is part of a single procedure, each individual component is shown separately below, followed by the complete solution.

Creating a New Document

```
Dim objNewDoc As Document

Set objNewDoc = Application.Documents.Add
```

Since this document is not based on a template (although it could be), no parameters are required to create it. The `objNewDoc` variable is used to hold a reference to the newly created document, so that there is a way to work with the document later on in the code.

Opening and Closing All the Documents

```
Dim FileArray() As String
Dim i As Integer

'Initialize our array
ReDim FileArray(0)

FindFiles sFolder, FileArray(), "*.doc"

For i = 1 To UBound(FileArray)

   Dim objDoc As Document

   Set objDoc = Application.Documents.Open _
      (FileArray(i), AddToRecentFiles:=False)

   objDoc.Close wdDoNotSaveChanges
   Set objDoc = Nothing

Next .i
```

Notice the additional parameter used when opening the document (in the `Documents.Open` statement), `AddToRecentFiles`. This parameter specifies whether or not the file you are opening should be added to the recent files list, as displayed at the bottom of the **File** menu. In the case of this project, since we are opening a large number of documents, it is unlikely the user would like or need to have all the documents we're opening added to their menu, and only the last few would be displayed anyway. So, by setting this parameter to `False`, the files we open will not appear on that list, unless they are already present.

Closing the document is critical in this procedure, if the line (`objDoc.Close`) was not present, then there could be hundreds of documents left open when the code ends. The line directly below closing the document is a method of ensuring that an object is no longer valid. By setting `objDoc` equal to `Nothing`, any reference it still held to the document is removed. Closing the document should be sufficient, but it is good programming practice to set all your objects equal to `Nothing` when you are done using them to release any memory resources used by the object.

Retrieving the Document's Properties

The properties required for this project were not specified exactly, and could be almost any of the values. We will be using the following four values: Author, Number of Pages, Date Created, and Date Modified. There isn't a specific property for the Date Modified, but the date the document was last saved is suitable for the purposes of this project:

```
Dim sAuthor As String
Dim iNumberPages As Integer
Dim dtDateCreated As Date
Dim dtDateModified As Date

sAuthor = objDoc.BuiltInDocumentProperties(wdPropertyAuthor)
```

```
objDoc.Repaginate

iNumberPages = objDoc.ComputeStatistics(wdStatisticPages)

dtDateCreated = objDoc.BuiltInDocumentProperties _
     (wdPropertyTimeCreated)
dtDateModified = objDoc.BuiltInDocumentProperties _
     (wdPropertyTimeLastSaved)
```

The code above contains a call to `Repaginate`, one of the methods of the `Document` object. This is required at this point because, as you may have noticed, the page count for a document that has just been opened is often incorrect. Without this line in place we would receive page counts of 1 or 2 for almost every document, regardless of their actual size. The same effect would occur going through `ComputeStatistics` (as above) or through the `BuiltInDocumentProperties` collection.

There are many other document properties that would be well suited for creating a document summary, or any other form of document management, including Subject, Title, Category and Comments. All of these properties are available to the user through the Properties dialog, but (for the average user) they are seldom used:

If you wish to increase the number of documents that have values for these and other properties, there is a setting that will help to accomplish this. Under the Save tab of Word's Options dialog there is a setting labeled Prompt for document properties. If this setting is checked, then when a new document is saved for the first time, the Properties dialog will appear, giving the user a chance to enter information about this document:

Although this option doesn't require that any values be set, it brings the dialog and its contents to the attention of the user, which will increase the number of documents in your organization that have property values.

Inserting the Values into the Summary Document

```
objNewDoc.Range.InsertAfter objDoc.FullName & _
    vbTab & sAuthor & vbTab & iNumberPages & _
    vbTab & Format(dtDateCreated, "Short Date") & _
    vbTab & Format(dtDateModified, "Short Date") & vbCrLf
```

The formatting and order of these values is completely dependent on your needs and preferences and has nothing to do with the development of the project. The code above inserts the values one by one onto a single line, separated by tabs. This choice of formatting means that the results of this code could be easily transferred into a database or spreadsheet if desired. The InsertAfter method of the Range object places text at the end of the range, which in this case is the end of the document.

The Complete Procedure

Putting all the separate pieces of code together produces a single procedure that builds
the complete summary document:

```
Public Sub MakeSummary()

Dim objNewDoc As Document
Dim FileArray() As String
Dim i As Integer
Dim sFolder As String

    Do

        sFolder = ChooseFolder("Choose Directory to Summarize")

        If sFolder = "" Then

            If MsgBox("Abort Scan?", _
            vbYesNo Or vbQuestion, _
            "No Folder Entered") = vbYes Then

                Exit Sub

            End If

        End If

    Loop Until sFolder <> ""


    Set objNewDoc = Application.Documents.Add


    'Initialize our array
    ReDim FileArray(0)

    FindFiles sFolder, FileArray(), "*.doc"

    Dim iTotalPages As Integer
    iTotalPages = 0

    For i = 1 To UBound(FileArray)

        Dim sAuthor As String
        Dim iNumberPages As Integer
        Dim dtDateCreated As Date
        Dim dtDateModified As Date

        Dim objDoc As Document

        Set objDoc = Application.Documents.Open(FileArray(i), _
            AddToRecentFiles:=False)

        sAuthor = objDoc.BuiltInDocumentProperties(wdPropertyAuthor)
        objDoc.Repaginate
        iNumberPages = objDoc.ComputeStatistics(wdStatisticPages)

        iTotalPages = iTotalPages + iNumberPages

        dtDateCreated = objDoc.BuiltInDocumentProperties _
            (wdPropertyTimeCreated)
        dtDateModified = objDoc.BuiltInDocumentProperties_
            (wdPropertyTimeLastSaved)

        objNewDoc.Range.InsertAfter objDoc.FullName & _
            vbTab & sAuthor & vbTab & iNumberPages & _
            vbTab & Format(dtDateCreated, "Short Date") & _
            vbTab & Format(dtDateModified, "Short Date") & vbCrLf

        objDoc.Close wdDoNotSaveChanges
        Set objDoc = Nothing

    Next i
```

```
    objNewDoc.Range.InsertAfter vbCrLf & vbCrLf
    objNewDoc.Range.InsertAfter iTotalPages

End Sub
```

The code listed above includes the user choosing a folder, and the call to `FindFiles`, with all the retrieval code following directly after. An additional bit of functionality has also been added, the calculation of a total page count, which is then added to the new document after all the other information.

> This is the finished version of **TestFindFiles**, which was started earlier in this chapter, but its name has been changed (to **MakeSummary**) to reflect its new purpose.

Prettying it up

At this point, the code in `MakeSummary` is functionally complete, but the document it produces (shown below) is very unappealing. In any form of development, appearance is extremely important, and the results of this code are not acceptable.

Output from `MakeSummary`:

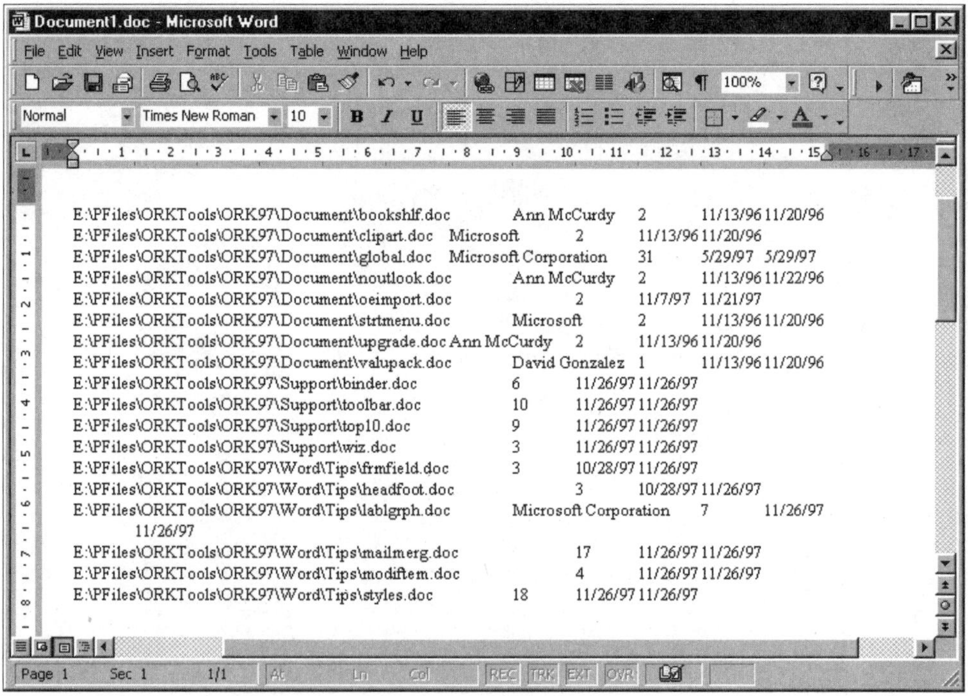

With Word there are many different ways we could improve on the appearance of this output; different fonts, font sizes, formatting, tables or even lines would all be potential methods for making this look professional. For our purposes though, we will look at improving it with only a few quick code changes. The biggest problem facing that output is the length of each document's path, which makes it very difficult to read, and that problem can be fixed through grouping. Grouping describes the division of a large number of items into smaller units based on some shared attribute. In this case, we will rewrite the code to group the documents by their paths, creating the following output:

```
E:\PFiles\ORKTools\ORK97\Document\
        bookshlf.doc    Ann McCurdy     2    11/13/96 11/20/96
        clipart.doc     Microsoft       2    11/13/96 11/20/96
        global.doc      Microsoft       31   5/29/97  5/29/97
        noutlook.doc    Ann McCurdy     2    11/13/96 11/22/96
        oeimport.doc    Microsoft       2    11/7/97  11/21/97
        strtmenu.doc    Microsoft       2    11/13/96 11/20/96
        upgrade.doc     Ann McCurdy     2    11/13/96 11/20/96
        valupack.doc    David Gonzalez  1    11/13/96 11/20/96

E:\PFiles\ORKTools\ORK97\Support\
        binder.doc      Microsoft       6    11/26/97 11/26/97
        toolbar.doc     Microsoft       10   11/26/97 11/26/97
        top10.doc       Microsoft       9    11/26/97 11/26/97
        wiz.doc Microsoft       3       11/26/97 11/26/97

E:\PFiles\ORKTools\ORK97\Word\Tips\
        frmfield.doc    Microsoft Corporation   3    10/28/97 11/26/97
        headfoot.doc    Microsoft Corporation   3    10/28/97 11/26/97
        lablgrph.doc    Microsoft Corporation   7    11/26/97 11/26/97
        mailmerg.doc    Microsoft Corporation   17   11/26/97 11/26/97
        modiftem.doc    Microsoft Corporation   4    11/26/97 11/26/97
        styles.doc      Microsoft Corporation   18   11/26/97 11/26/97
```

> If you were intending to transfer this information into another program, such as a database, then you won't want to make this modification. Grouped data is easier for humans to read, but almost impossible for most computer software to understand.

This output isn't perfect, but it is much more readable than the previous attempt. To accomplish this modification, we will follow a few steps. For each document, we will inspect its path, and then if that path is not the same as the previous document, we create our header. We then write out the document information. The modifications only effect the second half of MakeSummary, and the changed version is shown below:

```
Dim iTotalPages As Integer
    Dim sPrevPath As String

    sPrevPath = ""

    iTotalPages = 0

    For i = 1 To UBound(FileArray)

        Dim sAuthor As String
        Dim iNumberPages As Integer
        Dim dtDateCreated As Date
        Dim dtDateModified As Date

        Dim objDoc As Document

        Set objDoc = Application.Documents.Open _
            (FileArray(i), AddToRecentFiles:=False)

        sAuthor = objDoc.BuiltInDocumentProperties(wdPropertyAuthor)
        objDoc.Repaginate
        iNumberPages = objDoc.ComputeStatistics(wdStatisticPages)

        iTotalPages = iTotalPages + iNumberPages

        dtDateCreated = objDoc.BuiltInDocumentProperties _
            (wdPropertyTimeCreated)
        dtDateModified = objDoc.BuiltInDocumentProperties _
            (wdPropertyTimeLastSaved)

        If sPrevPath <> objDoc.Path Then

            'Make Header

            objNewDoc.Range.InsertAfter vbCrLf

            objNewDoc.Range.InsertAfter objDoc.Path & vbCrLf

            sPrevPath = objDoc.Path

        End If

        objNewDoc.Range.InsertAfter vbTab & objDoc.Name & _
            vbTab & sAuthor & _
            vbTab & iNumberPages & _
            vbTab & Format(dtDateCreated, "Short Date") & _
            vbTab & Format(dtDateModified, "Short Date") & vbCrLf

        objDoc.Close wdDoNotSaveChanges
        Set objDoc = Nothing

    Next i
```

With that final addition, all that is left is giving your users a way to run the code, which could be accomplished through a menu item or a toolbar button. In Chapter 8, we will cover the use of tables, which could be used to good effect in this project.

Project 7B Batch Processing Files

In the last project, we wrote code that could find all files in a certain directory (and everything under that location), and then demonstrated how to loop through those files and perform actions on each file. That code has many different uses, allowing you to perform whatever type of batch processing you want on any number of documents. Some of the more common applications would be to convert a series of documents from one file format to another, to merge several files into one, or to perform edits to multiple files such as adding or replacing some text. This project will demonstrate the first type of project, converting a large number of files from one format to another. In this case, the conversion will be a series of Word documents into HTML documents.

The Scenario

Often, much of the information that a company wants to put on their web site, such as technical notes, software manuals, press releases, etc already exist as Word documents. Java Jitters Inc. is no different, they have an entire directory structure of files that need to be converted and placed onto the website on a regular basis. Although they haven't moved to a completely automated system, (they still want a person to determine when to update the site), but they want to make it a one button process.

The files are organized into a set of sub-folders on the local machine and need to be uploaded to the same directories on the Java Jitters web site. Any files that already exist on the web server should be replaced with the converted file. The other special requirement for this conversion is that any spaces that exist within file and pathnames should be removed for use on the website. Many web browsers and servers can handle spaces in paths (replacing them with the special code %20 when referring to them), but it is safer to avoid the issue and remove or replace (with underscore characters, for example) the spaces.

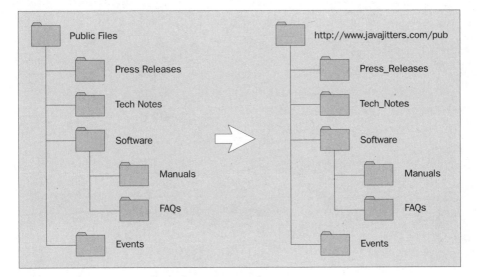

The Code

The code to accomplish this can be written in two phases; one where we build code to loop through the documents and generate appropriate new filenames, and a second where we actually save the document to the website as HTML. We will be using the code we created in 7A, above, including the FindFiles routine, and a bit of the code from Chapter 6, the NameWithoutExtension function.

Phase One: Finding the Files

The first phase is actually quite similar to the code from the previous project, but simpler as it has a fixed folder path and no need to create a new document. After filling an array with all the documents found within the local folder structure, each document is opened. Before the document can be converted, we have to convert its path and filename appropriately, replacing the spaces and the path separators, and then replacing the original extension (.doc) with one for html files (.htm in this example, but .html could be used). Whatever local path is used for the file search it is considered to be equivalent to the "pub" directory of the website, so it is stripped off and replaced appropriately. Although it is unlikely, please note that code below could potentially open a non-Word document (and fail) if that document had a .doc file extension:

```
Public Sub UploadFiles()

Dim FileArray() As String
Dim i As Integer
Dim sFolder As String
Dim sNewPath As String
Dim sNewName As String
Dim objDoc As Document

    'Initialize our array
    ReDim FileArray(0)

    sFolder = "C:\Public Web Files\"

    FindFiles sFolder, FileArray(), "*.doc"

    For i = 1 To UBound(FileArray)

        Set objDoc = Application.Documents.Open _
            (FileArray(i), AddToRecentFiles:=False)

        sNewPath = Replace(objDoc.Path, Application.PathSeparator, "/")
        sNewName = NameWithoutExtension(objDoc.Name) & ".htm"

        sNewPath = Mid(sNewPath, Len(sFolder) + 1)

        sNewPath = "http://www.javajitters.com/pub/" & sNewPath

        If Right(sNewPath, 1) <> "/" Then

            sNewPath = sNewPath & "/"

        End If

        sNewPath = Replace(sNewPath, " ", "_")
        sNewName = Replace(sNewName, " ", "_")

        MsgBox sNewPath & sNewName

        objDoc.Close wdDoNotSaveChanges
        Set objDoc = Nothing

    Next i

End Sub
```

To move on to the second phase, and complete this project, we need to replace the MsgBox command with the Document object's SaveAs method.

Phase Two: The SaveAs Method

The Document object has several ways in which documents can be saved:

❏ The Save method, which simply saves the document to wherever it was already saved

❏ The Close method, which will save changes and can convert between non-Word format documents and Word documents by specifying False for the OriginalFormat parameter

❏ The SaveAs method which will save a file into any format (supported by Word) and location, regardless of its previous format or path

So, only the SaveAs method will allow us to convert a Word document into another format, or to specify a particular location. The SaveAs method takes several parameters, each of which are described below:

Parameter	Description
FileName	Specifies the file name and path, including an extension.
FileFormat	Takes a constant to specify the file format to save the file in, one of the following choices:
	wdFormatDocument (Word document)
	wdFormatDOSText (DOS formatted text file)
	wdFormatDOSTextLineBreaks (DOS formatted text file with line breaks)
	wdFormatEncodedText (Text encoded using a specific character set, such as UTF-8 for Unicode, EUC-JP for Japanese, or EUC-TW for Chinese, usually only used for multi-lingual applications).
	wdFormatHTML (Saved as a HyperText Markup Language file, also known as a web page)
	wdFormatRTF (Saves the file using Rich-Text Format)
	wdFormatTemplate (Saves the file as a Word template)
	wdFormatText (Saves the file as a Windows text file)
	wdFormatTextLineBreaks (Saves the file as a Windows text file with line breaks)
	wdFormatUnicodeText (Saves as a Unicode character set text file)
	There are many other file formats available to you, but they must be specified using special numerical codes. These other formats are discussed later in this chapter in the section "Converting Files".

Table Continued on Following Page

Parameter	Description
LockComments	True or False, determines if locked for comments. (Through Word's Insert Comment feature).
Password, WritePassword	Strings containing passwords for opening the document and modifying it, respectively.
AddToRecentFiles	Same as for the Open method of the Documents collection, this parameter takes a True or False value and determines if this document should appear in the list of recent files on the File menu. This has no effect on whether or not it appears in the Documents folder on the Start menu.
ReadOnlyRecommended	An interesting option, if True is specified for this argument the file is not saved as Read-Only, but when it is opened Word will suggest that it should be Read-Only and give the user the option of opening it as such. Generally, if you want it to be Read-Only, this isn't the way to go about it, but it can be useful when you have generated a document that isn't intended for modification, but you want the user to have the option.
EmbedTrue_ TypeFonts	There is some legal and ethical controversy surrounding this feature. This option, if set to True, includes the fonts used for the document into the document's file. With this option, users on other machines will be able to view and print your document using the intended fonts, even if they do not have those fonts installed on their machines. The issue with this technology is that the font information is being transferred, and if someone were to figure out how that information was being stored, they might be able to extract it for their own use.
SaveNative_ PictureFormat	In the case of this option, native means Word's internal picture format, and this setting controls how pictures embedded in a document are saved.
SaveFormsData	When using Word forms (not covered in this book, but a useful feature), this option allows you to save only the data from the form as comma-delimited text.
SaveAsAOCELetter	This option allows you to save the document's associated mailer information along with the document.

To complete the code for uploading our documents, we just need to replace the MsgBox statement with a call to SaveAs:

```
objDoc.SaveAs FileName:=sNewPath & sNewName, FileFormat:=wdFormatHTML
```

The completed code has hard coded both the local and web paths, which make it less flexible and difficult to reuse. A few changes can change it into a generic routine that uploads any local directory to any web site (that you have security permissions on). The complete, generic routine is shown below with the modifications highlighted:

```
Public Sub UploadFiles(SourcePath As String, _
    TargetPath As String, TargetPathSeparator As String)

Dim FileArray() As String
Dim i As Integer
Dim sNewPath As String
Dim sNewName As String
Dim objDoc As Document

    'Initialize our array
    ReDim FileArray(0)

    FindFiles SourcePath, FileArray(), "*.doc"

    For i = 1 To UBound(FileArray)

        Set objDoc = Application.Documents.Open _
            (FileArray(i), AddToRecentFiles:=False)

        sNewPath = Replace(objDoc.Path, Application.PathSeparator, _
            TargetPathSeparator)

        sNewName = NameWithoutExtension(objDoc.Name) & ".htm"

        sNewPath = Mid(sNewPath, Len(SourcePath) + 1)

        sNewPath = TargetPath & sNewPath

        If Right(sNewPath, 1) <> TargetPathSeparator Then

            sNewPath = sNewPath & TargetPathSeparator

        End If

        sNewPath = Replace(sNewPath, " ", "_")
        sNewName = Replace(sNewName, " ", "_")

        objDoc.SaveAs FileName:=sNewPath & sNewName, _
            FileFormat:=wdFormatHTML

        objDoc.Close wdDoNotSaveChanges
        Set objDoc = Nothing

    Next i

End Sub
```

A third argument was added to account for the possibility that you may be saving locally or to a web site, requiring different path separators for each. Note that the file extension for the local files is still a hard coded value (.doc), to be truly flexible you could pass the local extension in as an argument as well.

General Notes on Converting to Web Pages

Converting to HTML is a technique that has many issues specific to this file format. A brief discussion of several of these issues is provided within this section, and a discussion about conversion in general is covered immediately after.

Web Folders and FTP Locations

When building any Word application to work with Internet sites, whether they are web or FTP based, you should set up the locations before attempting to run code against them. In the case of web sites, this means creating a **Web Folder** for that specific site (or sub-directory under a site), using the Explorer interface to the Web Folders:

Web Folders are a new method of defining a specific web location, and allowing you to browse, edit, delete and add to the files present on the web server. For this feature to function properly you need to have the Microsoft Office Server Extensions installed on the web server you are connecting to, which may require the assistance of the site's administrator (unless you are the site admin, which can make things more convenient).

> It appears that the Front Page 98 Server Extensions are really the same as the new Office Extensions, as servers with only those extensions installed still work correctly as Web Folders. Either way, software needs to be installed on the web server for this feature to work correctly.

All the details about these web sites are specified when you create the web folder, using the **Add Web Folder** wizard. This includes the server name (such as `http://www.wrox.com`) the specific directory you wish to refer to, unless you wish to deal with the entire site, and you will be prompted to enter any security information.

> Security issues are the most common problem when attempting to upload files to a web server. If you do not have sufficient access rights to create a file, the `SaveAs` will fail. Your attempt to upload will also fail i the directory you are trying to save your files into does not exist; it will not be automatically created.

FTP sites are very similar, but work through a different method. Office applications allow you to specify FTP sites as locations to open from or save to. This is accomplished through the **Look in** combo box in the regular **Open** or **Save** dialogs, allowing you to select, add or modify FTP locations:

For each site you add to the list (through the Add/Modify FTP Locations option), you can specify username and password information, along with the site address:

Both Web Folders and FTP locations can be referred to directly in your code by using them like regular file system paths. The format of these paths is in the generic URL format, `ftp://ftp.servername.com` for the FTP sites, and `http://www.servername.com` for the Web Folders. There is no special syntax required to tell Word that you intend to use the special FTP location or Web Folder, it will do so by default, if one exists.

Related Files for HTML documents

Unlike a Word document, or most other file formats, images and other elements of an HTML document are stored external to the document itself. When you save a Word document as an HTML page (and this is really a normal Word function, not a development issue), it creates images files and other related external files based on the contents of your document. All of these external files are stored into a folder named `<filename>_files`. One folder is therefore created for each such file; all the necessary files are placed into that folder and linked appropriately into the original document. Uploading 50 complex files to a web server could therefore create thousands of separate files, and 50 separate folders, which is a lot of information to transfer across the Internet.

It is advisable to work with small files when converting to HTML, which simplifies the work involved for Word, and also produces smaller, simpler, HTML files which is generally considered preferable. With the same goal of simplifying the work involved, many people also convert files locally first (saving them to a different local directory) and then upload them to the web site using Front Page or FTP client software. None of these are requirements for conversion to HTML; they are suggestions to make your life and work less difficult.

Converting Files

The code above was designed for converting files into HTML, but there are many other file formats you may want to work with, and most of them are not provided as constants for the `SaveAs` method. All the formats listed when you choose **Save As** in Word are available through code as constants (for the formats listed earlier in this chapter) or as numerical codes. Each of the formats is represented by a `FileConverter` object, and is part of the `FileConverters` collection, which is a property of the `Application` object. The following code demonstrates how to access this collection and it will (there needs to be an open document when you run this code) list the formats and their corresponding codes into the `ActiveDocument`:

```
Public Sub FileFormats()

Dim objFileConverters As FileConverters
Dim objCurrentFC As FileConverter

Set objFileConverters = Application.FileConverters

Application.Selection.InsertAfter "Internal Name" & _
    vbTab & "Display Name" & _
    vbTab & "Class Name (Index)" & _
    vbTab & "Numeric Code" & vbCrLf

For Each objCurrentFC In objFileConverters
```

```
    If objCurrentFC.CanSave Then

        Application.Selection.InsertAfter objCurrentFC.Name _
            & vbTab & objCurrentFC.FormatName _
            & vbTab & objCurrentFC.ClassName _
            & vbTab & objCurrentFC.SaveFormat & vbCrLf

    End If

Next

Dim objTable As Table

Set objTable = Application.Selection.ConvertToTable(wdSeparateByTabs)

objTable.Rows(1).Range.Bold = True

objTable.Borders.OutsideLineStyle = wdLineStyleNone
objTable.Borders.InsideLineStyle = wdLineStyleNone

End Sub
```

A little bit of formatting is included, and this is the result when the code is run:

Internal Name	Display Name	Class Name (Index)	Numeric Code
TXTLYT32.CNV	MS-DOS Text with Layout	MS-DOS Text with Layout	8
TXTLYT32.CNV	Text with Layout	Text with Layout	9
html32.cnv	HTML Document	HTML	10
WNWRD232.CNV	Word 2.x for Windows	MSWordWin2	12
WPFT532.CNV	WordPerfect 5.0	WrdPrfctDOS50	13
WPFT532.CNV	WordPerfect 5.1 for DOS	WrdPrfctDOS51	14
WPFT532.CNV	WordPerfect 5.x for Windows	WrdPrfctWin	15
WPFT532.CNV	WordPerfect 5.1 or 5.2 Secondary File	WrdPrfctDat	16
WPFT532.CNV	WordPerfect 5.0 Secondary File	WrdPrfctDat50	17
WRITE32.CNV	Windows Write 3.0	MSWinWrite30	18
DOSWRD32.CNV	Word for MS-DOS 3.x - 5.x	MSWordDOS	19
DOSWRD32.CNV	Word for MS-DOS 6.0	MSWordDOS6	20
works432.cnv	Works 4.0 for Windows	MSWorksWin4	21
MACWRD32.CNV	Word 4.0 for Macintosh	MSWordMac4	22
MACWRD32.CNV	Word 5.0 for Macintosh	MSWordMac5	23
MACWRD32.CNV	Word 5.1 for Macintosh	MSWordMac51	24
works332.cnv	Works 3.0 for Windows	MSWorksWin3	27
WRD6EX32.CNV	Word for Windows (Generic)	WRD6	11
wrd6ex32.cnv	Word 6.0/95	MSWord6Exp	26
wrd6er32.cnv	Word 97 & 6.0/95 - RTF	MSWord6RTFExp	25

When you need to use a specific file format in your code, WordPerfect 5.0 for instance, you should not use the code displayed above, but instead retrieve the code at run time using the format's class name as an index in the FileConverters collection.

```
objDoc.SaveAs FileName:=sFileName, _
    FileFormat:=Application.FileConverters("WrdPrfctDOS50").SaveFormat
```

Working in this method protects your development against any changes in the format codes, as the class names will not change. The FileConverters collection has the standard properties and methods of a collection (Count, Item, etc), and the most useful properties of the FileConverter object are documented in the table below:

Property	Description
CanSave, CanOpen	Return True or False to indicate if Word can save and/or open files in this format
Extensions	Returns a string containing the valid extension(s) for this file format
Creator	Designed for the Macintosh, this returns the 32-bit numeric equivalent of the document's 4 character Creator Code
ClassName	Returns the string code for this converter, such as MSWorksWin3 for Works for Windows 3.0
FormatName	Descriptive name for the format, such as WordPerfect 5.0
OpenFormat	Numeric code for use in opening files of this format
SaveFormat	Numeric code for use in saving files to this format, see example above
Path	Supposedly the path to the converter, but blank for most converters
Name	An internal name, usually blank but sometimes contains the name of a conversion file

Project 7C Working with Custom Document Properties

In the first project in this chapter, we summarized a set of documents based on their properties. The collection of properties is a powerful feature of Office documents, but those properties may not contain the information that you or your company needs. This project isn't really a project, but instead a series of quick examples of how you can use and customize those document properties to suit your organization.

Introduction to Custom Properties

Document properties, both built-in and custom, are an Office-wide feature. Every Office document has them, and every one works with them in the same way. The purpose of document properties is to provide a common way to describe any document, and custom properties enhance that ability by allowing you to define your own properties. In the **Properties** dialog, there is an area dedicated to viewing, creating, and setting these custom properties, providing the non-programmatic interface to this feature:

Chapter 7.doc Properties

General | Summary | Statistics | Contents | Custom

Name:

Checked by
Client
Date completed
Department
Destination
Disposition

Type: Text

Value: ☐ Link to content

Properties: | Name | Value | Type |

Add
Delete

OK   Cancel

Properties are assigned a name, a data type (Text, Date, Boolean, or Number), and a value. The names provided for you are only suggestions; you can enter any name you wish, as long as it is not already taken. All of the features of this dialog box are also available through code, allowing you to create properties as needed.

Creating Custom Properties

To create a custom document property you can do it through the standard Word interface, or through the Add method of the CustomDocumentProperties collection, as shown below:

```
Dim objCustomProperties As DocumentProperties

Set objCustomProperties = ActiveDocument.CustomDocumentProperties

objCustomProperties.Add Name:="ProjectCode", _
        Type:=msoPropertyTypeNumber, Value:=34, _
        LinkToContent:=False
```

The Type argument can be one of:

- ❑   msoPropertyTypeNumber, for integer values

- ❑   msoPropertyTypeFloat, for real numbers

- ❑   msoPropertyTypeBoolean, for True/False values

- ❑   msoPropertyTypeDate, for date/time values

- ❑   msoPropertyTypeString, for text values

Depending on the purpose for which you are creating the property, you can choose not to set the value at this time, and then set it later on through code or the regular Word interface.

Setting and Retrieving Custom Properties

The same CustomDocumentProperties collection through which you created the new custom property is also used to retrieve or set their values. The individual properties can be accessed using an index value into the collection, which can be a numeric value (representing each property's relative position in the collection) or the name of the property itself. The name value is usually preferred as the numeric index of a particular property changes as others are added or removed:

```
iProjectCode = objCustomProperties("ProjectCode").Value
```

Overall the custom document property feature of Office gives you a powerful method of storing company specific information with any document. It is often used to store your own project codes or other form of tracking data with the document, and can then be used manually or programmatically as part of a document management program. The possibilities are nearly endless. Note, however, that the maximum length of a custom property is 256 characters.

Summary

This chapter has covered various topics relating to document management, which is a very large and important field of development. The ability to process a multitude of Word documents without user intervention can allow you to build systems that hel track the huge amount of information being stored as Word documents. This chapter also covered how to convert documents from one format to another through code, which can be used to move information between mediums (such as for the Web or the Macintosh) and between software (from Microsoft Word to Word Perfect, for instance).

Word development is the perfect environment to use for document management, with so many built-in features, and the ability to work with external objects. The upcoming chapters on databases and the customization of the Microsoft Word environment will provide even more information related to this and other types of programming.

Databases

Introduction

Databases are an enormous topic, it is possible that every bit of Word development you do will involve one in some way, as they are the main form of information technology in use at most corporations. Regardless of whether it is a web-based program, a Windows application, or a mainframe, most business applications are front-ends to a database. With this technology being present everywhere, using it to produce Word documents is a very common application, and a very important one.

Having said all that, you might be wondering why more of this book isn't focused on database-oriented development, and that is an understandable question. The answer is that the book is focused on that type of development, but there is a lot more to building database-driven Word applications than working with the database itself. To create an invoice based on a database involves working with bookmarks, templates, document properties and many more of the topics covered in the non-database chapters of this book, and the same applies to most Word development projects.

This chapter is going to cover only the database side of this type of development, showing you how to connect to the database, retrieve selected information, and even add or change records in your database, all from VBA. A single project in this chapter, and two more in the next, will be provided to demonstrate the various techniques related to database-driven Word development.

As all the projects are built on top of the same database, the structure and description of that database will be provided first, separate from the projects. Java Jitters will once again form the model for the documents, the database, and the sample data, but the information being stored could be applied with few modifications to almost any company that sells products or services. Before we even get into the actual database though, we'll start by introducing some database-related terms and technology.

A Database Primer

This is a reference book, so don't worry, we won't be spending too much time reviewing the basic concepts, but it is often good to make sure we are all using the same terms and thinking about the same things before getting deep into a topic.

What is a Database?

As we mentioned above, databases are the most common type of information system, and they are built on many different computers using many different languages, but at the most basic level they are all the same. A database is a way to store information, nothing else. Using, adding, editing, or deleting data is up to the programs using the database, not the database itself. Databases are made up of several key objects:

- ❑ **Tables** are collections of information that have some logical reason to fit together, like all the names and addresses of customers.

- ❑ **Records** are the individual entries in a table, like all the details for one particular customer. These are also referred to as rows.

- ❑ **Fields** are the items that make up a complete record, like the first name portion of a customer's address. These are also known as columns.

Together, these objects are used to hold all the data stored into a database. For our example company of Java Jitters Inc., the database will consist of four tables (`Customer`, `Invoice`, `InvoiceItem`, and `Product`), structured as shown in the following diagram:

Customer	Invoice	InvoiceItem	Product
<u>ID</u>	<u>ID</u>	Invoice ID	<u>ID</u>
Name	Date	Product ID	Name
Address	Customer	Quantity	Price
City	Notes		Cost
Province			
Postal Code			
Country			

This database, complete with sample data is available from the Wrox Press web site at `http://www.wrox.com/`

Queries

Data is retrieved from the database through the use of **queries**, specially formatted requests for data, which are written using a language known as **SQL**. SQL stands for **Structured Query Language** and can be used to specify which columns you wish to retrieve from your database, and to specify which rows by providing certain criteria (i.e. Customers who live in South Dakota).

Simple Queries

The basic syntax of an SQL query is:

```
SELECT <Columns> FROM <Tables> WHERE <Criteria>
```

The columns are specified as a list of field names, separated by commas, like this: `Name, Address, City`. Field names that consist of more than one word (`First Name`, for instance) have to be surrounded in square brackets: `[First Name]`, `[Street Address]`, `City`. To specify that all columns should be returned, you use an asterisk (*) in place of the field names. These syntax details are specific to Microsoft Access, each database can have its own particular conventions.

Tables are specified in a similar manner, using a comma-separated list, using brackets if the table's name contains more than one word. At this point your SQL statement is complete, as the specifying of criteria is optional:

```
SELECT Name, Address, City FROM Customer
```

The criteria section of the SQL statement, although it is optional, is used to restrict the rows returned to only those that match certain conditions. A condition is specified as a Boolean expression, in a similar manner to those used in `If` statements, checking the value of one of the table's fields. The expressions can use most of the common operators (=, <, >, <>, etc) and some that are not available in regular code (`BETWEEN`, for instance). Multiple criteria expressions can be used, and are connected using `AND` or `OR` operators, to create a single multi-part Boolean expression.

The end result defines the complete set of data that you wish to retrieve. For instance, to retrieve all the columns of all the records from the `Customer` table where the `City` field was equal to `"Los Angeles"` and the `State` was equal to `"CA"`, the following SQL statement (once again using Access syntax) would be required:

```
SELECT * FROM Customer WHERE (City = "Los Angeles") AND (State = "CA")
```

> Note that you can specify criteria using fields that you are not returning from the query.

The result of this statement would be a set of records that matched the above criteria, which could be anywhere from no records to all the records in the `Customer` table. This set of records is represented in our code as a **recordset**, a special type of database object that we will be using throughout our code.

Multiple Table Queries

Returning to the example database for this chapter, you will notice that the `Invoice` table doesn't contain the customer's name, only their ID. This is because our database is a **relational database**, and one of the rules governing these types of databases is that you shouldn't repeat information. If we were to put all the customer's information in with the invoice, then that information would exist in several places (in the `Customer` table, and in every `Invoice` record for that customer). If the customer were to ever change his or her name, that name would have to be changed in many places; instead, by only placing the ID in with the invoice, the name will only exist in one location. The downside to this method of storing data is that you will have to perform a query to retrieve all the information you need about an invoice. This query needs to **join** the two related tables based on their common fields (`Customer` and `ID`), which is accomplished through the use of an appropriate `WHERE` clause in the SQL statement:

```
SELECT Customer.Name, Customer.City, Invoice.ID, Invoice.Date, Invoice.Notes
FROM Customer, Invoice WHERE Customer.ID = Invoice.[Customer] AND
Customer.City = "Los Angeles"
```

> In your SQL statements, you can specify the table name in front of a field name to prevent any confusion. This is required if a field by the same name exists in more than one of the tables involved in the query. If the table name consists of more than one word, you should place it within brackets (`[` & `]`), separate from the field name.

This query will return a recordset consisting of the requested columns from both `Invoice` and `Customer` for all the customers from Los Angeles. The diagram below shows the relationships between the four tables in our sample database. The connectors that go from one line to three lines signify **One-To-Many** relationships, where there can be several records in one table for every one record in the other.

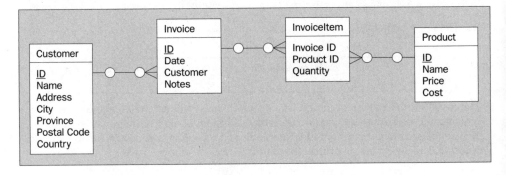

If you require more information on SQL or on databases in general, there are many sources of reference material on both databases and SQL, including Instant SQL Programming by Joe Celko (1-874416-50-8) and Beginning Access 2000 VBA by Smith & Sussman (1-861001-76-2) both published by Wrox Press.

Database Access Layers

When you program in VBA, you don't use databases directly, you go through an intermediate level, a data access layer. This layer is here to simplify the task of retrieving and modifying databases by providing a common interface to any one of several different database engines. You program using the interface provided by this data access layer, and the data access layer translates your requests appropriately for Microsoft SQL Server, Oracle, Sybase, Microsoft Access, or whichever other database you are using.

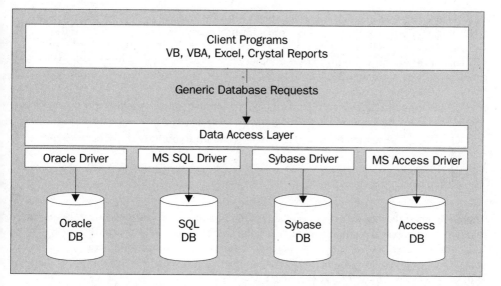

This insertion of a layer between you and the database serves two important purposes:

❑   Making your code generic, it can be used against any database supported by the data access layer.

❑   Making your code simpler. As the data access layer has to work against many different database engines, they tend to consist of straightforward methods for performing the most commonly needed tasks.

Some programmers do not use these layers, they write code to talk directly to the database because they need access to features of the database engine that are not provided by the data access layer, or because the data access layer is too slow. For most purposes, today's data access layers (such as OLE DB, which we are going to cover below) provide every bit of functionality you need, and the difference in performance isn't significant enough to justify the extra programming.

ADO

ActiveX Data Objects, or **ADO**, is the latest and greatest data access layer from Microsoft. This set of objects defines a very simple and generic database interface. ADO has replaced **DAO** (**Data Access Objects**) as the data access layer of choice, due to its simple interface, which is designed to provide the most common database services with low resource (memory, processor time, etc) usage. If this is your first exposure to database programming from VB or VBA, then you don't have to worry about what ADO is replacing but keep it mind in case you run into some older code.

ADO is also popular because it is really just a simple interface to another Microsoft technology called **OLE DB**, and therefore supports accessing non-traditional data sources. This book will only cover ADO, as it is currently the best data access layer available, but you may run into DAO in older code or other reference material. ADO consists of three main objects:

- ❑ `Connection`, which represents the actual link to the database through which you retrieve and work with data
- ❑ `Command`, which represents a single command you intend to execute against the database
- ❑ `Recordset`, which represents a group of records, anywhere from no records to thousands

There are several other objects, and each of them is important, but we can get by using just two of the objects available from ADO, the `Connection` object, and the `Recordset` object, so we will only focus on those particular items. Appendix C at the end of the book provides a quick reference to the complete ADO object model, and the Wrox Press book, *"ADO 2.0 Programmer's Reference"* is available if complete coverage of this technology is required.

Creating a Reference to the ADO Library

Before we can declare any variable as ADO objects, we need to add a reference to ADO to our project. This is accomplished through the References menu option (under the Tools menu in the Visual Basic editor), which will bring up the References dialog. To make a reference to ADO, the Microsoft ActiveX Data Objects 2.x Library item must be checked, as shown:

Once this reference is in place, the ADO objects will appear as options when you declare a variable, allowing you to create instances of these objects as needed:

```
(General)                          ▼   (Declarations)                    ▼

Dim dbMain as ADODB.c|
                      ╔═══════════════════════════════════╗
                      ║ ⌐P CEResyncEnum                    ║
                      ║ ⌐ Command                          ║
                      ║ ⌐P CommandTypeEnum                 ║
                      ║ ⌐P CompareEnum                     ║
                      ║ ▓ Connection                       ║
                      ║ ⌐P ConnectModeEnum                 ║
                      ║ ⌐P ConnectOptionEnum               ║
                      ╚═══════════════════════════════════╝
```

With this reference in place, you can also use the Object Browser (press *F2* when in the Visual Basic editor) to view all of the ADO objects and their various properties and methods:

```
╔═ Object Browser ═══════════════════════════ _□X ╗
║ ADODB                    ▼   ◄ ►  ⧉ ⧆  ?        ║
║                          ▼   ♯ ∨                ║
║ Classes              │ Members of 'Connection'   ║
║ ⌐P CEResyncEnum    ▲ │ ⌐ Attributes          ▲  ║
║ ⌐ Command            │ ⊸ BeginTrans              ║
║ ⌐P CommandTypeEnur   │ ∮ BeginTransComplete      ║
║ ⌐P CompareEnum       │ ⊸ Cancel                  ║
║ ▓ Connection         │ ⊸ Close                   ║
║ ⌐P ConnectModeEnum   │ ⌐ CommandTimeout          ║
║ ⌐P ConnectOptionEnur │ ⊸ CommitTrans             ║
║ ⌐P ConnectPromptEnur▼│ ∮ CommitTransComplete  ▼  ║
║ ─────────────────────────────────────────────── ║
║ Class **Connection**                             ║
║    Member of <u>ADODB</u>                        ║
╚══════════════════════════════════════════════════╝
```

The Connection Object

This object represents the link between your program and the database you are using. In our database-related projects we will always start by creating an instance of a `Connection` object and opening a connection to our database. When declaring your `Connection` variable, you need to use the `New` keyword, to specify that a new instance of this object type should be created. Here is an example of this type of declaration:

```
Dim dbMain As New ADODB.Connection
```

This object supports two methods that we will be concerned with in this chapter, `Open` and `Close`, which link the object to a specific database and remove that link, respectively.

Connection Strings

The link to a particular database is accomplished through a textual description of that link which is known as a **connection string**. This string's formatting and contents are quite complicated and require the introduction of some background information before they can be explained.

OLE DB Providers

As was mentioned earlier, ADO is a wrapper around a larger and more complex technology, OLE DB. This underlying technology works through the concept of **data providers** and **data consumers**, with every different type of database or other data source having a corresponding provider so that it can communicate with OLE DB consumers (such as ADO, and, indirectly, your program). These individual providers, which are database (and even version) specific, are known as **OLE DB providers** and represent the layer of drivers shown in our data access layer diagram:

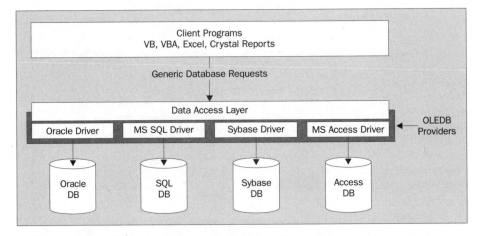

For you to be able to connect to a database using ADO, there must be an OLE DB provider that supports that type of data source, and that provider must be installed on your machine. As ADO is relatively new, not every data source has a provider available, but a generic **ODBC (Open Database Connectivity**, a special standard set up by Microsoft to allow a single set of interfaces to many different databases) provider is available that allows you to connect to any data source that supports that older, more established technology. The exact providers available can be different on every machine, but you will have at least a provider for Microsoft Jet 4.0 (Access 2000 databases), Microsoft SQL Server, Oracle databases, ODBC databases, and several others.

Database Specific Information

When connecting to a database, you have to connect through the appropriate OLE DB provider, but that provider requires certain information to find and connect to the database. The exact information required is different for each provider but generally consists of security information (a user ID and password for the database, if there is one), location information (a path to the .mdb file for Jet databases, or the Server name for SQL Server and others), and other connection options (Timeout values, etc).

Constructing the Connection String

The connection string consists of the combination of both the above values. Each OLE DB provider has a specific name that identifies it (`"Microsoft.Jet.OLEDB.4.0"` is the name of the provider for Access 2000 databases, for instance), which forms the main part of the connection string along with any security or option settings. Here is a sample connection string, specifying that the Microsoft SQL Server OLE DB provider should be used to connect to the WEBSERVER server with a user ID of `"sa"` and a blank password:

```
Provider=SQLOLEDB.1;Persist Security Info=False;User ID=sa;Initial
Catalog=pubs;Data Source=WEBSERVER
```

Using the Data Link File

This is a file that represents the same connection information that is contained in a connection string, but provides a graphical interface for generating that information. It would be possible to describe some of the available providers and the various options for those specific providers, but there is an easier way of creating these strings. When ADO is installed on your system, you gain the ability to create a special type of file called a **Microsoft Data Link File**. To take advantage of this feature, you need to right-click somewhere inside a Windows Explorer folder (or on the desktop), and select the Ne**w** menu option:

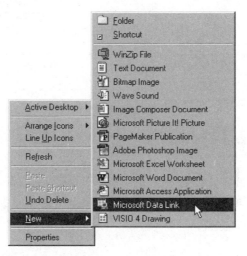

A list of files that can be created will be displayed, select Microsoft Data Link to create a new file of this type. A new file will be created on your drive in whichever folder you right-clicked, with a name of New Microsoft Data Link.UDL.

New Microsoft
Data Link.UDL

This file represents all the information required to connect to a data source, but it is currently empty. Double-click it to bring up a property dialog that will allow you to specify all the necessary connection options. The first tab of the displayed dialog is used to specify which OLE DB Provider you wish to use:

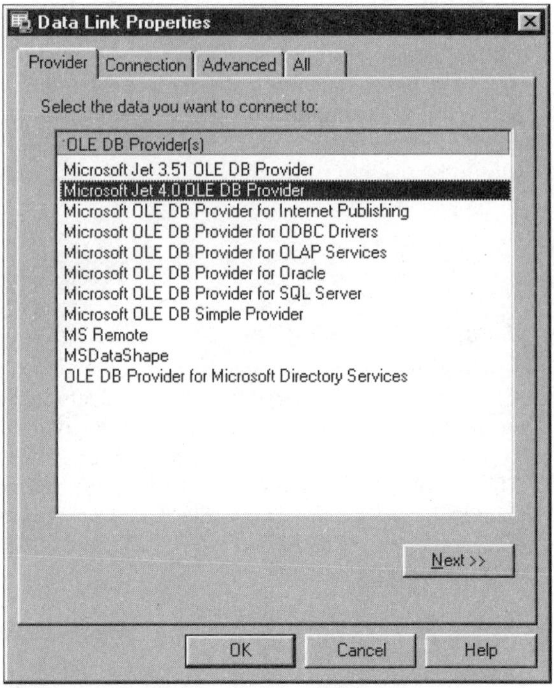

The exact list of providers displayed on this tab is dependent on what has been installed on your machine.

Clicking Next will take you to the next tab which allows you to specify the most common settings for this provider. The fields available on this tab are dependent on the provider selected, as every provider may require different connection information, two versions are shown here; the first is for Microsoft Jet 4.0 databases, and the other is for a Microsoft SQL Server database:

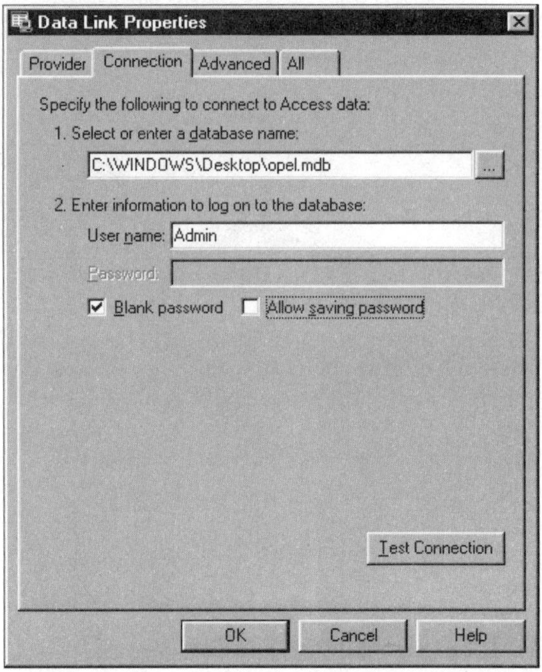

Notice the **Test Connection** button that is shown in both images. This button is available for all providers and performs a test of your settings, confirming that OLE DB can connect to the database with those values. If possible (i.e. the database is available when you set up this information), always use this self-test feature before going on in your development. If your connection information is wrong, nothing else will work.

The remaining two tabs are used for specifying advanced features and are not usually necessary. Once you have set up your connection using this dialog, click OK to close and save the information. To get this connection information out of the now complete data link file, you just have to open it with a text editor. You can do this easily with Notepad or Wordpad, or even Word itself, whatever is easier. Regardless of the method used, the file will contain text in the following format:

```
[oledb]
; Everything after this line is an OLE DB initstring
Provider=Microsoft.Jet.OLEDB.4.0;Persist Security Info=False;Data
Source=C:\WINDOWS\Desktop\opel.mdb
```

The line of text starting with `Provider` is the connection string you need for your code, select it and copy it to the clipboard.

The Open Method

Now that you have your connection string, you can use it to open your database connection. The `Open` method of the `Connection` object is relatively simple, it needs only a single parameter - the connection string. Given the string shown earlier, this code would declare a new connection variable and open a connection to the Jet database located at `"C:\Windows\Desktop\training.mdb"`:

```
Public Sub OpenDatabaseConnection()

Dim dbMain As New ADODB.Connection

    dbMain.Open "Provider=Microsoft.Jet.OLEDB.4.0;" & _
        "Persist Security Info=False;" & _
        "Data Source=C:\WINDOWS\Desktop\training.mdb"

End Sub
```

> **Actually, you don't need to supply even the single parameter to the `Open` method; if you wish you can set the `Connection` object's `ConnectionString` property first and then call `Open` without any parameters.**

Once you have an open connection, you can use it as part of opening a new recordset of data from this database, which will be detailed below, under the `Recordset` object.

The Close Method

Using the `Close` method of the `Connection` object doesn't require any instruction; it takes no parameters and is called in the exact same manner as any other method:

```
Public Sub OpenDatabaseConnection()

Dim dbMain As New ADODB.Connection

    dbMain.Open "Provider=Microsoft.Jet.OLEDB.4.0;" & _
        "Persist Security Info=False;" & _
        "Data Source=C:\WINDOWS\Desktop\training.mdb"

    dbMain.Close

End Sub
```

This method should always be called when you are done with your database connection, as it frees up certain system resources (memory, etc). Theoretically, a `Close` will be performed automatically when the connection variable goes out of scope (the program or procedure in which the variable is declared comes to completion), but it is better not to depend on such things, and call the `Close` method yourself.

The Recordset Object

The `Connection` object makes our link to the database, but it is through the `Recordset` object that we will retrieve, add, and modify actual data. Regardless of how we are going to use it, we will usually start with declaring a new `Recordset` variable and then use its `Open` method to execute a SQL statement.

Declaring a Recordset

For our declaration, we will be using the New keyword again, to create an instance of this object type:

```
Dim rsCustomer As New ADODB.Recordset
```

Opening the Recordset

Once you have an instance of a Recordset object, retrieving data involves the Recordset's Open method and the appropriate SQL statement. The Open method takes several important parameters:

Parameter	Description
Source	The SQL statement that the Recordset should execute to retrieve its data.
ActiveConnection	The Connection object that represents the database to be used, or a connection string, which would cause a new connection to be created just for this recordset.
CursorType	Specifies which type of recordset should be opened. The choices are: adOpenDynamic adOpenForwardOnly adOpenKeyset adOpenStatic For our purposes, you need remember only that Dynamic indicates one that we can modify (change the content of fields, delete records, add records, etc), and Static is for opening the data as read-only.

Table Continued on Following Page

Parameter	Description
LockType	This parameter controls how the database handles record locking for edits performed on this recordset. The choices for this option are: adLockBatchOptimistic adLockOptimistic adLockPessimistic adLockReadOnly The three choices are really Optimistic, Pessimistic, and ReadOnly. The Batch setting is only useful in certain advanced situations, and can be ignored for now. Optimistic locking means that the database only locks the record (prevents other users from editing that record) when you go to save changes to it, providing the least amount of locking. Pessimistic locking causes the database to lock the record as soon as you start working with it, resulting in a longer locking time. ReadOnly specifies that no locking is required, as changes to records will not be allowed.
Options	Allows the specification of certain additional settings, not necessary for most situations and won't be used in any of our code.

Once we determine our SQL statement, we need to decide what we will be doing with the data before we can decide how to set the other parameters. If we had decided to retrieve a list of all the customers from our database, and we won't be editing, deleting, or adding to that list, then the SQL statement and Open method would be called like this:

```
Public Sub OpenDatabaseConnection()

Dim dbMain As New ADODB.Connection
Dim rsCustomer As New ADODB.Recordset
Dim SQL As String

    dbMain.Open "Provider=Microsoft.Jet.OLEDB.4.0;" & _
        "Persist Security Info=False;" & _
        "Data Source=C:\WINDOWS\Desktop\training.mdb"

    SQL = "SELECT * FROM Customer"

    rsCustomer.Open SQL, dbMain, adOpenStatic, adLockReadOnly

    rsCustomer.Close
    dbMain.Close

End Sub
```

If we planned on editing some of the customer information, we would open the recordset as `Dynamic`, and specify `Optimistic` locking.

```
rsCustomer.Open SQL, dbMain, adOpenDynamic, adLockOptimistic
```

> Note that the second piece of code would work for the first example, even though it isn't `ReadOnly`. You could open all your recordsets with the options `adOpenDynamic` and `adLockOptimistic`; everything works against a wide-open recordset. It is better, though, for performance, to open a recordset with only the necessary options. If you only need a read-only recordset, then open it that way.

Working with the Recordset

The `Recordset` object has several methods that allow you to add new records, move between records, etc. Each of the most useful methods and properties is described in the table below:

Method/Property	Description
MoveNext	Moves the record pointer to the next record (see below for more information on the record pointer), causes an error if there isn't a next record (you are at the very last record, or there aren't any records).
MovePrevious	Moves to the previous record, causes an error if there isn't a previous record (you are at the very first record, or there aren't any records).
MoveFirst	Moves to the very first record in the recordset, causes an error only if there aren't any records.
MoveLast	Moves to the last record, causing an error only if there aren't any records.
EOF	This method returns `True`/`False` to indicate if the record pointer is currently located at the end of the available records. Stands for **End Of File**.
BOF	Standing for **Beginning of File**, this method returns `True` if the record pointer is at the very start of the recordset.
AddNew	Creates a new blank record for you to place values in.

Table Continued on Following Page

Method/Property	Description
Update	Saves changes to a record back to the recordset, must be called after any modifications and after using the AddNew function.
Delete	Deletes the current record, causes an error if there isn't a current record.
RecordCount	Property returning the number of records in the recordset. To ensure that the correct value is returned, you should call the Recordset's MoveLast method first, otherwise this property may just return -1.

Retrieving Field/Column Values

The values stored in the current record of the recordset can be retrieved or set through the use of the field's name as an index. The code below gives an example of opening a recordset, displaying some field values and then making several modifications.

```
Public Sub OpenDatabaseConnection()

Dim dbMain As New ADODB.Connection
Dim rsCustomer As New ADODB.Recordset
Dim SQL As String

    dbMain.Open "Provider=Microsoft.Jet.OLEDB.4.0;" & _
        "Persist Security Info=False;" & _
        "Data Source=C:\WINDOWS\Desktop\training.mdb"

    SQL = "SELECT * FROM Customer"

    rsCustomer.Open SQL, dbMain, adOpenDynamic, adLockOptimistic

    MsgBox "The Customer's Name Is: " & rsCustomer("Name")
    MsgBox "The Customer's City Is: " & rsCustomer("City")

    rsCustomer("Country") = "United States"
    rsCustomer("Name") = rsCustomer("Name") & " Jr."

    rsCustomer.Update

    rsCustomer.Close

    dbMain.Close

End Sub
```

Although it appears that the Recordset must be a form of collection object (since we are using an index of the field name, with it), it is not. The code above is using a short form of the real statement. rsCustomer("Name") is actually equivalent to rsCustomer.Fields.Item("Name").Value. Each of the properties in use in the longer statement is the default property of its object, allowing each to be skipped. The result is the much shorter version that we use on a regular basis.

The Record Pointer

When working with recordsets, it is important to understand the concept of the current record. A recordset is a collection of individual records, but you only access the contents of a single record at a time. This record is the current record, the location of the **record pointer**:

		ID	Name	Address	City
		1	George Popoli	349 Main St.	Chamberlain
Result of MovePrevious →		2	Margaret Mead	482 Broadway Avenue	Saskatoon
Current Record →		3	Lori Mackle	4300 9th Street West	San Franciso
Result of MoveNext →		4	William Wesrock	73 Campfire Lane	San Antonio
		5	Lori Handle	266 Reef St	San Antonio
		6	Joshua Wallace	507 May St.	Hartford
		7	Laura Thompson	Apt 6 - 1199 Pine St.	Flint
		8	Manny Donaldson	34 W. 54th Street	Waterford
		9	Crystal Bell	1308 Nelson Pl	Toronto
		10	Sadi Bims	348 Haroldson Dr.	Burlason

Record: 3 of 23

When you use `Recordset` methods, such as `MoveNext` and `MovePrevious`, they change the position of the record pointer, allowing you to work with the contents of a different record. The two properties, `EOF` and `BOF`, are used to determine when you have moved beyond the available records. If you are on the very last record and you call `MoveNext`, `EOF` will become `True`. The same will occur with `BOF` and `MovePrevious`.

Any attempt to work with the current record (retrieve the value of field, delete the record, etc) when either one of these properties is `True` will result in an error. If both `BOF` and `EOF` are `True`, then the recordset is empty, as these two properties cannot be true at the same time otherwise.

Looping through the Records

The most common task a developer needs to perform when working with a recordset is to loop through the available records, from first to last, performing some actions for each record. This is accomplished with a combination of a `Do While` loop, the recordset's `EOF` property, and the `MoveNext` method, and is shown in the sample code below:

```
Public Sub OpenDatabaseConnection()
Dim dbMain As New ADODB.Connection
Dim rsCustomer As New ADODB.Recordset
Dim SQL As String

    dbMain.Open "Provider=Microsoft.Jet.OLEDB.4.0;" & _
        "Persist Security Info=False;" & _
        "Data Source=C:\WINDOWS\Desktop\training.mdb"

    SQL = "SELECT * FROM Customer"

    rsCustomer.Open SQL, dbMain, adOpenDynamic, adLockOptimistic
```

```
Do While Not rsCustomer.EOF

    'Processing for each record goes here

    rsCustomer.MoveNext

Loop

    rsCustomer.Close
    dbMain.Close

End Sub
```

> If your code seems to enter an infinite loop when executing code similar
> to what is shown above, the MoveNext method call has probably been
> missed. Without that line, the loop would never hit EOF and would
> continue executing on the same record continuously. To stop code
> execution, use the keyboard combination *Ctrl + Break* to cause VBA to
> enter break mode, allowing you to fix the problem.

Editing Records

To edit your recordset's current record, you simply assign new values to the record's
fields, and then call the recordset's Update method when you are finished. For
programmers used to working with DAO (the database access layer provided by
Microsoft Jet), this method is a little different. In ADO, there is no Edit method, you
do not have to explicitly enter an edit mode before you can change field values.

Adding Records

The procedure for adding records to a recordset consists of three steps:

❑ Call the AddNew method

❑ Set each field to the desired value

❑ Call the Update method to save your changes to the database

Project 8A Simple Database Access

Now that you have had an introduction to databases and ADO, we'll move on to a
quick database-driven Word project that will demonstrate the key concepts that have
just been covered. This project will build a special template that will generate a
product price list every time it is opened. To program this yourself, you will need the
sample database described earlier in this chapter. This database is available from the
Wrox Press web site at http://www.wrox.com/ and should be downloaded, as it is
full of sample data that would be difficult and time consuming for you to recreate.

Document Events

To build this project, we are going to create a new blank template. This can be quickly accomplished by selecting <u>N</u>ew from the <u>F</u>ile menu, which will bring up this dialog:

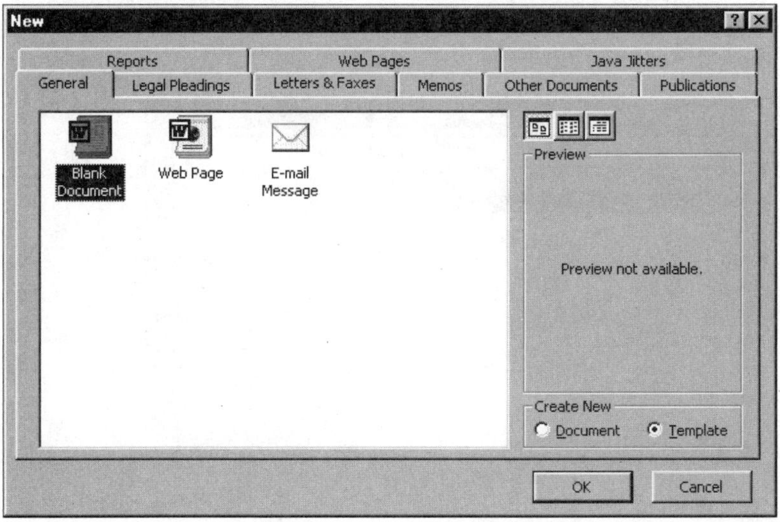

Select the Blank Document icon, and ensure that <u>T</u>emplate is selected under Create New. Click OK and a new blank template will be created. Save this template as `Product List.dot` under the `Java Jitters` folder in your templates location.

The code we are going to add to this template has to run every time a new document is created from it, which is possible through Document events. In the VBA editor, there will be a project labeled TemplateProject (Product List), select it and expand it by clicking on the small square plus sign.

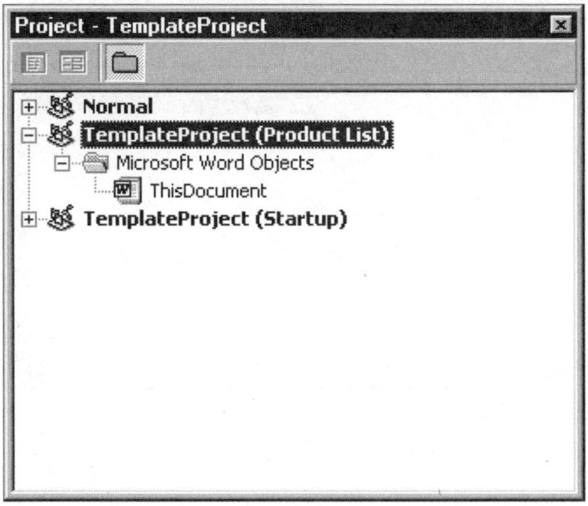

Under the sub folder **Microsoft Word Objects** there is a single item labeled **ThisDocument**, which is a `Document` object representing the template itself. Double-clicking this item will bring up a code module that exists for the object, similar to the code object behind a User Form. Like any module, this window has two drop-down list boxes along its top edge, one that represents object and the other representing procedure. As this is the code module for this `Document` object, there will be a **Document** object in the list on the left.

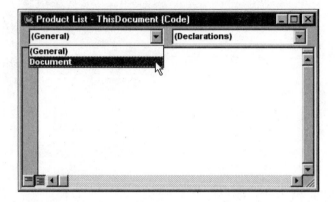

Picking this object will place you inside code for the `Document`'s events, and the right-hand list will contain the events that are available for this object. Picking one of these events will display the corresponding event procedure, code that will execute when this event occurs. The three events available for a `Document` object are:

- `Close`
- `Open`
- `New`

The Open event occurs whenever this document is opened, the Close event occurs when it is closed, and the New event occurs whenever a new document is created based on this template. It is that third event that we want, so select it and view its event procedure. To test out our concept, place a MsgBox call inside the event procedure, like this:

```
Private Sub Document_New()

    MsgBox "Test of Document New event"

End Sub
```

Now switch back to the new template document (in Word) and close it, making sure you answer Yes to save changes. Create a new document based on this template by selecting File I New and selecting Product List.dot from the Java Jitters tab:

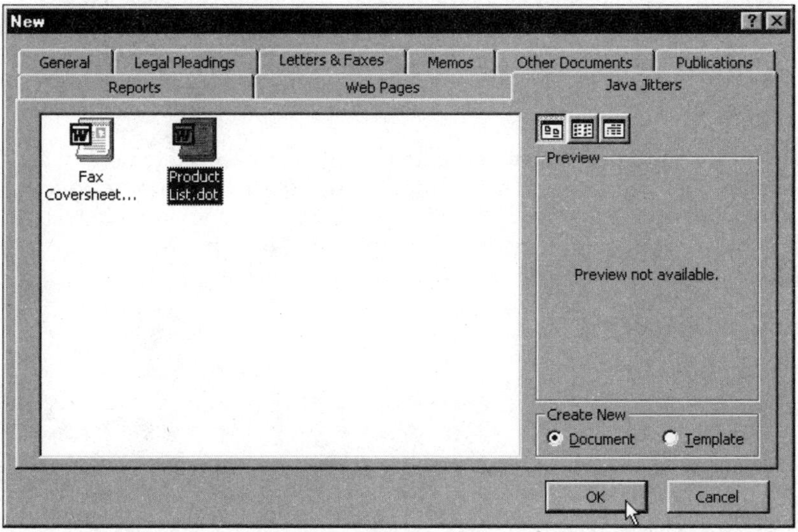

When you click OK, a new document will be created, and a MsgBox will be displayed, demonstrating that our code was run at this point:

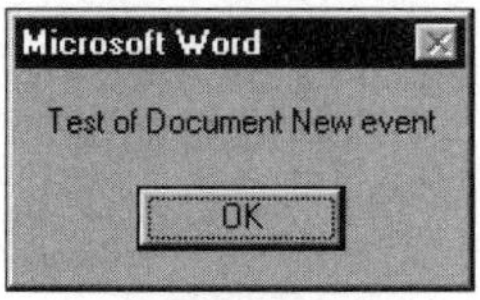

The ability to place code into a template that will run the instant someone creates a new document from that template, opens up many different possibilities; wizards that run to help the user fill out the template, document management programs that log the creation of the file, or (the technique we will be using) documents that generate their own content when you create them.

A product price list is something that should always be as current as possible, and by building the document at the exact moment it is created, it is guaranteed current as of that point. An application that simply displayed the list of products from the database would be one of the only ways to be more current, but such an application probably couldn't be emailed, or copied onto a floppy disk for giving to a client. Overall, this single document event gives you the power to build complete little applications that exist as document templates, easily used and managed.

For our particular project, the code is rather straightforward, and replaces the sample MsgBox call that is currently in the Document_New event:

❑ A Connection object is created and opened, creating a link to our sample database

❑ A Recordset object is created and used to retrieve the complete list of products and their prices

❑ Those names and prices are quickly and simply dumped into the document, completing the task

The complete code is listed below, but to run it yourself you will need to modify the path to the sample database, and add a reference to the ADO library to your project. For details on how to add the reference, see the section on that topic earlier in this chapter. The connection string used here is also explained earlier in this chapter, and is actually the same string that is demonstrated in that earlier section.

```
Private Sub Document_New()

Dim Conn As New Connection
Dim rsProducts As New Recordset
Dim SQL As String

Dim sDBPath As String
Dim sConnection As String
Dim sLine As String

    sDBPath = "C:\Word 2000 VBA\Chapter8.mdb"

    sConnection = "Provider=Microsoft.Jet.OLEDB.4.0;" & _
            "Persist Security Info=False;" & _
            "Data Source=" & sDBPath

    Conn.Open sConnection

    SQL = "SELECT Name, Price FROM Product"

    rsProducts.Open SQL, Conn, adOpenStatic, adLockReadOnly

    Do While Not rsProducts.EOF

        sLine = rsProducts("Name") & vbTab & _
            Format(rsProducts("Price"), "Currency") & vbCrLf

        ActiveDocument.Range.InsertAfter sLine

        rsProducts.MoveNext

    Loop

End Sub
```

> If desired, this code could produce slightly nicer results by simply converting all the document's text to a table after inserting the product information. To do this, add a line after the end of the `Do...While Loop` that calls `ActiveDocument.Range.ConvertToTable`

To run this code, close the document template (saving the changes) and create a new document based on it (as demonstrated earlier with the test `MsgBox` call), the document will open and fill with the following information:

```
Document3 - Microsoft Word

File  Edit  View  Insert  Format  Tools  Table  Window  Help

        Beans, Brazil Bourbons (20 lbs)        $50.00
        Beans, Celebes Kalossi (20 lbs)        $50.00
        Beans, Colombia Excelso (20 lbs)       $50.00
        Beans, Colombia Supremo (20 lbs)       $60.00
        Beans, Costa Rica Tarrazu (20 lbs)     $50.00
        Beans, Ethiopian Harrar-Moka (20 lbs)       $47.00
        Beans, Guatemala Antigua (20 lbs)      $50.00
        Beans, Indian Mysore (20 lbs)          $55.00
        Beans, Jamaican Blue Mountain (20 lbs)      $50.00
        Beans, Java Estate Kuyumas (20 lbs)    $50.00
        Beans, Kenya AA (20 lbs)       $50.00
        Beans, Kona Extra Prime (20 lbs)       $55.00
        Beans, Mexico Pluma Altura (20 lbs)    $50.00
        Beans, Mocha Mattari (Yemen) (20 lbs)       $50.00
        Beans, New Guinea (20 lbs)     $50.00
        Beans, Panama Organic (20 lbs)         $50.00
        Beans, Sumatra (20 lbs)        $50.00
        Beans, Tanzania Peaberry (20 lbs)      $50.00
        Beans, Zimbabwe (20 lbs)       $55.00
        Beans, Kenya AA (100 lbs)      $225.00
        Beans, House Blend (100 lbs)   $250.00
        Ground, Brazil Bourbons (10 lbs)       $20.00
        Ground, Celebes Kalossi (10 lbs)       $20.00

Page 1     Sec 1        1/1    At 2.5cm   Ln 1    Col 1      REC TRK EXT OVR
```

Summary

The result of this chapter's project isn't exactly professional looking, but it demonstrates the use of databases from Word VBA, and shows the power of document events. The next chapter will continue with two more projects using ADO and the sample Java Jitters database, including the first project, which will improve the results of our simple product price list. To make it look professional, the next chapter will introduce the programmatic creation and formatting of tables, which come in handy when working with databases.

For another demonstration of an auto-generating document, one that has nothing to do with databases but is pretty cool, download the `FontSamples.dot` template from the Wrox web site. When you create a document based on this template, it will automatically fill with a sample of every font available to Word, which is actually rather useful, though a little big to print out. The code for this template isn't locked and includes some interesting features, so feel free to take a look.

More Databases

Introduction

In the last chapter, we covered the basics of databases, and introduced ADO, a technology that allows you to use databases from within your Word development. A quick project was included after all that theory, just to show the code required to quickly integrate some database content into a Word document, and the concept of auto-generating documents was introduced. All of these concepts are going to be touched on and expanded in this chapter as we build an enhanced product listing and produce an invoice.

In addition to the continued discussion of databases, we will be covering the extremely useful topic of tables in Word, creating and formatting them to fit our needs. Tables are especially important when working with databases (though do not confuse Word tables with databases tables), and are necessary for many different types of projects.

Project 9A   Enhanced Product Listing

In Chapter 8, we showed the database code required to produce a quick and dirty price listing, which was completely functional but didn't look very professional. The need for a professional appearance is more than just esthetics; it allows this document to be used direct from Word to a customer. An important goal, especially for dynamic information such as a price list, is to avoid professional printing (actual printing press type of work) wherever possible, and by producing a proper looking document right from the start, you can accomplish that goal. For our price listing, we will start first on what we can change with only minimal changes to the code, and then move onto the topic of tables.

Polishing Your Auto-Generated Documents

Back in Chapter 5, we covered some reasons why you should use templates for your
development, and the best reason was that people can change the template's
appearance without changing your code. This is still true, and fits the current
implementation of our project, which is based completely on a template. Starting with
our `Product List.dot` template file, we can simply add some info at the top of the
page to improve the overall look. What you add is up to you, but a logo and some
heading text seems appropriate, like this:

Adding this isn't as easy as it should be though, due to the way our project currently
works. The portion of our code that inserts values into our document uses the
`InsertAfter` method of the `ActiveDocument.Range` object. This method always
adds information after the last character of the document, which is where we can run
into problems:

```
Do While Not rsProducts.EOF

    sLine = rsProducts("Name") & vbTab & _
        Format(rsProducts("Price"), "Currency") & vbCrLf

    ActiveDocument.Range.InsertAfter sLine
```

```
        rsProducts.MoveNext

    Loop

    ActiveDocument.Range.ConvertToTable
```

If, when formatting your template, you decide to add a block of text that is intended to
follow the price listings, it won't work. Regardless of where you put it, the prices will
follow afterwards, and will likely take on the formatting of that last piece of content. If
you are not careful with how you leave the end portion of your document, the inserted
text could end up inside a table, starting halfway along a line (if you didn't end with a
blank line), or somewhere else it was not intended to be. To get around any of these
problems, and allow you to completely control the formatting and location of your
inserted text, we will change our code and our template to use a single bookmark. This
bookmark will be used to indicate the desired area of text to replace, and the
formatting currently applied to that text will then be used for your inserted content.
Later on, when we start looking at tables, we'll see how to work with the format of
your content after you have inserted it, but for now, this is a quick way to accomplish
the desired results.

So, after adding a single line, "Insert Products Here" (the content does not matter), a
couple of lines below our logo and title, we bookmark that line as InsertHere, and
change our code to the following:

```
Private Sub Document_New()

Dim Conn As New Connection
Dim rsProducts As New Recordset
Dim SQL As String

Dim sDBPath As String
Dim sConnection As String
Dim sLine As String

Dim rngInsertHere As Range

    'Replace with the DB's path
    sDBPath = "C:\Windows\Desktop\Chapter8.mdb"

    sConnection = "Provider=Microsoft.Jet.OLEDB.4.0;" & _
            "Persist Security Info=False;" & _
            "Data Source=" & sDBPath

    Conn.Open sConnection

    SQL = "SELECT Name, Price FROM Product"

    rsProducts.Open SQL, Conn, adOpenStatic, adLockReadOnly

    Set rngInsertHere = ActiveDocument.Bookmarks("InsertHere").Range

    rngInsertHere.Text = ""

    Do While Not rsProducts.EOF

        sLine = rsProducts("Name") & _
            vbTab & Format(rsProducts("Price"), "Currency") & vbCrLf

        rngInsertHere.Text = rngInsertHere.Text & sLine

        rsProducts.MoveNext

    Loop
```

```
rngInsertHere.ConvertToTable

End Sub
```

There are a couple of key changes being made here. First, we are no longer using the
`ActiveDocument.Range` object, it represented the entire document contents and we
only want to deal with the bookmark. Second, we are not using the `InsertAfter`
method; we are simply replacing the contents of the bookmark (using the `Text`
property), which is done so that our `Range` object will always be referring to all of the
text we have added. This second change allows us to use the same `Range` object at the
end of the procedure, when we call `ConvertToTable`. With these changes done, you
can adjust the template however you wish; as long as a bookmark with that name stays
available, the code will still work. In the next section, we are going to cover the
manipulation and creation of tables, using this project as the example.

Tables

Each individual table in a Word document is represented by a `Table` object, a complex
structure that allows access to all the rows, columns, and individual cells of the
corresponding table. The most useful properties, methods and collections of the `Table`
object are listed below. A complete listing is available in Appendix A.

Properties

Name	Returns	Description
AllowAutoFit	Boolean	Controls whether the table columns will automatically adjust depending on the text, a useful alternative to setting the column widths individually.
AllowPageBreaks	Boolean	Determines whether the table will be allowed to break across pages.
ID	String	Sets or returns a string value assigned to a table to identify it. This value has nothing to do with the table's index in the `Tables` collection.
Range	Range	Returns a `Range` object that represents the entire table, useful for applying formatting information to the complete object.

Methods

AutoFormat

Parameters	Description
[Format] [ApplyBorders] [ApplyShading] [ApplyFont] [ApplyColor] [ApplyHeadingRows] [ApplyLastRow] [ApplyFirstColumn] [ApplyLastColumn] [AutoFit]	Reformats the entire table based on the parameters. The key setting for this method is the Format parameter, which determines which set of formatting information is applied to the table. Th Format parameter can be set using any one of the following constants: wdTableFormatSimple (Default) wdTableFormatNone wdTableFormat3DEffects1 wdTableFormat3DEffects2 wdTableFormat3DEffects3 wdTableFormatClassic1 wdTableFormatClassic2 wdTableFormatClassic3 wdTableFormatClassic4 wdTableFormatColorful1 wdTableFormatColorful2 These formats, including those not listed, correspond to the Table AutoFormat dialog, which will display a sample of each format as well. The remainder of the arguments to this method correspond to the various checkboxes on this form, and take true/false arguments.

Cell

Returns	Parameters	Description
Cell	Row As Long, Column As Long	Returns the cell in the table using the Row, Column parameters. Discussed below under "Creating New Tables".

ConvertToText

Returns	Parameters	Description
Range	[Separator], [NestedTables]	Converts the table to text using a particular separator (tabs, commas, etc.) and returns a Range object corresponding to the resulting text. The NestedTables parameter specifies whether any tables nested inside of this one should also be converted.

Delete

Deletes the table.

Select

Selects the table in the document.

Sort, SortAscending, SortDescending

Parameters	Description
Various	Provides methods for easily sorting the data in your table. Covered in detail below under "Sorting".

Split

Returns	Parameters	Description
Table	BeforeRow	Splits the table into two tables at the specified row by placing a blank paragraph (not part of a table) between the tables. The existing `Table` object (the one referring to the table before the split) now refers to the first of two resulting tables, and the result of this method is a `Table` object that refers to the other resulting table. The diagram below illustrates how the split occurs and the two results:

Collections

As a complex object, the `Table` object has many different sub-collections available as properties. Those collections are described in the list below:

Collection	Description
Rows	Represents the collection of all rows contained within the table. This is a one-based collection, starting at `Rows(1)`. Each row is represented by a separate `Row` object.
Columns	Represents all the columns contained within the table. As for `Rows`, `Columns` is a one-based collection, starting with `Columns(1)`. Each column is represented by a separate `Column` object.
Tables	In the same manner as the `Tables` collection of the `Range` object or the `Document` object, this collection contains all the tables that are contained within this table. This collection allows access to any tables that have been created within another table, also known as nested tables. This collection is also one-based.
Cell	Although this is actually a method, and was mentioned in that section above, it fits best in with these collections. This method takes two parameters, `Row` and `Column`, and returns the `Cell` object corresponding to those co-ordinates. This collection is also one-based.

Between the two collections, Rows and Columns, and the method Cell, it is possible to work with any particular part of the table desired. The three different ways of dividing up a table are illustrated in this diagram:

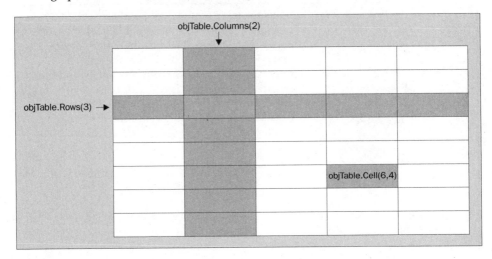

Each of the code snippets illustrated above return an object representing the appropriate portion of the table: a Row, Column, or Cell object.

Common Properties

Each of those objects (returned by the collections described above) is individually described in Appendix A, but there are certain common properties that cover the most common programming needs:

Property	Description
Range	Returns a Range object representing the appropriate object and can be used to manipulate the format settings for that object and its contents. Often used to return the contents of a cell: `objTable.Cell(6,4).Range.Text` Oddly, there is an exception to this, although there should not be. The Column object does not have a Range property, an exclusion that causes many problems.

Property	Description
Borders	Represents the various borders around the object (left, top, bottom, right, outside, inside) and controls the appearance of those borders. The code below shows an example of how these object can be manipulated, turning off all the borders on a particular table:

```
objTable.Borders.OutsideLineStyle _

    = wdLineStyleNone

objTable.Borders.InsideLineStyle _

    = wdLineStyleNone
```

And this code demonstrates the manipulation of a single border element by specifying that member of the collection:

```
objTable.Borders(wdBorderBottom). _

    LineWidth = wdLineWidth300pt

objTable.Borders(wdBorderBottom). _

    LineStyle = wdLineStyleDoubleWavy
```

There are many different values for each of the border settings, all of which will be automatically listed for you when you reach the appropriate point in your code.

Property	Description
Shading	Returns a `Shading` object that allows the manipulation of the texture, background and foreground color of the object. The most common properties of this object are: `BackgroundPatternColor` and `ForegroundPatternColor`, which take a color constant (such as `wdColorRed`).

The `Row` and `Column` object have another useful property in common; `Cells`. This property returns a collection of all the cells in that particular row or column, allow you to refer to any one of them by position. The two lines of code below show different ways to insert a value into the same table cell:

```
objTable.Rows(3).Cells(1).Range.Text = "Cell 3,1"
objTable.Cell(3, 1).Range.Text = "Cell 3,1"
```

Inserting and Removing Columns and Rows

A common need when working with a table is to add additional rows to that table. It is less common to remove rows, or change the number of columns in any way, but all of these things can be done through the methods of the Rows and Columns collection and the Row and Column objects.

Inserting

Adding rows or columns to a table is done through the Add method of either the Rows or Columns collection. The method, in either case, simply takes a parameter of another row or column that indicates where the insertion is to take place. The code below inserts a row between the 2nd and 3rd rows of a table, and inserts a column between the 1st and 2nd existing columns. In each case, the parameter for the Add method specifies that the insertion is to occur **before** that item:

```
objTable.Rows.Add objTable.Rows(3)  'Insert a row before Row 3

objTable.Columns.Add objTable.Columns(2)  'Insert a column before Column 2
```

A faster way of adding many rows at one time is to use the InsertRows, InsertRowsAbove, or InsertRowsBelow methods of the Selection object. The Selection object represents whatever portion of the active document is currently selected and, if that includes a row or rows of your table, allows you to use one of these three methods to perform a bulk insertion. The code below selects the third row of your table and then inserts 50 rows after that point:

```
objTable.Rows(3).Select
Selection.InsertRowsBelow 50
```

The same bulk procedures can be accomplished for columns through the InsertColumns and InsertColumnsRight methods (note that there is no InsertColumnsLeft method).

Removing

Removing a row or column is easily accomplished through the Delete method of the corresponding Row or Column object, as shown below:

```
objTable.Rows(5).Delete
objTable.Columns(2).Delete
```

or, alternatively:

```
Set objRow = objTable.Rows(5)
objRow.Delete

Set objCol = objTable.Columns(2)
objCol.Delete
```

In either case, the row or column (and its contents) will be removed from the table. An error occurs if the specified item doesn't exist, such as objTable.Rows(5).Delete when there are only 4 rows in the table.

Sorting

Once you have a Table object to work with, having either created one or obtained one from the `Tables` collection, you can use one of the object's three sorting methods to reorder the items in the table. These three methods are: `Sort`, `SortAscending`, and `SortDescending`. `Sort` is the main method, taking several different parameters, the most common of which are listed below:

Parameter	Description
`ExcludeHeader`	Controls (through a `True` or `False` value) whether or not the first row should be included in the sorting. If it is `False` (the default value), then that first row is reordered just like any other row, and if it is `True` then the first row is not effected by the sort. Be sure to set this parameter if you have a header row in your table or you will likely find your header relocated to another location.
`FieldNumber`, `FieldNumber2`, `FieldNumber3`	Specifies which field, or column, is to be used for sorting. If nothing is specified then the sort is assumed to take place on the first column. To specify more than one column, such as to allow sorting by Last Name, then First Name, you supply the second and (if desired) third column numbers through the `FieldNumber2` and `FieldNumber3` parameters. Due to the large number of parameters to this method, it is best to use **named parameters** when you call it, such as: `objTable.Sort _` `SortOrder:=wdSortOrderAscending`

`SortFieldType`, `SortFieldType2`, `SortFieldType3`	Specifies the nature of the data within each of the sorting columns, one of:
	
	`wdSortFieldAlphanumeric`
	
	`wdSortFieldDate`
	
	`wdSortFieldJapanJIS`
	
	`wdSortFieldKoreaKS`
	
	`wdSortFieldNumeric`
	
	`wdSortFieldStroke`
	
	`wdSortFieldSyllable`
	
	This parameter allows Word to perform the sorting correctly for that particular type of data, for instance, it will correctly place January 12th before February 9th if you specify that the information is date information, not alphanumeric (which is the default).

Table Continued on Following Page

Parameter	Description
SortOrder, SortOrder2, SortOrder3	One of wdSortOrderAscending or wdSortOrderDescending, this option specifies how the corresponding column is to be sorted. The default, if nothing is specified for this parameter, is wdSortOrderAscending.
CaseSensitive	Controls whether case is considered when sorting, False by default.
IgnoreThe	Specifies, through a True or False value, whether or not a leading "The" is ignored when sorting.
IgnoreDiacritics	Determines whether **diacritics**, (special modified versions of characters with additional accent marks, used in some languages, such as French and Spanish), are treated as their regular character equivalents for the purpose of this sort. Most useful when dealing with non-English text.

SortAscending and SortDescending are simpler versions of this command. They take no parameters and just perform the sort based only on the first column, and in the appropriate order (ascending or descending, depending on the method). The same results, and more, can be achieved using only the Sort method.

Name	Group	City	Date of Birth
Mackenzie	1	Winnipeg	06/23/56
Johnson	2	New Orleans	08/29/72
Martins	1	Toronto	03/12/90
Franklin	3	Thomasville	12/15/85
Singh	2	New York	11/19/76

The following code will sort the table above, based on the 2nd and the 1st columns (column 2 first, then column 1), both in descending order, ignoring the header row, and specifying that column 1 is numeric, and column 2 is alphanumeric. The result is shown immediately following the code. To try this code yourself, create the table above, and then place this code into a procedure and run it:

```
Dim objTable as Word.Table

Set objTable = ActiveDocument.Tables(1)
objTable.Sort ExcludeHeader:=True, FieldNumber:=2, _
    SortFieldType:=wdSortFieldNumeric, _
    SortOrder:=wdSortOrderDescending, _
    FieldNumber2:=1, SortFieldType2:=wdSortFieldAlphanumeric, _
    SortOrder2:=wdSortOrderDescending, CaseSensitive:=False
```

Name	Group	City	Date of Birth
Franklin	3	Thomasville	12/15/85
Singh	2	New York	11/19/76
Johnson	2	New Orleans	08/29/72
Martins	1	Toronto	03/12/90
Mackenzie	1	Winnipeg	06/23/56

Although the ability to Sort a table has many uses in the development of Word-based utilities and other types of macros, it isn't really required for database programming. When retrieving data from a database, it is possible to specify the order in which it should be returned, removing the need to sort it after the fact. The order is specified through an Order By clause at the end of your SQL statement, such as:

```
SELECT Name, Group, City, BirthDate FROM SalesReps
ORDER BY Group DESC, Name DESC
```

The Tables Collection

The Word Document object and the Range object both have a collection that represents all the Table objects contained within them. This collection is accessed through the Tables property and can be used to create new tables within the Document or Range, or to obtain any one of the individual tables for use in code.

Working with Existing Tables

The following code shows how the Tables collection of a Document can be used to access the individual Table objects within that Document. The code first displays a count of the tables in the active document and then goes on to change the background color of each table to red. To try this code out, create a macro containing these lines and then run that macro with an unimportant document open, one that hopefully contains several tables:

```
Dim objTable As Table
Dim i As Integer

MsgBox "This Document Contains: " & _
        ActiveDocument.Tables.Count & _
        " Tables"

For i = 1 To ActiveDocument.Tables.Count

    Set objTable = ActiveDocument.Tables(i)

    objTable.Shading.BackgroundPatternColor = wdColorRed

Next i
```

Creating New Tables

The `Tables` collection has an `Add` method, which allows for the creation of new `Table` objects within the `Range` or `Document` you are working with. This method takes several important parameters:

Parameter	Description
Range	Specifies the location of the new table. The existing contents of the `Range` supplied (whatever they may be) are replaced by the new table.
NumRows	Specifies how many rows should be in the new table, although rows can be deleted and added later (see "Inserting and Removing Columns and Rows" above).
NumColumns	Specifies the number of columns in the new table.

The following line of code would create a new table, replacing the entire contents of the active document, with 15 rows and 3 columns. Note that this code assumes that there isn't a table present in the document already:

```
ActiveDocument.Tables.Add ActiveDocument.Range, 15, 3
```

This method returns a `Table` object that, if you choose to use it, allows you to immediately have access to the new table. The code below demonstrates this, and sets the value of a few cells of the newly created table:

```
Dim objTable As Table

Set objTable = ActiveDocument.Tables.Add(ActiveDocument.Range, 15, 3)

objTable.Cell(1, 1).Range.Text = "Cell 1, 1"
objTable.Cell(1, 2).Range.Text = "Cell 1, 2"
```

Using the returned `Table` object is much easier than attempting to find the appropriate table within the `Tables` collection after it is created, as you may not know the index value to use.

Back to Project 9A

Armed with the concept of tables, including the ability to create them and work with their cells, rows, and columns, we could rewrite the code for our price list. The code below would replace the existing `Document_New` code in the `Product List.dot` template:

```
Private Sub Document_New()

Dim Conn As New Connection
Dim rsProducts As New Recordset
Dim SQL As String
```

```
Dim sDBPath As String
Dim sConnection As String
Dim sLine As String

Dim rngInsertHere As Range

Dim objTable As Table
Dim NumProducts As Integer
Dim CurrentRow As Integer

    sDBPath = "C:\Windows\Desktop\Chapter8.mdb"

    sConnection = "Provider=Microsoft.Jet.OLEDB.4.0;" & _
            "Persist Security Info=False;" & _
            "Data Source=" & sDBPath

    Conn.Open sConnection

    SQL = "Select Name, Price From Product"

    rsProducts.Open SQL, Conn, adOpenStatic, adLockReadOnly

    rsProducts.MoveLast

    NumProducts = rsProducts.RecordCount

    rsProducts.MoveFirst

    Set rngInsertHere = ActiveDocument.Bookmarks("InsertHere").Range

    Set objTable = ActiveDocument.Tables.Add _
        (rngInsertHere, NumProducts + 1, 2)

    CurrentRow = 1

    objTable.Cell(CurrentRow, 1).Range.Text = "Name"
    objTable.Cell(CurrentRow, 2).Range.Text = "Price"

    CurrentRow = 2

    Do While Not rsProducts.EOF

        objTable.Cell(CurrentRow, 1).Range.Text = rsProducts("Name")
        objTable.Cell(CurrentRow, 2).Range.Text = Format _
            (rsProducts("Price"), "Currency")

        rsProducts.MoveNext
        CurrentRow = CurrentRow + 1

    Loop

    With objTable.Rows(1).Range
        .Font.Bold = True
        .Shading.BackgroundPatternColor = wdColorBlack
        .Font.Color = wdColorWhite
    End With

    objTable.Rows(1).HeadingFormat = True

    objTable.Borders.InsideLineStyle = wdLineStyleNone

End Sub
```

This code would create a table replacing the specified bookmark, containing the appropriate number of rows and columns, and then fill that table with the results of your query. The header row is formatted appropriately, with a black background and white text, and its `HeadingFormat` property is set to `True` which causes this row to be repeated if the table crosses a page boundary. The result is shown below, but the number of rows would change if products were added or removed from the database:

Project 9B Produce an Invoice

Most companies produce invoices, and they usually do it based on a computer system. Java Jitters is no exception, but they want to produce their invoices through Microsoft Word. There are several advantages to using Word to produce any printed report, including invoices, over using a system that can simply print the invoice onto paper; some of these advantages are listed below:

❑   Flexibility in document movement, storage and sharing. Word files are more easily emailed, placed on a corporate server, and reprinted than a paper hard copy.

❑ Advanced formatting options. Although many current reporting tools are capable of very complex formatting, there is really no limit on what can be accomplished with Word. Invoices can be produced with any appearance desired, using color, graphics, multiple fonts, and anything else required.

❑ Almost universal printer compatibility. By using Word, you are only limited by the printers supported by Windows, which, as a consumer product, has a substantially larger customer base than most custom accounting solutions.

For these reasons, Java Jitters has requested that some VBA code be written that, given an invoice number, will produce an invoice. To do this, we need to take another look at the database diagram we saw back in chapter 8:

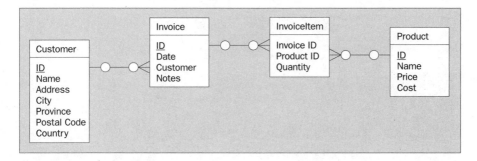

To produce an invoice with all the information we want (customer name and address, list of the products purchased, and the date), we will need records from more than one table. As was discussed earlier, back in chapter 5, a good step towards a solution is to build a test piece of code that obtains at least part of the correct result. In this case, we will start by retrieving the data we need.

Building the Query

Using Access 2000, we can design and run a query that retrieves the desired information:

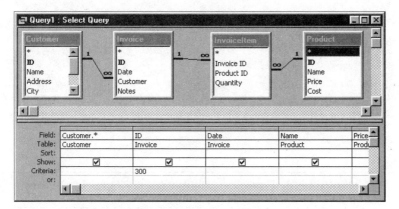

Once designed (and easily tested within Access), it is a simple matter to switch to SQL View and copy the text out for use in our code:

```
SELECT Customer.*, Invoice.ID, Invoice.Date, Product.Name, Product.Price,
InvoiceItem.Quantity FROM Product INNER JOIN ((Customer INNER JOIN Invoice ON
Customer.ID = Invoice.Customer) INNER JOIN InvoiceItem ON Invoice.ID =
InvoiceItem.[Invoice ID]) ON Product.ID = InvoiceItem.[Product ID] WHERE
(((Invoice.ID)=300));
```

Testing Our Concept

Next, we will quickly build a macro that just retrieves the results of this query, and dumps those results out into a new document. The start of this procedure, along with most other procedures that access databases, will appear almost identical to the first section of our `Product List.dot` code. Different SQL text will be used, but otherwise the same actions are being performed. The completed code is shown below:

```
Public Sub SampleInvoiceInformation()

Dim Conn As New Connection
Dim rsInvoice As New Recordset
Dim SQL As String

Dim sDBPath As String
Dim sConnection As String

Dim objNewDoc As Document
Dim sOutput As String

    sDBPath = "C:\Windows\Desktop\Chapter8.mdb"

    sConnection = "Provider=Microsoft.Jet.OLEDB.4.0;" & _
            "Persist Security Info=False;" & _
            "Data Source=" & sDBPath

    Conn.Open sConnection

    SQL = "SELECT Customer.*, Invoice.ID, Invoice.Date, " & _
        "Product.Name, Product.Price, InvoiceItem.Quantity " & _
        "FROM Product INNER JOIN ((Customer INNER JOIN Invoice ON " & _
        "Customer.ID = Invoice.Customer) INNER JOIN InvoiceItem ON " & _
        "Invoice.ID = InvoiceItem.[Invoice ID]) ON " & _
        "Product.ID = InvoiceItem.[Product ID] " & _
        "WHERE (((Invoice.ID)=300))"

    rsInvoice.Open SQL, Conn, adOpenStatic, adLockReadOnly

    Do While Not rsInvoice.EOF

        sOutput = sOutput & rsInvoice("Customer.Name") & vbTab _
            & rsInvoice("Date") & vbTab & rsInvoice("Product.Name") _
            & vbTab & rsInvoice("Quantity") & vbTab _
            & rsInvoice("Price") & vbCrLf

        rsInvoice.MoveNext

    Loop

    Set objNewDoc = Documents.Add

    objNewDoc.Range.Text = sOutput

End Sub
```

> You will have to modify the code if your copy of our sample database (`Chapter8.mdb`) is not located at the same path shown above.

Which, when run against the sample database, produces the following results:

```
Document1.doc - Microsoft Word                                    _ □ X
File  Edit  View  Insert  Format  Tools  Table  Window  Help              X

  Peter Saul    8/22/99    Beans, Kenya AA (20 lbs)       27      50
  Peter Saul    8/22/99    Ground, Zimbabwe (10 lbs)      28      23
  Peter Saul    8/22/99    Ground, Java Estate Kuyumas (10 lbs)     22    20
  Peter Saul    8/22/99    Ground, Kenya AA (10 lbs)      7       20
  Peter Saul    8/22/99    Ground, Java Estate Kuyumas (10 lbs)      3    20
  Peter Saul    8/22/99    Beans, House Blend (100 lbs)41    250
  Peter Saul    8/22/99    Beans, House Blend (100 lbs)24    250
  Peter Saul    8/22/99    Ground, Zimbabwe (10 lbs)      2       23
  Peter Saul    8/22/99    Beans, Celebes Kalossi (20 lbs)     31     50
  Peter Saul    8/22/99    Beans, House Blend (100 lbs)28    250
  Peter Saul    8/22/99    Ground, Kona Extra Prime (10 lbs)  43    22
  Peter Saul    8/22/99    Beans, Kona Extra Prime (20 lbs)    24     55

Page 1     Sec 1      1/1      At       Ln      Col     REC  TRK  EXT  OVR
```

This test code proves that we can and have obtained the necessary invoice information, and we can move on to building the true invoice, starting with an appropriate template. The template can take on any appearance you like, but it needs to have the following bookmarks: `BillingAddress`, `InvoiceNumber`, `InvoiceDate`, `Total` (which will have to be calculated). The only information left to put in the invoice is the list of actual products that were purchased, which really belong in a table, so a bookmark should exist that indicates where that table should be created. A template for this purpose has been created and, like the rest of the materials from these chapters, is available on the Wrox Press web site. This template, `Invoice.dot`, contains all the bookmarks required, along with the Java Jitters logo and other formatting elements. The code to actually build the invoice isn't anything that we haven't covered before, until we get to the product table, so we'll cover it separately and then put it all together.

The Product Table

On our invoice we need to have a list of the products purchased, the quantity and price of each, and the total price paid for that invoice item. This information will look the best if organized into a table, which we will create, populate, and format appropriately. The code to create this table will eventually be part of the complete solution but we can work on it independently until it is completed. Modifying our sample code to produce a table filled with the appropriate information involves only a few lines of code:

```
Public Sub SampleInvoiceInformation()

Dim Conn As New Connection
Dim rsInvoice As New Recordset
Dim SQL As String

Dim sDBPath As String
Dim sConnection As String

Dim objNewDoc As Document

Dim objTable As Table
Dim NumRows As Integer
Dim i As Integer
Dim Total As Currency

    sDBPath = "C:\Windows\Desktop\Chapter8.mdb"

    sConnection = "Provider=Microsoft.Jet.OLEDB.4.0;" & _
            "Persist Security Info=False;" & _
            "Data Source=" & sDBPath

    Conn.Open sConnection

    SQL = "SELECT Customer.*, Invoice.ID, Invoice.Date, " & _
        "Product.Name, Product.Price, InvoiceItem.Quantity " & _
        "FROM Product INNER JOIN ((Customer INNER JOIN Invoice ON " & _
        "Customer.ID = Invoice.Customer) INNER JOIN InvoiceItem ON " & _
        "Invoice.ID = InvoiceItem.[Invoice ID]) ON " & _
        "Product.ID = InvoiceItem.[Product ID] " & _
        "WHERE (((Invoice.ID)=300))"

    rsInvoice.Open SQL, Conn, adOpenStatic, adLockReadOnly

    rsInvoice.MoveLast
    rsInvoice.MoveFirst

    NumRows = rsInvoice.RecordCount

    Set objNewDoc = Documents.Add

    Set objTable = objNewDoc.Tables.Add _
        (objNewDoc.Range, NumRows + 1, 4)

    i = 1

    objTable.Cell(i, 1).Range.Text = "Quantity"
    objTable.Cell(i, 2).Range.Text = "Product"
    objTable.Cell(i, 3).Range.Text = "Each"
    objTable.Cell(i, 4).Range.Text = "Total"

    Do While Not rsInvoice.EOF

        i = i + 1

        objTable.Cell(i, 1).Range.Text = rsInvoice("Quantity")
        objTable.Cell(i, 2).Range.Text = rsInvoice("Product.Name")
        objTable.Cell(i, 3).Range.Text = rsInvoice("Price")
        objTable.Cell(i, 4).Range.Text = rsInvoice _
            ("Quantity") * rsInvoice("Price")

        rsInvoice.MoveNext

    Loop

End Sub
```

The result is in a table, but its appearance leaves a lot to be desired:

Quantity	Product	Each	Total
27	Beans, Kenya AA (20 lbs)	50	1350
28	Ground, Zimbabwe (10 lbs)	23	644
22	Ground, Java Estate Kuyumas (10 lbs)	20	440
7	Ground, Kenya AA (10 lbs)	20	140
3	Ground, Java Estate Kuyumas (10 lbs)	20	60
41	Beans, House Blend (100 lbs)	250	10250
24	Beans, House Blend (100 lbs)	250	6000
2	Ground, Zimbabwe (10 lbs)	23	46
31	Beans, Celebes Kalossi (20 lbs)	50	1550
28	Beans, House Blend (100 lbs)	250	7000
43	Ground, Kona Extra Prime (10 lbs)	22	946
24	Beans, Kona Extra Prime (20 lbs)	55	1320

Adjusting Column Widths

To start with, the column widths are all inappropriate, which can be corrected using the individual Column objects. Each Column object has a Width property that sets or retrieves the width of that particular column in **points**. Points are the unit of measure that Word likes to use and most property settings dealing with measurements must be set to a value in these units. Points do not lend themselves well to human measurements, as we prefer to deal in inches, centimeters, and lines. For this reason, we often have to convert between a unit of measure that we use (such as inches) to Word's preferred units (points). One inch is equivalent to 72 points, allowing for an easy conversion, but it is actually even simpler as a set of functions are provided for us to convert to and from points as required. Each of these functions is listed below, and their purposes are self-explanatory:

- ❑ CentimetersToPoints
- ❑ InchesToPoints
- ❑ LinesToPoints
- ❑ MillimetersToPoints

- ❑ `PicasToPoints`
- ❑ `PixelsToPoints`
- ❑ `PointsToCentimeters`
- ❑ `PointsToInches`
- ❑ `PointsToLines`
- ❑ `PointsToMillimeters`
- ❑ `PointsToPicas`
- ❑ `PointsToPixels`

With these functions to aid us, we can easily adjust the width of our new table's columns to a specific inch-based size. This code can be executed at any time after the table is created; it is not effected by any changes to the content or number of rows.

```
objTable.Columns(1).Width = InchesToPoints(0.8)
objTable.Columns(2).Width = InchesToPoints(4)
objTable.Columns(3).Width = InchesToPoints(1)
objTable.Columns(4).Width = InchesToPoints(1.3)
```

To determine exactly the width that you want, you can run these lines over and over again with different values, until it looks just right. The next formatting change that will improve our table is to adjust the alignment of our columns.

Adjusting Column Alignment

Unfortunately, the `Column` object does not return a `Range` object, which means there is no easy way to refer to the formatting information for an entire column, such as font, style or alignment. To get around this annoying problem, we must work in two steps - select the column (using the `Select` method) and then work with the `Selection` object.

The code to adjust the alignment of our columns would therefore be written like this:

```
objTable.Columns(1).Select
Selection.ParagraphFormat.Alignment = wdAlignParagraphRight

objTable.Columns(2).Select
Selection.ParagraphFormat.Alignment = wdAlignParagraphLeft

objTable.Columns(3).Select
Selection.ParagraphFormat.Alignment = wdAlignParagraphRight

objTable.Columns(4).Select
Selection.ParagraphFormat.Alignment = wdAlignParagraphRight
```

> To avoid the added confusion that this two step process creates, you could create a small function that returns a `Range` for a specific column, and then use it just like the `Range` property of the `Row` and `Cell` objects.

Formatting the Contents

After our columns are the correct width and alignment, the next set of changes to our table would be to format the cell contents as desired. Fortunately, unlike the `Column` object, both the `Row` and `Table` objects possess a `Range` property, so formatting them is easy. For this particular table, we will format the entire table and then reformat the first row as a header:

```
objTable.Range.Font.Name = "Arial"
objTable.Range.Font.Size = 8
objTable.Range.Font.Bold = False

objTable.Rows(1).Range.Font.Size = 10
objTable.Rows(1).Range.Font.Bold = True
objTable.Rows(1).Range.Font.Color = wdColorWhite

objTable.Rows(1).Shading.BackgroundPatternColor = wdColorBlack
objTable.Rows(1).HeadingFormat = True
```

The "Each" and "Total" columns could also use some special formatting, to give them the proper appearance of currency. This can easily be accomplished using the VBA function, `Format`, which takes a value and a special formatting string and returns the result, the correctly formatted value. For currency values we use the formatting string `"Currency"`, as in `Format(Value, "Currency")`. Modifying the code inside our `Do ... Loop` to include this formatting produces the following result:

```
Do While Not rsInvoice.EOF

    i = i + 1

    objTable.Cell(i, 1).Range.Text = rsInvoice("Quantity")
    objTable.Cell(i, 2).Range.Text = rsInvoice("Product.Name")

    objTable.Cell(i, 3).Range.Text = _
        Format(rsInvoice("Price"), "Currency")
    objTable.Cell(i, 4).Range.Text = _
        Format(rsInvoice("Quantity") * rsInvoice("Price"), _
            "Currency")

    rsInvoice.MoveNext

Loop
```

With all this code together, we have almost everything we need to complete an actual invoice. Modifying our code to create a new document based on our `Invoice.dot` template involves changing only the document creation code from:

```
Set objNewDoc = Documents.Add
```

To:

```
'Path for User Templates
sUserTemplates = Options.DefaultFilePath(wdUserTemplatesPath)

'Create Fax Coversheet
Set objNewDoc = Documents.Add _
        (sUserTemplates & "\Java Jitters\Invoice.dot")
```

> The code above assumes that you have placed the `Invoice.dot` template in the same Java Jitters folder as for the Fax Coversheet and Product List.

Next, the various bookmarks on our invoice need to be filled in with the proper data, each corresponding to a particular field in our `rsInvoice` recordset. This can easily be done with just a few lines and using the `SetBookmark` procedure that we created in Chapter 6:

```
SetBookmark objNewDoc, "InvoiceDate", rsInvoice("Date")
SetBookmark objNewDoc, "InvoiceNumber", rsInvoice("Invoice.ID")

sBillingAddress = rsInvoice("Customer.Name") & vbCrLf & _
                  rsInvoice("Address") & vbCrLf & _
                  rsInvoice("City") & ", " & _
                  rsInvoice("Province") & vbCrLf & _
                  rsInvoice("Postal Code")

SetBookmark objNewDoc, "BillingAddress", sBillingAddress
```

Now, using the template's bookmark that indicates where to place our list of products, we modify the code that adds our table and add that code to our original procedure:

```
Set objTable = objNewDoc.Tables.Add(objNewDoc.Bookmarks _
    ("ItemTable").Range, NumRows + 1, 4)
```

The only remaining piece of information left is the invoice total, represented by the "Total" bookmark and designed to hold the sum of all our individual line totals. Code is added to the `Do ... Loop` to calculate this sum and then a call to `SetBookmark` allows it to be placed onto the invoice:

```
Do While Not rsInvoice.EOF

    i = i + 1

    objTable.Cell(i, 1).Range.Text = rsInvoice("Quantity")
    objTable.Cell(i, 2).Range.Text = rsInvoice("Product.Name")
    objTable.Cell(i, 3).Range.Text = _
        Format(rsInvoice("Price"), "Currency")
    objTable.Cell(i, 4).Range.Text = _
        Format(rsInvoice("Quantity") * rsInvoice("Price"), _
        "Currency")

    Total = Total + (rsInvoice("Quantity") * rsInvoice("Price"))

    rsInvoice.MoveNext

Loop

SetBookmark objNewDoc, "Total", Format(Total, "Currency")
```

The only remaining thing is to change this procedure into the final version, a procedure that takes an Invoice ID and can produce the appropriate output. This involves two changes - adding an argument to the procedure's declaration (and changing its name at the same time):

```
Public Sub GenerateInvoice(ID As Long)
```

And, second, modifying the SQL string so that it is using this new parameter for its WHERE clause instead of always using the number 300:

```
SQL = "SELECT Customer.*, Invoice.ID, Invoice.Date, Product.Name, " & _
    "Product.Price, InvoiceItem.Quantity " & _
    "FROM Product INNER JOIN ((Customer INNER JOIN Invoice ON " & _
    "Customer.ID = Invoice.Customer) INNER JOIN InvoiceItem ON " & _
    "Invoice.ID = InvoiceItem.[Invoice ID]) ON " & _
    "Product.ID = InvoiceItem.[Product ID] " & _
    "WHERE (((Invoice.ID)=" & ID & "))"
```

The end result, listed below in its entirety, can be called from other code, or from the Immediate window, to generate any invoice that exists:

```
Public Sub GenerateInvoice(ID As Long)

Dim Conn As New Connection
Dim rsInvoice As New Recordset
Dim SQL As String

Dim sDBPath As String
Dim sConnection As String
Dim sUserTemplates As String

Dim objNewDoc As Document
Dim sBillingAddress As String

Dim objTable As Table
Dim NumRows As Integer
Dim i As Integer

Dim Total As Currency

    sDBPath = "C:\Windows\Desktop\Chapter8.mdb"

    sConnection = "Provider=Microsoft.Jet.OLEDB.4.0;" & _
            "Persist Security Info=False;" & _
            "Data Source=" & sDBPath

    Conn.Open sConnection

    SQL = "SELECT Customer.*, Invoice.ID, Invoice.Date, " & _
        "Product.Name, Product.Price, InvoiceItem.Quantity " & _
        "FROM Product INNER JOIN ((Customer INNER JOIN Invoice ON " & _
        "Customer.ID = Invoice.Customer) INNER JOIN InvoiceItem ON " & _
        "Invoice.ID = InvoiceItem.[Invoice ID]) ON " & _
        "Product.ID = InvoiceItem.[Product ID] " & _
        "WHERE (((Invoice.ID)=" & ID & "))"

    rsInvoice.Open SQL, Conn, adOpenStatic, adLockReadOnly

    rsInvoice.MoveLast
    rsInvoice.MoveFirst

    NumRows = rsInvoice.RecordCount

    'Path for User Templates
    sUserTemplates = Options.DefaultFilePath(wdUserTemplatesPath)

    'Create Fax Coversheet
    Set objNewDoc = Documents.Add _
        (sUserTemplates & "\Java Jitters\Invoice.dot")

    SetBookmark objNewDoc, "InvoiceDate", rsInvoice("Date")
    SetBookmark objNewDoc, "InvoiceNumber", rsInvoice("Invoice.ID")

    sBillingAddress = rsInvoice("Customer.Name") & vbCrLf & _
                    rsInvoice("Address") & vbCrLf & _
                    rsInvoice("City") & ", " & _
                    rsInvoice("Province") & vbCrLf & _
                    rsInvoice("Postal Code")

    SetBookmark objNewDoc, "BillingAddress", sBillingAddress

    Set objTable = objNewDoc.Tables.Add(objNewDoc.Bookmarks _
      ("ItemTable").Range, NumRows + 1, 4)

    i = 1

    objTable.Cell(i, 1).Range.Text = "Quantity"
    objTable.Cell(i, 2).Range.Text = "Product"
    objTable.Cell(i, 3).Range.Text = "Each"
    objTable.Cell(i, 4).Range.Text = "Total"

    Do While Not rsInvoice.EOF

        i = i + 1
```

```
          objTable.Cell(i, 1).Range.Text = rsInvoice("Quantity")
          objTable.Cell(i, 2).Range.Text = rsInvoice("Product.Name")
          objTable.Cell(i, 3).Range.Text = _
            Format(rsInvoice("Price"), "Currency")
          objTable.Cell(i, 4).Range.Text = _
            Format(rsInvoice("Quantity") * rsInvoice("Price"), _
            "Currency")

          Total = Total + (rsInvoice("Quantity") * rsInvoice("Price"))

          rsInvoice.MoveNext

      Loop

      SetBookmark objNewDoc, "Total", Format(Total, "Currency")

      objTable.Columns(1).Width = InchesToPoints(0.8)
      objTable.Columns(2).Width = InchesToPoints(4)
      objTable.Columns(3).Width = InchesToPoints(1)
      objTable.Columns(4).Width = InchesToPoints(1.3)

      objTable.Columns(1).Select
      Selection.ParagraphFormat.Alignment = wdAlignParagraphRight
      objTable.Columns(2).Select
      Selection.ParagraphFormat.Alignment = wdAlignParagraphLeft
      objTable.Columns(3).Select
      Selection.ParagraphFormat.Alignment = wdAlignParagraphRight
      objTable.Columns(4).Select
      Selection.ParagraphFormat.Alignment = wdAlignParagraphRight

      objTable.Range.Font.Name = "Arial"
      objTable.Range.Font.Size = 8
      objTable.Range.Font.Bold = False

      objTable.Rows(1).Range.Font.Size = 10
      objTable.Rows(1).Range.Font.Bold = True
      objTable.Rows(1).Range.Font.Color = wdColorWhite

      objTable.Rows(1).Shading.BackgroundPatternColor = wdColorBlack
      objTable.Rows(1).HeadingFormat = True

  End Sub
```

> Note that this procedure, as it is, is not capable of handling invalid input. If it is called with a non-existent ID, it will cause an error. Adding the ability to deal with this possibility would be relatively easy, (simply checking if EOF is True immediately after the recordset has been opened), and would greatly increase the durability of this code.

Summary

Between the two examples in this chapter, producing a list of items or placing the contents of a single record into a custom template, we covered most of the possible situations in which you will be using databases and Word together. In the next chapter, we will move on to the more complex topic of accessing external applications (eg Outlook and Excel) from your Word VBA code.

External Applications

Introduction

This book is focused on developing in Word 2000, but no application exists in a vacuum. Other applications are likely available to you and each of these programs can give you access to powerful features and functions. This chapter covers how to find and use those other applications from Word, and even discusses the reverse; how to control Word from other programs. By adding the power of other applications, there is really no limit to what you can do with Word development.

What Applications Are Available

Not every application can be controlled from your VBA code, only those that are **COM** objects. COM stands for **Component Object Model** and refers to a set of standards, created by Microsoft, that define how different applications and application components can communicate. Word and VBA are both built around this framework, so they are capable of communicating with any other object built in the same way. If there are objects on your machine that are designed to support COM and that have been installed correctly, then you can use the References dialog (available under the Tools menu in the Visual Basic Editor) to determine what is available. Not every one of these objects is necessarily available for your use; the list will display objects that are installed for other applications and for which you do not have a design-time license (required for use in development).

Using the References Dialog

The References dialog displays a list of every properly installed COM object available on your machine. Every machine may have a different list of objects, but you can usually count on certain ones being available. In the References dialog (available through the VBA Editor's Tools menu) shown below, you can see an item that represents Outlook 2000:

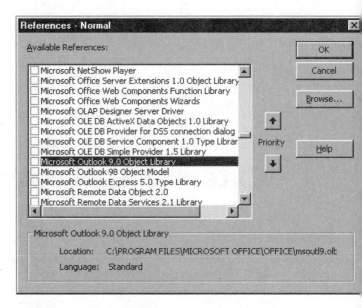

Depending on the installation objects chosen, several of these objects should be available on every machine that has Office 2000 on it. If, in your company, you know that every machine has Excel, Word, and PowerPoint installed on it, then you can count on having those objects available to your code. Determining which applications on your machine are capable of being controlled through your code involves looking carefully through the References dialog for object names. When you have highlighted a particular item, the corresponding file on your computer is displayed below the list box:

Knowing the filename and/or location that corresponds to a particular object can help you to determine which application is associated with each one. Some of the more common applications that support this form of development are listed below:

❑ Microsoft Excel, Word, Access, PowerPoint, Outlook

❑ Visio

❑ AutoCad

❑ Adobe Photoshop (4.0)

❑   Internet Explorer

❑   Outlook Express (version 5.0 +)

In each case, it may only be the latest version of the product that supports the COM interface, so you will have to do your own research to determine what is available.

Other Types of COM Objects (DLLs vs. EXEs)

Applications, which are represented on your machine by `.exe` files, are not the only type of file that can be a COM object. There is another type of file that shares this ability, the **DLL** (**Dynamic Linked Library**), which is just a library of code routines that can be built to meet the COM specifications. Libraries like this can be created in several development programs, including Visual Basic and Visual C++, and are a common method of sharing and distributing code routines. A programmer could build a set of statistical functions in Visual Basic that they want to be available to all the other developers in their company, some of which use VB, some VBA (in Word, for instance) and some use other tools entirely, like Borland's Delphi tool. By creating a COM DLL in Visual Basic, this programmer could place all their code into this single file that (once installed onto each machine) would be available to all the other developers. Overall, the ability to use code stored in EXEs and DLLs can greatly add to the power of your Word development.

What Can the Object Do?

Once we have determined that an object is available, that a certain application or DLL exists and is COM-compliant we need to find out what that object is capable of. One way to discover this information is through VBA's Object Browser. This tool, available through the View menu in the Visual Basic Editor (or with the F2 key), displays all the available functions, methods, and properties of every referenced object. Once we have checked an item in the References dialog, as shown below with the Microsoft Excel object, we can explore the exposed features of that object through the Object Browser:

At the top of the Browser's dialog is a dropdown list that allows you to select a single library for viewing. This list will contain an entry for every item selected in the References dialog, including Excel, which we just checked. Selecting the Excel library displays all the individual objects available as part of this library in the left hand list box, and, when one of these items is selected, the right hand list box will display all the available properties, methods, and events of that object:

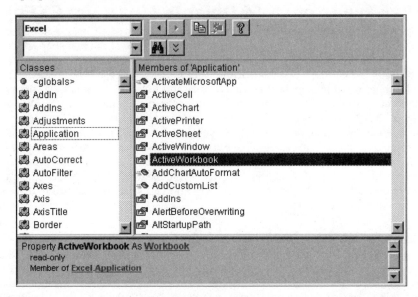

All of the object, properties, and methods of Word 2000 and VBA are also available through the **Object Browser**. This provides an excellent way to familiarize yourself with what is available.

Talking to Other Applications (Creating an Instance)

Setting a reference to another application, or to a DLL, is the first step towards using those resources in your program. The next step is to actually create (or obtain) an **instance** of the desired object. An instance of an object is a single copy of that code in memory, such as a single copy of Microsoft Word running on your machine. If Word were to be run more than once, there would be more than one instance of the application. There are several different ways to create a new instance of an object for your own use:

❑ Declaring the object variable using the New keyword:

```
Dim objExcel As New Excel.Application
```

> This method is the least recommended method, although it is the
> simplest. It is notorious for creating memory leaks.

❑ Declaring it without the New keyword and then using the New keyword later
on in code:

```
Dim objExcel As Excel.Application
Set objExcel = New Excel.Application
```

❑ Declaring it without the New keyword and then using the CreateObject
statement in code:

```
Dim objExcel As Excel.Application
Set objExcel = CreateObject("Excel.Application")
```

In each case, the object you are creating is specified using a name (in our example this
was Excel.Application) known as its **ProgID** a string consisting of two parts that
together identify a single object from a particular library. In our example, we are
creating an instance of the Application object from the Excel library.

Each of the three methods shown above will correctly create an instance of the desired
object, but they are not all equal. The first method, using the New keyword directly in
the variable declaration, is the simplest in terms of code but it causes a great deal of
complexity behind the scenes and is therefore the least efficient. The second method is
both easy and efficient, and is the one that you should use for most circumstances. The
third method uses the CreateObject statement, which takes a string parameter
specifying the object to create and returns a new instance of that object. The purpose
and power of this method is due to the fact that it uses a string to identify the object,
which means that the object being created doesn't have to be known at design time
(when you are coding it). Consider the following example of how this ability could be
used:

```
Dim objOfficeApp As Object
Dim sObjectID As String

sObjectID = Text1.Text & "." & Text2.Text

Set objOfficeApp = CreateObject(sObjectID)
```

From a database, or user input, or based on the results of a calculation, your code
could create an object of any type it wished. The Object data type, used to declare
objOfficeApp in the example, is a generic data type that is capable of representing
any created object.

> Having the user type in the object's ProgID is not always going to work.
> The information has to be exactly correct, and an error will result if you
> call CreateObject with an ID that doesn't exist.

CreateObject vs. GetObject

All of different methods shown above for creating objects will create a new instance of that object. This is generally what you want, but consider the result of using code like this to perform many different tasks with Microsoft Excel. Every time you called `CreateObject`, or declared a variable `As New`, a new copy of Excel would start running. After a while, you could have so many copies of Excel running that the computer may run out of available memory. You can always cause each copy to end when you are done with it (using the `Excel.Application` object's `Quit` method), but what if the user already had Excel running? Wouldn't it have been nice, not to mention better on memory and faster, to have just used that copy?

To allow for the reuse of existing instances of objects, VBA provides the `GetObject` statement, which works a little differently than `CreateObject`. Calling `GetObject` with the name of an object or application as its second parameter (the first argument, path name, is optional,so just put a comma to skip it), will return the instance of that object that is already running, into your object variable. If there isn't an existing instance, this statement would fail, which isn't very handy. What you probably want is some way to code the following:

```
If there already is an instance of Object available, give me that, otherwise
create an new instance of Object.
```

It is possible to code this in VBA due to a special characteristic of object variables; they start out equal to the special keyword `Nothing` and keep that value until an associated object instance is created and if `GetObject` fails, the object variable is still equal to `Nothing`. The code shown below shows how this special value can be used to properly get or create an object variable:

```
Public Sub GetExcel()
On Error Resume Next
'On Error statement stops a Run-Time error from
'occurring if the GetObject call fails
Dim objExcel As Excel.Application

    Set objExcel = GetObject(, "Excel.Application")

    If objExcel Is Nothing Then

        Set objExcel = New Excel.Application

    End If

End Sub
```

These lines of code will get an existing instance of Excel if one exists, otherwise the `If` statement is executed and a new instance is created. This code will work for any object you need to create, simply replace the `Excel.Application` portions with the appropriate object's class name.

> If you have to create a new instance of an object, that object will close automatically when the variable that refers to it ceases to exist (such as when the procedure ends or, for global variables, when your application is closed). You can also force VBA to release the object instance at any time by setting the variable equal to Nothing:
>
> ```
> Set objExcel = Nothing
> ```

Controlling Office 2000 Components

The most common external applications you will be using will be the other programs that make up the Office 2000 suite. This section provides a quick guide to the most common tasks you will need to perform with two of those programs, but isn't intended to be any form of complete reference to these applications. The programs we will cover are Excel and Outlook, providing details on performing all of the basic tasks. If you require more information on a particular application, there is a corresponding VBA Programmer's Reference available from Wrox that will provide all the details.

Common Programming Considerations

Many of the techniques involved in working with a single Office 2000 product, apply to all of them. This includes:

- Making an object reference
- Creating an instance of the desired application
- Scope issues with object references
- Converting code from the external application's VBA

We will cover each of these issues separately from the discussion of each individual application, to avoid repetition.

Adding a Reference to Your Project

A **reference** is the first step to working with one of the other Office applications; it provides the ability to browse through the available objects, properties, and methods of that application, as well as being a necessary part of creating your object instance. You must remember to set up the appropriate reference(s) for each project you are working with, as the settings from the References dialog are specific to an individual project. You can avoid having to set up commonly used references every time you start a project by making those references in a document template.

> Making a reference to an external application is not always necessary. You can successfully use any external application by declaring your variable "As Object" and using the CreateObject command to create your instance. There is a downside to this flexibility though; you will not have any of the handy dropdown lists of object properties, or tool tips displaying the arguments for methods, and no checking will be done by VB to ensure that you have spelt property names correctly. It is best to work without a reference only when you have no choice.

Creating an Instance

Creating an **instance** can be done in several ways, but we will only discuss two. The deciding factor between the two variations is whether you want to reuse an existing instance of the application (if there is one) or always create a new copy. If a new copy is desired, then the following code (modified to use the appropriate object name) will accomplish the desired goal:

```
Dim objAccess as Access.Application
Set objAccess = New Access.Application
```

The other alternative is for when you wish to ensure that any existing instance of the application will be used before a new one would be created. This procedure (once again, modified to use the correct object name) will provide that functionality, reusing an existing instance if available, and creating a new one if an instance is not available:

```
Public Sub OpenAccess()
On Error Resume Next
Dim objAccess As Access.Application
    Set objAccess = GetObject(, "Access.Application")
    If objAccess Is Nothing Then
        Set objAccess = CreateObject("Access.Application")
    End If
End Sub
```

The first line of this procedure, On Error Resume Next, is very important. This line tells VBA to just ignore any error that occurs when executing each line of this procedure. If an error occurs (such as if GetObject fails because there isn't an existing instance), VBA will just continue with the next line. Without this line, VBA would simply halt at the GetObject call and display a message box with the following error information:

Microsoft Visual Basic

Run-time error '429':

ActiveX component can't create object

| Continue | End | Debug | Help |

> Note that creating an instance does not always make the application visible, in fact for most applications (including those in Office 2000), it doesn't. To actually see the instance of Excel or Access that you have created you have to set their `Visible` property to `True`.

Scope Issues

When dealing with external applications, there is usually a variable in use to represent the object instance you have created (like `objAccess` from the previous code example). If this variable goes out of **scope** the object instance is destroyed, causing the application (Access, Excel, etc) to also close. If you wish to have more than one routine working with this same object variable (for instance, a single procedure could always be used to create an instance of Excel), then this becomes a problem. To avoid having the instance close almost immediately after you create it, use a `Public` (or `Global`) variable to store the object reference and then modify your code appropriately:

```
'In General Declarations Section
Public objAccess As Access.Application

Public Sub OpenAccess()

On Error Resume Next

    Set objAccess = GetObject(, "Access.Application")

    If objAccess Is Nothing Then

        Set objAccess = CreateObject("Access.Application")

    End If

End Sub
```

By using this method, storing your object references as `Public` variables, any application instance you create will exist until your application ends or you explicitly destroy the reference (`Set objAccess = Nothing`).

> Note that if you do not create the object instance, if you merely obtain an already existing instance (using `GetObject`), then that instance does not end when your variable goes out of scope or your application ends.

Microsoft Excel 2000

Here are code samples and explanations of how to accomplish some of the most common actions in Microsoft Excel 2000 from your Word VBA code. Excel is often used from other applications due to several key features:

❑ The ability to read and convert many file formats unavailable to Word or to Visual Basic

❑ Complex financial functions for calculating amortizations, interest and investments

❑ Easily manipulated by many business people, making it a good output format for your programs

The first actions required, as with controlling any external application are to make a reference from your project to Excel (using the **References** dialog) and to create an instance using a public variable. The code for creating your Excel instance is shown below:

```
'Variable declared in General Declarations section
Dim objExcel As Excel.Application

Public Sub OpenExcel()
On Error Resume Next

    Set objExcel = GetObject(, "Excel.Application")

    If objExcel Is Nothing Then

        Set objExcel = New Excel.Application

    End If

End Sub
```

Once you have your instance, you can start working with the `objExcel` variable, which is now an instance of `Excel.Application`. Each of the following common tasks will be covered for this object:

❑ Opening a file (regardless of the format)

❑ Saving a file

❑ Saving a file as a different name or format

❑ Printing a file or portion of a file

❑ Referencing the contents of a particular cell, which is demonstrated in the section "Converting Internal VBA Code to External Programming" below

Opening a File into Excel 2000

Similar to Word's `Documents` collection, Excel has a `Workbooks` collection. This collection has an `Open` method, allowing the opening of existing document from disk into Excel. A Word VBA function that takes a filename as a parameter and opens the corresponding file is shown below:

```
Public Sub OpenExcelDocument(sFileName As String)
Dim objWRK As Excel.Workbook

    OpenExcel

    Set objWRK = objExcel.Workbooks.Open(sFileName)

End Sub
```

Saving a File

Saving an Excel `Workbook` is done through the `Save` method of that object, which takes no parameters, making it very easy to program. Saving as a different file format or name is done through the `SaveAs` method, which needs more information, including the file path and, if appropriate, the new file format. The code below opens an Excel document and saves it as a comma-delimited text file:

```
Public Sub ConvertFile(sOriginalFile As String, sNewFile As String)

Dim objWRK As Excel.Workbook

    OpenExcel

    Set objWRK = objExcel.Workbooks.Open(sOriginalFile)

    objWRK.SaveAs sNewFile, xlCSV

End Sub
```

Printing an Excel File

Printing can be simple or complex through Excel; depending on how many options
you wish to set. At its easiest the following code will open and print an Excel
workbook:

```
Public Sub PrintFile(sFileName As String)

Dim objWRK As Excel.Workbook

    OpenExcel

    Set objWRK = objExcel.Workbooks.Open(sFileName)

    objWRK.PrintOut

End Sub
```

More control and options are available through the parameters of the `PrintOut`
method, including:

❑ `From` and `To` page numbers

❑ `ActivePrinter`, controlling which of your installed printers is used (useful
for when you store different types of paper in each, or when you wish to
specify a color printer, etc)

❑ Specifying the number of `Copies`

❑ Others are listed in Excel 2000 VBA Programmer's Reference, also published
by Wrox Press

If you need even more control over what is printed, the other option is to set a **print
range**, which is a range of cells that should be printed. This feature, demonstrated
below, allows you to print only a column or a small section of your document as is
accessed through the `PageSetup.PrintArea` property of an individual Worksheet:

```
Public Sub PrintRange(sFileName As String)
Dim objWRK As Excel.Workbook
Dim objWKS As Excel.Worksheet

    OpenExcel

    objExcel.Visible = True

    Set objWRK = objExcel.Workbooks.Open(sFileName)
```

```
    Set objWKS = objWRK.ActiveSheet

    objWKS.PageSetup.PrintArea = "$A$1:$A$5"

    objWKS.PrintPreview

End Sub
```

> It is easy to confuse the two terms, but (in Excel) a Workbook is a complete Excel file, which may contain more than one Worksheet.

Converting Internal VBA Code to External Programming

It is difficult to know exactly how to code the desired result in many different applications, but there is a powerful tool available in each of these programs that can make it a great deal easier, the Macro Recorder. Like in Word 2000, Excel, Access, PowerPoint and Outlook all contain their own Macro Recorders. These recorders allow you to create procedures in VBA that take advantage of the particular functions and objects available from within that particular application. The code created by these recorders is similar to the code we have been creating as part of our Word 2000 development, as shown by this sample Excel 2000 macro that records the entry of data into a series of cells:

```
Sub Macro3()
'
' Macro3 Macro
' Macro recorded 1/12/1999 by Duncan Mackenzie
'
    Range("A1").Select
    ActiveCell.FormulaR1C1 = "Special"
    Range("A2").Select
    ActiveCell.FormulaR1C1 = "Entry"
    Range("A3").Select
    ActiveCell.FormulaR1C1 = "Into"
    Range("A4").Select
    ActiveCell.FormulaR1C1 = "These"
    Range("A5").Select
    ActiveCell.FormulaR1C1 = "Cells"
    Range("A6").Select

End Sub
```

This is a perfectly correct procedure, in Excel 2000, but it will not function at all inside your Word VBA. Your program would generate errors when it attempted to understand of the objects from above (`Range` and `ActiveCell`). This is because code written inside (in internal VBA development) an individual application takes advantage of certain assumptions to simplify development. The code above could also be written like this (in Excel 2000):

```
Sub Macro3()
'
' Macro3 Macro
' Macro recorded 1/12/1999 by Duncan Mackenzie
'
    Application.Range("A1").Select
    Application.ActiveCell.FormulaR1C1 = "Special"
    Application.Range("A2").Select
    Application.ActiveCell.FormulaR1C1 = "Entry"
    Application.Range("A3").Select
    Application.ActiveCell.FormulaR1C1 = "Into"
```

```
      Application.Range("A4").Select
      Application.ActiveCell.FormulaR1C1 = "These"
      Application.Range("A5").Select
      Application.ActiveCell.FormulaR1C1 = "Cells"
      Application.Range("A6").Select

End Sub
```

It is still 100% correct Excel 2000 VBA code, but it is no longer taking advantage of the
shortcut (present in all of these applications) that allows you to skip the `Application`
object because it is assumed. This code still would not work inside Word as is, but the
change required is much clearer; we have to replace any reference to `Application`
with our object variable that contains an instance of `Excel.Application`, like this
(correct code for Word 2000 now):

```
Sub Macro3()
'
' Macro3 Macro
' Macro recorded 1/12/1999 by Duncan Mackenzie
'
Dim objExcel As New Excel.Application
Dim objWrk As Excel.Workbook

Set objWrk = objExcel.Workbooks.Add

objExcel.Visible = True

      objExcel.Range("A1").Select
     .objExcel.ActiveCell.FormulaR1C1 = "Special"
      objExcel.Range("A2").Select
      objExcel.ActiveCell.FormulaR1C1 = "Entry"
      objExcel.Range("A3").Select
      objExcel.ActiveCell.FormulaR1C1 = "Into"
      objExcel.Range("A4").Select
      objExcel.ActiveCell.FormulaR1C1 = "These"
      objExcel.Range("A5").Select
      objExcel.ActiveCell.FormulaR1C1 = "Cells"
      objExcel.Range("A6").Select
End Sub
```

Now this would be correct code for use outside of Excel, from within Word, Access,
etc. The conversion process covered here is relatively simple, and allows you to use the
internal Macro Recorders of any external application to generate code that you can
then take back into Word to control that external program.

> Note that this code could be made much simpler by the use of a `With`
> `objExcel ... End With` statement, but was intentionally left in the
> longer form for clarity.

Microsoft Outlook 2000

Here are code samples and explanations of how to accomplish some of the most
common actions in Microsoft Outlook 2000 from your Word VBA code. Linking your
application with Outlook provides you with the ability to view and modify your user's
calendar and contact information (a powerful benefit) and, of course, access to all the
email features of Outlook. The common tasks for Outlook cover a wider ground than
those for Excel, including the following:

❑ Sending an email message (with or without a file attachment).

❑ Looping through items in Outlook, including mail items, contact items, and journal entries.

❑ Adding new items to the various Outlook folders. Covers adding an appointment, adding a contact, adding a journal entry and adding a task.

Just like with Excel, above, the first actions required are to make a reference from you project to the **Microsoft Outlook 9.0 Object Library** and then to create a `Public` instance of that library. The code to do this with Outlook is shown below:

```
'Variable declared in the General Declarations section
Dim objOutlook As Outlook.Application

Public Sub OpenOutlook()
On Error Resume Next

    Set objOutlook = GetObject(, "Outlook.Application")

    If objOutlook Is Nothing Then

        Set objOutlook = New Outlook.Application

    End If

End Sub
```

Once you have your instance of Outlook, you can start to work with it. For the purposes of programming, you will want to have Outlook running before executing any code, as it can take quite some time to load. Outlook is actually very different than most applications you will control; you have to go through several layers before you can work with its standard items. The first example we will cover for outlook will demonstrate that process.

The Outlook Object Model

Without attempting to cover this information in complete detail, your programming of Outlook will usually consist of working with two major objects: `Folders` (Inbox, Contacts, etc) and `Items` (individual contacts, appointment's, mail messages, etc). When we open Outlook we have access to many different folders, some that were created for us (such as the Inbox and Outbox) and most likely a few that we have created ourselves. All of these folders are available through an object called a `NameSpace`. This object represents all the contents of the Outlook/Exchange storage space, including the folders and all the items. The following code demonstrates how to get to this `NameSpace` object through the `Outlook.Application` instance:

```
Public Sub OutlookNameSpace()
Dim nsMAPI As Outlook.NameSpace

    OpenOutlook

    Set nsMAPI = objOutlook.GetNameSpace("MAPI")

End Sub
```

The GetNameSpace function takes only a single parameter, defining the type of namespace you are attempting to retrieve. "MAPI" is the only possibility at the moment, although different types may become available in the future. This particular type returns a namespace that consists of all the information available through **MAPI**, the **Messaging Application Programming Interface**. Once you have that NameSpace object, you can get at all the useful objects of Outlook.

Looping through Folders

From the NameSpace object, you can obtain a Folders collection, representing the folders directly under this object. These are the top level of folders in Outlook, the parent of the Inbox folder and others:

```
Public Sub ListFolders()
Dim nsMAPI As Outlook.NameSpace
Dim objFolder As Outlook.MAPIFolder

OpenOutlook

    Set nsMAPI = objOutlook.GetNameSpace("MAPI")

    For Each objFolder In nsMAPI.Folders

        ActiveDocument.Range.InsertAfter objFolder.Name & vbCrLf

    Next

End Sub
```

This code will place the names of each of the top-level folders, returning "Mailbox - Duncan Mackenzie" and "Public Folders" for the Outlook system shown here, into your currently active document:

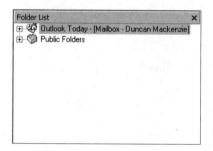

Each folder has within it another Folders collection, representing any sub-folders of that particular item. By using two separate procedures and a bit of **recursion** (a programming technique explained back in Chapter 7), our code can be modified to produce a list of all of these items, using tab characters (the constant vbTab) to create a well formatted list showing the relationship between all the folders:

```
Public Sub ListFolders()
Dim nsMAPI As Outlook.NameSpace
Dim objFolder As Outlook.MAPIFolder

OpenOutlook

    Set nsMAPI = objOutlook.GetNameSpace("MAPI")

    ListSubFolders nsMAPI.Folders, ""

End Sub
```

```
Public Sub ListSubFolders(objFolders As Outlook.Folders, _
       sIndent As String)
'the sIndent argument allows you to create the hierarchal effect
Dim objFolder As Outlook.MAPIFolder

If objFolders.Count > 0 Then

   For Each objFolder In objFolders

       ActiveDocument.Range.InsertAfter _
           sIndent & objFolder.Name & vbCrLf

       ListSubFolders objFolder.Folders, _
           sIndent & vbTab

   Next

End If

End Sub
```

Running this code will produce a listing of every folder that exists within Outlook, this will be different for each machine but an example of its results are shown below:

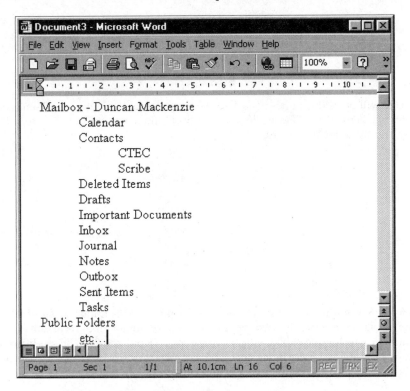

Each `Folder` object has several useful properties, other than just its `Folders` collection and its `Name`. From a `Folder` object you can obtain a collection of all the items it contains (`Items`) and even a count of the unread items within it (shown within Outlook as a number in brackets next to the folder name) through the `UnReadItemCount` property.

Obtaining Particular Folders

Looping through all the `Folders` available is one way to work with Outlook, but you are more likely to want a particular folder. There are three main ways to retrieve a single `Folder` object, through three separate functions of the `NameSpace` object.

❏   `GetDefaultFolder`, which allows you to obtain one of the main Outlook folders: Calendar, Contacts, Deleted Items, Drafts, Inbox, Journal, Notes, Outbox, Sent Mail, or Tasks. Very commonly used.

This piece of example code demonstrates obtaining the Inbox folder through the `GetDefaultFolder` function:

```
Public Sub UnReadItems()
Dim nsMAPI As Outlook.NameSpace
Dim objInbox As Outlook.MAPIFolder

OpenOutlook

    Set nsMAPI = objOutlook.GetNameSpace("MAPI")

    Set objInbox = nsMAPI.GetDefaultFolder(olFolderInbox)
    'the constant olFolderInbox specifies which default folder to
    'open there are similar constants for the Tasks, Calendar,
    'Journal, etc...

    MsgBox "There are " & objInbox.UnReadItemCount & _
        " Unread Item(s) in your Inbox.", _
        vbInformation, "Outlook Example"

End Sub
```

❏   `GetFolderFromID`, which takes a special identifying value (obtained from the `Folder`'s `EntryID` property) and returns that particular folder. Not much use if you don't already have the `EntryID`.

❏   `PickFolder`, a very useful function that displays a dialog box containing a hierarchal listing of all the available folders and returns the folder corresponding to the user's choice.

This code demonstrates the usage of `PickFolder`:

```
Public Sub UserChoice()
Dim nsMAPI As Outlook.NameSpace
Dim objPicked As Outlook.MAPIFolder

OpenOutlook

    Set nsMAPI = objOutlook.GetNameSpace("MAPI")

    Set objPicked = nsMAPI.PickFolder

    MsgBox "You chose the " & objPicked.Name & " Folder!", _
        vbInformation, "Outlook Example"

End Sub
```

This code produces the following dialog box from which the user can choose a particular folder, or even create a new one. An error occurs if they press Cancel.

Sending a Mail Message

Mail messages, Contacts, Tasks and Appointments are all represented in Outlook by `Items`, and it is through these objects that we can accomplish those various programming tasks listed at the beginning of the Outlook section.

When programming Outlook, we send a new message by creating a new item inside the Outbox, when we save it, it is automatically sent. Creating a new item is accomplished through the `Add` method of a folder's `Items` collection, returning an object of the appropriate type (`Outlook.MailItem`, `Outlook.ContactItem`, etc). Once you have your new item, you can set its various properties (too numerous to cover in this book) and then `Save` the item (or `Send` it, in the case of a new message). The routine below is a procedure that you can call (with the appropriate parameters) from anywhere else in your code and it will send a message with the appropriate information:

```
Public Sub SendMessage(sRecipient As String, sSubject As String, _
            sBody As String, sFileName As String)

Dim nsMAPI As Outlook.NameSpace
Dim objOutbox As Outlook.MAPIFolder
Dim objNewMessage As Outlook.MailItem

OpenOutlook

    Set nsMAPI = objOutlook.GetNameSpace("MAPI")

    Set objOutbox = nsMAPI.GetDefaultFolder(olFolderOutbox)

    Set objNewMessage = objOutbox.Items.Add

    With objNewMessage

        .To = sRecipient
        .Subject = sSubject
        .Body = sBody

        If sFileName <> "" Then

            If Dir(sFileName) <> "" Then 'File Exists!
```

```
            .Attachments.Add sFileName

      End If

      End If

      .Send

   End With
End Sub
```

> Note that the routine sets only the bare minimum number of properties;
> no Cc recipients are set, no priority, nothing but the recipient, the
> subject, the body (message), and a single attachment. You will have to
> modify this code, or create your own, if you need additional features
> such as multiple file attachments.

Word already has email functionality built into it, so you may wonder why you would
want to use Outlook for this purpose. The code below demonstrates the two ways in
which you could send a document, through Word first and then second through our
email routine that uses Outlook:

```
Public Sub SendDocument(objDoc As Word.Document)

   objDoc.Save

   'Method 1, through Word

   objDoc.SendMail

   'Method 2, through Outlook
   SendMessage "Duncan Mackenzie", "This File", _
            "Here it is!", objDoc.FullName

End Sub
```

Now, just from this code you can see that the Word method (Method 1) is simpler, and if you add in the code required to create the `SendMessage` routine, there is no doubt that less work is required if you use Word's `SendMail` command. The problem is in how the `SendMail` routine works, it doesn't accept any arguments (such as who to send the document to, etc) because it works by creating a new message in Outlook and then popping up the regular email dialog for the user to fill in the required information:

This is good for standard usage, but not very useful in programs that are intended to run without user intervention.

Adding other Items

The code above (SendMessage) showed you how to create a new MailItem, and the procedure is similar for each of the other types of items, using the appropriate Items collection's Add method. You can also create items directly into the appropriate default folder using the Outlook.Application's CreateItem method, which takes a parameter to specify which type of item to create. This method works well for some types of items (and could have been used for the SendMessage routine) but is less flexible allowing you to only create the item in the default folder. This code below takes two parameters (a Type, such as "Fax", and a Subject) and creates a new JournalItem in the default Journal folder:

```
Public Sub CreateNewJournalEntry(sType As String, sSubject As String)
Dim objJournal As Outlook.JournalItem

OpenOutlook

    Set objJournal = objOutlook.CreateItem(olJournalItem)

    With objJournal

        .Type = sType

        .Subject = sSubject

        .Close olSave

    End With

End Sub
```

Using Word from other Applications

Although this might be obvious from the discussions above, it is possible to control Word from other applications that support the COM standard, in exactly the same fashion as controlling Excel and Access was detailed above. To accomplish this from another VBA application or from Visual Basic itself (for use as part of a Visual Basic application) you have to follow three steps:

❑   Make a reference to the **Word 2000 Object Library** from the other application

❑   Create or obtain an instance of Word.Application in your code

❑   Use the instance you just created in exactly the same fashion as the Word Application object to control Word from within your code

Of course, just like the example above under "Converting Internal VBA Code to External Programming", you can convert existing Word VBA code for use from another application. The code below shows how one of our earlier projects (the Fax Coversheet from Chapter 6) would convert for use from outside of Word itself:

```
Public Sub CreateFaxCoversheet()

Dim objWord As Word.Application

Set objWord = GetObject(, "Word.Application")

Dim objCurrentDoc As Word.Document
Dim objNewDoc As Word.Document

Dim sUserTemplates As String

Dim sTitle As String
Dim iNumberofPages As Integer
Dim sUserName As String

Dim sToName As String
Dim sToFax As String

    If objWord.Documents.Count > 0 Then

        Set objCurrentDoc = objWord.ActiveDocument

        'Get information for fax coversheet
        sTitle = NameWithoutExtension(objCurrentDoc.Name)
        iNumberofPages = objCurrentDoc.ComputeStatistics _
            (wdStatisticPages) + 1
        sUserName = objWord.UserName

        'Project 6C -- GetAddress Information
        If MsgBox("Retrieve Recipient Information from Address" & _
            " Book ?", vbQuestion Or vbYesNo, "Coversheet Generator") _
            = vbYes Then

            Do
                sToName = objWord.GetAddress _
                    (AddressProperties:="<PR_DISPLAY_NAME>")

            Loop Until sToName <> ""

            sToFax = objWord.GetAddress _
                    (AddressProperties:="<PR_BUSINESS_FAX_NUMBER>" _
                , DisplaySelectDialog:=2)

        End If

        'Path for User Templates
        sUserTemplates = objWord.Options.DefaultFilePath _
                (wdUserTemplatesPath)

        'Create Fax Coversheet
        Set objNewDoc = objWord.Documents.Add(sUserTemplates & _
                "\Java Jitters\Fax Coversheet.dot")

        SetBookmark objNewDoc, "Subject", sTitle
        SetBookmark objNewDoc, "Pages", CStr(iNumberofPages)
        SetBookmark objNewDoc, "From", sUserName

        If sToName <> "" Then

            SetBookmark objNewDoc, "To", sToName
            SetBookmark objNewDoc, "ToFax", sToFax
            objNewDoc.Bookmarks("Comments").Select

        Else

            objNewDoc.Bookmarks("To").Select

        End If

    End If

End Sub
```

> Code that is added or changed in the above procedure is indicated in bold or gray. In addition to those modifications, the two helper procedures `SetBookmark` and `NameWithoutExtension` have to be copied and pasted into the module (in Excel for example) but their code requires no changes. Note that this code assumes that there is an existing instance of Word 2000 available (it uses only `GetObject`), as this would be required for this particular code to function correctly (it depends on the presence of an active document).

Due to the common language (VBA) shared by so many applications, the code shown above would work in any of the other Office 2000 products, and in many others. In fact, although VB uses a language that is slightly different than VBA, that code is 100% compatible with VB as well and could be placed directly into a Visual Basic project with no changes. Whichever application you put it into though, do not forget that you must still add a reference to the Word 2000 (version 9.0) object library for the code to function:

Summary

To completely understand how to control Excel, Access, or any other application is beyond the scope of this book, but the examples and techniques above detail the process from a Word developer's point of view. Adding the abilities of other applications into your programs can provide you with nearly endless possibilities, so experiment and enjoy. For more detailed information on a specific application's object model and other programming information see one of these references:

❑   Outlook 2000 VBA Programmer's Reference (186100253X)

❑   Excel 2000 VBA Programmer's Reference (1861002548)

❑   Beginning Access 2000 VBA (1861001762)

This is the last actual chapter in this book, but there is a great deal more information still to come in the appendices. Appendix A (next) provides a very thorough reference to the enormous Word 2000 Object Model, Appendix B covers the various functions, statements and structures available in VBA, Appendix C covers ActiveX Database Objects (ADO), and Appendix D provides a quick guide to programming with one of the shared Office 2000 features, the Office Assistant.

Word 2000 Object Model

Complete Object Model

What follows is the complete object model for Word 2000. The gray boxes represent collection objects, the white boxes represent objects and the small, dark gray circles mean that an object is described in full detail elsewhere in the diagram.

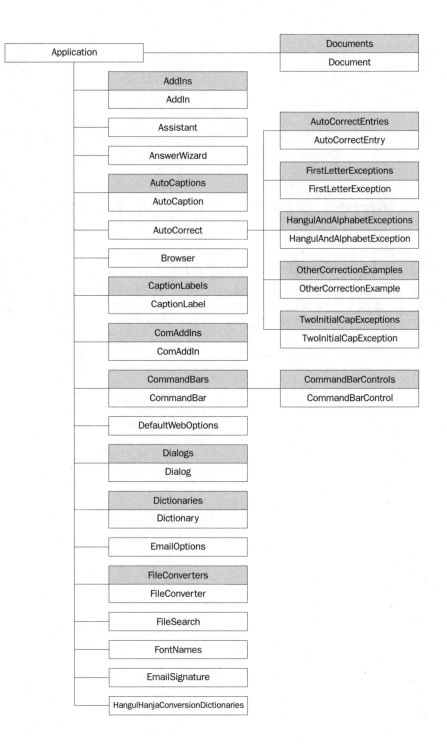

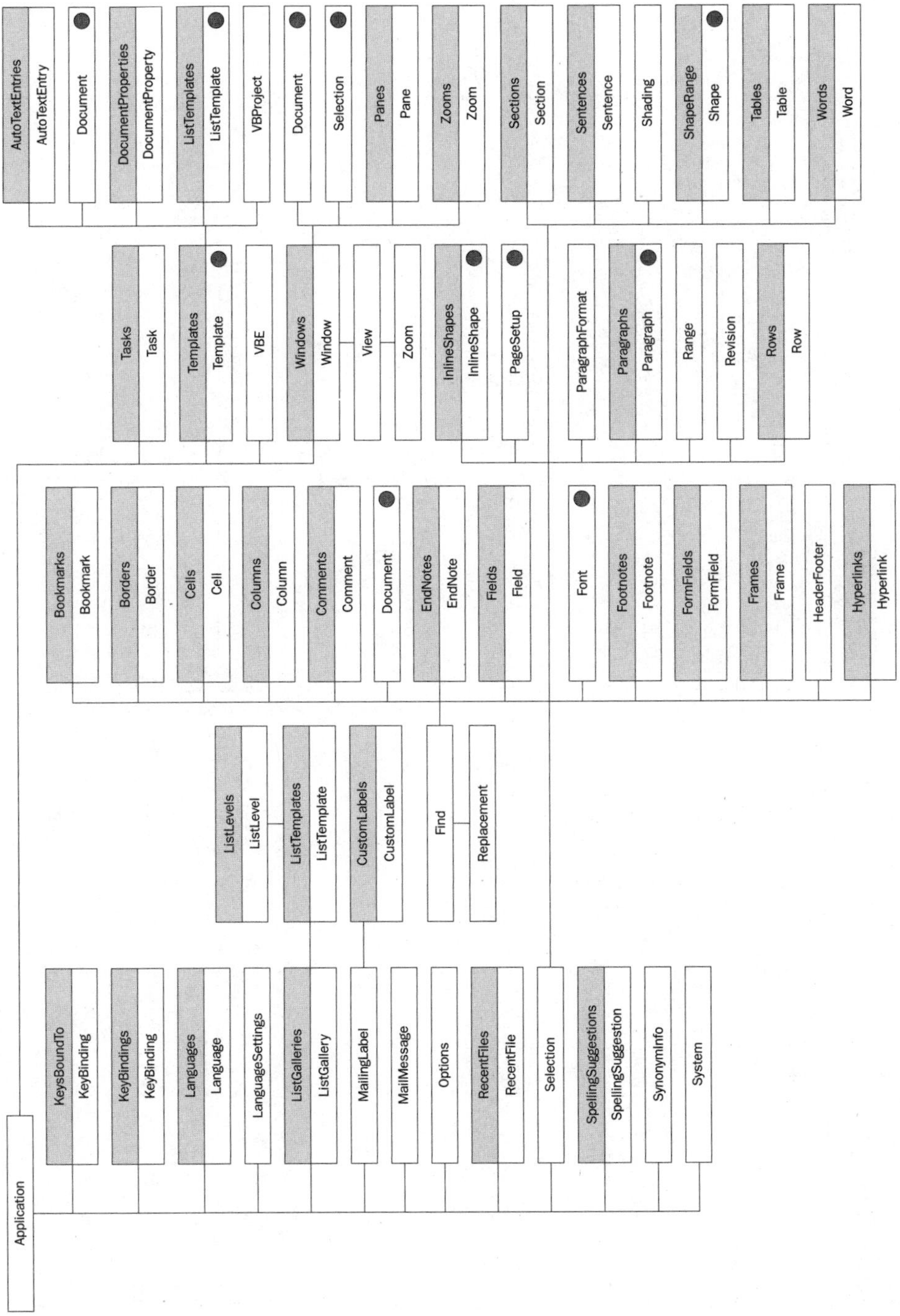
Application
KeysBoundTo
KeyBinding
KeyBindings
KeyBinding
Languages
Language
LanguageSettings
ListGalleries
ListGallery
MailingLabel
MailMessage
Options
RecentFiles
RecentFile
Selection
SpellingSuggestions
SpellingSuggestion
SynonymInfo
System
ListLevels
ListLevel
ListTemplates
ListTemplate
CustomLabels
CustomLabel
Find
Replacement
Bookmarks
Bookmark
Borders
Border
Cells
Cell
Columns
Column
Comments
Comment
Document
EndNotes
EndNote
Fields
Field
Font
Footnotes
Footnote
FormFields
FormField
Frames
Frame
HeaderFooter
Hyperlinks
Hyperlink
Tasks
Task
Templates
Template
VBE
Windows
Window
View
Zoom
InlineShapes
InlineShape
PageSetup
ParagraphFormat
Paragraphs
Paragraph
Range
Revision
Rows
Row
AutoTextEntries
AutoTextEntry
Document
DocumentProperties
DocumentProperty
ListTemplates
ListTemplate
VBProject
Document
Selection
Panes
Pane
Zooms
Zoom
Sections
Section
Sentences
Sentence
Shading
ShapeRange
Shape
Tables
Table
Words
Word

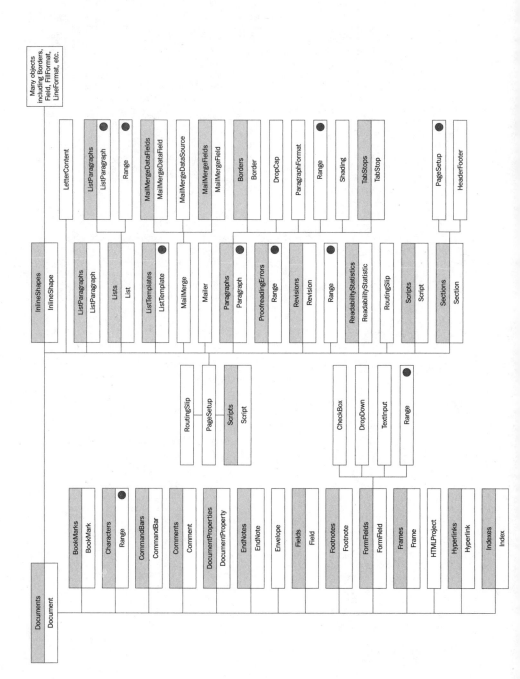

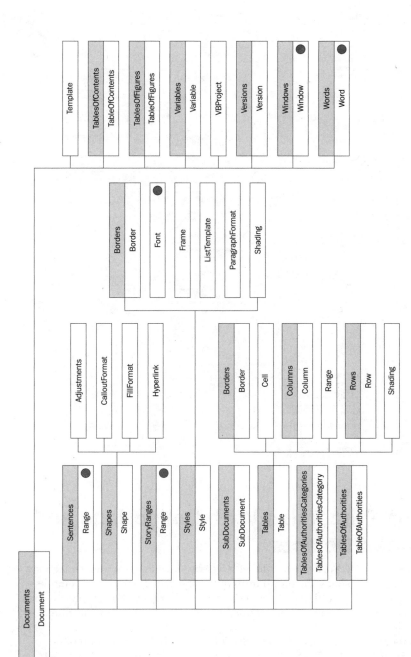

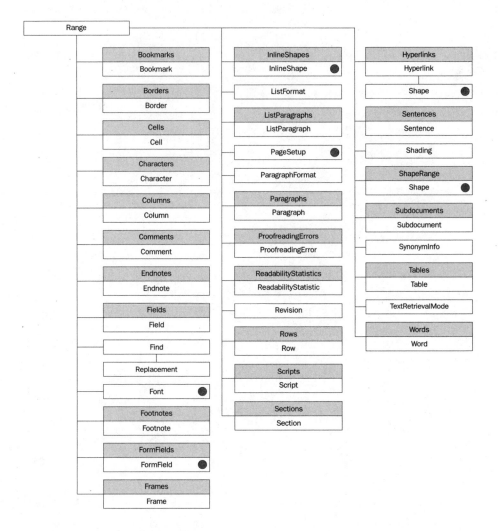

Common Properties With Collections and Associated Objects

Most of the objects in the Word Object Model have objects with associated collections. The collection object is usually the plural form of the associated object. For example, the Documents collection holds a collection of Document objects. For simplicity, each object and associated collection will be grouped together under the same heading.

In most cases the purpose of the collection object is only to hold a collection of the same objects. To avoid redundancy all objects and associated collections have been grouped under the same title. The common properties and methods of the collection objects are listed below. Only unique properties, methods or events will be mentioned in each object sections.

Common Collection Object Properties

Name	Returns	Description
Application	Application	Read-Only. Returns a reference to the owning `Application` object of the current object.
Count	Long	Read-Only. Returns the number of objects in the collection.
Creator	Long	Read-Only. Returns a Long number that describes whether the object was created in Word or not.
Parent	Object	Read-Only. The `Parent` object is the owning object of the collection object.

Common Collection Object Methods

Name	Returns	Parameters	Description
Item	Single	Index As Variant	Returns the object from the object collection either through it's position or by it's name.

Objects also have some common properties. To avoid redundancy the common properties and methods of all objects are listed below. They will be mentioned in each object description as existing but are only defined here.

Common Object Properties

Name	Returns	Description
Application	Application	Read-Only. Returns a reference to the owning `Application` object of the current object.
Creator	Long	Read-Only. Returns a Long number that describes whether the object was created in Word.
Parent	Object	Read-Only. The owning object of the current object.

Objects and their Properties, Methods and Events

The objects are listed in alphabetical order. Each object has a general description of the object and possible parent objects. This is followed by a table format of each of the object's properties, methods and events. The last section of each object describes some code examples of the object's use.

AddIn Object and the AddIns Collection

The `AddIns` collection holds a collection of `AddIn` objects. Each `AddIn` object represents a global template or Word add-in library (files with a .WLL extension). It does not matter whether the `AddIn` is currently loaded or not for it to be an item in the `AddIns` collection.

> The items in the `AddIns` collection are displayed in the **Templates and Add-Ins** dialog box from the **Tools** menu.

In addition to the usual properties and methods the `AddIns` collection has two additional methods. The `Add` method adds a file specified by the `FileName` parameter to this list of available add-ins. The `Unload` method removes all loaded add-ins, if the `RemoveFromList` parameter is set to `True`, then these add-ins will also be removed from the `AddIns` collection. Some of the following property, method and object names are extremely long. We have split some of the names over two lines for printing purposes. However, they should all be typed as if one word.

AddIn Common Properties

The `Application, Creator,` and `Parent` properties are defined at the beginning of this section.

AddIn Properties

Name	Data Type	Description
Autoload	Boolean	Read-Only. `True` if the add-in starts up automatically when Word starts up.
Compiled	Boolean	Read-Only. `True` if the add-in is a Word add-in library. `False` if the add-in is a template.
Index	Long	Read-Only. The position number in the `AddIns` collection.
Installed	Boolean	`True` if add-in is installed and loaded in the current Word session.
Name	String	Read-Only. The name of the `AddIn`. Also the filename associated with the template or add-in library.
Path	String	Read-Only. The path to the template or add-in library.

Addln Methods

Name	Returns	Parameters	Description
Delete	N/A		Deletes the AddIn object from the current AddIns collection.

Examples

Display the number of add-ins in the Word and then display the names of all the add-ins:

```
Dim ai As AddIn

MsgBox Application.AddIns.Count
For Each ai In Application.AddIns
    MsgBox ai.Name
Next
```

Adjustments Object

The Adjustments object holds a collection of numeric values used to adjust the adjustment 'handles' of the parent Shape object. Each Shape object can have up to 8 different adjustments. Each specific adjustment handle can have one or two adjustments associated with it depending on whether it can be moved both horizontally and vertically (two) or just in one dimension.

Adjustments Common Properties

The Application, Creator, and Parent properties are defined at the beginning of this section.

Adjustments Properties

Name	Returns	Description
Count	Long	Read-Only. Returns the number of adjustment values in the Adjustments object associated with the parent Shape object.
Item	Single	Index as long parameter. Set/Get the adjustment value specified by the Index parameter.

Examples

Display the number of adjustments associated with the first shape in the active document:

```
MsgBox ActiveDocument.Shapes(1).Adjustments.Count
```

Application Object

The `Application` object is the top-level object of the Word Object Model. All other object references must go through the `Application` object. However, some objects, such as the `ActiveDocument` object and the `CommandBars` object, are considered `Global` in that they do not require the `Application` object qualifier to access their properties. Typically the `Application` object is used to do the following:

- ❏ Access all of the objects in the Word Object Model.

- ❏ Use Word defaults such as the `UserName` or `UserInitials` of the Word session.

- ❏ Understand how the current Word environment is set up. For example, you can use properties like `International` to see the information about international settings, and `Height` to see or set the height of the application window for Word.

When controlling Word from another application, such as Visual Basic, the `Application` object is almost always referenced first. It is required to use the `Application` object when using the `GetObject` or `CreateObject` function to control Word from another application. Note that `Application` object events are not automatically available for use by the developer. The following three steps must be completed **first**:

1. Declare a public object variable in a class, say called `AppObject`, to respond to events. For example:

```
Public WithEvents AppObject As Word.Application
```

2. Now the `Application` object events will be available in the class for `AppObject`. Write the appropriate event handling code in the class. For example if you wanted a user not to be able to close a document then you could write the following:

```
Private Sub AppObject_DocumentBeforeClose(Doc As Document, _
                                    Cancel As Boolean)
    'Cancel any attempt to close a document
    Cancel = True
End Sub
```

3. Finally, instantiate the class created above with a current `Application` object in a procedure:

```
Private App As New clsAppObject 'class with the above code snippets

Sub RegisterAppEvents()
     Set App.AppObject = Word.Application
End Sub
```

Application Common Properties

The `Application`, `Creator`, and `Parent` properties are defined at the beginning of this section.

Application Properties

Name	Returns	Description
Active Document	Document	Read-Only. A `Document` object referring to the current document that has focus in the Word session. An error occurs if no documents are open.
Active Printer	String	Set/Get the printer that will be used to print. To set the active printer you must know the exact name of the printer, including references to network drives if applicable.
Active Window	Window	Read-Only. A `Window` object referring to the current window that has focus in the Word session. An error occurs if no windows are open.
AddIns	AddIns	Read-Only. An `AddIns` collection object representing all of the add-ins available, including global templates and add-in libraries.
Answer Wizard	Answer Wizard	Read-Only. An `AnswerWizard` object representing the Answer Wizard.
Assistant	Assistant	Read-Only. An `Assistant` object representing the Office Assistant.
Auto Captions	Auto Captions	Read-Only. The `AutoCaptions` collection object representing a list of all the captions that are used when tables and drawings are added to a document.
Auto Correct	Auto Correct	Read-Only. An `AutoCorrect` object holding all of the AutoCorrect entries and options. Equivalent to the AutoCorrect tab of AutoCorrect dialog box.
Background Printing Status	Long	Read-Only. Returns the number of documents that are being queued up for background printing in Word.
Background Saving Status	Long	Read-Only. Returns the number of documents that are being queued up for background saving in Word.

Table Continued on Following Page

Name	Returns	Description
Browse ExtraFile Types	String	Set the type of files that can be browsed inside of Word. Currently used to open hyperlinked HTML files inside Word instead of the default browser.
Browser	Browser	Read-Only. A Browser object used to move back and forth through a document by table, page, section and other ways.
Build	String	Read-Only. Returns the version number and build number for Word.
CapsLock	Boolean	Read-Only. True if the *Caps Lo* is on for the keyboard.
Caption	String	Set/Get the caption for the Word session.
Caption Labels	Caption Labels	Read-Only. A CaptionLabels collection object holding all caption labels available to Word.
Check Language		True if the language you are using is checked as you type. Word must be set up for multilingual editing for this property to be true.
COMAddIns	COMAddIns	Read-Only. A COMAddIns collection object representing all of the registered COM Add-ins.
Command Bars	Command Bars	Read-Only. A CommandBars collection object representing all of the menus and toolbars available in Word.
Custom Dictionaries	Dictionaries	Read-Only. A Dictionaries collection object holding all of the custom Dictionary objects.
Customization Context	Object	Set/Get the document or template object that refers to the document or template where CommandBar and KeyBinding changes are saved. Use with the CommandBars and KeyBindings collection to change CommandBar and KeyBinding items.

Name	Returns	Description
DefaultSave Format	String	Set/Get the default **Save As** file format. This property is equivalent to the **Save as type** textbox in the **Save As** dialog box (**File** | **Save As** menu item). Internal types used for the String value include "" for Word documents, "Dot" for templates, "Text" for text only, and "Rtf" for Rich Text Format files
DefaultTable Separator	String	Set/Get the default character that is used to create separate cells when converting text into a table. This value can be overridden by using the Separator parameter of the Range.ConvertToTable or Selection.ConvertToTable method.
Dialogs	Dialogs	Read-Only. A Dialogs collection object holding all of the dialog boxes used in Word.
Display Alerts	WdAlert Level	Sets up how certain messages and error messages are handled when a macro is running. Possible values are wdAlertsNone (no messages or error messages will pop up), wdAlertsMessageBox (only messages pop up), and wdAlertsAll (both messages and error messages will pop up).
DisplayAuto Complete Tips	Boolean	Set/Get whether Word displays auto-completion tips when a user is typing common names, dates, and places.
Display RecentFiles	Boolean	Set/Get whether Word displays a list of the most recently opened files under the File menu.
Display ScreenTips	Boolean	Set/Get whether comments, footnotes, endnotes and hyperlinks are displayed as tips.
Display ScrollBars	Boolean	Set/Get whether at least one document window is displaying scrollbars. Use the DisplayHorizontalScrollBar and the DisplayVerticalScrollBar properties of the Window object to set or return individual window scrollbar visibility.

Table Continued on Following Page

Name	Returns	Description
Display StatusBar	Boolean	Set/Get whether Word's status bar is displayed.
Documents	Documents	Read-Only. A Documents collection object holding all of the currently open documents.
EmailOptions	Email Options	Read-Only. Returns a reference to an EmailOptions collection object.
EnableCancel Key	WdEnable Cancel Key	Set/Get how pressing *Ctrl + Break* effects running macros. Possible values are wdCancelDisabled (macro cannot be canceled by *Ctrl + Break*), and wdCancelInterrupt (macro can be canceled by *Ctrl + Break*. Property changes will be in effect for the entire Word session.
Feature Install	Mso Feature Install	Set/Get how Word handles programmatic access to Word features that have not been installed. Possible values are msoFeatureInstallNone (an automation error message is displayed), msoFeatureInstallOnDemand (a message pops up prompting the user to install the needed features), or msoFeatureInstallOnDemandWith UI (a progress bar is displayed to the user showing installation progress). This property works along with the DisplayAlerts property.
File Converters	File Converters	Read-Only. A FileConverters collection holding all of the file converters available in Word.
FileSearch	FileSearch	Read-Only. Returns a FileSearch object that is used to search for physical files.

Name	Returns	Description
FindKey	KeyBinding	Read-Only. `KeyCode` as a `Long` parameter, `KeyCode2` as an optional `Variant` parameter. Returns a `KeyBinding` object specified by a certain key combination. The key combination is passed using `KeyCode` and `KeyCode2`. The parameters have to be one of the `WdKey` constants. This property is typically used to alter or display specific customized key assignments.
FocusInMail Header	Boolean	Read-Only. This property is `True` if insertion point is in a WordMail header field like the To: or Cc: fields.
FontNames	FontNames	Read-Only. A `FontNames` collection object listing all of the fonts available in Word.
HangulHanja Dictionaries	Hangul Hanja Dictionaries	Read-Only. Returns a reference to the `HangulHanjaDictionaries` collection object holding all of the Asian Dictionary objects.
Height	Long	Set/Get the height of Word's application window.
International	Variant	Read-Only. `WdInternational Index` as a parameter. Returns information about the country settings currently being used by Word. The parameter is used to choose the information returned. Possible values for the parameter include `wd24HourClock` (property returns `True` if a 24-hour clock is being used) and `wdDecimal Separator` (property returns the character used for the decimal separator). Other parameter values are `wdCurrencyCode`, `wdDate Separator`, `wdInternationalAM`, `wdInternationalPM`, `wdListSeparator`, `wdProductLanguageID`, `wdThousandsSeparator`, and `wdTimeSeparator`.

Table Continued on Following Page

Name	Returns	Description
IsObject Valid	Boolean	Read-Only. Object as parameter. True if the object reference passed in the parameter is a valid object, False if the object pertaining to the passed object reference has been deleted.
Key Bindings	KeyBindings	Read-Only. A KeyBindings collection holding all the customized key assignments. Used in conjunction with the CustomizationContext property.
Keys BoundTo	KeysBoundTo	Read-Only. KeyCategory, Command and OptionalCommandParameter as parameters. A KeysBoundTo object listing all of the key combinations assigned to the command passed in as a parameter. The KeyCategory parameter must be one of the following WdKeyCategory constants: wdKeyCategoryAutoText, wdKeyCategoryCommand, wdKeyCategoryFont, wdKeyCategoryMacro, wdKeyCategoryStyle, or wdKeyCategorySymbol. The CommandParameter parameter can hold any required parameters for the command specified by the Command string.
Landscape FontNames	FontNames	Read-Only. A FontNames object listing all of the available landscape-oriented fonts.
Language	MsoLanguage ID	Read-Only. Returns the current language used by Word.
Languages	Languages	Read-Only. Returns the list of proofing languages available in Word.
Language Settings	Language Settings	Read-Only. Returns a LanguageSettings object listing all of the different language settings used in Word. For example the user interface may be French but the Help language may be English.
Left	Long	Set/Get the horizontal position of the active document.

Name	Returns	Description
List Galleries	List Galleries	Read-Only. Returns a `ListGalleries` collection object holding the three list template galleries (associated with the **Bullets And Numbering** dialog box).
Macro Container	Object	Read-Only. Returns a `Template` or `Document` object that contains the currently running code.
Mailing Label	Mailing Label	Read-Only. Returns a `MailingLabel` object that represents a mailing label. Typically used to create new mailing label documents.
Mail Message	Mail Message	Read-Only. Returns a reference to the active WordMail message.
Mail System	WdMail System	Read-Only. Returns the different mail systems that are installed on the machine hosting the running code. Possible values are `wdMAPI`, `wdMAPIandPowerTalk`, `wdPowerTalk`, and `wdNoMailSystem`.
MAPI Available	Boolean	Read-Only. True if the MAPI mail system is installed.
Math Coprocessor Available	Boolean	Read-Only. True if a math coprocessor is installed on the host machine.
Mouse Available	Boolean	Read-Only. True if a mouse is available on the host machine.
Name	String	Read-Only. Always returns "Microsoft Word".
Normal Template	Template	Read-Only. A `Template` object that represents Word's **Normal** template.
NumLock	Boolean	Read-Only. `True` if the *Num Lock* key is on for the keyboard.
Options	Options	Read-Only. An `Options` object representing all of the application settings that can be made in Word.

Table Continued on Following Page

Name	Returns	Description
Path	String	Read-Only. This property returns the directory path of Microsoft Word without the backslash path separator at the end. Use this property with the Path Separator and Name properties to get the full path to Microsoft Word.
Path Separator	String	Read-Only. This property returns the file path separator being used. Returns a backslash (\) in Windows and a colon (:) in Macintosh.
Portrait FontNames	FontNames	Read-Only. A FontNames object listing all the available portrait-oriented fonts.
Print Preview	Boolean	Check if the current view in Word is print preview or change the current view from/to print preview.
Recent Files	RecentFil es	Read-Only. A RecentFiles collection object representing a list of all the recently opened files (using RecentFile objects).
Screen Updating	Boolean	Set or check whether Word updates its display while a procedure is running. This property can be used to speed up procedure code by turning off screen updates (setting the property to False) during processing. Use with the ScreenRefresh method to manually refresh the screen. You should always set this property back to True when you are finished with it.
Selection	Selection	Read-Only. References a Selection object representing the selected text in the document or the position of the insertion point.
ShowVisual BasicEditor	Boolean	Set or check whether the Visual Basic editor is visible (True) or not.
SpecialMode	Boolean	Read-Only. If Word is in a *Special Mod* like CopyText or MoveText mode then this property is True. If Word is in a special mode then using code to cut or copy text may cause an error. Use SendKey "*ESC*" to change SpecialMode from True to False.

Name	Returns	Description
StartupPath	String	Set or check the path to the Startup folder for Word. Use with the PathSeparator property to get the path with a backslash at the end. All templates and add-ins in the Startup folder run when Word starts up.
StatusBar	String	Set but **not** check the text in Word's status bar.
SynonymInfo	SynonymInfo	Read-Only. A string and an optional language ID parameter. Returns a SynonymInfo object representing a list of synonyms, antonyms, and related words of the first string parameter. The second parameter, language ID, specifies which language to use for the thesaurus using a WdLanguageID constant.
System	System	Read-Only. A System object holding general information about the host computer like disk space, screen resolution. The System object can also map network drives.
Tasks	Tasks	Read-Only. A Tasks collection object representing the full list of tasks running on the host system. Each task can be manipulated through the individual Task objects. With this collection you can change the active task (e.g. from Word to Access), close tasks and shutdown Windows.
Templates	Templates	Read-Only. A Templates collection object representing all the templates that can be used by Word in the current session. Global templates, open templates, and attached open templates are the usual list of templates available as Template objects through the Templates collection.
Top	Long	Set/Get the vertical position of the active document.

Table Continued on Following Page

Name	Returns	Description
UsableHeight	Long	Read-Only. Returns the vertical space available in Word's main window, in points, that is available to a document Window. The value will be 1 if there is no space available.
UsableWidth	Long	Read-Only. Returns the horizontal space available in Word's main window, in points, that is available to a document Window. This property's value will be invalid if no space is available. Check the value of the UsableHeight property to check to see if there is any space available (>1).
UserAddress	String	Set/Get the mailing address of the current Word user. This property specifies what the return address is for envelopes.
UserControl	Boolean	Read-Only. True if the user started the current Word session, and False if the Word session was started programmatically through Automation. Used by applications using Word programmatically.
UserInitials	String	Set/Get the initials of the current Word user.
UserName	String	Set/Get the name of the current Word user.
VBE	VBE	Read-Only. The returning VBE object represents the Visual Basic Editor allowing access to the programming environment.
Version	String	Read-Only. Returns Microsoft Word's version number.
Visible	Boolean	Set/Get whether Word is visible to the user (True) or not (False).
Width	Long	Set/Get the width of Word's application window.
Windows	Windows	Read-Only. Returns a collection of all the document windows that are open through the Windows collection.

Name	Returns	Description
WindowState	WdWindowState	Set the state of all of Word's document windows. If all of the document windows are of the same state (wdWindowStateMaximize, wdWindowStateMinimize) then the correct state value returns, otherwise wdWindowStateNormal is returned.
WordBasic	Object	Read-Only. Returns an object that allows access to WordBasic commands and function found in older versions of Word (Word 6.0).

Application Methods

Name	Returns	Parameters	Description
Activate	N/A		Makes Word's active document window the topmost window.
Add Address	N/A	TagID() As String, Value() As String	Adds an entry to the address book in Word. The first parameter is a string array of tag IDs for the different parts of an address. The second parameter is a string array of ID values associated with each Tag ID.
Automatic Change	N/A		Causes Word to AutoFormat what the Office Assistant suggested. If the Office Assistant has no suggestions an error occurs.
BuildKey Code	Long	Arg1 As WdKey, [Arg2], [Arg3], [Arg4]	Creates a unique value for keyboard combination given up to four WdKey keyboard parameters. Use with the FindKey property to create KeyCodes.

Table Continued on Following Page

Name	Returns	Parameters	Description
Centimeters ToPoints	Single	Centimeters As Single	Converts the Centimeters parameter to points where 1 cm = 28.35 points.
ChangeFile Open Directory	N/A	Path As String	Changes the document path shown in the File | Open dialog to the Path parameter.
CheckGrammer	Boolean	String As String	Checks the String parameter for grammatical mistakes. Returns True if there are no errors, False if there are errors.
Check Spelling	Boolean	Word As String, [Custom Dictionary], [Ignore Uppercase], [Main Dictionary], [Custom Dictionary2], ... , [Custom Dictionary10]	Checks the Word parameter for spelling mistakes. Returns True if there are no errors, False if there are errors. The names of custom and main dictionaries or dictionary objects can be set using the CustomDictionary parameters and MainDictionary parameters. Capitalization can be ignored by setting the IgnoreUppercase parameter to True.
CleanString	String	String As String	Changes any nonprintable characters like line feeds and bullets in the String parameter to spaces and returns the result.
DDEExecute	N/A	Channel As Long, Command As String	Sends a command to an application using DDE through the given Channel number.

Name	Returns	Parameters	Description
DDEInitiate	Long	App As String, Topic As String	Returns a channel number to use for DDE given an application name and the DDE topic.
DDEPoke	N/A	Channel As Long, Item As String, Data As String	Sends data to an item in an application using DDE through the given Channel number.
DDERequest	String	Channel As Long, Item As String	Returns information, given a specific DDE channel and a requested item.
DDETerminate	N/A	Channel As Long	Closes the specified DDE channel.
DDE TerminateAll	N/A		Closes all the DDE channels opened using Word. The properties starting with DDE are associated with the older technology, Dynamic Data Exchange, which was used to share data between applications.
DefaultWeb Options	Defaul tWebOp tions		Returns the DefaultWebOptions object, which contains application-level attributes used by Word when you save a document as a web page. Allows programmatic changes to items associated with the Web Options dialog.

Table Continued on Following Page

Name	Returns	Parameters	Description
Get Address	String	[Name], [Address Properties], [UseAuto Text], [Display Select Dialog], [Select Dialog], [CheckNames Dialog], [Recent Addresses Choice], [Update Recent Addresses]	Searches for an address in the address book given the name of the addressee with the Name parameter. Returns an address string containing either a custom address string or a generic address depending if the AddressProperties and UseAutoText parameters are used. The address selection dialog can be hidden using the DisplaySelectDialog or displayed in a different manner using the SelectDialog parameter.
GetDefault Theme	String	DocumentType As WdDocument Medium	Returns the name of the default theme that Word uses for your new documents, e-mail messages and web pages. Themes are a set of unified elements such as colors, fonts and graphics. Themes are unlike templates in that they do not contain macros, Autotext entries and shortcut keys.

Name	Returns	Parameters	Description
Get Spelling Suggestions	Spelling Suggestions	(Word As String, [Custom Dictionary], [Ignore Uppercase], [Main Dictionary], [Suggestion Mode], [Custom Dictionary2], [Custom Dictionary3], ... [Custom Dictionary10]	Checks the Word parameter for spelling mistakes. Returns a Spelling Suggestions collection representing the list of suggested spellings for the word. The names of custom and main dictionaries or dictionary objects can be set using the Custom Dictionary parameters and Main Dictionary parameters. Setting the Ignore Uppercase parameter to True will ignore capitalization.
GoBack	N/A		Moves back through the active document to the last three locations where the document was edited. Equivalent to pressing *Shift* + *F5*

Table Continued on Following Page

Name	Returns	Parameters	Description
GoForward	N/A		Moves forward through the active document to the last three locations where the document was edited.
Help	N/A	HelpType	Invokes online help for Word. The HelpType parameter is used to open up different parts of the help system. Two examples of parameter values are WdHelp for the Help topics dialog or WdHelpAbout for Word's about screen.
HelpTool	N/A		Changes the mouse pointer from the regular pointer to a question mark. The user can then get context sensitive help on whatever is clicked next.
InchesTo Points	Single	Inches As Single	Converts the Inches parameter to points and returns the new value. (1 inch = 72 points)
Keyboard	Long	(LangID as Long)	The optional LangID parameter specifies the language and layout settings to which Word should set the keyboard. If the LangID parameter is omitted Keyboard will return the current language and layout setting.
KeyboardBidi	N/A		Sets the keyboard language to one that is right-to-left and sets the text-entry direction to right-to-left also.

Name	Returns	Parameters	Description
Keyboard Latin	N/A		The reverse of KeyboardBidi. Sets the keyboard language to one that is left-to-right and the text-entry direction to left-to-right.
KeyString	String	KeyCode As Long, [KeyCode2]	Returns an English-like phrasing for a given KeyCode where a KeyCode is a unique value representing a keyboard combination (e.g. value returned could be *Shift + F2*).
LinesTo Points	Single	Lines As Single	Converts the Lines parameter to points and returns the new value (1 line = 12 points).
List Commands	N/A	ListAll Commands As Boolean	A new document is created with a table listing of all the Word commands with the keyboard shortcuts and menu locations. If the parameter is True then all Word commands are listed, if it is False only customized commands are listed.
LookupName Properties	N/A	Name As String	Searches for the Name parameter in address book and returns with the address book's **Properties** dialog box if one name is found. If more then one name is found the **Check Names** dialog is returned.
Millimeters ToPoints	Single	Millimeters As Single	Converts the Millimeters parameter to points and returns the new value (1 mm = 2.85 points).

Table Continued on Following Page

Name	Returns	Parameters	Description
Mount Volume	Integer	Zone As String, Server As String, Volume As String, [User], [User Password], [Volume Password]	Connects to network drive on a Macintosh. Generates an error in Windows.
Move	N/A	Left As Long, Top As Long	Moves the active document window's left edge to the Left value and top edge to the Top value.
NewWindow	Window		Creates a new window with the same document as the active window. A colon (:) and a number are tagged on to the old window's caption to create the new window's caption.
NextLetter	N/A		Used in Macintosh systems with PowerTalk mail extensions to open the oldest unread letter from the In Tray. Generates an error in Windows.
OnTime		When, Name As String, [Tolerance]	Used to start a macro passed by the Name parameter at a later time or date. The When parameter must be either a string specifying the time/date or a serial number.

Name	Returns	Parameters	Description
Organizer Copy	N/A	Source As String, Destination As String, Name As String, Object As WdOrganizer Object	Copies a toolbar, style, macro project or AutoText entry named by the Name parameter from the Source template or document to the Destination template or document. The type of object being copied is specified by Object.
Organizer Delete	N/A	Source As String, Name As String, Object As WdOrganizer Object	Deletes a toolbar, style, macro project or AutoText entry named by the Name parameter from the Source template or document. The type of object being deleted is specified by Object.
Organizer Rename	N/A	Source As String, Name As String, NewName As String, Object As WdOrganizer Object	Renames a toolbar, style, macro project or AutoText entry named by the Name parameter from the Source template or document to the NewName parameter. The type of object being renamed is specified by Object.
PicasTo Points	Single	Picas As Single	Converts the Picas parameter to points and returns the new value (1 pica = 12 points).
PixelsTo Points	Single	Pixels As Single, [fVertical]	Converts the Pixels parameter to points and returns the new value. If fVertical is True then converts vertical pixels, else horizontal pixels.

Table Continued on Following Page

Name	Returns	Parameters	Description
PointsTo Centimeters	Single	Points As Single	Converts the Points parameter to centimeters and returns the new value (1 cm = 28.35 points).
PointsTo Inches	Single	Points As Single	Converts the Points parameter to inches and returns the new value (1 inch = 72 points).
PointsTo Lines	Single	Points As Single	Converts the Points parameter to lines and returns the new value (1 line = 12 points).
PointsTo Millimeters	Single	Points As Single	Converts the Points parameter to millimeters and returns the new value (1 mm = 2.835 points).
PointsTo Picas	Single	Points As Single	Converts the Points parameter to picas and returns the new value (1 pica = 12 points).
PointsTo Pixels	Single	Points As Single, [fVertical]	Converts the Points parameter to pixels and returns the new value. If fVertical is True then converts vertical pixels, else horizontal pixels.

Name	Returns	Parameters	Description
PrintOut	N/A	[Background], [Append], [Range], [OutputFile Name], [From], [To], [Item], [Copies], [Pages], [PageType], [PrintTo File], [Collate], [FileName], [Active PrinterMacGX], [ManualDuplex Print], [PrintZoom...]	Prints either part or all of the active document or, if specified, the document from the FileName parameter. If True is passed in the Background parameter then the macro keeps running while the document prints. The other parameters are equivalent to correspondingly named fields in the Print dialog box.
Product Code	String		Microsoft Word's (Globally Unique Identifier) GUID product ID is returned as a string. This ID uniquely identifies a particular Microsoft Word package against other packages of Microsoft Word.
Quit	N/A	[SaveChanges], [Original Format], [Route Document]	Quits the current Word session. Unsaved changes can be saved, ignored, or user-prompted with the SaveChanges parameter. The original format can be saved or ignored with the OriginalFormat parameter.
Repeat	Boolean	[Times]	Repeats the last editing action done. The Times parameter can specify how many times to repeat the last editing action.

Table Continued on Following Page

Name	Returns	Parameters	Description
Reset IgnoreAll	N/A		Resets the list of words that were ignored during the previous spell checks for the active document.
Resize	N/A	Width As Long, Height As Long	Resizes the active document window to the Width and Height parameters.
Run	N/A	MacroName As String,, [varg1], [varg2], ...[varg30]	Runs the macro (Sub procedure) specified in the MacroName parameter. This method can run procedures that require up to 30 parameters.
Screen Refresh	N/A		Refreshes the screen with the latest video information. Typically used when the ScreenUpdating property is set to False.
SendFax	N/A		Starts the process for sending a fax by starting the Fax Wizard.
Set Default Theme	N/A	Name, DocumentType As WdDocument Medium	Sets the default theme or look of next document you create. The Name parameter specifies the name of the theme; DocumentType specifies whether you are assigning the theme to new documents, emails or web pages. Themes are a set of unified elements such as colors, fonts and graphics. Themes are unlike templates in that they do not contain macros, Autotext entries and shortcut keys.

Name	Returns	Parameters	Description
Show Clipboard	N/A		Shows the clipboard on Macintosh systems. Generates an error in Windows.
ShowMe	N/A		If more help is available for a topic then the office assistant or online help pops up. If there is no more information a message pops up stating that no associated Help topic exists.
Substitute Font	N/A	Unavailable Font As String, Substitute Font As String	Substitutes the UnavailableFont parameter with the SubstituteFont parameter. Equivalent to the Font Substitution dialog box in the Options dialog box.
Toggle Keyboard			Switches the keyboard setting between right-to-left and left-to-right.

Application Events

Name	Parameters	Description
Document Before Close	Doc As Document, Cancel As Boolean	Triggered when the user tries to close a document. Set the Cancel parameter to True to cancel the close. Doc is the document the user is trying to close.
Document Before Print	Doc As Document, Cancel As Boolean	Triggered when the user tries to print a document. Set the Cancel parameter to True to cancel the print. Doc is the document the user is trying to print.
Document Before Save	Doc As Document, SaveAsUI As Boolean, Cancel As Boolean	Triggered when the user tries to save a document. Set the Cancel parameter to True to cancel the save. Doc is the document the user is trying to save. If SaveAsUI is set to True the Save As dialog box is shown.

Table Continued on Following Page

Name	Parameters	Description
Document Change		Triggered when a new document is created, when an open document is activated, or when an existing document is opened.
Document Open	Doc As Document	Triggered when a user opens up a document. Doc is the recently opened document.
New Document	Doc As Document	Triggered when a user creates a new document. Doc is the recently created document.
Quit		Triggered when the user quits Word.
Window Activate	Doc As Document, Wn As Window	Triggered when the user activates a document window. Doc is the document displayed in the activated window, Wn.
Window Before Double Click	Sel As Selection, Cancel As Boolean	Triggered when a users tries to double click in a document window. The selected text as a result of the double-click is the Selection object Sel. This action can be canceled by setting the Cancel parameter to True.
Window Before Right Click	Sel As Selection, Cancel As Boolean	Triggered when a users tries to right click in a document window. The selected text as a result of the right-click is the Selection object Sel. This action can be canceled by setting the Cancel parameter to True.
Window Deactivate	Doc As Document, Wn As Window	Triggered when a document window has lost focus.
Window Selection Change	Sel As Selection	Triggered when a user changes the selected text. Sel is the newly selected text.

Examples

All of the examples in this appendix have the `Application` object as their parent. Usually the `Application` reference is left out. For example, the following code adds a shape to the active document. The `Application` reference could easily be removed:

```
Application.ActiveDocument.Shapes.AddShape _
    (msoShapeSmileyFace, 143.85, 153, 126, 72).Select

With Application.Selection.ShapeRange
    .Fill.Visible = msoTrue
    .Fill.Solid
    .Fill.ForeColor.RGB = RGB(255, 255, 255)
    .Fill.Transparency = 0
    .Left = CentimetersToPoints(1.9)
    .Top = CentimetersToPoints(0.07)
    .LockAnchor = False
    .WrapFormat.AllowOverlap = True
    .WrapFormat.Side = wdWrapBoth
    .WrapFormat.DistanceTop = CentimetersToPoints(0)
    .WrapFormat.DistanceBottom = CentimetersToPoints(0)
    .WrapFormat.DistanceLeft = CentimetersToPoints(0.32)
    .WrapFormat.DistanceRight = CentimetersToPoints(0.32)
    .WrapFormat.Type = 3
    .ZOrder 5
End With
```

AutoCaption Object and the AutoCaptions Collection

The `AutoCaptions` collection represents the list of captions that are automatically added whenever certain items like tables, pictures, and other insertable OLE objects are added to documents. Each `AutoCaption` object represents one of the items that can have captions automatically added. To access an `AutoCaption` object use the `AutoCaptions` collections and pass it an insertable item name. Besides the regular collection properties and methods the `AutoCaptions` collection has an additional method called `CancelAutoInsert`. **Invoking this method disables all automatic adding of captions.**

> The items in the `AutoCaptions` collection are displayed in the **AutoCaption** dialog box from the **Insert Caption** menu item.

AutoCaption Common Properties

The `Application`, `Creator`, and `Parent` properties are defined at the beginning of this section.

AutoCaption Properties

Name	Returns	Description
AutoInsert	Boolean	Set/Get whether a caption will be added automatically when this object type is added to a Word document.

Table Continued on Following Page

Name	Returns	Description
CaptionLabel	Variant	Set/Get the caption label that will be added automatically like 'Figure' or 'Table'. The WdCaptionLabelID constants can also be used instead of a string.
Index	Long	Read Only. The position of the current object in the AutoCaptions collection.
Name	String	Read Only. The name of the caption, e.g. "Microsoft Word Table".

Example

Turning on the AutoCaption for Microsoft tables and set the caption to "Table":

```
AutoCaptions("Microsoft Word Table").AutoInsert = True
AutoCaptions("Microsoft Word Table").CaptionLabel = "Table"
```

AutoCorrect Object

Provides the functionality equivalent to the AutoCorrect feature in Word.

AutoCorrect Common Properties

The Application, Creator, and Parent properties are defined at the beginning of this section.

AutoCorrect Properties

Name	Returns	Description
Correct CapsLock	Boolean	Set/Get whether Word automatically corrects typing mistakes made by leaving the *Caps Lo* key on.
Correct Days	Boolean	Set/Get whether Word automatically capitalizes the initial letter of days of the week.
CorrectHangul AndAlphabet	Boolean	Set/Get whether Word automatically applies the correct font to non-Asian words typed in the middle of hangul text and vice versa. (Hangul is the script used for Korean words.)
CorrectInital Caps	Boolean	Set/Get whether Word will automatically change the second letter of a word to lowercase if the first letter is uppercase.

Name	Returns	Description
Correct Keyboard Setting	Boolean	Set/Get whether Word automatically changes words to their native alphabet if text is typed in a language other than the one currently set as the keyboard language. To use the `CorrectKeyboardSetting` property, the `CheckLanguage` property must first be set to `True`.
Correct Sentence Caps	Boolean	Set/Get whether Word will automatically change the first letter of each sentence to uppercase.
Entries	Auto Correct Entries	Read Only. Returns a collection representing the list of current AutoCorrect entries in Word.
FirstLetter AutoAdd	Boolean	Set/Get whether Word automatically adds abbreviations to the `FirstLetterExceptions` collection.
FirstLetter Exceptions	First Letter Exceptions	Read Only. Returns a `FirstLetterExceptions` collection representing the list of abbreviations where Word will not automatically capitalize the letter following the abbreviation.
HangulAnd Alphabet AutoAdd	Boolean	Set/Get whether Korean AutoCorrect exceptions are automatically added.
HangulAnd Alphabet Exceptions	HangulAnd Alphabet Exceptions	Read Only. Returns a collection representing the list of Korean words that will not be `AutoCorrect`ed.
Other Corrections AutoAdd	Boolean	Set/Get whether Word automatically adds words to the `OtherCorrectionsExceptions` collection.
Other Corrections Exceptions	Other Corrections Exceptions	Read Only. Returns an `OtherCorrectionsExceptions` collection representing the list of words that Word will not automatically correct.

Table Continued on Following Page

Name	Returns	Description
ReplaceText	Boolean	Set/Get whether Word will automatically replace certain words with words from the AutoCorrect list.
ReplaceText FromSpelling Checker	Boolean	Set/Get whether Word will automatically replace certain words with words from the current spell check dictionaries.
TwoInitial CapsAutoAdd	Boolean	Set/Get whether Word automatically adds words to the TwoInitialCapExceptions collection.
TwoInital Caps Exception	TwoInitial Caps Exceptions	Read Only. Returns a TwoInitialCapExceptions collection representing the list of words where Word will not automatically change capitalized second letters to lowercase.

AutoCorrectEntry Object and the AutoCorrectEntries Collection

The AutoCorrectEntries collection holds a list of words and their AutoCorrect entries. The Entries property of the AutoCorrect object has to be used to access the AutoCorrectEntries collection.

Besides the regular properties and methods associated with collections, the AutoCorrectEntries has two methods to add AutoCorrect entries and create AutoCorrectEntry objects. The Add method of the AutoCorrectEntries collection adds AutoCorrect entries using the Name and Value parameters. The AddRichText method uses the Name and Range parameters to add AutoCorrect entries while preserving formatting.

AutoCorrectEntry Common Properties

The Application, Creator, and Parent properties are defined at the beginning of this section.

AutoCorrectEntry Properties

Name	Returns	Description
Index	Long	Read Only. The position of the current object in the parent collection.
Name	String	Set/Get the name of the AutoCorrect entry e.g. "The".

Name	Returns	Description
Rich Text	Boolean	Set/Get whether formatting is saved with the AutoCorrect value.
Value	String	Set/Get the value of the AutoCorrect entry e.g. "The".

AutoCorrectEntry Methods

Name	Returns	Parameters	Description
Apply	N/A	Range As Range	Substitute the range specified by the Range parameter with the AutoCorrectEntry's Value property.
Delete	N/A		Deletes the AutoCorrectEntry object.

Example

Adding an AutoCorrect entry to the AutoCorrectEntries collection, displaying a message box with the value of the entry and then deleting it:

```
Dim  AutEntry As AutoCorrectEntry

Set AutEntry = AutoCorrect.Entries.Add("Manger", "Manager")
MsgBox "Value is " & AutEntry.Value
AutEntry.Delete
```

AutoTextEntry Object and the AutoTextEntries Collection

Provides the functionality equivalent to the AutoText feature of Word. Used to keep 'boilerplate' text and associated formatting for often-used phrases, such as legal phrases and closings in letters.

The AutoTextEntries collection has two additional methods available to it besides the regular collection properties and methods. The Add method of the AutoTextEntries collection adds an AutoText entry to the existing list using the Name and Range parameters. An AutoTextEntry object is returned by the Add method. The AppendToSpike method of the AutoTextEntries collection adds the text and formatting specified by a Range parameter to the built-in "Spike" AutoTextEntry object and deletes the Range in the original document.

> The items in the AutoTextEntries collection are displayed in the **AutoText** tab of the **AutoCorrect** dialog box under the **Tools** menu.

AutoTextEntry Common Properties

The Application, Creator, and Parent properties are defined at the beginning of this section.

AutoTextEntry Properties

Name	Returns	Description
Index	Long	Read Only. The position of the current object in the AutoTextEntries collection.
Name	String	Set/Get the AutoText entry name.
StyleName	String	Read Only. The style name of the formatting applied to the AutoText entry.
Value	String	Set/Get the AutoText entry's text value.

AutoTextEntry Methods

Name	Returns	Parameters	Description
Delete	N/A		Deletes the AutoTextEntry object.
Insert	Range	Where As Range, [RichText]	Inserts the contents of the AutoText entry into the Range parameter provided.

Example

Adding an AutoText entry specified by the selected text, displaying the value of the AutoText, and then inserting it back into the current selection:

```
Dim AutText As AutoTextEntry

Set AutText = NormalTemplate.AutoTextEntries.Add("CurText", _
                    ActiveDocument.Range)
MsgBox "Value is " & AutText.Value
AutText.Insert ActiveDocument.Range
```

Bookmark Object and the Bookmarks Collection

Provides the functionality equivalent to the Bookmark feature of Word. The Bookmarks collection represents a list of bookmarks associated with the Selection, Range, or Document.

The Bookmarks collection has two properties and two methods besides the usual collection properties and methods: the DefaultSorting property, ShowHidden property, Add method, and the Exists method. The DefaultSorting property uses the WdBookmarkSortBy constants to set the order that bookmarks will be displayed in the Bookmark dialog box. If the ShowHidden property is set to True then hidden bookmarks are listed in the Bookmarks collection and displayed in the Bookmark dialog box.

The `Add` method adds a `Bookmark` to the `Bookmarks` collection using the `Name` and `Range` parameters. The `Exists` method is used to check if the bookmark named in the `Name` parameter exists.

> The items in the `Bookmarks` collection are displayed in the **Bookmark** dialog box (**Insert** menu).

Bookmark Common Properties

The `Application`, `Creator`, and `Parent` properties are defined at the beginning of this section.

Bookmark Properties

Name	Returns	Description
Column	Boolean	Read Only. Returns whether the `Bookmark` object is a table column.
Empty	Boolean	Read-Only. Returns whether the `Bookmark` object marks just a location and not a selection of text.
End	Long	Set/Get the end position of the `Bookmark` object.
Name	String	Read Only. Returns the bookmark name.
Range	Range	Read Only. Returns the part of the document that the bookmark is associated with.
Start	Long	Set/Get the start position of the `Bookmark` object.
StoryType	WdStoryType	Read Only. Returns one of the `WdStoryType` constants describing the area of the document that the bookmark is located in (e.g. `wdFootNotesStory`, or `wdMainTextStory`).

Bookmark Methods

Name	Returns	Parameters	Description
Copy	Bookmark	Name As String	Sets the `Bookmark` object to the bookmark named in the `Name` parameter.
Delete	N/A		Deletes the `Bookmark` object.
Select	N/A		Selects the bookmark specified by the `Bookmark` object.

Examples

Display the end location of the bookmark named "One" and then delete it:

```
MsgBox ActiveDocument.Bookmarks("One").End
ActiveDocument.Bookmarks("One").Delete
```

Border Object and the Borders Collection

The `Borders` collection represents all of the borders that are around a specific object. The types of objects that can have borders are: `Cell`, `Cells`, `Column`, `Columns`, `Font`, `Frame`, `InlineShape`, `Paragraph`, `ParagraphFormat`, `Paragraphs`, `Range`, `Row`, `Rows`, `Section`, `Selection`, and `Table`. The number of `Border` objects in a `Borders` collection depends on the parent object and cannot be changed. Using one of the `WdBorderType` constants accesses individual `Border` objects.

The `Borders` collection has one method and many properties besides the normal properties and methods associated with a collection. The `ApplyPageBordersToAllSections` method applies the page border format in the current `Border` object to all the sections of the documents. The properties are detailed in the following table:

Borders Collection Special Properties

Name	Returns	Description
AlwaysInFront	Boolean	Set/Get whether page borders are displayed in front of text.
DistanceFrom	WdBorder Distance From	Set/Get if a page border is measured from the page edge or from the inner text edge.
DistanceFromBottom, DistanceFromLeft, DistanceFromRight, DistanceFromTop	Long	Set/Get the space between the appropriate borders and either the text or the page edge.
Enable	Long	Set/Get either a `Boolean` value on whether formatting is applied to the `Borders` collection or a `WdLineStyle` constant describing the line style associated with the borders.
EnableFirstPage InSection, EnableOtherPage InSection	Boolean	Set/Get whether a border is around the first page (EnableFirstPageInSection) and other pages (EnableOtherPageInSection).

Name	Returns	Description
HasHorizontal, HasVertical	Boolean	Read Only. Return whether horizontal borders can be applied to the object and whether vertical borders can be applied.
InsideColor, OutsideColor	WdColor	Set/Get the colors of the inside borders and outside borders respectively using the WdColor constants or a value returned by the RGB function.
InsideColor Index, Outside ColorIndex	WdColor Index	Set/Get the colors of the inside borders and outside borders respectively using the WdColorIndex constants.
InsideLine Style, OutsideLine Style	WdLine Style	Set/Get whether styles are applied the to the inside/outside borders (True or False) or a WdLineStyle constant describing the line style associated with the inside/outside borders.
InsideLine Width, Outside LineWidth	WdLine Width	Set/Get whether line widths are applied the to the inside/outside borders (True or False) or a WdLineWidth constant describing the line width associated with the inside/outside borders.
JoinBorders	Boolean	Set/Get whether table and paragraph borders become attached to page borders by the removal of the table and paragraph vertical borders.
Shadow	Boolean	Set/Get whether shadows are part of the formatting associated with borders.
SurroundFooter, SurroundHeader	Boolean	Set/Get whether page borders surround headers or footers.

Border Common Properties

The Application, Creator, and Parent properties are defined at the beginning of this section.

Border Properties

Name	Returns	Description
ArtStyle	WdPageBorder Art	Set/Get the art design of the page border if the current Border object is a page Border object.

Table Continued on Following Page

Name	Returns	Description
ArtWidth	Long	Set/Get the width of the art style page border.
Color	WdColor	Set/Get the color of the border using the WdColor constants or the RGB function.
ColorIndex	WdColorIndex	Set/Get the color of the border using the WdColorIndex constants.
Inside	Boolean	Read Only. Return whether the border is an inside border.
LineStyle	WdLineStyle	Set/Get the line style of the border using the WdLineStyle constants.
LineWidth	WdLineWidth	Set/Get whether line widths are applied to the border (True or False) or a WdLineWidth constant describing the line width associated with the border.
Visible	Boolean	Set/Get whether the border is visible.

Examples

Set the overall line style of a table to wdLineStyleDot and then set the color of all the borders of the first cell in the first table to red:

```
Dim brd As Border
With ActiveDocument.Tables(1).Borders
        .InsideLineStyle = wdLineStyleDot
        .OutsideLineStyle = wdLineStyleDot
End With

For Each brd in ActiveDocument.Tables(1).Cell(0, 0).Borders
        Brd.Color = wdColorRed
Next
```

Browser Object

The Browser object represents the navigation tool used to move around a document in Word. The Browser object is represented by the three navigation buttons on the vertical scroll bar. The type of navigation includes movement by endnote, footnote, comment, found text, edit, heading, graphic, table, page, section and field.

Browser Common Properties

The Application, Creator, and Parent properties are defined at the beginning of this section.

Browser Properties

Name	Returns	Description
Target	WdBrowse Target	Set/Get the type of movement through a document.

Browser Methods

Name	Returns	Parameters	Description
Next	N/A		Moves the selection to the next point as specified by the Target property.
Previous	N/A		Moves the selection to the previous point as specified by the Target property.

Examples

Go to the beginning of next table from the current position of the insertion point:

```
Application.Browser.Target = wdBrowseComment
Application.Browser.Next
```

CalloutFormat Object

The CalloutFormat object represents the modifications that can be made to line callouts.

CalloutFormat Common Properties

The Application, Creator, and Parent properties are defined at the beginning of this section.

CalloutFormat Properties

Name	Returns	Description
Accent	MsoTri State	Set/Get whether a vertical accent bar is used to separate the callout box from the line. (True/False)
Angle	MsoCallout AngleType	Set/Get the angle of the callout line in relation to the callout box.
Auto Attach	MsoTri State	Set/Get whether a callout line automatically changes where it is attached to on callout box depending on the where the line is pointing (left or right of the callout box).

Table Continued on Following Page

Name	Returns	Description
AutoLength	MsoTri State	Read Only. Return whether the callout line changes sizes automatically if the multi-segment callout box is moved.
Border	MsoTri State	Set/Get whether the callout box has a border around it.
Drop	Single	Read Only. Returns the distance from the callout box to the spot where the callout line is pointing.
DropType	Mso Callout DropType	Read Only. Returns the spot on the callout box that attaches to the callout line.
Gap	Single	Set/Get the distance between the callout line end and the callout box.
Length	Single	Read Only. Returns the length of the first part of a callout line. AutoLength must be False.
Type	Mso Callout Type	Set/Get the type of line callout used.

CalloutFormat Methods

Name	Returns	Parameters	Description
Automatic Length	N/A		Sets the AutoLength property to True.
Custom Drop	N/A	Drop As Single	Sets the distance from the callout box to the spot where the callout line is pointing using the Drop parameter.
Custom Length	N/A	Length As Single	Sets the length of the first part of a callout line to the Length parameter and sets AutoLength to False.
Preset Drop	N/A	DropType As MsoCallout DropType	Sets the spot on the callout box that attaches to the callout line using the DropType parameter.

Example

Turn the borders off on the first callout shape (say the first shape) on the current document and then change the type of callout to the third type of callout:

```
ActiveDocument.Shapes(1).Callout.Border = False
ActiveDocument.Shapes(1).Type = msoCalloutThree
```

CaptionLabel Object and the CaptionLabels Collection

The CaptionLabels collection represents all the caption labels in the application. Caption labels are captions that can automatically be added to tables, figures, equations and other insertable objects. The WdCaptionLabelID constants can be used to access built-in CaptionLabel objects.

Besides the common collection properties and methods the CaptionLabels collection has an Add method. The Add method adds a custom caption label using the Name parameter for the custom label name.

CaptionLabel Common Properties

The Application, Creator, and Parent properties are defined at the beginning of this section.

CaptionLabel Properties

Name	Returns	Description
BuiltIn	Boolean	Read Only. Returns whether the CaptionLabel object is one built into Word or is a custom one.
Chapter Style Level	Long	Set/Get which heading style will be used for chapter numbers in the caption labels. Set IncludeChapterNumber to True first.
ID	WdCaption LabelID	Read Only. If the caption label is built-in then this property returns the type of caption label.
Include Chapter Number	Boolean	Set/Get whether chapter numbers are included with the caption label.
Name	String	Read Only. Returns the caption label name.
Number Style	WdCaption Number Style	Set/Get the number style of the caption label.
Position	WdCaption Position	Set/Get the position of the text of the caption label.
Separator	WdSeparato rType	Set/Get the separator between the chapter number and the sequence number.

CaptionLabel Methods

Name	Returns	Parameters	Description
Delete	N/A		Deletes the `CaptionLabel` object.

Examples

Set the caption labels for all figures to include chapter numbers and the position of the caption labels to be above the figure:

```
With CaptionLabels(wdCaptionFigure)
    .IncludeChapterNumber = True
    .Position = wdCaptionPositionAbove
End With
```

Cell Object and the Cells Collection

The `Cells` collection represents an aggregation of `Cell` objects in a table, row, column, certain selection or a range. The `Parent` of the `Cells` collection determines what the current aggregation is made up of. Each `Cell` object represents a cell in a table.

Besides the regular collection properties and methods, the following table describes other properties and methods that are unique to the `Cells` collection.

Cells Collection Special Properties

Name	Returns	Description
Borders	Borders	Set/Get the borders around the cells in the current parent object.
Height, Width	Single	Set/Get the height of all the `Cell` objects in the `Cells` collection.
HeightRule	WdRow HeightRule	Set/Get the height rules associated with `Cell` objects (e.g. exact height).
Nesting Level	Long	Read Only. Returns how deep the current cells' table is nested within other tables.
Preferred Width	Single	Set/Get the preferred width of the specified cells in the measure set by `PreferredWidthType`.
Preferred WidthType	WdPreferre dWidthType	Set/Get the measure used by `PreferredWidth`.
Shading	Shading	Read Only. Returns an object used to manipulate shading formats.

Name	Returns	Description
Vertical Alignment	WdCellVert icalAlignm ent	Set/Get the vertical alignment of the text in the Cell objects.

Cells Collection Special Methods

Name	Returns	Parameters	Description
Add	Cell	[Before Cell]	Adds a Cell object to the existing collection and optionally places it before the BeforeCell cell object.
AutoFit			Changes the size of the columns associated with the collection to fit to the size of the text, if there is room on the page.
Delete		[Shift Cells]	Deletes the Cells collection and optionally how the remaining cells in the table should be shifted using WdDeleteCells constants.
Distribute Height, Distribute Width			Adjusts the row height or the column width of the Cells collection to be equally distributed among each other.
Merge			Merges all the cells in the Cells collection into one cell.
SetHeight		RowHeight As Single, [Height Rule As WdRow Height Rule]	Sets the height of the cells.

Table Continued on Following Page

Name	Returns	Parameters	Description
SetWidth		ColumnWidth As Single, RulerStyle As WdRulerStyle	Sets the width of the cells.
Split		NumRows As Variant, NumColumns As Variant, MergeBefore Split As Variant	Splits the cells in the Cells collection into rows specified by NumRows and the columns specified by NumColumns. All the cells can be merged first by setting MergeBeforeSplit to True.

Cell Common Properties

The Application, Creator, and Parent properties are defined at the beginning of this section.

Cell Properties

Name	Returns	Description
Borders	Borders	Set/Get the borders around the cell.
BottomPadding	Single	Set/Get the bottom margin for a cell.
Column	Column	Read Only. Returns the Column object that the current cell belongs to.
ColumnIndex	Long	Read Only. Returns the column number that the current cell belongs to.
FitText	Boolean	Set/Get whether the text will fit in the cell by shrinking the font.
Height	Single	Set/Get the height of the cell.
HeightRule	WdRow Height Rule	Set/Get the height rules associated with the cell (e.g. exact height).
ID	String	Set/Get the unique ID for the cell.
LeftPadding	Single	Set/Get the left margin for a cell.
NestingLevel	Long	Read Only. Returns how deep the current cell's table is nested within other tables.

Name	Returns	Description
Next	Cell	Read Only. Returns the next cell after the current cell.
Preferred Width	Single	Set/Get the preferred width of the table in the measure set by PreferredWidthType.
Preferred WidthType	WdPreferred WidthType	Set/Get the measure used by PreferredWidth.
Previous	Cell	Read Only. Returns the previous cell before the current cell.
Range	Range	Read Only. Returns the part of the document that the cell is part of.
Right Padding	Single	Set/Get the right margin for a cell.
Row	Row	Read Only. Returns the Row object that the current cell belongs to.
RowIndex	Long	Read Only. Returns the row number that the current cell belongs to.
Shading	Shading	Read Only. Returns an object used to manipulate shading formats.
Tables	Tables	Read Only. Returns all the tables in the current cell.
TopPadding	Single	Set/Get the top margin for a cell.
Vertical Alignment	WdCell Vertical Alignment	Set/Get the vertical alignment of the text in the cell.
Width	Single	Set/Get the width of the cell.
WordWrap	Boolean	Set/Get whether the text in the cell wraps to the next line.

Cell Methods

Name	Returns	Parameters	Description
AutoSum	N/A		Makes the current cell a Formula field, summing up the cells above or to the left of the current cell.

Table Continued on Following Page

Name	Returns	Parameters	Description
Delete	N/A	[ShiftCells]	Deletes the cell and optionally determines how the remaining cells in the table should be shifted using WdDeleteCells constants.
Formula		[Formula], [NumFormat]	Makes the current cell a Formula field optionally using the Formula parameter as the formula and setting the number format with NumFormat.
Merge		MergeTo As Cell	Merges the current cell with the MergeTo cell.
Select		﹨	Selects (highlights) the current cell allowing manipulation using the Selection object.
Set Height		RowHeight As Single, HeightRule As WdRowHeight Rule	Sets the row height of the cell.
SetWidth		ColumnWidth As Single, RulerStyle As WdRulerStyle	Sets the column width of the cell.
Split		[NumRows], [NumColumns]	Splits the current cells into the rows specified by NumRows and the columns specified by NumColumns.

Examples

Please see the Tables object and the Tables collection for examples.

Characters Collection

The Characters collection holds the collection of characters that make up the parent object. A Range object represents each character.

Characters Common Properties

The Application, Creator, and Parent properties are defined at the beginning of this section.

Characters Properties

Name	Returns	Description
First	Range	Read Only. Returns the first character in the collection.
Last	Range	Read Only. Returns the last character in the collection

Characters Methods

Name	Returns	Parameters	Description
Item	Range	Index As Long	Returns the character in the collection specified by the index in a Range object.

Checkbox Object

A Checkbox object is a certain type of a form field that looks similar to a checkbox. The Checkbox object is only accessed from the FormField object.

Checkbox Common Properties

The Application, Creator, and Parent properties are defined at the beginning of this section.

Checkbox Properties

Name	Returns	Description
AutoSize	Boolean	Set/Get whether the size of the checkbox is set by the fonts of the nearby text (True) or is set by the Size property (False).
Default	Boolean	Set/Get what the default value is for the Checkbox. True = Checked.
Size	Single	Set/Get the size of the checkbox. See AutoSize property.
Valid	Boolean	Read Only. Returns whether the current form field is a valid checkbox form field.
Value	Boolean	Set/Get whether the checkbox is checked. True = Checked.

Examples

Check to see if the first form field is a valid checkbox and not a different type of form field. If it is valid, then set the default value to checked:

```
If ActiveDocument.FormFields(1).CheckBox.Valid = True Then
    ActiveDocument.FormFields(1).CheckBox.Default = True
End If
```

ColorFormat Object

The `ColorFormat` object represents a specific single color used in a gradient or patterned fill.

ColorFormat Common Properties

The `Application`, `Creator`, and `Parent` properties are defined at the beginning of this section.

ColorFormat Properties

Name	Returns	Description
RGB	Long	Set/Get the RGB (red-green-blue) color number using the RGB function.
Type	MsoColorType	Read Only. Returns the color type.

Column Object and the Columns Collection

The `Columns` collection represents an aggregation of `Column` objects in a table, row, certain `Selection` or a `Range`. The `Parent` of the `Columns` collection determines what the current aggregation is made up of. Each `Column` object represents a column in a table.

Besides the regular collection properties and methods, the following table describes other properties and methods that are unique to Columns collections.

Columns Collection Special Properties

Name	Returns	Description
Borders	Borders	Set/Get the borders around the columns in the current parent object.
First, Last	Columns	Read Only. Returns the first and last columns in the collection respectively.
Nesting Level	Long	Read Only. Returns how deep the columns' table is nested within other tables.

Name	Returns	Description
Preferred Width	Single	Set/Get the preferred width of the columns in the measure set by `PreferredWidthType`.
Preferred WidthType	WdPreferred WidthType	Set/Get the measure used by `PreferredWidth`.
Shading	Shading	Read Only. Returns an object used to manipulate shading formats.
Width	Single	Set/Get the width of the columns in the collection.

Columns Collection Special Methods

Name	Returns	Parameters	Description
Add	Column	[Before Column]	Adds a column object to the existing collection and optionally places it after the `BeforeColumn` column object.
AutoFit			Changes the size of the columns in the collection to fit to the size of the text, if there is room on the page.
Delete			Deletes the `Columns` collection.
Distribute Width			Adjusts the column width of the columns to be equally distributed among each other.
Select			Selects (highlights) the columns in the `Columns` collection.
SetWidth		ColumnWidth As Single, RulerStyle As WdRulerStyle	Sets the column width of the columns.

Column Common Properties

The `Application`, `Creator`, and `Parent` properties are defined at the beginning of this section.

Column Properties

Name	Returns	Description
Borders	Borders	Set/Get the borders around the column.
Cells	Cells	Read Only. Returns the `Cells` collection that makes up the column.
Index	Long	Read Only. Returns the column's position in the `Columns` collection.
IsFirst	Boolean	Read Only. Returns whether the column is the first column of the table.
IsLast	Boolean	Read Only. Returns whether the column is the last column of the table.
Nesting Level	Long	Read Only. Returns how deep the current column's table is nested within other tables.
Next	Column	Read Only. Returns the next column after the current column.
Preferred Width	Single	Set/Get the preferred width of the column in the measure set by `PreferredWidthType`.
Preferred WidthType	WdPreferredWidthType	Set/Get the measure used by `PreferredWidth`.
Previous	Column	Read Only. Returns the previous column before the current column.
Shading	Shading	Read Only. Returns an object used to manipulate shading formats.
Width	Single	Set/Get the width of the column.

Column Methods

Name	Returns	Parameters	Description
AutoFit	N/A		Changes the size of the columns in the collection to fit to the size of the text, if there is room on the page.
Delete	N/A		Deletes the current `Column` object.

Name	Returns	Parameters	Description
Select	N/A		Selects (highlights) the current column.
Set Width		ColumnWidth As Single, RulerStyle As WdRulerStyle	Sets the column width of the column.
Sort		[Exclude Header], [SortField Type], [SortOrder], [Case Sensitive], [BidiSort], [IgnoreThe], [Ignore Kashida], [Ignore Diacritics], [IgnoreHe], [LanguageID]	Sorts the cells in the column. Set ExcludeHeader to True to exclude the first row of the column from the sort. The type of sort (alphanumeric, dates) can be defined using SortFieldType and the WdSortFieldType constants. The sort order can be set using SortOrder and the WdSortOrder constants. Set CaseSensitive to True to do a case sensitive sort. Set BidiSort to True to do a sort in a right-to-left language. IgnoreThe, IgnoreKashida, IgnoreDiacritics and IgnoreHe are all used when sorting right-to-left languages. LanguageID specifies the sorting language and can be one of the WdLanguageID constants.

Examples

See Table object and the Tables collection for examples.

COMAddIn Object and the COMAddIns Collection

The COMAddIns collection represents the list of COM components available to Word. Each COMAddIn object is equivalent to a single COM add-in available in Word.

Besides the typical properties and methods associated with a collection object, the COMAddIns collection has an Update method. The Update method updates the list of COMAddIn objects in the COMAddIns collection with the current list of add-ins stored in the Windows registry.

COMAddln Common Properties

The `Application`, `Creator`, and `Parent` properties are defined at the beginning of this section.

COMAddln Properties

Name	Returns	Description
Connect	Boolean	Set/Get whether the COM add-in is active or 'connected' in Word.
Description	String	Set/Get the description of the COM add-in.
Guid	String	Read Only. Return the GUID (globally unique identifier) for the COM add-in.
Object	Object	Set/Get the COM object that makes up the COM add-in.
ProgID	String	Read Only. Returns the ProgID (programmatic identifier) for the COM add-in.

Examples

Display the description of each COM add-in currently connected in Word:

```
Dim cm As COMAddIn
For Each cm In Application.COMAddIns
    If cm.Connect = True Then
        MsgBox cm.Description
    End If
Next
```

Comment Object and the Comments Collection

A `Comments` collection represents the list of comments in a document, range or selection. Each `Comment` object represents a single comment in a document, range, or selection.

The `Collection` object has a `ShowBy` property and an `Add` method besides the typical collection attributes. The `ShowBy` property along with an `Author` parameter displays the list of comments associated with a particular author. The `Add` method adds a `Comment` object to the `Comments` collection.

Comment Common Properties

The `Application`, `Creator`, and `Parent` properties are defined at the beginning of this section.

Comment Properties

Name	Returns	Description
Author	String	Set/Get the author name for a comment. Changing the Author for one comment will change Author for ALL comments in the document.
Index	Long	Read Only. Returns the position number of the Comment object in the collection.
Initial	String	Set/Get the initials of the author for a comment.
Range	Range	Read Only. Returns the comment.
Reference	Range	Read Only. Returns the part of the document that contains a comment reference mark.
Scope	Range	Read Only. Returns the part of the document that contains the text marked by the comment.
ShowTip	Boolean	Set Get whether a screen tip is displayed when the user hovers over a comment.

Comment Methods

Name	Returns	Parameters	Description
Delete	N/A		Deletes the current comment object.

Examples

Display the first comment and the author of the comment on the active document:

```
MsgBox ActiveDocument.Comments(1).Range.Text
MsgBox ActiveDocument.Comments(1).Author
```

CustomLabel Object and the CustomLabels Collection

The CustomLabels collection represents a list of all custom labels available in Word. Each CustomLabel object represents a single custom-mailing label found in the Label Options dialog box.

The CustomLabel collection has an Add method besides the usual collection properties and methods. The Add method adds a CustomLabel object to the collection using a Name property.

CustomLabel Common Properties

The Application, Creator, and Parent properties are defined at the beginning of this section.

CustomLabel Properties

Name	Returns	Description
DotMatrix	Boolean	Read Only. True if the custom label is for a dot matrix printer.
Height	Single	Set/Get the height of the custom label.
Horizontal Pitch	Single	Set/Get the horizontal gap between the left edge of one custom label and the left edge of the next custom label.
Index	Long	Read Only. Returns the position number of the CustomLabel object in the collection.
Name	String	Set/Get the name of the custom label.
Number Across	Long	Set/Get the number of custom labels across a page.
NumberDown	Long	Set/Get the number of custom labels down a page.
PageSize	WdCustom LabelPage Size	Set/Get the page size for the custom labels.
SideMargin	Single	Set/Get the side margin for the page containing custom labels.
TopMargin	Single	Set/Get the top margin for the page containing custom labels.
Valid	Boolean	Read Only. Indicates that the properties of the label are valid as a whole.
Vertical Pitch	Single	Set/Get the vertical gap between the top of one custom label and the top of the next custom label.
Width	Single	Set/Get the width of the custom label.

CustomLabel Methods

Name	Returns	Parameters	Description
Delete	N/A		Deletes the current CustomLabel object.

Examples

Set the number of labels across and down a page to 5 for a custom label named WroxLabel:

```
Application.MailLabel.CustomLabels("WroxLabel").NumberAcross = 5
Application.MailLabel.CustomLabels("WroxLabel").NumberDown = 5
```

DefaultWebOptions Object

Allows programmatic changes to items associated with the default settings of the Web Options dialog. The `DefaultWebOptions` contains the application-level attributes used by Word when a document is saved as a web page. The attributes specified in `DefaultWebOptions` can be overridden by the document-level attributes held with the `WebOptions` object.

DefaultWebOptions Common Properties

The `Application`, `Creator`, and `Parent` properties are defined at the beginning of this section.

DefaultWebOptions Properties

Name	Returns	Description
AllowPNG	Boolean	Set/Get whether Portable Network Graphics Format (PNG) is allowed as an output format when you save a document as a web page. PNG is a file format for the lossless, portable, well-compressed storage of images.
AlwaysSave InDefault Encoding	Boolean	Set/Get whether Web pages are always saved in the default encoding.
BrowserLevel	WdBrowser Level	Set/Get what the browser settings to optimize for are (e.g. IE5).
CheckIfOffice IsHTMLEditor	Boolean	Set/Get whether Word checks if Office is the default web editor for Office created pages.
CheckIfWordIs Default HTMLEditor	Boolean	Set/Get whether Word checks if it is the default web editor for non-Office created pages.
Encoding	Mso Encoding	Set/Get the type of encoding to save a document as.

Table Continued on Following Page

Name	Returns	Description
FolderSuffix	String	Read Only. If the OrganizeInFolder and UseLongFileNames properties are set to True, this property returns the folder suffix that Word uses when you save a document as a web page.
Fonts	WebPage Fonts	Read Only. Returns the WebPageFonts collection. This collection represents the set of fonts that Word uses if a web page is opened and there is either no font information specified in the web page or the current default font cannot display the character set.
OptimizeFor Browser	Boolean	Set/Get whether the document should be optimized for the browser specified in the BrowserLevel property.
OrganizeIn Folder	Boolean	Set/Get whether supporting files are organized in a folder.
PixelsPer Inch	Long	Set/Get the density of graphics images and table cells on the web page.
RelyOnCSS	Boolean	Set/Get whether Cascading Style Sheets (CSS) is used for font formatting.
RelyOnVML	Boolean	Set/Get whether image files are not generated from drawing objects when you save a document. You can reduce file sizes by not generating images for drawing objects and relying on VML. Vector Markup Language (VML) is used to display graphics in some browsers (including Internet Explorer 5.0). VML is an XML-based format for high-quality vector graphics on the Web. You should set this property to False if you targeting older web browsers.
ScreenSize	Mso Screen Size	Set/Get the ideal minimum screen size that should be used when viewing the saved document.
UpdateLinks OnSave	Boolean	Set/Get whether links are updated every time the document is saved.
UseLongFile Names	Boolean	Set/Get whether long file names are used whenever possible. If UseLongFileNames is set to False the DOS file name format of 8.3 is used instead.

Dialog Object and the Dialogs Collection

The `Dialogs` collection represents the list of dialog boxes that are built into word. The `WdWordDialog` constants are used to access an individual `Dialog` objects in the `Dialogs` collection. A `Dialog` object represents a single built-in Word dialog box. Each Dialog object will have additional custom properties depending on what type of Dialog object it is.

Dialog Common Properties

The `Application`, `Creator`, and `Parent` properties are defined at the beginning of this section.

Dialog Properties

Name	Returns	Description
CommandName	String	Read Only. Returns the name of the command associated with the dialog box.
DefaultTab	WdWord DialogTab	Set/Get the active tab in the dialog box.
Type	WdWord Dialog	Read Only. Returns the dialog box type.

Dialog Methods

Name	Returns	Parameters	Description
Display	Long	[TimeOut]	Displays the dialog box but does not execute the dialog box settings.
Execute	N/A		Executes the dialog box settings.
Show	Long	[TimeOut]	Displays and executes the dialog box settings.
Update	N/A		Updates the values in the dialog box.

Examples

Display a File Open dialog box:

```
Application.Dialogs(wdDialogFileOpen).Show
```

Dictionary Object and the Dictionaries Collection

The Dictionaries collection represents the list of custom dictionaries currently active in the Word session. Each Dictionary object represents a single custom dictionary active in Word. The CustomDictionaries property of the Application object is used to access the Dictionaries collection containing the currently active dictionaries in the active document. A Dictionary object can also be associated with languages. Each Language object in the Languages collection holds a list of all the different types of dictionaries associated with a specific language. Each type of dictionary in the Languages collection is a Dictionary object.

The Dictionaries collection has some other properties and methods besides the common properties and methods. The ActiveCustomDictionary property is used to specify which Dictionary object will have new words added to it. The Maximum property returns the maximum amount of custom dictionaries that Word can use at a time. The Add method is used to add Dictionary objects to the Dictionaries collection. The ClearAll method is used to clear all of the Dictionary objects from the Dictionaries collection.

The Languages collection is discussed in Languages Collection.

Dictionary Common Properties

The Application, Creator, and Parent properties are defined at the beginning of this section.

Dictionary Properties

Name	Returns	Description
LanguageID	WdLanguage ID	Set/Get the language associated with the dictionary.
Language Specific	Boolean	Set/Get whether only text of the language specified by the LanguageID is checked.
Name	String	Read Only. Returns the dictionary's file name.
Path	String	Read Only. Returns the dictionary's file path.
ReadOnly	Boolean	Read Only. Returns whether the dictionary is a main dictionary that cannot be altered (True) or a custom dictionary that can be changed (False).
Type	Wd Dictionary Type	Read Only. Returns the type of dictionary (e.g. grammar, spelling).

Dictionary Methods

Name	Returns	Parameters	Description
Delete	N/A		Deletes the current Dictionary object.

Examples

Add a custom dictionary and set it to be the active custom dictionary:

```
Dim Dict As Dictionary
Set Dict = Application.CustomDictionaries.Add("Wrox.dic")
Application.CustomDictionaries.ActiveCustomDictionary = Dict
```

Document Object and the Documents Collection

This object and collection represent the second most important object of the Word Object Model (the first being the Application object). Most VBA programming in Word will involve the Documents collection and the Document object. The Documents collection holds the list of currently open documents in Word. Each open document in Word is equivalent to a Document object.

The Documents collection is the main programmatic way to open, close, and create documents. There should be no surprise that there are additional methods besides the standard collection methods. The table below outlines the four important methods of the Documents collection:

Documents Collection Special Methods

Name	Returns	Parameters	Description
Add	Document	[Template], [New Template], [Document Type], [Visible]	Adds a Document object to the current Documents collection and displays it in Word if the Visible parameter is set to True. The Template parameter specifies the template to base the new document on (NormalTemplate by default). If the NewTemplate parameter is True then the new document is opened as a new template. The DocumentType parameter uses the wdDocumentType constants to specify the type of document to create.

Table Continued on Following Page

Name	Returns	Parameters	Description
Close		[Save Changes], [Original Format], [Route Document]	Closes all of currently open documents. Unsaved changes can be saved, ignored, or user prompted with the SaveChanges parameter. The original format can be saved or ignored with the OriginalFormat parameter.
Open	Document	FileName, [Confirm Conversions], [ReadOnly], [AddToRecent Files], [Password Document], [Password Template], [Revert], [Write Password Document], [Write Password Template], [Format], [Encoding], [Visible]	Adds a Document object to the Documents collection and opens up the document specified by the FileName. Whether to open the file as read only, convert the file automatically, add it to the recent files list and other File Open options can be specified with the other parameters.
Save		[NoPrompt], [Original Format]	Saves all the documents in the Documents collection and can optionally suppress the user prompt.

Document Common Properties

The Application, Creator, and Parent properties are defined at the beginning of this section.

Document Properties

Document Properties

Name	Returns	Description
ActiveTheme	String	Read Only. Returns name of current theme in use on this document. Themes are sets of unified design elements (fonts, colors and graphics) that enhance the appearance of your documents, emails and web pages.
ActiveThem DisplayName	String	Read Only. Returns the descriptive name of active theme.
ActiveWindow	Window	Read Only. Returns the Window object that contains the document.
Active WritingStyle	String	LanguageID parameter. Set/Get the writing style associated with the language in the LanguageID parameter.
Attached Template	Variant	Set/Get the Template object that is associated with the document.
Auto Hyphenation	Boolean	Set/Get whether hyphenation is automatic for the current document.
Background	Shape	Read Only. Returns the background image being used for the document.
Bookmarks	Bookmarks	Read Only. Returns the list of bookmarks in the document.
BuiltIn Document Properties	Object	Read Only. Returns a DocumentProperties collection representing all of the Word defined attributes of the document (e.g. Author).
Characters	Characters	Read Only. Returns the collection of characters for the entire document.
ClickAnd Type Paragraph Style	Variant	Read and Write. Used to define text style and format used for the new "Click and Type" utility in Word 2000, if enabled.
CodeName	String	Read Only. Returns the name the document uses in VBA macros (e.g. ThisDocument).
CommandBars	Command Bars	Read-Only. A CommandBars collection object representing all of the menus and toolbars available in Word.

Table Continued on Following Page

351

Name	Returns	Description
Comments	Comments	Read Only. The collection of comments for the document.
Compatibility	Boolean	Type As WdCompatibilty parameter. Whether the current document compatible features described by the Type parameter are turned on.
Consecutive HyphensLimit	Long	Set/Get the maximum number of lines in a row that can have hyphenation at the end of the line.
Container	Object	Read Only. Returns the OLE object containing the Word document.
Content	Range	Read Only. Returns the Range of the main document body.
Custom Document Properties	Object	Read Only. Returns the DocumentProperties collection, allowing manipulation and addition of custom document properties.
DefaultTab Stop	Single	Set/Get the number of points between the default tab stops in the document.
Email	Email	Read Only. Returns an Email object.
EmbedTrue TypeFonts	Boolean	Set/Get whether TrueType fonts are saved with the document.
Endnotes	Endnotes	Read Only. A collection of all the end notes for the document.
Envelope	Envelope	Read Only. Returns the envelope used for the current document.
FarEastLine BreakLanguage	WdFarEast LineBreak Language ID	Set/Get the East-Asian line break language.
FarEastLine BreakLevel	WdFarEast LineBreak Level	Set/Get the line break control level.
Fields	Fields	Read Only. Returns the collection of fields in the document.
Footnotes	Footnotes	Read Only. Returns the collection of footnotes in the document.

Name	Returns	Description
FormFields	FormFields	Read Only. Returns the collection of form fields in the document.
FormsDesign	Boolean	Read Only. Returns whether the document is in form design mode.
Frames	Frames	Read Only. Returns the collection of frames in the document.
Frameset	Frameset	Read Only. Returns a Frameset object that represents a single frame on a frames page or an entire frames page.
FullName	String	Read Only. Returns the path and document filename.
Grammar Checked	Boolean	Set/Get whether the grammar has been checked for the document.
Grammatical Errors	Proofreading Errors	Read Only. Returns the sentence collection of grammatical errors in the document.
GridDistance Horizontal	Single	Set/Get the horizontal space between Word's AutoShape or East Asian character gridlines.
GridDistance Vertical	Single	Set/Get the vertical space between Word's AutoShape or East Asian character gridlines.
GridOrigin FromMargin	Boolean	Set/Get whether the character grid starts from the upper left margin.
GridOrigin Horizontal	Single	Set/Get horizontal start of Word's AutoShape or East Asian character gridlines.
GridOrigin Vertical	Single	Set/Get vertical start of Word's AutoShape or East Asian character gridlines.
GridSpace Between Horizontal Lines	Long	Set/Get the horizontal space between Word's print layout gridlines.
GridSpace Between VerticalLines	Long	Set/Get the vertical space between Word's print layout gridlines.

Table Continued on Following Page

Name	Returns	Description
HasMailer	Boolean	Indicates whether or not document has associated mailing information (label, etc).
HasPassword	Boolean	Read Only. Return whether a password is required to open the document.
HasRouting Slip	Boolean	Set/Get whether a routing slip is attached to the document.
HTMLProject	HTMLProject	Read Only. Returns the HTML project that the Word document is associated with.
Hyperlinks	Hyperlinks	Read Only. Returns the collection of hyperlinks in the document.
HyphenateCaps	Boolean	Set/Get whether words that are capitalized can be hyphenated.
Hyphenation Zone	Long	Set/Get the point that hyphenation starts at the end of a line.
Indexes	Indexes	Read Only. Returns the collection of indexes in the document.
InlineShapes	InlineShapes	Read Only. Returns the collection of inline shapes in the document.
IsMaster Document	Boolean	Read Only. Returns whether the current document is a master document that includes subdocuments.
IsSubdocument	Boolean	Read Only. Returns whether the current document is a subdocument.
Justification Mode	WdJustificat ionMode	Set/Get the amount of spacing used between letters.
KerningBy Algorithm	Boolean	Set/Get whether kerning of half-width characters is executed.
Kind	WdDocumentKi nd	Set/Get whether the document is an email or letter 'kind'.
Language Detected	Boolean	Set/Get whether multiple languages are detected in the document.
List Paragraphs	List Paragraphs	Read Only. Returns the collection of numbered paragraphs in the document.

Name	Returns	Description
Lists	Lists	Read Only. Returns the collection of lists in the document.
ListTemplates	List Templates	Read Only. Returns the collection of list formats in the document.
Mailer	Mailer	Read Only Returns an object manipulating mailing properties. Macintosh only.
MailMerge	MailMerge	Read Only. Returns an object that can creates mail merges for the document.
Name	String	Read Only. The document filename.
NoLineBreak After	String	Set/Get the kinsoku characters after which Word should not break a line.
NoLineBreak Before	String	Set/Get the kinsoku characters before which Word should not break a line.
OpenEncoding	Mso Encoding	Read Only. Return the file-encoding format (character set and other formatting information) of the file at time of opening, such as UTF8, Japanese, etc...
OptimizeFor Word97	Boolean	Set/Get whether the document is optimized for Word 97.
PageSetup	PageSetup	Read Only. Returns an object that allows manipulation of the page setup for the current document.
Paragraphs	Paragraphs	Read Only. Returns the collection of paragraphs in the document.
Password	String	Sets the password that will be needed to open the document.
Path	String	Read Only. The path of the document.
PrintForms Data	Boolean	Set/Get whether Word prints the data on a Word form to the printer (not the Form picture itself).
Print Fractional Widths	Boolean	Set/Get whether the document uses fractional point spacing. Macintosh specific.

Table Continued on Following Page

Name	Returns	Description
PrintPost ScriptOver Text	Boolean	Set/Get whether special characters are used when printing if the document has PRINT field instructions.
Print Revisions	Boolean	Set/Get whether revisions are printed with the document.
Protection Type	WdProtection Type	Read Only. Returns the type of protection used on a document.
Readability Statistics	Readability Statistics	Read Only. Returns an object holding the readability statistics on the current document.
ReadOnly	Boolean	Read Only. Returns whether document changes can be saved (False).
ReadOnly Recommended	Boolean	Set/Get whether a message box pops up every time the user opens up the document recommending to be opened read-only.
Revisions	Revisions	Read Only. Returns a collection of all of the changes made to the document (TrackRevisions must be True).
Routed	Boolean	Read Only. Returns whether the document has been routed to the next recipient.
RoutingSlip	RoutingSlip	Read Only. Returns an object holding the routing slip information.
Saved	Boolean	Set/Get whether the document has been saved.
SaveEncoding	MsoEncoding	See OpenEncoding (above). Defines encoding format used to save document.
SaveFormat	Long	Read Only. Returns how the document will be saved using either the WdSaveFormat constants or an external file converter number.
SaveFormsData	Boolean	Set/Get whether form data is saved as tab-delimited data.

Name	Returns	Description
SaveSubset Fonts	Boolean	Set/Get whether a part of the full TrueType font is saved with the document.
Scripts	Scripts	Read Only. Returns the collection of HTML scripts associated with the document.
Sections	Sections	Read Only. Returns the collection of sections in the document.
Sentences	Sentences	Read Only. Returns the collection of sentences in the document.
Shapes	Shapes	Read Only. Returns the collection of shapes in the document.
Show Grammatical Errors	Boolean	Set/Get whether grammatical errors are shown to the user with green wavy lines.
Show Revisions	Boolean	Set/Get whether revisions are shown to the user.
ShowSpelling Errors	Boolean	Set/Get whether spelling errors are shown to the user with red wavy lines.
ShowSummary	Boolean	Set/Get whether an automatic summary is displayed.
SnapToGrid	Boolean	Set/Get whether AutoShapes and East Asian characters align automatically to the grid.
SnapToShapes	Boolean	Set/Get whether AutoShapes or East Asian characters align automatically with other AutoShapes or East Asian characters.
Spelling Checked	Boolean	Set/Get whether the current document has been spell checked.
Spelling Errors	Proofreading Errors	Read Only. Returns the collection of spelling errors in the document.
StoryRanges	StoryRanges	Read Only. Returns the collection of all the stories (document sections) in the document.
Styles	Styles	Read Only. Returns the styles collection for a document.

Table Continued on Following Page

Name	Returns	Description
Subdocuments	Subdocuments	Read Only. Returns a list of all the subdocuments of the current document.
Summary Length	Long	Set/Get the percentage of summary length compared to document length.
Summary ViewMode	WdSummary Mode	Set/Get how a summary is viewed (e.g. key points highlighted).
Tables	Tables	Read Only. Returns the collection of tables in the document.
TablesOf Authorities	TablesOf Authorities	Read Only. Returns the collection of table of authorities in the document.
TablesOf Authorities Categories	TablesOf Authorities Categories	Read Only. Returns the collection of tables of authority categories in the document.
TablesOf Contents	TablesOf Contents	Read Only. Returns the tables of contents for the document.
TablesOf Figures	TablesOf Figures	Read Only. Returns the tables of figures for a document.
Track Revisions	Boolean	Set/Get whether revisions are tracked.
Type	WdDocument Type	Set/Get what the current document type is (e.g. template).
UpdateStyles OnOpen	Boolean	Set/Get whether styles in a document are updated from the attached template every time a document is opened.
UserControl	Boolean	True if the current document was started by the user and False if the current document was started programmatically through Automation. Used by applications using Word programmatically.
Variables	Variables	Read Only. Returns the collection of variables used in a document.
VBASigned	Boolean	Read Only. Return whether the VBA macro code has been digitally signed.
VBProject	VBProject	Read Only. Returns an object allowing access to the VB project associated with the document.

Name	Returns	Description
Versions	Versions	Read Only. Returns the collection of versions associated with the current document.
WebOptions	WebOptions	Read Only. Returns an object manipulating the web options in Word.
Windows	Windows	Read Only. Returns the collection of Windows associated with the current document (e.g. `Wrox.doc:1`, `Wrox.doc:2`).
Words	Words	Read Only. Returns the collection of words in the document.
WritePassword	String	Write Only. Sets the password so changes can't be saved to the document.
WriteReserved	Boolean	Read Only. Returns whether a `WritePassword` is associated with the document (i.e. can changes be made to the document).

Document Methods

Name	Returns	Parameters	Description
AcceptAllRevisions			Accepts all of the revisions made to a document.
Activate			Activates the document making it the document with focus.
AddToFavorites			Adds a shortcut of the document to the Favorites folder.
ApplyTheme		Name	Applies style elements associated with the named theme to the current document.
AutoFormat			Formats the document to the property set by the `Kind` property.

Table Continued on Following Page

Name	Returns	Parameters	Description
Auto Summarize	Range	[Length], [Mode], [Update Properties]	Creates a summary of the document. Same as the AutoSummarize feature in Word's Tools menu.
Check Consistency			Searches the text of a Japanese language document. Shows all instances of inconsistent character usage for the same word.
Check Grammar			Checks the grammar for the current document.
Check Spelling		[Custom Dictionary], [Ignore Uppercase], [Always Suggest], [Main Dictionary], [Custom Dictionary2], ..., [Custom Dictionary10]	Checks the spelling for the current document. The names of custom and main dictionaries or dictionary objects can be set using the CustomDictionary parameters and MainDictionary parameters. Capitalization can be ignored by setting the IgnoreUppercase parameter to True.
Close		[Save Changes], [Original Format], [Route Document]	Closes the document. Unsaved changes can be saved, ignored, or user-prompted with the SaveChanges parameter. The original format can be saved or ignored with the OriginalFormat parameter.
ClosePrint Preview			Closes the print preview screen in the document.

Name	Returns	Parameters	Description
Compare		Name As String	Compares the current document to the one specified in the Name parameter. Revisions are used to show the differences.
Compute Statistics	Long	Statistic As WdStatistic, [Include FootnotesAnd EndNotes]	Calculates certain statistics as specified by the Statistic parameter and returns the computed value.
Convert NumbersTo Text		[NumberType]	Converts all the list numbers and paragraph numbers in a document to text.
CopyStyles FromTemplate		Template	Copies the styles from the Template parameter to the current document.
Count Numbered Items	Long	[Number Type], [Level]	Returns the number of bullets or numbered lists in the document. The NumberType parameter can be used with the WdNumberType constants to specify the type of numbering to count. The Level parameter is used to only count a certain level in the numbered list.
CreateLetter Content	Letter Content	Many	Creates a LetterContent object equivalent to the letter wizard. The RunLetterWizard method can then be used to actually create the letter.

Table Continued on Following Page

Name	Returns	Parameters	Description
DataForm			Shows the Data Form dialog to the end user, usually used in mail mergers or delimited text processing.
Detect Language			Detect the language associated with the document.
Edition Options		Type As WdEdtionType, Option As WdEdtionOption, Name As String, [Format]	Sets options for the selected publisher. Not available on Windows platforms.
FitToPages			Word tries to decrease the total document pages by one by decreasing font sizes.
Follow Hyperlink		Address, [SubAddress], [NewWindow], [AddHistory], [ExtraInfo], [Method], [HeaderInfo]	Opens up the target document specified by the address. May be a local document or a URL. Setting NewWindow to True opens up a new window with the target document. Set AddHistory to True to display the item in history folder. Use the Method parameter to choose if the ExtraInfo parameter is sent as a Get or a Post.
GetCross Reference Items	Variant	ReferenceType	Returns an array of variants for the specified ReferenceType. See the Cross-reference dialog box in the Insert menu.

Name	Returns	Parameters	Description
GetLetter Content	LetterCo ntent		Allows access to the LetterContent object.
Goto	Range	[What], [Which], [Count], [Name]	Goes to a certain spot in a document returning a Range object specifying the start of the new spot. This method can be used to go to a certain type of thing (What), moving a specific way (Which) a number of times (Count) or to a certain named object (Name).
Make Compatibility Default			Makes the items in the Compatibility tab (under Tools I Options) the default settings for new documents.
Manual Hyphenation			Goes through all the potential hyphenations in a document and allows the user to use suggestions or not.
Merge		FileName As String	Merges the revision-marked changes in the current document into the FileName document.
Post			Posts the current document to a user-prompted Microsoft Exchange folder.
PresentIt			Opens the current document in PowerPoint.

Table Continued on Following Page

Name	Returns	Parameters	Description
PrintOut		[Background], [Append], [Range], [OutputFile Name], [From], [To], [Item], [Copies], [Pages], [PageType], [PrintToFile], [Collate], [ActivePrinter MacGX], [ManualDuplex Print], [PrintZoom...]	Prints either part or the entire document. If True is passed in the Background parameter then the macro keeps running while the document prints. The other parameters are equivalent to correspondingly named fields in the Print dialog box.
Print Preview			Invokes Word's print preview.
Protect		Type As WdProtection Type, [NoReset], [Password]	Protects the current document from certain or all modifications as specified by the Type parameter. A 'full access' password can be specified with the Password parameter.
Range	**Range**	[Start], [End]	Returns a Range object specified by the starting character position and ending character position.
Redo	**Boolean**	[Times]	Reverses what was undone by the Undo method. The number of redone actions can be [Times].
RejectAll Revisions			Rejects all the revisions made to the document.
Reload			Refreshes the hyperlinked document from its source.

Name	Returns	Parameters	Description
ReloadAs		Encoding As MsoEncoding	Refreshes the document using the specified document encoding (Unicode, Arabic, etc).
Remove Numbers		[NumberType]	Removes all or only NumberType numbering and bullets in lists and paragraphs from the current document.
Remove Theme			Removes the styles applied through the theme feature. See the Theme menu option under the Format menu.
Repaginate			Repaginates the document.
Reply			If document is a mailed item, this method is used to initiate a reply.
ReplyAll			As above, but all recipients are included.
Route			Routes the document using the information specified by the RoutingSlip object.
RunAuto Macro		Which As Long	Runs one of the Auto macros specified by the WdAutoMacros constants.
RunLetter Wizard		[LetterConten t], [WizardMode]	Runs the Letter Wizard. If a LetterContent object is supplied the Letter Wizard will have these items prefilled.
Save			Saves the current document.

Table Continued on Following Page

Name	Returns	Parameters	Description
SaveAs		[FileName], [FileFormat], [LockComments], [Password], [AddToRecent Files], [Write Password], [ReadOnly Recommended], [EmbedTrueType Fonts], [SaveNative PictureFormat], [SaveForms Data], [SaveAsAOCE Letter]	Saves the current document with the path and filename in the FileName parameter and with the FileFormat format. Set a password with the Password parameter. The other parameters are used in the same way as in the **Save As** dialog box.
Select			Selects the entire document.
SendFax		Address As String, [Subject]	Sends the current document as a fax.
SendMail			Sends the current document through MAPI mail server. See the SendMailAttach property of the Options object for more on how the document is sent.
Send Mailer		[FileFormat], [Priority]	Macintosh Only. Sends the current document by using the PowerTalk mailer.
SetLetter Content		[LetterContent]	Sets the LetterContent object used by the document and inserts LetterContent into the document.
Toggle Forms Design			Toggle whether the form design view is on or not.

Name	Returns	Parameters	Description
Undo	Boolean	[Times]	Undoes the last action done to the document. The number of actions that are undone can be [Times].
UndoClear			Clears the actions that can be undone.
Unprotect		[Password]	Unprotects the current document from whatever editing restrictions were put on it. A password can be passed as a parameter.
Update Styles			The styles in a document are updated from the attached template.
Update Summary Properties			Updates the values in the Properties dialog box (under File) with the most current data.
ViewCode			If the document is being controlled by OLE automation then this method displays the code window for the ActiveX control currently selected.
View Property Browser			If the document is being controlled by OLE automation then this method displays the property window for the ActiveX control currently selected.
WebPage Preview			Invokes Word's web page preview.

Document Events

Name	Parameters	Description
Close		Triggered when a document is closed.
New		Triggered when a document is created based on a template with this event.
Open		Triggered when a document is opened.

Examples

Create a new document and type the text "This is a Wrox Document." in it. Set a write password of "Wrox" on the document; print it out, and save the document as `Wrox.Doc`:

```
Dim NewDoc As Document
    Dim Sel As Selection
    Set NewDoc = Documents.Add

    NewDoc.Range.Select
    Selection.TypeText "This is a Wrox Document."
    NewDoc.WritePassword = "Wrox"
    NewDoc.SaveAs "C:\Wrox.Doc"
    NewDoc.PrintOut

    NewDoc.Close
```

DropCap Object

The `DropCap` object is used to create a dropped capital letter of the first letter in a paragraph. Only one `DropCap` object can be a child for a `Paragraph` object.

> A `DropCap` object is equivalent to the **Drop Cap** dialog box from the **F̲ormat** menu.

DropCap Common Properties

The `Application`, `Creator`, and `Parent` properties are defined at the beginning of this section.

DropCap Properties

Name	Returns	Description
DistanceFro mText	Single	Set/Get the horizontal distance between the dropped capital letter and the rest of the paragraph.
FontName	String	Set/Get the font name of the dropped capital letter.
LinesToDrop	Long	Set/Get how many lines high the dropped capital letter is.
Position	WdDropPosi tion	Set/Get how the dropped capital letter appears in the paragraph.

DropCap Methods

Name	Returns	Parameters	Description
Clear			Sets the dropped capital letter back to a normal letter.
Enable			Sets the dropped capital letter for the parent paragraph.

Examples

Sets a dropped capital letter with four lines of height for the first paragraph in the active document:

```
ActiveDocument.Paragraphs(1).DropCap.Enable
ActiveDocument.Paragraphs(1).DropCap.LinesToDrop = 4
```

DropDown Object

A DropDown object is a certain type of a form field that looks like a dropdown combo box. The DropDown object is only accessed from the FormField object.

DropDown Common Properties

The Application, Creator, and Parent properties are defined at the beginning of this section.

DropDown Properties

Name	Returns	Description
Default	Long	Set/Get what the default value is for the DropDown as an index.
ListEntries	List Entries	Read Only. Returns the list of items contained in the Dropdown.
Valid	Boolean	Read Only. Returns whether the current form field is a valid dropdown form field.
Value	Long	Set/Get the number of the currently selected dropdown item.

Examples

Display the current item number that is currently selected in a dropdown:

```
MsgBox ActiveDocument.FormFields(1).DropDown.Value
```

Email, EmailAuthor, EmailOptions and EmailSignature Objects

These objects all relate to mailing options when using Word as your email editor. The different objects are detailed in the following tables.

Email, EmailAuthor, EmailOptions and EmailSignature Common Properties

The `Application`, `Creator`, and `Parent` properties are defined at the beginning of this section.

Email Properties

The `Email` object represents an email message. There can only be one `Email` object for each `Document` object.

Name	Returns	Description
Current EmailAuthor	Email Author	Read-Only. Returns the details associated with the current author.

EmailAuthor Properties

The `EmailAuthor` object represents the author of the email message. There can only be one `EmailAuthor` object for each `Email` object.

Name	Returns	Description
Style	Style	Read Only. Returns the format style details associated with the author.

EmailOptions Properties

The `EmailOptions` object holds the application-level attributes used by Word when you create and edit email messages.

Name	Returns	Description
Compose Style	Style	Read Only. Returns the style formatting associated with the email.
Email Signature	Email Signature	Read Only. Returns the signature details.
Mark Comments	Boolean	Set/Get whether to mark the user's comments in the email messages.
Mark Comments With	String	Set/Get what string Word uses to mark the comments.

Name	Returns	Description
Reply Style	Style	Read Only. Returns the style properties associated with a reply.
ThemeName	String	Set/Get the name of the HTML theme and its formatting options to use for email.
UseTheme Style	Boolean	Set/Get whether to use the style defined by the default theme.

EmailSignature Properties

The EmailSignature object holds information about the signatures used by Word in email messages. There is only one EmailSignature object for each EmailOptions object.

Name	Returns	Description
NewMessage Signature	String	Set/Get the signature for a new message.
ReplyMessage Signature	String	Set/Get the signature used when replying to messages.

Endnote Object and the Endnotes Collection

An Endnotes collection represents the list of endnotes in a document, range or selection. Each Endnote object represents a single endnote in a document, range, or selection.

The Endnotes collection has many properties and methods besides the typical ones for collections. The properties and methods are listed below:

Endnotes Collection Special Properties

Name	Returns	Description
Continuation Notice	Range	Read Only. Returns the range in the text containing the endnote continuation notice.
Continuation Separator	Range	Read Only. Returns the range in the text containing the endnote continuation separator.
Location	WdEndnote Location	Set/Get where the endnotes are going to be put (e.g. end of document).

Table Continued on Following Page

Name	Returns	Description
Numbering Rule	WdNumbering Rule	Set/Get how endnote numbering is effected after section breaks.
Numbering Style	WdNote Numbering Style	Set/Get what the number style is for the endnotes.
Separator	Range	Read Only. Returns the range in the text containing the endnote separator (e.g. a line).
Starting Number	Long	Set/Get the starting number for the endnotes.

Endnotes Collection Special Methods

Name	Returns	Parameters	Description
Add	Endnote	Range As Range, [Reference], [Text]	Adds an endnote (Text) at the Range parameter with the Reference mark.
Convert			Converts an endnote to a footnote.
Reset Continuation Notice			Resets the continuation notice to the default notice.
Reset Continuation Separator			Resets the continuation separator to the default separator.
Reset Separator			Resets the separator to the default separator.
SwapWith Footnotes			Converts all endnotes to footnotes and vice versa.

Endnote Common Properties

The Application, Creator, and Parent properties are defined at the beginning of this section.

Endnote Properties

Name	Returns	Description
Index	Long	Read Only. Returns the position number of the Endnote object in the collection.
Range	Range	Read Only. Returns the spot in the document with the endnote text.
Reference	Range	Read Only. Returns the spot in the document that is marked as having an endnote.

Endnote Methods

Name	Returns	Parameters	Description
Delete			Deletes the current Endnote object.

Examples

Set endnotes to appear at the end of the document and set the text color of the first endnote comment to blue:

```
ActiveDocument.Endnotes.Location = wdEndOfDocument
ActiveDocument.Endnotes(1).Range.Font.ColorIndex=wdBlue
```

Envelope Object

The Envelope object represents the single envelope available for a Document object.

> An Envelope object should always be inserted into a document first before using it to avoid errors accessing properties such as Address, AddressFromleft, AddressFromTop, FeedSource, ReturnAddress, ReturnAddressFromLeft, ReturnAddressFromTop, and UpdateDocument.

Envelope Common Properties

The Application, Creator, and Parent properties are defined at the beginning of this section.

Envelope Properties

Name	Returns	Description
Address	Range	Read Only. Returns the spot in the associated document that contains the delivery address of the envelope.

Table Continued on Following Page

Name	Returns	Description
AddressFrom Left	Single	Set/Get the horizontal distance between the left edge of the envelope and the delivery address.
AddressFrom Top	Single	Set/Get the vertical distance between the top edge of the envelope and the delivery address.
AddressStyle	Style	Read Only. Returns the styles associated with the delivery address.
DefaultFace Up	Boolean	Set/Get whether the envelope is feed face up in the printer by default.
Default Height	Single	Set/Get the default height of the envelope.
DefaultOmit Return Address	Boolean	Set/Get whether the returns address is omitted by default.
Default Orientation	Wd Envelope Orientation	Set/Get the default placement of an envelope when feeding the envelope to the printer (e.g. wdRightLandscape).
DefaultPrint BarCode	Boolean	Set/Get whether the U.S. POSTNET bar code is added to the envelope by default.
DefaultPrint FIMA	Boolean	Set/Get whether a Facing Identification Mark (FIM-A) is added to envelopes by default. For U.S. only.
DefaultSize	String	Set/Get the default paper size for envelopes (e.g. Size 10).
DefaultWidth	Single	Set/Get the default width of the envelope.
FeedSource	WdPaperTray	Set/Get the how the envelopes are fed into the printer.
Return Address	Range	Read Only. Returns the spot in the associated document that contains the return address of the envelope
Return AddressFrom Left	Single	Set/Get the horizontal distance between the left edge of the envelope and the return address.

Name	Returns	Description
Return AddressFrom Top	Single	Set/Get the vertical distance between the top edge of the envelope and the return address.
Return AddressStyle	Style	Read Only. Returns the styles associated with the return address.

Envelope Methods

Name	Returns	Parameters	Description
Insert		Many	Inserts an envelope into the beginning of the parent Document object. The parameters correspond to the properties mentioned above.
PrintOut		Many	Prints an envelope but does not add it to the parent Document object. The parameters are the same as the Insert method.
Update Document			Updates the envelope contained in the parent Document object with the current property settings.

Examples

Insert an envelope into the active document and sets the delivery address to be the first three paragraphs:

```
Dim rng As Range
Dim lStart As Long
Dim lEnd As Long

'Find the point that starts the first paragraph
lStart = ActiveDocument.Range.Paragraphs(1).Range.Start
'Find the point that ends the third paragraph
lEnd = ActiveDocument.Range.Paragraphs(3).Range.End
'Put the points together to define the range of the
'first three paragraphs
Set rng = ActiveDocument.Range(lStart, lEnd)
'Insert the address at the specified range
ActiveDocument.Envelope.Insert Address:=rng.Text
```

Field Object and the Fields Collection

A Fields collection represents the list of fields in the parent document, range or selection. Each Field object represents a single field in the parent collection.

The Fields collection has a few properties and methods besides the typical ones for collections. The properties and methods are listed below.

Fields Collection Special Property

Name	Returns	Description
Locked	Long	Set/Get whether editing is allowed for all the Field objects in the collection.

Fields Collection Special Methods

Name	Returns	Parameters	Description
Add	Field	Range As Range, [Type], [Text], [Preserve Formatting]	Adds a Field object to the Fields collection at the Range position. The Type of field and whether formatting is preserved can also be specified.
Toggle Show Codes			Toggle between showing the field code and showing the visual part or the result part of the field for all fields.
Unlink			Converts all fields in the collection to text or graphics.
Update	Long		Updates all the field results.
Update Source			Method. Saves the results of INCLUDETEXT fields back to the source.

Field Common Properties

The Application, Creator, and Parent properties are defined at the beginning of this section.

Field Properties

Name	Returns	Description
Code	Range	Set/Get the Range object containing the field's code.
Data	String	Set/Get the data for an ADDIN field only.
Index	Long	Read Only. Returns the position number of the Field object in the collection.

Name	Returns	Description
Inline Shape	Inline Shape	Read Only. Returns a reference to a picture or other insertable object in an INCLUDEPICTURE or EMBED field.
Kind	WdField Kind	Read Only. Returns the type of link of the field.
Link Format	LinkFormat	Read Only. Returns the linking options for a field that has files or pictures linked to it.
Locked	Boolean	Set/Get whether editing is allowed in the field.
Next	Field	Read Only. Returns the next field in the collection.
OLEFormat	OLEFormat	Read Only. Returns the OLE properties for the field.
Previous	Field	Read Only. Returns the previous field in the collection.
Result	Range	Set/Get the spot in the document that contains the results of the field.
ShowCodes	Boolean	Toggle between showing the field code and showing the visual part or the result part of the field.
Type	WdField Type	Read Only. Returns the type of the current Field object.

Field Methods

Name	Returns	Parameters	Description
Copy			Copies the Field object to the clipboard.
Cut			Copies the Field object to the clipboard and deletes the original from the document.
Delete			Deletes the current Field object
DoClick			Triggers the 'click' reaction of a Field object if any.
Select			Selects the Field object in the document.

Table Continued on Following Page

Name	Returns	Parameters	Description
Unlink			Converts the field to text or graphics.
Update	Boolean		Updates the field results.
Update Source			Saves the results of INCLUDETEXT field back to the source.

Examples

Add a field holding the name of the current document to the current selection point overwriting the existing contents:

```
ActiveDocument.Fields.Add Selection.Range, wdFieldFileName
```

FileConverter Object and the FileConverters Collection

A `FileConverters` collection holds all of the file converters available in Word. The `FileConverter` object represents one of the file converters in Word such as a `WordPerfect` file converter.

The `FileConverters` collection has one additional property besides the typical collection properties and methods: the `ConvertMacWordChevrons` property. This property is used to set or get how Word treats chevron characters (<< >>). Chevron characters are used in Word for Mac 4.5 and 5.0 to enclose mail merge fields. This property helps decide whether to convert chevron-enclosed text as mail-merge fields.

FileConverter Common Properties

The `Application`, `Creator`, and `Parent` properties are defined at the beginning of this section.

FileConverter Properties

Name	Returns	Description
CanOpen	Boolean	Read Only. Returns whether the file converter is used to open files.
CanSave	Boolean	Read Only. Returns whether the file converter is used to save files.
ClassName	String	Read Only. Returns the underlying unique name for the file converter.
Extensions	String	Read Only. Returns the file extensions associated with the file converter.

Name	Returns	Description
FormatName	String	Read Only. Returns the descriptive name for the file converter.
Name	String	Read Only. Returns the file converter file name.
OpenFormat	Long	Read Only. Returns an internal (use one of the WdOpenFormat constants) or external (number) file converter format.
Path	String	Read Only. Returns the file converter file path.
SaveFormat	Long	Read Only. Returns an internal (use one of the WdSaveFormat constants) or external (number) file converter format.

Examples

Display a message box describing whether the first file format can or cannot be used when opening files:

```
If Application.FileConverters(1).CanOpen Then
    MsgBox "File converter named " & _
    FileConverters(1).FormatName & _
    " can be used when opening files."
Else
    MsgBox "File converter named " & _
    FileConverters(1).FormatName & _
    " cannot be used when opening files."
End If
```

FillFormat Object

The FillFormat object represents the fill effects available for shapes. A FillFormat object can only be access through a Shape object.

FillFormat Common Properties

The Application, Creator, and Parent properties are defined at the beginning of this section.

FillFormat Properties

Name	Returns	Description
BackColor	ColorFormat	Read Only. Returns the background color through the ColorFormat object.
ForeColor	ColorFormat	Read Only. Returns the foreground color through the ColorFormat object.
Gradient ColorType	MsoGradient ColorType	Read Only. Returns what type of gradient fill color concept is used.

Table Continued on Following Page

Name	Returns	Description
Gradient Degree	Single	Read Only. Returns how dark or light the gradient fill is.
Gradient Style	MsoGradient Style	Read Only. Returns the orientation of the gradient that is used.
Gradient Variant	Long	Read Only. Returns the variant (equivalent to the Variants displayed on the Gradient tab of the Fill Effects dialog box) used for the gradient as an integer from 1 to 4. If GradientStyle is msoGradientFromCenter, either 1 or 2 will be returned.
Pattern	MsoPattern Type	Read Only. Returns the pattern used for the fill, if any.
Preset GradientType	MsoPreset GradientType	Read Only. Returns the type of preset gradient that is used.
Preset Texture	MsoPreset Texture	Read Only. Returns the non-custom texture of the fill.
TextureName	String	Read Only. Returns the custom texture name of the fill.
TextureType	MsoTexture Type	Read Only. Returns whether the texture is custom, preset, or mixed.
Transparency	Single	Set/Get how transparent the fill is, from 0 (opaque) to 1 (clear)
Type	MsoFillType	Read Only. Returns if the fill is a texture, gradient, solid, background, picture or mixed.
Visible	MsoTriState	Set/Get whether the fill options are visible in the parent shape.

FillFormat Methods

Name	Returns	Parameters	Description
OneColor Gradient		Style As MsoGradient STyle, Variant As Long, Degree As Single	Set the style, variant and degree for a one color gradient fill.

Name	Returns	Parameters	Description
Patterned		Pattern As MsoPattern Type	Set the pattern for a fill.
Preset Gradient		Style As MsoGradient Style, Variant As Long, Preset Gradient Type As MsoPreset GradientType	Choose the style, variant, and preset gradient type for a gradient fill.
Preset Textured		PresetTexture As MsoPreset Texture	Set the preset texture for a fill.
Solid			Set the fill to a solid color.
TwoColor Gradient		Style As MsoGradient Style, Variant As Long	Set the style for a two-color gradient fill.
User Picture		PictureFile As String	Set the fill to the picture in the PictureFile format.
User Textured		TextureFile As String	Set the custom texture for a fill with the TextureFile format.

Examples

Add a star pattern to the active document and set the pattern to dark vertical lines:

```
With ActiveDocument.Shapes.AddShape(msoShape8pointStar, 50, 50, 150,
150).Fill
    .Patterned msoPatternDarkVertical
End With
```

Find Object

The Find object represents the <u>F</u>ind And Replace dialog box in Word. The same functionality is provided as the dialog box. The Find object can be accessed from the Range and Selection objects.

Find Common Properties

The Application, Creator, and Parent properties are defined at the beginning of this section.

Find Properties

Name	Returns	Description
Correct HangulEndings	Boolean	Set/Get if Word automatically corrects hangul endings when replacing hangul text.
Font	Font	Set/Get the font type to search for.
Format	Boolean	Set/Get whether formatting is included when doing a search.
Forward	Boolean	Set/Get whether the search will move forward from the current selection point.
Found	Boolean	Read Only. Returns whether the searched item was found.
Frame	Frame	Read Only. Returns an object allowing search criteria for text in frames
Highlight	Long	Set/Get whether highlighted text is also searched.
LanguageID	WdLanguageID	Set/Get the language to search for.
LanguageID FarEast	WdLanguageID	Set/Get the East Asian language to search for.
LanguageID Other	WdLanguageID	Set/Get the language to search for. Microsoft recommends using this property to set/get the language of Latin (e.g. English, Spanish, German etc) text in a document that has been created in a right-to-left language version of Word.
MatchAlef Hamza	Boolean	Set/Get whether certain characters are included in search. Relates to a specific form of letter combination within the Arabic language, similar in some respects to the concept of Diacritics.
MatchAllWord Forms	Boolean	Set/Get whether different grammatical word forms (e.g. tense and plurals) of the Text property are searched.
MatchByte	Boolean	Set/Get whether the search is "half-width characters" sensitive.
MatchCase	Boolean	Set/Get whether the search and replace is case sensitive.

Name	Returns	Description
MatchControl	Boolean	Set/Get whether search ignores bidirectional control characters in a right-to-left language document.
Match Diacritics	Boolean	Set/Get whether accent marks are ignored or used in a search of a right-to-left language document.
MatchFuzzy	Boolean	Set/Get whether nonspecific Japanese searches can be used.
MatchKashida	Boolean	Set/Get whether certain characters are included in search. Relates to the use of Arabic within Word.
MatchSounds Like	Boolean	Set / Get whether words that sound like the Text property are searched for as well.
MatchWhole Word	Boolean	Set / Get whether only whole words that match the Text property are searched for.
Match Wildcards	Boolean	Set/Get whether wildcards can be used in the Text property.
NoProofing	Long	Set/Get whether Word finds or replaces text that the spelling and grammar checker has ignored.
Paragraph Format	Paragraph Format	Set/Get the paragraph formatting that is searched for.
Replacement	Replacement	Read Only. Returns an object that allows you to set the replacement option for a find and replace operation.
Style	Variant	Set/Get the style format that is searched for.
Text	String	Set/Get the search text.
Wrap	WdFindWrap	Set/Get what should happen if the search reaches the end or beginning of the document.

Find Methods

Name	Returns	Parameters	Description
ClearAll Fuzzy Options			Clears all of the nonspecific Japanese search criteria.
Clear Formatting			Clears any previously set formatting search criteria.
Execute	Boolean	Many	Executes a search returning True if the search was successful. The parameters correspond to the properties mentioned in the Properties section.
SetAll Fuzzy Options			Sets all of the nonspecific search criteria in Japanese text.

Examples

Find the word "One" in the current document:

```
With Selection.Find
    .Text = "One"
    .Forward = True
    .MatchWholeWord = True
End With
If Selection.Find.Execute=True Then
    MsgBox "Find Successful"
Else
    Msgbox "Find Failed"
Endif
```

FirstLetterException Object and the FirstLetterExceptions Collection

The FirstLetterExceptions collection represents the list of exceptions to the 'Capitalize the first letter after a period' rule of the AutoCorrect object. Each FirstLetterException object represents an abbreviation that is not included in the AutoCorrect object capitalization rule. The FirstLetterExceptions collection can only be accessed through the AutoCorrect object.

The FirstLetterExceptions collection has an Add method in addition to the regular collection properties and methods. The Add method is used to add FirstLetterException objects to the collection.

FirstLetterException Common Properties

The Application, Creator, and Parent properties are defined at the beginning of this section.

FirstLetterException Properties

Name	Returns	Description
Index	Long	Read Only. Returns the position of the FirstLetterException object in the collection.
Name	String	Read Only. Returns the name of the FirstLetterException object, which is the word itself.

FirstLetterException Methods

Name	Returns	Parameters	Description
Delete			Deletes the · FirstLetterException object.

Examples

Add an exception to the First Letter Capitalization rule for the abbreviation "mgmt.":

```
Application.AutoCorrect.FirstLetterExceptions.Add "mgmt."
```

Font Object

The Font object contains all the different information associated with a font. For example the font name, size and effects are stored in the Font object. Find, ListLevel, Range, Replacement, Selection and Style objects can be the parents of the Font object. Some of the following properties only apply to some parent objects.

Font Common Properties

The Application, Creator, and Parent properties are defined at the beginning of this section.

Font Properties

Name	Returns	Description
AllCaps	Long	Set/Get whether the selected font will only contain capital letters.
Animation	WdAnimation	Set/Get the animation type associated with the selected font.
Bold	Long	Set/Get whether the selected font is bold.

Table Continued on Following Page

Name	Returns	Description
BoldBi		Set/Get whether the selected font is bold. This property applies to text written in right-to-left languages.
Borders	Borders	Set/Get the borders around the selected font.
Color	WdColor	Set/Get the color of the selected font.
ColorIndex	WdColor Index	Set/Get the color of the selected font.
ColorIndex Bi	WdColor Index	Set/Get the color of the selected font. This property applies to text written in right-to-left languages.
Diacritic Color	WdColor	Set/Get a separate color for accent marks on the selected characters.
Disable Character SpaceGrid	Boolean	Set/Get whether Word ignores the setting for the number of characters per line on the Document Grid tab of the Page Setup dialog. The character spacing grid is used in East Asian versions of Word.
Double Strike Through	Long	Set/Get whether the selected font has a double strikethrough effect.
Duplicate	Font	Read Only. Duplicates the font's characteristics with the returned Font object.
Emboss	Long	Set/Get whether the selected font has an embossed effect.
Emphasis Mark	WdEmphasis Mark	Set/Get the emphasis mark for a specific character or characters.
Engrave	Long	Set/Get whether the selected font has an engraved effect.
Hidden	Long	Set/Get whether the selected font is hidden.
Italic	Long	Set/Get whether the selected font has an italic effect.
ItalicBi	Long	Set/Get whether the selected font has an italic effect. This property applies to text written in a right-to-left language.

Name	Returns	Description
Kerning	Single	Set/Get how small the font can be for Word to still adjust kerning.
Name	String	Set/Get the name of the font.
NameAscii	String	Set/Get the name of the font used for ASCII characters (character set 0-127).
NameBi	String	Set/Get a font name in a document written in a right-to-left language.
NameFar East	String	Set/Get a Far East font name.
NameOther	String	Set/Get the name of the font used for non-ASCII characters (character set >127).
Outline	Long	Set/Get whether the selected font has an outline effect.
Position	Long	Set/Get how high (positive value) or low (negative value) a font is from a base line.
Scaling	Long	Set/Get how wide or narrow a font is as a percentage of its original value.
Shading	Shading	Read Only. Returns an object used to manipulate shading formats.
Shadow	Long	Set/ Get whether the selected font has a shadow effect.
Size	Single	Set/Get the size of the selected font.
SizeBi	Single	Set/Get the size of the selected font. This property applies to text written in a right-to-left language.
SmallCaps	Long	Set/Get whether the selected font is formatted as small capital letters.
Spacing	Single	Set/Get the spacing between characters in the font.
Strike Through	Long	Set/Get whether the selected font has a strikethrough effect.
Subscript	Long	Set/Get whether the selected font is a subscript.

Table Continued on Following Page

Name	Returns	Description
Superscript	Long	Set/Get whether the selected font is a superscript.
Underline	WdUnderline	Set/Get whether the selected font has an underline effect and its type.
Underline Color	WdColor	Set/Get the color of the underline for underline text.

Font Methods

Name	Returns	Parameters	Description
Grow			Increases the size of the font to next available size.
Reset			Removes any formatting not set by the font's style.
SetAs Template Default			Set the current font as the Normal style font for the template that the current document is based on.
Shrink			Decreases the size of the font to next available size.

Examples

Set the font of the current selection to bold Times New Roman:

```
Selection.Font.Bold = True
Selection.Font.Name = "Times New Roman"
```

FontNames Object

The FontNames object returns a list of all the available fonts in Word. The FontNames object is really a collection of strings. The collection has the same properties and methods associated with a regular collection.

Examples

Display the first font in the FontName object:

```
MsgBox FontNames(1)
```

Footnote Object and the Footnotes Collection

A Footnotes collection represents the list of footnotes in a document, range or selection. Each Footnote object represents a single footnote in a document, range, or selection.

The Footnotes collection has many properties and methods besides the typical ones for collections. The properties and methods are listed below:

Footnotes Collection Special Properties

Name	Returns	Description
Continuation Notice	Range	Read Only. Returns the range in the text containing the footnote continuation notice.
Continuation Separator	Range	Read Only. Returns the range in the text containing the footnote continuation separator.
Location	WdFootnote Location	Set/Get where the footnotes are going to be put (e.g. bottom of page).
NumberingRule	WdNumbering Rule	Set/Get how footnote numbering is effected after page or section breaks.
NumberStyle	WdNoteNumber Style	Set/Get what the number style is for the footnote.
Separator	Range	Read Only. Returns the range in the text containing the footnote separator (e.g. a line).
StartingNumber	Long	Set/Get the starting number for the footnotes.

Footnotes Collection Special Methods

Name	Returns	Parameters	Description
Add	Footnote	Range As Range, [Reference], [Text]	Adds a footnote (Text) at the Range parameter with the Reference mark.
Convert			Converts a footnote to an endnote.

Table Continued on Following Page

Name	Returns	Parameters	Description
Reset Continuation Notice			Resets the continuation notice to the default notice.
Reset Continuation Separator			Resets the continuation separator to the default separator.
Reset Separator			Resets the separator to the default separator.
SwapWith Endnotes			Converts all footnotes to endnotes and vice versa.

Footnote Common Properties

The `Application`, `Creator`, and `Parent` properties are defined at the beginning of this section.

Footnote Properties

Name	Returns	Description
Index	Long	Read Only. Returns the position number of the `Footnote` object in the collection.
Range	Range	Read Only. Returns the spot in the document with the footnote text.
Reference	Range	Read Only. Returns the spot in the document that is marked as having a footnote.

Footnote Methods

Name	Returns	Parameters	Description
Delete			Deletes the current `Endnote` object.

Examples

Set footnotes to appear at the end of the page and set the text color of the first footnote comment to red:

```
ActiveDocument.Footnotes.Location = wdEndOfPage
ActiveDocument.Footnotes(1).Range.Font.ColorIndex = wdRed
```

FormField Object and the FormFields Collection

A `FormFields` collection represents the list of form fields in a document, range or selection. Each `FormField` object represents a single form field in a document, range, or selection. A form field can be a `CheckBox`, a `DropDown`, or a `TextInput` type of form field.

The FormFields collection has an `Add` method and a `Shaded` property besides the typical properties and methods associated with a collection. The `Add` method adds a `FormField` object of the `Type` type (either a `DropDown`, `TextInput`, or `Checkbox` type) at the spot specified by the `Range` parameter. The `Shaded` property sets whether the form fields are shaded or not. The FormFields collection can be accessed from the `Document`, `Range`, and `Selection` objects.

FormField Common Properties

The `Application`, `Creator`, and `Parent` properties are defined at the beginning of this section.

FormField Properties

Name	Returns	Description
CalculateOn Exit	Boolean	Set/Get whether any fields that reference the current field should have their references updated whenever exiting the current field.
CheckBox	CheckBox	Read Only. Returns an object allowing manipulation of the checkbox form field.
DropDown	DropDown	Read Only. Returns an object allowing manipulation of the drop-down form field.
Enabled	Boolean	Set/Get whether the data in the form field can be changed.
EntryMacro	String	Set/Get the macro to run whenever the form field gets focus.
ExitMacro	String	Set/Get the macro to run whenever the form field loses focus.
HelpText	String	Set/Get the *F1* help associated with the form field.
Name	String	Set/Get the name of the form field.
Next	FormField	Read Only. Returns the next form field in the parent collection.

Table Continued on Following Page

Name	Returns	Description
OwnHelp	Boolean	Set/Get where *F1* help comes from. True for the HelpText property to be the help, False for the AutoText entry named in HelpText to be the help.
OwnStatus	Boolean	Set/Get where the status bar text comes from. True for the StatusText property to be the text, False for the AutoText entry named in StatusText to be the text.
Previous	FormField	Read Only. Returns the previous form field in the parent collection.
Range	Range	Read Only. Returns the spot in the document that contains the form field.
Result	String	Set/Get the content results of the form field.
StatusText	String	Set/Get the status bar text for the form field.
TextInput	TextInput	Read Only. Returns an object allowing manipulation of the text input form field.
Type	WdField Type	Read Only. Returns the type of form field (e.g. checkbox).

FormField Methods

Name	Returns	Parameters	Description
Copy			Copies the FormField object to the clipboard.
Cut			Cuts the FormField object to the clipboard.
Delete			Deletes the FormField object.
Select			Highlights the spot in the document specified by the form field.

Examples

Add a drop-down form field to the current selection:

```
Selection.FormFields.Add Range:=Selection.Range, _
        Type:=wdFieldFormDropDown
```

Frame Object and the Frames Collection

A `Frames` collection represents the list of frames in a document, range or selection. Each `Frame` object represents a single frame in a document, range, or selection.

The `Frames` collection has two methods besides the typical properties and methods of a collection. The `Add` method adds a `Frame` to the spot in the document specified by the `Range` parameter. The `Delete` method deletes all of the frames in the `Frames` collection.

Frame Common Properties

The `Application`, `Creator`, and `Parent` properties are defined at the beginning of this section.

Frame Properties

Name	Returns	Description
Borders	Borders	Set/Get the borders of the current `Frame` object.
Height	Single	Set/Get the height of the `Frame` object.
HeightRule	WdFrameSizeRule	Set/Get if the height of the frame changes depending on the text inside the frame.
Horizontal Distance FromText	Single	Set/Get how far away regular text will be from the frame.
Horizontal Position	Single	Set/Get the horizontal distance between the edge of the frame and the item specified by the `RelativeHorizontalPosition` property. Can be a measurement in points or one of the `WdFramePosition` constants.
LockAnchor	Boolean	Set/Get whether a frame's position can be changed (`True` = No).
Range	Range	Read Only. Returns the spot in the document containing the frame.
Relative Horizontal Position	WdRelative Horizontal Position	Set/Get from where the `HorizontalPosition` property is measured.
Relative Vertical Position	WdRelative Vertical Position	Set/Get from where the `VerticalPosition` property is measured.

Table Continued on Following Page

Name	Returns	Description
Shading	Shading	Read Only. Returns an object used to manipulate shading formats.
TextWrap	Boolean	Set/Get whether outer document text wraps around the frame.
Vertical Distance FromText	Single	Set/Get how far away regular text will be from the frame.
Vertical Position	Single	Set/Get the vertical distance between the edge of the frame and the item specified by RelativeVerticalPosition. Can be a measurement in points or one of the WdFramePosition constants.
Width	Single	Set/Get the width of the Frame object.
WidthRule	WdFrameSize Rule	Set/Get the rule determining the width of the frame.

Frame Methods

Name	Returns	Parameters	Description
Copy			Copies the Frame object to the clipboard.
Cut			Cuts the Frame object to the clipboard.
Delete			Deletes the Frame object.
Select			Highlights the spot in the document specified by the Frame.

Examples

Add a Frame object to the active document's current selection point and set the width of the frame to always be at least 50 points:

```
Dim frm As Frame
Set frm = ActiveDocument.Frames.Add(Selection.Range)
With frm
    .Height = 50
    .HeightRule = wdFrameAtLeast
End With
```

Frameset Object

The `Frameset` object can represent a frames page (known as a frameset) or a single frame on a frames page. A frameset is a web page that is divided into two or more frames. Each frame in the frameset points to another web page or frameset. To access the properties and methods of all the frames on the frames page, use the `Document` object's `Frameset` object (`ActiveWindow.Document.Frameset`). To access the properties and methods of a single frame on the frames page, use the `Pane` object's `Frameset` object (`ActiveWindow.ActivePane.Frameset`).

Frameset Common Properties

The `Application`, `Creator`, and `Parent` properties are defined at the beginning of this section.

Frameset Properties

Name	Returns	Description
ChildFrameset Count	Long	Read Only. Returns the number of child `Frameset` objects of the specified `Frameset` object.
ChildFrameset Item	Frameset	Read Only. Returns the child `Frameset` object specified by the required `Index As Long` parameter.
FrameDefault URL	String	Set/Get the web page or document to be displayed in the specified frame when the frameset is opened.
FrameDisplay Borders	Boolean	Set/Get whether the frames in the frameset have borders displayed.
FrameLinkTo File	Boolean	Set/Get whether the item specified by `FrameDefaultURL` is an external file to which the frame has a link.
FrameName	String	Set/Get the name of the specified frame on the frames page.
FrameResizable	Boolean	Set/Get whether a specified frame can be resized by the user when the frameset is viewed in a web browser.
FrameScrollbar Type	WdScrollbar Type	Set/Get when scroll bars are available for a specified frame when the frameset is viewed in a web browser.

Table Continued on Following Page

Name	Returns	Description
FramesetBorder Color	WdColor	Set/Get the color of the frame borders in the frames page.
FramesetBorder Width	Single	Set/Get the width of the borders of the frames (in points) in the frameset.
Height	Long	Set/Get the height of the Frameset object.
HeightType	WdFramesetSi zeType	Set/Get the height type used by the Height property.
ParentFrameset	Frameset	Read Only. Returns the parent Frameset object of the specified Frameset object.
Type	WdFramesetTy pe	Read Only. Returns the type of Frameset object.
Width	Long	Set/get the width of the Frameset object.
WidthType	WdFramesetSi zeType	Set/Get the width type used by the Width property.

Frameset Methods

Name	Returns	Parameters	Decription
AddNew Frame	Frameset	Where As WdFrameset NewFrame Location	Add a new frame to the frames page. Where sets the location of the new frame in relation to the specified frame.
Delete			Deletes the specified Frameset object.

Examples

Set the borders of the frames in the frames page to be 10 points wide and sea green in color:

```
With ActiveWindow.Document.Frameset
    .FramesetBorderColor = wdColorSeaGreen
    .FramesetBorderWidth = 10
End With
```

Make the frame in the active pane show scrollbars if needed:

```
With ActiveWindow.ActivePane.Frameset
    .FrameScrollbarType = wdScrollbarTypeAuto
End With
```

FreeformBuilder Object

The FreeformBuilder object is used by the parent Shapes collection object to create new 'free hand' shapes. The BuildFreeform method of the Shapes collection is used to return a FreeformBuilder object.

FreeformBuilder Common Properties

The Application, Creator, and Parent properties are defined at the beginning of this section.

FreeformBuilder Methods

Name	Returns	Parameters	Description
AddNodes	N/A	SegmentType As MsoSegmentType, EditingType As MsoEditingType, X1 As Single, Y1 As Single, [X2] As Single, [Y2] As Single ...	This method adds a point in the current shape being drawn. A line is drawn from the current node being added to the last node added. SegmentType describes the type of line to add between the nodes. X1, Y1, X2, Y2, X3, Y3 are used to define the position of the current node being added. The coordinates are taken from the upper-left corner of the document.
Convert ToShape	Shape	[Anchor]	Converts the nodes added above into a Shape object.

Examples

Create a square using the FreeformBuilder object:

```
With ActiveDocument.Shapes.BuildFreeform(msoEditingAuto, 100, 100)
    .AddNodes msoSegmentLine, msoEditingAuto, 200, 100
    .AddNodes msoSegmentLine, msoEditingAuto, 200, 200
    .AddNodes msoSegmentLine, msoEditingAuto, 100, 200
    .AddNodes msoSegmentLine, msoEditingAuto, 100, 100
    .ConvertToShape
End With
```

Global Object

The Global object represents all the methods and properties that can be accessed independently without specifying the Application object parent. Please see the Application object for a definition of all the following properties and methods.

Global Common Properties

The `Application`, `Creator`, and `Parent` properties are defined at the beginning of this section.

Global Properties

Name	Returns
ActiveDocument	Document
ActivePrinter	**String**
ActiveWindow	Window
AddIns	AddIns
AnswerWizard	AnswerWizard
Assistant	Assistant
AutoCaptions	AutoCaptions
AutoCorrect	AutoCorrect
CaptionLabels	CaptionLabels
CommandBars	CommandBars
CustomDictionaries	Dictionaries
CustomizationContext	**Object**
Dialogs	Dialogs
Documents	Documents
FileConverters	FileConverters
FindKey	KeyBinding
FontNames	FontNames
HangulHanjaDictionaries	HangulHanjaConversion Dictionaries
IsObjectValid	**Boolean**
KeyBindings	KeyBindings
KeysBoundTo	KeysBoundTo
LandscapeFontNames	FontNames
Languages	Languages
LanguageSettings	LanguageSettings
ListGalleries	ListGalleries
MacroContainer	**Object**

Name	Returns
Name	String
NormalTemplate	Template
Options	Options
PortraitFontNames	FontNames
PrintPreview	Boolean
RecentFiles	RecentFiles
Selection	Selection
ShowVisualBasicEditor	Boolean
StatusBar	String
SynonymInfo	SynonymInfo
System	System
Tasks	Tasks
Templates	Templates
VBE	VBE
Windows	Windows
WordBasic	Object

Methods

Name	Returns
BuildKeyCode	Long
CentimetersToPoints	Single
ChangeFileOpenDirectory	N/A
CheckSpelling	Boolean
CleanString	String
DDEExecute	N/A
DDEInitiate	Long
DDEPoke	N/A
DDERequest	String
DDETerminate	N/A

Table Continued on Following Page

Name	Returns
DDETerminateAll	N/A
GetSpellingSuggestions	SpellingSuggestions
Help	N/A
InchesToPoints	Single
KeyString	String
LinesToPoints	Single
MillimetersToPoints	Single
NewWindow	Window
PicasToPoints	Single
PixelsToPoints	Single
PointsToCentimeters	Single
PointsToInches	Single
PointsToLines	Single
PointsToMillimeters	Single
PointsToPicas	Single
PointsToPixels	Single
Repeat	Boolean

GroupShapes Collection Object

A GroupShapes collection represents the collection of Shape objects that make up the parent Shape object. The GroupItems property of a Shape object returns the GroupShapes collection. The properties and methods of the GroupShapes collection are the same as those of a regular collection.

Examples

Iterate through the grouped shapes that make up the first shape in the Shapes collection and display the name of each shape:

```
Dim shp As Shape
For Each shp In ActiveDocument.Shapes(1).GroupItems
     MsgBox shp.Name
Next
```

HangulAndAlphabetException Object and the HangulAndAlphabetExceptions Collection

These objects are used in the Korean version of Word. The HangulAndAlphabetExceptions object represents the collection of HangulAndAlphabetException objects. The HangulAndAlphabetException object represents a single hangul or alphabet AutoCorrect exception. The HangulAndAlphabetExceptions collection is accessible via the HangulAndAlphabetExceptions property of the AutoCorrect object.

In addition to the usual properties and methods the HangulAndAlphabetExceptions collection has an Add method, which adds a new AutoCorrect exception that Word should not correct. The Add method takes a Name parameter, a string that is the word that should not be automatically corrected.

HangulAndAlphabetException Common Properties

The Application, Creator, and Parent properties are defined at the beginning of this section.

HangulAndAlphabetException Properties

Name	Returns	Description
Index	Long	Read Only. Returns the position of the HangulAndAlphabetExceptions object in the collection.
Name	String	Read Only. Returns the word that should be ignored by the AutoCorrect feature.

HangulAndAlphabetException Methods

Name	Returns	Parameters	Description
Delete			Deletes the HangulAndAlphabetException AutoCorrect entry.

Example

Using HangulAndAlphabetException is very similar to using the OtherCorrectionsException object. Please see OtherCorrectionsException.

HangulHanjaConversionDictionaries Collection

This collection is used in the Korean version of Word. The
HangulHanjaConversionDictionaries collection represents the list of custom
dictionaries, including the hangul-hanja conversion dictionaries, currently active in the
Word session. Each dictionary has an associated Dictionary object. The
HangulHanjaDictionaries property of the Application object is used to access
the HangulHanjaConversionDictionaries collection.

The HangulHanjaConversionDictionaries collection has some other properties
and methods besides the common properties and methods, which are outlined below:

HangulHanjaConversionDictionaries Properties

Name	Returns	Description
ActiveCustom Dictionary	Dictionary	Set/Get which Dictionary object will have new words added to it.
Builtin Dictionary	Dictionary	Read Only. Returns the main dictionary Word uses when converting between hanja and hangul.
Maximum	Long	Read Only. Returns the maximum amount of conversion dictionaries that Word can use at a time.

HangulHanjaConversionDictionaries Methods

Name	Returns	Parameters	Description
Add	Dictionary	FileName As String	Adds Dictionary objects to the HangulHanjaConversionDictionaries collection as specified by the path given in FileName.
Clear All			Clears all of the Dictionary objects from the HangulHanjaConversionDictionaries collection.

Example

The HangulHanjaConversionDictionaries collection is used in a similar manner
to the Dictionaries collection. Please refer to the example given for using the
Dictionaries object.

HeaderFooter Object and the HeadersFooters Collection

The HeadersFooters collection represents the list of headers and footers in a particular section of a document. The parent object for a HeadersFooters collection is a Section object. The Headers property and Footers property returns the respective HeadersFooters collection. To access individual HeaderFooter objects in the parent collection use the WdHeaderFooterIndex constants.

HeaderFooter Common Properties

The Application, Creator, and Parent properties are defined at the beginning of this section.

HeaderFooter Properties

Name	Returns	Description
Exists	Boolean	Set/Get whether the header or footer exists in the document.
Index	WdHeader FooterIndex	Read Only. Returns the position number of the HeaderFooter object in the collection.
IsHeader	Boolean	Read Only. Returns whether the HeaderFooter object is a header.
LinkTo Previous	Boolean	Set/Get whether the current HeaderFooter object is linked to the previous HeaderFooter object (i.e. same content).
Page Numbers	Page Numbers	Read Only. Returns an object allowing page number manipulation.
Range	Range	Read Only. Returns the spot in the document that contains the header or footer.
Shapes	Shapes	Read Only. Returns the shapes contained in the header or footer.

Examples

Set the header of the active document to "My Document":

```
ActiveDocument.Sections(1).Headers(wdHeaderFooterPrimary). _
    Range.Text = "My Document"
```

HeadingStyle Object and the HeadingStyles Collection

The HeadingStyles collection represents the list of heading styles used to make up a table of contents or a table of figures. Each HeadingStyle object contains a style that can be used to create a table of contents or a table of figures. Possible parents of the HeadingStyles collection are the TableOfContents and the TableOfFigures objects. The HeadingStyles collection has an Add method besides the typical collection properties and methods. The Add method takes a Style object or style name and a heading level number to create a HeadingStyle object.

HeadingStyle Common Properties

The Application, Creator, and Parent properties are defined at the beginning of this section.

HeadingStyle Properties

Name	Returns	Description
Level	Integer	Set/Get the level for the heading style.
Style	Variant	Set/Get the style name, a WdBuiltinStyle constant, or the Style object for the heading style.

HeadingStyle Methods

Name	Returns	Parameters	Description
Delete			Deletes the HeadingStyle object.

Example

Set the "Heading1" style to be a level 1 heading style of the first Table of Contents in the active document:

```
ActiveDocument.TablesOfContents(1).HeadingStyles.Add "Heading1", 1
```

HorizontalLineFormat Object

The HorizontalLineFormat object allows formatting of a horizontal line. The HorizontalLineFormat object is accessible via the HorizontalLineFormat property of the InlineShape object.

HorizontalLineFormat Common Properties

The Application, Creator, and Parent properties are defined at the beginning of this section.

HorizontalLineFormat Properties

Name	Returns	Description
Alignment	WdHorizontal Line Alignment	Set/Get how the line is aligned on the page (e.g. left).
NoShade	Boolean	Set/Get whether the horizontal line should be drawn without 3D shading.
Percent Width	Single	Set/Get the length of the horizontal line as a percentage of the width of the window.
WidthType	WdHorizontal LineWidth Type	Set/Get whether the horizontal line is a fixed width or a percentage of the screen width.

Example

Add a horizontal line at the currently selected point. Draw the line with 3D shading and set its length to be 75% of the window width:

```
Dim inShape As InlineShape
Set inShape = Selection.InlineShapes.AddHorizontalLineStandard

inShape.HorizontalLineFormat.NoShade = False
inShape.HorizontalLineFormat.PercentWidth = 50
```

Hyperlink Object and the Hyperlinks Collection

The Hyperlinks collection represents the list of hyperlinks in a document, selection or range. Each Hyperlink object represents a single hyperlink in a document, selection or range. The Hyperlinks collection has an Add method besides the typical collection properties and methods. The Add method takes the text or graphic that is to be converted into a hyperlink (Anchor) and the URL address or filename (Address) and creates a Hyperlink object.

Hyperlink Common Properties

The Application, Creator, and Parent properties are defined at the beginning of this section.

Hyperlink Properties

Name	Returns	Description
Address	String	Set/Get the file name or URL address of the hyperlink.
Email Subject	String	Set/Get the email subject line if the address is an email address.

Table Continued on Following Page

Name	Returns	Description
ExtraInfo Required	Boolean	Read Only. Returns whether any further information is required by the hyperlink. The further information can be placed in the ExtraInfo parameter of the Follow method.
Name	String	Read Only. Returns the name of the hyperlink.
Range	Range	Read Only. Returns the spot in the document where the hyperlink is.
ScreenTip	String	Set/Get the text that appears when the mouse hovers over the hyperlink.
Shape	Shape	Read Only. Returns the shape associated with the hyperlink, if any.
SubAddress	String	Set/Get the spot in the target location that the hyperlink points to.
Target	String	Set/Get the frame or window in which to load the hyperlink.
TextTo Display	String	Set/Get the text that will be displayed in association with the hyperlink, if any.
Type	Mso Hyperlink Type	Read Only. Returns the hyperlink type (e.g. shape).

Hyperlink Methods

Name	Returns	Parameters	Description
AddTo Favorites			Creates a shortcut to the hyperlink and places it into the Favorites folder.
CreateNew Document		FileName As String, EditNow As Boolean, Overwrite As Boolean	Creates a new document with the FileName name from the results of the hyperlink's address. Set the EditNow property to True to open up the document in the appropriate editor. Set Overwrite to True to overwrite any existing document with the same name.

Name	Returns	Parameters	Description
Delete			Deletes the Hyperlink object.
Follow		[NewWindow], [AddHistory], [ExtraInfo], [Method], [HeaderInfo]	Opens up the target document specified by the Address property. Setting NewWindow to True opens up a new window with the target document. Set AddHistory to True to display the item in history folder. Use the Method parameter to choose if the ExtraInfo parameter is sent as a Get or a Post.

Examples

If a hyperlink exists then set the address to www.wrox.com and open up the URL in a new window:

```
If ActiveDocument.Hyperlinks.Count > 0 Then
    ActiveDocument.Hyperlinks(1).Address = "www.wrox.com"
    ActiveDocument.Hyperlinks(1).Follow NewWindow:=True
End If
```

Index Object and the Indexes Collection

The Indexes collection represents the list of indexes in a document. Each Index object represents a single index in a document. The following table lists the properties and methods of the Indexes collection besides the typical collection attributes.

Indexes Collection Special Property

Name	Returns	Description
Format	WdIndexFormat	Set/Get the way the index will look in the document.

Indexes Collection Special Methods

Name	Returns	Parameters	Description
Add	Index	Range As Range, [HeadingSeparator], [RightAlignPage Numbers], [Type], [NumberOfColumns], [AccentedLetters], [SortBy], [IndexLanguage]	Add an index to the document at the spot specified in the Range parameter, replacing the existing range contents. What shows up between different letters groups can be specified with HeadingSeparator. The Type parameter is used to define how subentries are displayed and the NumberOfColumns sets how many columns per page are used for the index.
AutoMark Entries		ConcordanceFileName As String	Uses a concordance file that contains a table of index terms and index entries to add index entry fields (XE) to the document.
MarkAll Entries	Field	Range As Range, [Entry], [EntryAutoText], [CrossReference], [CrossReferenceAuto Text], [BookmarkName], [Bold], [Italic]	Inserts an index entry field (XE) after all instances of the text specified in the Range parameter.
MarkEntry	Field	Range As Range, [Entry], [EntryAutoText], [CrossReference], [CrossReferenceAuto Text], [BookmarkName], [Bold], [Italic], [Reading]	Creates an index entry field (XE) after the spot in the document specified by the Range parameter.

Index Common Properties

The `Application`, `Creator`, and `Parent` properties are defined at the beginning of this section.

Index Properties

Name	Returns	Description
Accented Letters	Boolean	Set/Get whether accented letters get their own alphabetic group.
Filter	WdIndex Filter	Set/Get how the first characters of the entries are classified in the index.
Heading Separator	WdHeading Separator	Set/Get what will separate different alphabetic letter groupings.
Index Language	WdLanguag eID	Set/Get the language of the index.
NumberOf Columns	Long	Set/Get the number of columns per page used for the index page.
Range	Range	Read Only. Returns the spot in the document where the index is.
RightAlign PageNumbers	Boolean	Set/Get whether the page number will be right aligned.
SortBy	WdIndex SortBy	Set/Get how to sort the index.
TabLeader	WdTab Leader	Set/Get what appears between the entry and its page number.
Type	WdIndex Type	Set/Get the index type.

Index Methods

Name	Returns	Parameters	Description
Delete			Deletes the `Index` object.
Update			Updates changes made in the document to the index.

Examples

Add an index to the current selection in the active document. Set the index type to indented. Note that some entries have to have been marked first for an index page to appear:

```
Dim ind As Index
Set ind = ActiveDocument.Indexes.Add(Selection.Range)
ind.Type = wdIndexIndent
ind.Update
```

InlineShape Object and the InlineShapes Collection

The InlineShapes collection represents the list of inline shapes in a document, field, range or selection. Each InlineShape object represents a single inline shape in the current document, field, range or selection. The following table lists the properties and methods of the InlineShapes collection besides the typical collection attributes:

InlineShapes Collection Special Methods

Name	Returns	Parameters	Description
Add Horizontal Line	Inline Shape	FileName As String, [Range]	Creates a horizontal line based on an image file (specified by the FileName parameter) at the Range location.
Add Horizontal LineStandard	Inline Shape	[Range]	Creates a standard horizontal line at the Range location.
AddOLE Control	Inline Shape	[ClassType], [Range]	Creates an ActiveX control specified by ClassType at the Range spot and returns the InlineShape object containing the control.

Name	Returns	Parameters	Description
AddOLE Object	Inline Shape	[ClassType], [FileName], [LinkToFile], [DisplayAs Icon], [IconFile Name], [IconIndex], [IconLabel], [Range]	Creates an OLE object of the type specified by ClassType at the Range spot and returns the InlineShape object containing the control. FileName can specify the file containing the OLE object, however you cannot use both FileName and ClassType.
AddPicture	Inline Shape	FileName As String, [LinkToFile], [SaveWith Document], [Range]	Adds the picture specified by the FileName at the Range location and returns an InlineShape.
AddPicture Bullet	Inline Shape	FileName As String, [Range]	Adds the picture bullet specified by the FileName at the Range location and returns an InlineShape.
New	Inline Shape	Range As Range	Creates an empty, 1-inch square Word picture object, returned by this method as an InlineShape object.

InlineShape Common Properties

The Application, Creator, and Parent properties are defined at the beginning of this section.

InlineShape Properties

Name	Returns	Description
Alternative Text	String	Set/Get the text to appear if the image cannot be loaded (web pages).
Borders	Borders	Set/Get the border properties of the inline shape.

Table Continued on Following Page

Name	Returns	Description
Field	Field	Read Only. Returns the field associated with the inline shape.
Fill	Fill Format	Read Only. Returns an object allowing manipulation of the fill properties.
Height	Single	Set/Get the height of the inline shape.
HorizontalLineFormat	HorizontalLineFormat	Read Only. Returns an object containing the horizontal line formatting for the inline shape.
Hyperlink	Hyperlink	Read Only. Returns the hyperlink associated with the inline shape.
Line	LineFormat	Read Only. Returns an object containing the line formatting properties for the inline shape.
LinkFormat	LinkFormat	Read Only. Returns an object containing the link options for the inline shape.
LockAspectRatio	MsoTriState	Set/Get whether the image proportions are kept if the height or width is changed.
OLEFormat	OLEFormat	Read Only. Returns an object representing the OLE characteristics of the inline shape.
PictureFormat	PictureFormat	Set/Get the picture formatting properties associated the inline shape if relevant.
Range	Range	Read Only. Returns location of the inline shape in the document.
ScaleHeight	Single	Set/Get the height of the inline shape relative to the original image.
ScaleWidth	Single	Set/Get the width of the inline shape relative to the original image.
Script	Script	Read Only. Returns an object representing the script code associated with an inline shape.
TextEffect	TextEffectFormat	Read Only. Returns the text formatting properties for the inline shape.
Type	WdInlineShapeType	Read Only. Returns the type of the current inline shape.
Width	Single	Set/Get the width of the inline shape.

InlineShape Methods

Name	Returns	Parameters	Description
Activate			Opens up the inline shape for editing.
Convert ToShape	Shape		Converts the inline shape to a free-floating shape and returns the new Shape object.
Delete			Deletes the inline shape.
Reset			Resets any changes made to an inline shape back to its default settings
Select			Selects the inline shape.

Examples

Add a horizontal line to the current document at the current selection point and set its width to 10 points:

```
Dim inShape As InlineShape
Set inShape = ActiveDocument.InlineShapes.AddHorizontalLineStandard
inShape.Width = 10
```

KeyBinding Object and the KeyBindings Collection/KeysBoundTo Collection

The KeyBindings collection represents the list of custom keyboard settings for Word. The KeysBoundTo collection represents the list of custom keyboard settings for the current context specified by the CustomizationContext object. Both the KeyBindings collection and KeysBoundTo collection are made up of KeyBinding objects. KeyBinding object represents a single custom key assignment.

The KeyBindings collection and the KeysBoundTo collection have a few properties and methods besides the typical collection attributes. The Add method requires a KeyCategory, Command, and KeyCode parameter to create a new KeyBinding object. The ClearAll method clears all the custom keyboard settings for Word. The Key method returns a KeyBinding object for the given KeyCode parameter. The Context property returns where abouts the KeyBindings collection is being stored (e.g. template).

KeyBinding Common Properties

The Application, Creator, and Parent properties are defined at the beginning of this section.

KeyBinding Properties

Name	Returns	Description
Command	String	Read Only. Returns the command that is triggered by the key combination.
Command Parameter	String	Read Only. Returns any parameters needed by the Command property.
Context	Object	Read Only. Returns where the key binding is stored.
KeyCategory	WdKey Category	Read Only. Returns the category of the key binding (e.g. Style).
KeyCode	Long	Read Only. Returns a unique value representing a keyboard combination (e.g. value returned could be *SHIFT-F2*).
KeyCode2	Long	Read Only. Returns a unique value for a second key that is pressed.
KeyString	String	Read Only. Returns the string representation of the key combination.
Protected	Boolean	Read Only. Returns whether the key binding can be changed.

KeyBinding Methods

Name	Returns	Parameters	Description
Clear			Removes the KeyBinding object from the collection and may reset built-in command.
Disable			Disables the key-binding shortcut.
Execute			Triggers the Command property of the key binding.
Rebind		KeyCategory As WdKey Category, Command As String, [Command Parameter]	Rebinds the KeyBinding object with the specified KeyCategory and Command string.

Examples

Display all of the custom key bindings and all of their commands:

```
Dim keybnd As KeyBinding
For Each keybnd In Application.KeyBindings
    MsgBox keybnd.KeyString & " command: " & keybnd.Command
Next
```

Language Object and the Languages Collection

The Languages collection holds a list of all the languages that can have proofing and formatting abilities. The WdLanguageID constants or the name of the language is used to return a specific Language object in the Languages collection. A Language object contains all of the proofing and formatting abilities for a specific language.

Language Common Properties

The Application, Creator, and Parent properties are defined at the beginning of this section.

Language Properties

Name	Returns	Description
ActiveGrammar Dictionary	Dictionary	Read Only. Returns the dictionary used for grammar proofing for the language.
ActiveHyphenation Dictionary	Dictionary	Read Only. Returns the dictionary used for hyphenation proofing for the language.
ActiveSpelling Dictionary	Dictionary	Read Only. Returns the dictionary used for spell checking for the language.
ActiveThesaurus Dictionary	Dictionary	Read Only. Returns the dictionary used as a thesaurus for the language.
DefaultWriting Style	String	Set/Get the default writing style used by the grammar checker (e.g. Technical).
ID	WdLanguage ID	Read Only. Returns the ID for the language.
Name	String	Read Only. Returns the language name in the language.

Table Continued on Following Page

415

Name	Returns	Description
NameLocal	String	Read Only. Returns the local name of the language (e.g. Returns the English name for the language in U.S Word)
SpellingDictionary Type	WdDictionary Type	Set/Get the type of dictionary to use for spell checks.
WritingStyleList	Variant	Read Only. Returns a list of writing styles available for the language.

Examples

Display the local and language name of the Portuguese dictionary:

```
MsgBox Languages(wdPortuguese).Name
MsgBox Languages(wdPortuguese).NameLocal
```

LetterContent Object

The LetterContent object represents the different parts of a letter that Word's Letter Wizard uses to create letters. The LetterContent object is accessed through the Document object with the GetLetterContent and CreateLetterContent methods.

LetterContent Common Properties

The Application, Creator, and Parent properties are defined at the beginning of this section.

LetterContent Properties

Name	Returns	Description
Attention Line	String	Set/Get the attention line for the letter.
CCList	String	Set/Get the carbon copy list for the letter.
Closing	String	Set/Get the closing for the letter.
DateFormat	String	Set/Get the date for the letter.
Duplicate	Letter Content	Read Only. Returns a duplicate of the current LetterContent object.
Enclosure Number	Long	Set/Get the number of enclosures for the letter.

Name	Returns	Description
IncludeHeader Footer	Boolean	Set/Get whether the template in the PageDesign property is used to set the headers and footers for the letter.
InfoBlock	Boolean	Set/Get whether the information block is shown. Not used in U.S. Word.
Letterhead	Boolean	Set/Get whether their should be space left for printed letterhead.
Letterhead Location	WdLetterhead Location	Set/Get where the letterhead is located on the page.
Letterhead Size	Single	Set/Get the size of the letterhead.
LetterStyle	WdLetter Style	Set/Get the style of the letter as specified by the letter wizard.
Mailing Instructions	String	Set/Get the mailing instructions for the letter.
PageDesign	String	Set/Get the name of the template used to create the letter.
Recipient Address	String	Set/Get the recipient's mailing address.
RecipientCode	String	Set/Get the recipient's mailing code.
Recipient Gender	WdSalutation Gender	Set/Get the recipient's gender.
RecipientName	String	Set/Get the recipient's name.
Recipient Reference	String	Set/Get the reference line.
ReturnAddress	String	Set/Get the return address.
ReturnAddress ShortForm	String	Set/Get the return address short form.
Salutation	String	Set/Get the salutation used in the letter.
Salutation Type	WdSalutation Type	Set/Get the type of salutation to use in the letter (e.g. business)..
SenderCity	String	Set/Get the sender's city.
SenderCode	String	Set/Get the sender's mailing code.

Table Continued on Following Page

Name	Returns	Description
SenderCompany	String	Set/Get the sender's company.
SenderGender	WdSalutation Gender	Set/Get the sender's gender.
SenderInitials	String	Set/Get the sender's initials.
SenderJobTitle	String	Set/ Get the sender's job title.
SenderName	String	Set/Get the sender's name.
SenderReference	String	Set/Get the sender's reference.
Subject	String	Set/Get the subject line of the letter.

Examples

Run the letter wizard and set the date to 'December 7, 1998', no letterhead, and the recipient address to a certain address:

```
Dim ltr As LetterContent
Set ltr = New LetterContent
ltr.DateFormat = "December 7, 1998"
ltr.Letterhead = False
ltr.RecipientAddress = "1232 Black Street" & Chr(13) & Chr(10) & _
        "Winnipeg, MB" & Chr(13) & Chr(10) & "R3E 2X7"
ActiveDocument.RunLetterWizard ltr
```

LineFormat Object

The LineFormat object represents the formatting associated with the line of the parent Shape object. The Line property of the Shape object is used to access the LineFormat object. The LineFormat object is especially used to change line properties such as arrowhead styles and directions.

LineFormat Common Properties

The Application, Creator, and Parent properties are defined at the beginning of this section

LineFormat Properties

Name	Returns	Description
BackColor	ColorFormat	Read Only. Returns an object allowing manipulation of the background color of the line.
BeginArrowhead Length	MsoArrowhead Length	Set/Get the arrowhead length on the start of the line.

Name	Returns	Description
BeginArrowhead Style	MsoArrowhead Style	Set/Get how the arrowhead looks on the start of the line.
BeginArrowhead Width	MsoArrowhead Width	Set/Get the arrowhead width on the start of the line.
DashStyle	MsoLineDash Style	Set/Get the style of the line.
EndArrowhead Length	MsoArrowhead Length	Set/Get the arrowhead length on the end of the line.
EndArrowhead Style	MsoArrowhead Style	Set/Get how the arrowhead looks on the end of the line.
EndArrowhead Width	MsoArrowhead Width	Set/Get the arrowhead width on the end of the line.
ForeColor	ColorFormat	Read Only. Returns an object allowing manipulation of the background color of the line.
Pattern	MsoPattern Type	Set/Get the pattern used on the line.
Style	MsoLineStyle	Set/Get the line style.
Transparency	Single	Set/Get how transparent (1) or opaque (0) the line is.
Visible	MsoTriState	Set/Get whether the line is visible.
Weight	Single	Set/Get how thick the line is.

Examples

Add a line shape at the coordinates 100, 100 to 300,300 with a medium sized, triangular, wide arrowhead at the beginning of the line:

```
Dim ln As LineFormat

Set ln = ActiveDocument.Shapes.AddLine(100, 100, 300, 300).Line
ln.BeginArrowheadLength = msoArrowheadLengthMedium
ln.BeginArrowheadWidth = msoArrowheadWide
ln.BeginArrowheadStyle = msoArrowheadTriangle
```

LineNumbering Object

The LineNumbering object is used to view line numbers for each page or column. The line numbers are always located to the left of the text and do not become a permanent part of the actual document. The LineNumbering object can be accessed through the PageSetup object.

LineNumbering Common Properties

The `Application`, `Creator`, and `Parent` properties are defined at the beginning of this section

LineNumbering Properties

Name	Returns	Description
Active	Long	Set/Get whether line numbering is turned on.
CountBy	Long	Set/Get at which lines to display numbering (e.g. every 5th line).
DistanceFrom Text	Single	Set/Get how far away the line numbering is from the text.
RestartMode	WdNumbering Rule	Set/Get when numbering restarts (e.g. every page or section).
Starting Number	Long	Set/Get what the starting number is.

Examples

Set the active document to have line-numbering starting at 1 with every 5th line showing a number. The line numbers should restart every page:

```
With ActiveDocument.PageSetup.LineNumbering
    .Active = True
    .StartingNumber = 1
    .CountBy = 5
    .RestartMode = wdRestartPage
End With
```

LinkFormat Object

The `LinkFormat` object represents the linking attributes associated with an OLE object or picture. The `LinkFormat` object is associated with a `Shape`, `InlineShape` or `Field` object. Only parents that are valid OLE objects can access the `LinkFormat` object.

LinkFormat Common Properties

The `Application`, `Creator`, and `Parent` properties are defined at the beginning of this section.

LinkFormat Properties

Name	Returns	Description
AutoUpdate	Boolean	Set/Get whether the parent object is updated whenever the source file changes or when the parent object is opened.
Locked	Boolean	Set/Get whether the parent object does not update itself against the source file.
SavePictureWi thDocument	Boolean	Set/Get whether the parent object picture is saved with the document.
SourceFullNam e	String	Set/Get the path and filename of the parent object's source file.
SourceName	String	Read Only. Returns the filename of the parent object's source file.
SourcePath	String	Read Only. Returns the path of the parent object' s source file.
Type	WdLinkTyp e	Read Only. Returns the link type.

LinkFormat Methods

Name	Returns	Parameters	Description
BreakLink			Severs the link between the parent object and the source file.
Update			Updates the parent object with the source file data.

Examples

Display the source file's full name for the first shape object and break the link. First shape object must be a linked object for this example to work otherwise you will get a runtime error:

```
ActiveDocument.Shapes(1).LinkFormat.SourceFullName
ActiveDocument.Shapes(1).LinkFormat.BreakLink
```

ListEntry Object and the ListEntries Collection

The ListEntries collection holds a list of all the items in a drop down type form field. A ListEntry object contains a specific list item in a drop down type form field. The FormField object is always the parent of the ListEntries collection.

The ListEntries collection has a few properties and methods besides the typical collection attributes. The Add method requires a Name parameter to create a new ListEntry object in the associated drop down list. The Clear method clears all the list items (ListEntry objects) in the associated drop down list.

ListEntry Common Properties

The Application, Creator, and Parent properties are defined at the beginning of this section.

ListEntry Properties

Name	Returns	Description
Index	Long	Read Only. Returns the number associated with its place in the parent collection.
Name	String	Set/Get the name and the actual entry of the ListItem.

ListEntry Methods

Name	Returns	Parameters	Description
Delete			Deletes the list entry.

ListFormat Object

The ListFormat object represents the list formatting options that can be applied to the paragraphs in the parent Range object. The Range object is the only way to access the ListFormat object.

ListFormat Common Properties

The Application, Creator, and Parent properties are defined at the beginning of this section.

ListFormat Properties

Name	Returns	Description
List	List	Read Only. Returns the first List object in the specified range.
ListLevel Number	Long	Set/Get the level number for the first paragraph in the range.
ListString	String	Read Only. Returns a string representation of the list item number of the first paragraph in the range.

Name	Returns	Description
List Template	List Template	Read Only. Returns the list template associated with the first paragraph in the range.
ListType	WdListType	Read Only. Returns the type of list contained the ListFormat range.
ListValue	Long	Read Only. Returns the list item number of the first paragraph in the range.
SingleList	Boolean	Read Only. Returns whether the ListFormat range contains only one list.
SingleList Template	Boolean	Read Only. Returns whether the ListFormat range contains only one list template.

ListFormat Methods

Name	Returns	Parameters	Description
ApplyBullet Default		[DefaultList Behaviour]	Toggles the addition or subtraction of bullet formatting for the ListFormat.
ApplyList Template		ListTemplate As ListTemplate, [Continue PreviousList], [ApplyTo], [DefaultList Behavior]	Applies the formatting of the ListTemplate parameter to the current ListFormat. Optionally continues previous list numbering.
ApplyNumber Default		[DefaultList Behaviour]	Toggles the addition or subtraction of number formatting for the ListFormat.
ApplyOutline Number Default		[DefaultList Behaviour]	Toggles the addition or subtraction of outline number formatting for the ListFormat.

Table Continued on Following Page

Name	Returns	Parameters	Description
CanContinue PreviousList	Wd Continue	ListTemplate As ListTemplate	Checks to see if the list can continue the previous list using the list template formatting.
Convert Numbers ToText			Changes the entire list numbering into text.
Count Numbered Items	Long	[NumberType], [Level]	Sends back the number of items in the ListFormat.
ListIndent			Makes the level of the list items in the ListFormat higher.
ListOutdent			Makes the level of the list items in the ListFormat lower.
Remove Numbers			Removes the list numbers from the ListFormat.

Examples

Set the first three paragraphs of the active document to have bullet list formatting:

```
Dim rng As Range
Set rng =
ActiveDocument.Range(ActiveDocument.Paragraphs(1).Range.Start, _
            ActiveDocument.Paragraphs(3).Range.End)
rng.ListFormat.ApplyBulletDefault
```

ListGallery Object and the ListGalleries Collection

The ListGalleries collection holds the three list template galleries associated with the three tabs in the **Bullets** and **Numbering** dialog box. Each ListGallery object represents one of the three tabs in the **Bullets** and **Numbering** dialog box. The ListGallery object contains the seven ListTemplates associated with that particular tab. To access a particular ListGallery in the ListGalleries collection, use the wdListGalleryType constants.

ListGallery Common Properties

The Application, Creator, and Parent properties are defined at the beginning of this section.

ListGallery Properties

Name	Returns	Description
List Templates	List Templates	Read Only. Returns the seven list templates for the list gallery.
Modified	Variant	Read Only. Index parameter. Returns whether the list template number passed by the Index parameter has been modified from the original format.

ListGallery Methods

Name	Returns	Parameters	Description
Reset			Resets all the modified list templates in the gallery back to the original format.

Examples

If a list template has been modified then reset it to its original settings:

```
Dim lstGallery As ListGallery
Dim i As Integer
Const MAXGALLERIES = 7 'Only seven listtemplates per gallery

For Each lstGallery In ListGalleries
    For i = 1 To MAXGALLERIES
        If lstGallery.Modified(i) Then
            lstGallery.Reset (i)
        End If
    Next i
Next lstGallery
```

ListLevel Object and the ListLevels Collection

The ListLevels collection represents the list levels for a particular list template. The parent object is always a ListTemplate object. The number of list levels per list template varies depending on the type of list template. Each ListLevel object represents a single list level of a particular list template.

ListLevel Common Properties

The Application, Creator, and Parent properties are defined at the beginning of this section.

ListLevel Properties

Name	Returns	Description
Alignment	WdListLevel Alignment	Set/Get how the text in the list level is aligned.
Font	Font	Set/Get font properties for the list level.
Index	Long	Read Only. Returns the position number of the ListLevel object in the collection.
Linked Style	String	Set/Get the style name that is associated with the list level.
Number Format	String	Set/Get a number style from 1 to 9 with associated text representing the number style from the respective list level.
Number Position	Single	Set/Get where the number is positioned in the list level.
Number Style	WdListNumber Style	Set/Get the style of the number (e.g. Roman).
ResetOn Higher	Long	Set/Get whether the numbering restarts after an item at a higher list level.
StartAt	Long	Set/Get the number to start at.
Tab Position	Single	Set/Get the tab position for the list level.
Text Position	Single	Set/Get where the second and subsequent lines of text appears in a list level.
Trailing Character	WdTrailing Character	Set/Get what character appears after the list level number and before the list level text starts.

Examples

Set the alignment of the first list level in the first list template of the Bullet number list gallery to left aligned:

```
ListGalleries(wdBulletGallery).ListTemplates(1). _
    ListLevels(1).Alignment = wdListLevelAlignLeft
```

ListParagraphs Collection

The ListParagraphs collection represents the list of paragraphs in a document, list or range that are formatted with list formatting. The ListParagraphs collection attributes are made up of regular collection attributes.

Examples

Display the number of paragraphs in the current document with list formatting:

```
MsgBox ActiveDocument.ListParagraphs.Count
```

List Object and the Lists Collection

The `Lists` collection represents the collection of lists in a document. Possible parents of the `Lists` collection are the `Document` object and the `ListFormat` object. Each `List` object represents formatting options for a particular list.

List Common Properties

The `Application`, `Creator`, and `Parent` properties are defined at the beginning of this section.

List Properties

Name	Returns	Description
List Paragraphs	List Paragraphs	Read Only. Returns all of the formatted list paragraphs in the list.
Range	Range	Read Only. Returns the spot in the document that contains the list item.
SingleList Template	Boolean	Read Only. Returns whether the whole list uses the same list format.

List Methods

Name	Returns	Parameters	Description
ApplyList Template	Wd Continue	ListTemplate As ListTemplate, [Continue PreviousList], [DefaultList Behavior]	Applies the formatting of the ListTemplate parameter to the current list. Optionally continues previous list numbering.
CanContinue PreviousList	Wd Continue	ListTemplate As ListTemplate	Checks to see if the list can continue the previous list using the list template formatting.
Convert NumbersTo Text		[NumberType]	Changes the entire list numbering into text.

Table Continued on Following Page

427

Name	Returns	Parameters	Description
Count Numbered Items	Long	[NumberType], [Level]	Sends back the number of items in the list. Can specify to count only a certain number type (e.g. paragraph) or count a certain level.
Remove Numbers			Removes all the numbers from the list.

Examples

Change the first list in the active document to have the third list template style in the number list gallery:

```
ActiveDocument.Lists(1).ApplyListTemplate _
    ListGalleries(wdNumberGallery).ListTemplates(3)
```

ListTemplate Object and the ListTemplates Collection

The ListTemplates collection represents the collection of list templates for a particular list gallery. The ListTemplates collection is associated with all the items in a particular tab from the Bullets and Numbering dialog box. A ListTemplate object represents a particular list format. The ListTemplates collection can be accessed from the ListGallery, Document, ListFormat, Style and Template objects.

The ListTemplates collection has an Add method besides the typical collection attributes. The Add method adds a list template to the ListTemplates collection. The Add method cannot be used when the ListTemplates parent object is the ListGallery object.

ListTemplate Common Properties

The Application, Creator, and Parent properties are defined at the beginning of this section.

ListTemplate Properties

Name	Returns	Description
ListLevels	ListLevels	Read Only. Returns the list levels for the list template.
Name	String	Set/Get the name of the list template.
Outline Numbered	Boolean	Set/Get whether the list template has outline (multilevel) numbering.

ListTemplate Methods

Name	Returns	Parameters	Description
Convert	List Template	[Level]	Toggles between a multilevel list and a single level list. Optionally sets the level to the Level parameter. Cannot be used when accessing a ListTemplate through a ListGallery object.

Examples

See the ListGallery object, the ListLevel object and the List object for examples. Objects and their Properties, Methods and Events.

Mailer Object

The Mailer object represents the PowerTalk mailer for a document. It is only available on the Macintosh.

Common Properties

The Application, Creator, and Parent properties are defined at the beginning of this section

Mailer Properties

Name	Returns	Description
BCCRecipients	Variant	Set/Get the list of blind copies
CCRecipients	Variant	Set/Get the list of carbon copies.
Enclosures	Variant	Set/Get the list of enclosures.
Received	Boolean	Read Only. Return whether the mail message was received.
Recipients	Variant	Set/Get the list of recipients
SendDateTime	Date	Read Only. Return the date and time the message was sent.

Table Continued on Following Page

Name	Returns	Description
Sender	String	Read Only. Return the name of the mail message sender.
Subject	String	Set/Get the subject line of the mail message.

Example

Makes the Mailer object is available and sets the subject line:

```
With ActiveDocument
    .HasMailer = True
    .Mailer.Subject = "Hello, here is the chapter."
End With
```

MailingLabel Object

The MailingLabel object represents a mailing label in Word.

Common Properties

The Application, Creator, and Parent properties are defined at the beginning of this section.

MailingLabel Properties

Name	Returns	Description
CustomLabels	Custom Labels	Read Only. Returns an object that allows creation and manipulation of custom mailing labels.
DefaultLabel Name	String	Set/Get the name of the default mailing label.
DefaultLaser Tray	WdPaper Tray	Set/Get the default paper tray for the printer.
DefaultPrint BarCode	Boolean	Set/Get whether the POSTNET bar code is added the mailing label.

MailingLabel Methods

Name	Returns	Parameters	Description
CreateNew Document	Document	[Name], [Address], [AutoText], [Extract Address], [LaserTray]	Creates a new document as a mailing label document. Can specify the mailing label properties using the parameters.

Name	Returns	Parameters	Description
PrintOut		[Name], [Address], [ExtractAddress], [LaserTray], [SingleLabel], [Row], [Column]	Prints out a label or a page labels. Can specify the mailing label properties using the parameters or the location of the single label to print on the page.

Examples

Set the default label to 5097 Diskette label:

```
Application.MailingLabel.DefaultLabelName = "5097"
```

MailMerge Object

The MailMerge object allows access to the mail merge abilities of Word. The parent of the MailMerge object is the Document object.

MailMerge Common Properties

The Application, Creator, and Parent properties are defined at the beginning of this section.

MailMerge Properties

Name	Returns	Description
DataSource	MailMerge DataSource	Read Only. Returns the data source object for the mail merge.
Destination	WdMailMerge Destination	Set/Get the merged document destination.
Fields	MailMerge Fields	Read Only. Returns the collection of mail merge fields.
MailAddress FieldName	String	Set/Get the field name containing the list of email addresses.
MailAs Attachment	Boolean	Set/Get whether the merged documents are sent as email attachments.
MailSubject	String	Set/Get the subject line of the merged documents sent as email.
MainDocument Type	WdMailMerge MainDocType	Set/Get the merge document type.

Table Continued on Following Page

Name	Returns	Description
State	WdMailMerge State	Read Only. Returns what part of the mail merge process is currently happening.
SuppressBlank Lines	Boolean	Set/Get whether lines containing blank merge fields are suppressed.
ViewMailMerge FieldCodes	Long	Set/Get whether field codes are displayed (True) or field data (False).

MailMerge Methods

Name	Returns	Parameters	Description
Check			Test the mail merge process and reports any errors.
CreateData Source		[Name], [Password Document], [WritePassword Document], [HeaderRecord], [MSQuery], [SQLStatement], [SQLStatement1], [Connection], [LinkToSource]	Creates a table in a new Word document that will be used as the mail merge data source. The Name of the new document can be specified as well as a password. SQL statements and a data connection can also be used to create a data source.
CreateHeader Source		Name As String, [Password Document], [WritePassword Document], [HeaderRecord]	Creates a table in a new document that contains all of the header records for a mail merge. The Name of the new document must be specified.
EditData Source			Opens up or activates the data source of the mail merge.

Name	Returns	Parameters	Description
EditHeader Source			Opens up or activates the header source of the mail merge.
EditMain Document			Activates the main document in the mail merge.
Execute		[Pause]	Executes the mail merge.
OpenData Source		Name As String, [Format], [Confirm Conversions], [ReadOnly], [LinkToSource], [AddToRecentFiles], [PasswordDocument], [PasswordTemplate], [Revert], [WritePassword Document], [WritePassword Template], [Connection], [SQLStatement], [SQLStatement1]	Opens an existing data source and sets it as the data source of the current mail merge process.
OpenHeader Source		Name As String, [Format], [ConfirmConversions], [ReadOnly], [AddToRecentFiles], [PasswordDocument], [PasswordTemplate], [Revert], [WritePassword Document], [WritePassword Template]	Opens an existing header source and sets it as the header source of the current mail merge process.
UseAddress Book		Type	Sets the address book type used in the mail merge.

Examples

Merge the all the customers from the Northwind database with the active Word document into a new document. Make sure that the document has merge fields in it and then print the document out:

```
Dim objWord As Word.Document
Dim mmDatasource As MailMergeDataSource
Dim mmDatafield As MailMergeDataField
Dim rng As Range

Set objWord = ActiveDocument
' Make Word visible.
objWord.Application.Visible = True
' Set the mail merge data source as the Northwind database.
objWord.MailMerge.CreateDataSource Name:="C:\Program Files\Microsoft " &

"Office\Office\Samples\NWind.mdb", _
LinkToSource:=True, _
Connection:="TABLE Customers", _
SQLStatement:="Select * from [Customers]"
Set mmDatasource = objWord.MailMerge.DataSource
Set rng = ActiveDocument.Paragraphs.First.Range

'display the field names and add them to the current form as merge fields
For Each mmDatafield In mmDatasource.DataFields
    MsgBox "Field Name: " & mmDatafield.Name
    objWord.MailMerge.Fields.Add Selection.Range, mmDatafield.Name
    rng.Next (wdParagraph)
Next mmDatafield

' Execute the mail merge.
objWord.MailMerge.Destination = wdSendToNewDocument
objWord.MailMerge.Execute

Application.Options.PrintBackground = False
objWord.PrintOut
```

MailMergeDataField Object and the MailMergeDataFields Collection

The `MailMergeDataFields` collection represents all of the data fields being used by the parent mail merge data source. A single `MailMergeDataField` represents one mail merge data field of a mail merge data source. The `MailMergeDataSource` is always the parent of the `MailMergeDataFields` collection.

MailMergeDataField Common Properties

The `Application, Creator,` and `Parent` properties are defined at the beginning of this section.

MailMergeDataField Properties

Name	Returns	Description
Index	Long	Returns the position number of the MailMergeDataField object in the collection.
Name	String	Read Only. Returns the mail merge data field name.
Value	MailMergeData Fields	Read Only. Returns the field contents for the current record.

Examples

Display the name of the first datafield associated with the active document's data source.

```
MsgBox ActiveDocument.MailMerge.DataSource.DataFields(1).Name
```

MailMergeDataSource Object

The MailMergeDataSource object represents the properties of the mail merge data source. The parent of the MailMergeDataSource object is the MailMerge object.

MailMergeDataSource Common Properties

The Application, Creator, and Parent properties are defined at the beginning of this section.

MailMergeDataSource Properties

Name	Returns	Description
ActiveRecord	WdMailMerge ActiveRecord	Set/Get the active data record of the mail merge.
ConnectString	String	Read Only. Returns the connection string of the data source.
DataFields	MailMerge DataFields	Read Only. Returns an object allowing manipulation of the data fields.
FieldNames	MailMerge FieldNames	Read Only. Returns an object allowing manipulation of the field names.
FirstRecord	Long	Set/Get which record is the first record for the mail merge.

Table Continued on Following Page

Name	Returns	Description
HeaderSource Name	String	Read Only. Returns the name and path of the header source file or DSN name.
HeaderSource Type	WdMailMerge DataSource	Read Only. Returns the type of the header source.
LastRecord	Long	Set/Get which record is the last record for the mail merge.
Name	String	Read Only. Returns the name of the data source.
QueryString	String	Set/Get the SQL string used to create the data source.
Type	WdMailMerge DataSource	Read Only. Returns the type of the data source.

Examples

See the MailMerge object.

MailMergeField Object and the MailMergeFields Collection

The MailMergeFields collection represents the list of mail merge fields in a particular document. The parent object of the MailMergeFields collection is the MailMerge object. There are many methods associated with the MailMergeFields collection besides the typical collection attributes. All of the methods add mail merge fields to the parent document at the specified Range parameter and return a new MailMergeField. The following table shows the methods in the MailMergeFields collection:

MailMergeFields Collection Special Methods

Name	Returns	Parameters	Description
Add	MailMerge Field	Range As Range, Name As String	Adds a mail merge field.
AddAsk	MailMerge Field	Range As Range, Name As String, [Prompt], [DefaultAsk Text], [AskOnce]	Adds an ASK mail merge field prompting the user for text.

Name	Returns	Parameters	Description
AddFill In	MailMerge Field	Range As Range, [Prompt], [DefaultFill InText], [AskOnce]	Adds a **FILLIN** mail merge field prompting the user for text to insert at the field location.
AddIf	MailMerge Field	Range As Range, MergeField As String, Comparison As WdMailMerge Comparison, [CompareTo], [TrueAuto Text], [TrueText], [FalseAuto Text], [FalseText]	Adds an **IF** mail merge field inserting appropriate text depending how the Comparison matches.
AddMerge Rec	MailMerge Field	Range As Range	Adds a **MERGEREC** mail merge field.
AddMerge Seq	MailMerge Field	Range As Range	Adds a **MERGESEQ** mail merge field.
AddNext	MailMerge Field	Range As Range	Adds a **NEXT** mail merge field.
AddNextIf	MailMerge Field	Range As Range, MergeField As String, Comparison As WdMailMergeCo mparison, [CompareTo]	Adds a **NEXTIF** mail merge field.
AddSet	MailMerge Field	Range As Range, Name As String, [ValueText], [ValueAutoTex t]	Adds a **SET** mail merge field.

Table Continued on Following Page

Name	Returns	Parameters	Description
AddSkipIf	MailMerge Field	Range As Range, MergeField As String, Comparison As WdMailMergeCo mparison, [CompareTo]	Adds a SKIPIF mail merge field.

MailMergeField Common Properties

The `Application`, `Creator`, and `Parent` properties are defined at the beginning of this section.

MailMergeField Properties

Name	Returns	Description
Code	Range	Set/Get the `Range` object containing the merge field's code.
Locked	Boolean	Set/Get whether editing is allowed in the field.
Next	MailMerge Field	Read Only. Returns the next field in the collection.
Previous	MailMerge Field	Read Only. Returns the previous field in the collection.
Type	WdFieldType	Read Only. Returns the type of the current field object.

MailMergeField Methods

Name	Returns	Parameters	Description
Copy			Copies the field object to the clipboard.
Cut			Copies the field object to the clipboard and deletes the original from the document.
Delete			Deletes the current field object.
Select			Selects the field object in the document.

Examples

See the `MailMerge` object.

MailMergeFieldName Object and the MailMergeFieldNames Collection

The `MailMergeFieldNames` collection represents the list of field names for the parent `MailMergeDataSource` object. Each `MailMergeFieldName` object represents a single field name of a mail merge data source field.

MailMergeFieldName Common Properties

The `Application`, `Creator`, and `Parent` properties are defined at the beginning of this section.

MailMergeFieldName Properties

Name	Returns	Description
Name	String	Read Only. Returns the name of the mail merge field.
Index	Long	Read Only. Returns the position number of the `MailMergeFieldName` object in the collection.

MailMergeFieldName Examples

See the `MailMerge` object.

MailMessage Object

The `MailMessage` object represents the properties of an email message when using Word as the email editor.

MailMessage Common Properties

The `Application`, `Creator`, and `Parent` properties are defined at the beginning of this section.

MailMessage Methods

Name	Returns	Parameters	Description
CheckName			Makes sure the name in the To, Cc, or Bcc fields are valid email addresses.
Delete			Deletes the email message.

Table Continued on Following Page

Name	Returns	Parameters	Description
DisplayMove Dialog			Displays the **Move** dialog box for the email message.
Display Properties			Displays the **Properties** dialog box for the email message.
DisplaySelect NamesDialog			Display the **Select Name** dialog box for the email message.
Forward			Creates a new email message with the existing message attached.
GoToNext			Opens up the next email message in the current folder.
GoToPrevious			Opens up the previous email message in the current folder.
Reply			Creates a new email message as a reply to the existing message.
ReplyAll			Creates a new email message as a reply to all the people addressed in the existing message.
ToggleHeader			Toggles whether the email header is visible or not.

Examples

Display the properties of the current email message that uses Word as an email editor:

```
Application.MailMessage.DisplayProperties
```

OLEFormat Object

The OLEFormat object represents all of attributes associated with an OLE object, ActiveX object or a field except for linking. Linking characteristics are taken care of by the LinkFormat object. Possible parent objects of the OLEFormat object are the Shape, InlineShape, and Field object.

OLEFormat Common Properties

The `Application`, `Creator`, and `Parent` properties are defined at the beginning of this section

OLEFormat Properties

Name	Returns	Description
ClassType	String	Set/Get the class type for the parent OLE object. This property is read only for non DDE links.
DisplayAs Icon	Boolean	Set/Get whether the parent OLE object is displayed as an icon.
IconIndex	Long	Set/Get which icon to use as the icon of the parent OLE object.
IconLabel	String	Set/Get the icon label.
IconName	String	Set/Get the filename containing the icon.
IconPath	String	Read Only. Returns the file path containing the icon.
Label	String	Read Only. Returns the spot in the OLE source that is being linked.
Object	Object	Read Only. Returns a reference to the parent OLE object.
ProgID	String	Read Only. Returns the `ProgID` of the parent OLE object.

OLEFormat Methods

Name	Returns	Parameters	Description
Activate			Activates and opens the parent OLE object.
ActivateAs		[ClassType]	Changes what default application is used to open up the parent OLE object.
ConvertTo		[ClassType], [DisplayAs Icon], [IconFileName], [IconIndex], [IconLabel]	Changes the parent OLE object to a new class type and icon properties.

Table Continued on Following Page

441

Name	Returns	Parameters	Description
DoVerb		[VerbIndex]	Performs an action on the parent OLE object that triggers a reaction in the OLE object.
Edit			Opens up the parent OLE object in its default application for editing.
Open			Opens up the parent OLE object in its default application.

Examples

Add a bitmap object to the current selection point and display the object as the second Microsoft chat icon with an icon label of **Picture Room**. Note that Microsoft Chat must be located in the `"C:\Program Files\Microsoft Chat"` directory for this example to work.

```
Dim OLEObj As OLEFormat

    Set OLEObj = Selection.InlineShapes.AddOLEObject _
        ("Paint.Picture").OLEFormat

    OLEObj.DisplayAsIcon = True
    OLEObj.IconName = "C:\Program Files\Microsoft Chat\CChat.exe"
    OLEObj.IconIndex = 2 'Choose the second icon in the EXE
    OLEObj.IconLabel = "Picture Room"
```

Options Object

The Options object allows access to all of the Word options found in Word's **Options** dialog box. All of the following properties correspond to an equivalently named area of the **Options** dialog box.

Options Common Properties

The Application, Creator, and Parent properties are defined at the beginning of this section.

Options Properties

Name	Returns	Description
AddBi DirectionalMarks WhenSavingText File	Boolean	Set/Get if bi-directional control characters are added when saving a document as a text file.

Name	Returns	Description
AddControl Characters	Boolean	Set/Get if bi-directional control characters are added when cutting and copying text.
AddHebDouble Quote	Boolean	Set/Get if encloses number formats are enclosed in double quotation marks.
AllowAccented Uppercase	Boolean	Set/Get if accents are kept when French language characters are changed to uppercase.
AllowClickAnd TypeMouse	Boolean	Set/Get if Click and Type is enabled.
AllowCombined AuxiliaryForms	Boolean	Set/Get if auxillary verb forms are ignored when checking the spelling in a document written in Korean.
AllowCompound NounProcessing	Boolean	Set/Get if compound nouns are ignored when checking a document written in Korean.
AllowDragAnd Drop	Boolean	Set/Get if dragging and dropping is allowed when moving or copying a selection.
AllowFastSave	Boolean	Set/Get if Word only saves changes to a document. Reopening a document, Word will use the saved changes to reconstruct the document.
AllowPixel Units	Boolean	Set/Get if pixels are used as the default unit of measurement for HTML features.
AnimateScreen Movements	Boolean	Set/Get if Word animates mouse movements or other actions.
ApplyFarEast FontsToAscii	Boolean	Set/Get if East Asian fonts are applied to Latin text.
ArabicMode	WdAra Speller	Set/Get Arabic spell checker
ArabicNumeral	WdArabic Numeral	Set/Get the numeral style for the Arabic language.
AutoFormat ApplyBulleted Lists	Boolean	Set/Get if bullets replace characters (astericks, hyphens etc) at the beginning of list paragraphs when formatting automatically.

Table Continued on Following Page

Name	Returns	Description
AutoFormatApply FirstIndents	Boolean	Set/Get if a space is replaced with a first-line indent at the beginning of a paragraph when formatting automatically.
AutoFormatApply Headings	Boolean	Set/Get if styles are applied to headings automatically.
AutoFormatApply Lists	Boolean	Set/Get if styles are applied to lists automatically.
AutoFormatApply OtherParas	Boolean	Set/Get if styles are applied to paragraphs when formatting automatically.
AutoFormatAsYou TypeApplyBorders	Boolean	Set/Get if three or more hyphens, equal signs or underscore characters are replaced automatically when the ENTER key is pressed as you type.
AutoFormatAsYou TypeApply BulletedLists	Boolean	Set/Get if bullet characters are replaced by bullets (from the **Bullets And Numbering**) dialog box as you type.
AutoFormatAsYou TypeApply Closings	Boolean	Set/Get if the Closing style is automatically applied to letter closings as you type
AutoFormatAsYou TypeApplyDates	Boolean	Set/Get the Date style is applied to dates as you type.
AutoFormatAsYouT ypeApplyFirst Indents	Boolean	Set/Get if a space at the beginning of a paragraph is automatically replaced with a first line indent as you type.
AutoFormatAsYou TypeApply Headings	Boolean	Set/Get if styles are applied to headings as you type.
AutoFormatAsYou TypeApply Numbered Lists	Boolean	Set/Get if paragraphs are formatted automatically as a numbered list with a numbering scheme from the **Bullets And Numbering** dialog box as you type.
AutoFormatAsYou TypeApplyTables	Boolean	Set/Get if a plus sign, a series of hyphens, another plus sign etc, is automatically replaced by creating a table as you type.

Name	Returns	Description
AutoFormatAsYou TypeAutoLetter Wizard	Boolean	Set/Get if the users enter a letter salutation the Letter Wizard automatically starts as you type.
AutoFormatAsYou TypeDefineStyles	Boolean	Set/Get if Word automatically creates new styles based on manual formatting as you type.
AutoFormatAsYou TypeDeleteAuto Spaces	Boolean	Set/Get if are deleted automatically between Japanese and Latin text as yo type.
AutoFormatAsYou TypeFormatList ItemBeginning	Boolean	Set/Get if Character formatting is repeated to the beginning of a list item to the next list item as you type.
AutoFormatAsYou TypeInsert Closings	Boolean	Get/Set if a corresponding memo closing is inserted automatically when the user enters a memo heading as you type.
AutoFormatAsYou TypeInsertOvers	Boolean	Used for converting Japanese text.
AutoFormatAsYou TypeMatch Parentheses	Boolean	Get/Set if improperly paired parentheses is automatically corrected as you type.
AutoFormatAsYou TypeReplaceFar EastDashes	Boolean	Get/Set if long vowel sounds and dash use is automatically corrected as you type.
AutoFormatAsYou TypeReplace Fractions	Boolean	Set/Get if typed fractions are automatically replaced with fractions from the current character set as you type.
AutoFormatAsYou TypeReplace Hyperlinks	Boolean	Set/Get is hyperlinks automatically replace e-mail addresses, URL's etc as you type.
AutoFormatAsYou TypeReplace Ordinals	Boolean	Set/Get if superscript letters automatically replace ordinal number suffixes as you type.
AutoFormatAsYou TypeReplacePlain TextEmphasis	Boolean	Set/Get if character formatting replaces manual emphasis characters as you type.
AutoFormatAsYou TypeReplace Quotes	Boolean	Set/Get if smart quotation marks automatically replace straight quotation marks as you type.

Table Continued on Following Page

Name	Returns	Description
`AutoFormatAsYou TypeReplace Symbols`	Boolean	Set/Get if two consecutive hyphens are automatically replaced by en or em dashes as you type.
`AutoFormatDelete AutoSpaces`	Boolean	Set/Get if spaces are automatically deleted between Japanese and Latin text when formatting.
`AutoFormatMatch Parentheses`	Boolean	Set/Get if improperly paired parentheses are corrected when being formatted automatically.
`AutoFormatPlain TextWordMail`	Boolean	Set/Get if plain-text e-mail is formatted automatically.
`AutoFormat Preserve Styles`	Boolean	Set/Get if previously applied styles are preserved when automatically formating a range or a document.
`AutoFormatReplace FarEastDashes`	Boolean	Set/Get if long vowel sound and dash use is corrected when automatically formatting.
`AutoFormatReplace Fractions`	Boolean	Set/Get if typed fractions are replaced with fractions from the current character set when automatically
`AutoFormatReplace Hyperlinks`	Boolean	Set/Get if e-mail addresses, URL's etc are automatically formatted when Word AutoFormats a range or document.
`AutoFormatReplace Ordinals`	Boolean	Set/Get is superscript replaces ordinal number suffixes when automatically formatting.
`AutoFormatReplace PlainTextEmphasis`	Boolean	Set/Get if character formatting replaces manual emphasis characters when automatically formatting.
`AutoFormatReplace Quotes`	Boolean	Set/Get if curly quotation marks are replaced by straight quotation marks when automatically formatting.
`AutoFormatReplace Symbols`	Boolean	Set/Get if en or em dashes replace two consecutive hyphens when automatically formatting.
`AutoKeyboard Switching`	Boolean	Set/Get if automatic switch to the keyboard language to what you are typing.

Name	Returns	Description
AutoWord Selection	Boolean	Set/Get if dragging selects one word as opposed to one character.
Background Save	Boolean	Set/Get if documents in the background are saved.
BlueScreen	Boolean	Set/Get if text is displayed as white characters on a blue background.
ButtonField Clicks	Long	Set/Get the number of clicks required to run **GoToButton** or **MacroField**.
CheckGrammar AsYouType	Boolean	Set/Get if errors are marked and grammar is checked as you type.
CheckGrammar WithSpelling	Boolean	Set/Get if spelling and grammar are chacked consecutively.
CheckHangul Endings	Boolean	Set/Get if hangul endings are automatically detected and are ignored during conversion from hangul to hanja.
CheckSpelling AsYouType	Boolean	Set/Get if errors are marked and grammar is checked as you type
Confirm Conversions	Boolean	Set/Get if a Convert File dialog box is displayed before it opens or inserts a file that isn't a Word template or document.
ConvertHighAnsi ToFarEast	Boolean	Set/Get if East Asian fonts are converted to an appropriate font when opening a document.
CreateBackup	Boolean	Set/Get if a backup copy is created each time a document is saved.
CursorMovement	WdCursor Movement	Set/Get how the insertion poin progresses within bi-directional text.
DefaultBorder Color	WdColor	Set/Get default 24-bit color to use for new `Border` objects.
DefaultBorder ColorIndex	WdColor Index	Set/Get default color line for borders.
DefaultBorder LineStyle	WdLine Style	Set/Get default border line style.
DefaultBorder LineWidth	WdLine Width	Set/Get default line width of borders.

Table Continued on Following Page

Name	Returns	Description
DefaultFile Path	String	Set/Get default folders.
DefaultHighlight ColorIndex	WdColor Index	Set/Get color of highlighted text formatted with the **Highlight** button.
DefaultOpen Format	WdOpen Format	Set/Get default file converter used to open documents.
DefaultTray	String	Set/Get default tray the printer uses.
DefaultTrayID	WdPaper Tray	Set/Get default tray the printer uses.
DeletedTextColor	WdColor Index	Set/Get the deleted text color while change tracking is enabled.
DeletedTextMark	WdDeleted TextMark	Set/Get format of text while change tracking is enabled.
DiacriticColor Val	WdColor	Set/Get the diacritics 24-bit
DisplayGrid Lines	Boolean	Set/Get if document grid is displayed.
DocumentView Direction	Wd Document View Direction	Set/Get the reading order and alignment for the entire document.
EnableHangul HanjaRecent Ordering	Boolean	Set/Get if the most recently used words are displayed at the top of the suggestions list when converting between hangul hanja.
EnableMisused WordsDictionary	Boolean	Set/Get if checking for wrongly used words is performed when doing a spell/grammar check.
EnableSound	Boolean	Set/Get the computer to respond with a sound when an error occurs.
EnvelopeFeeder Installed	Boolean	Read Only. True if the current printer has a special feeder for envelopes.
GridDistance Horizontal	Single	Set/Get the horizontal space between the invisible grid lines when using Autoshapes or East Asian characters.
GridDistance Vertical	Single	Set/Get the vertical space between the invisible gridlines when using Autoshapes or East Asian characters.

Name	Returns	Description
GridOrigin Horizontal	Single	Set/Get the point (relative to the left edge of the page) where the invisible grid for working with Autoshapes/East Asian characters begins.
GridOrigin Vertical	Single	Set/Get the point (relative to the top of the page) where the invisible grid for working with Autoshapes/East Asian characters begins.
HangulHanja FastConversion	Boolean	Set/Get if automatically converts words (with only one suggestion) while converting between hangul and hanja.
HebrewMode	WdHeb Spell Start	Set/Get the Hebrew spell checker.
IgnoreInternet AndFileAddresses	Boolean	Set/Get if e-mail addresses. URL's etc are ignored during spell check.
IgnoreMixed Digits	Boolean	Set/Get if numbers within words are ignored during spell check.
IgnoreUppercase	Boolean	Set/Get if all uppercase letters are ignored during spell check.
IMEAutomatic Control	Boolean	Set/Get if the Japanese Input Method Editor (IME) opens and closes automatically.
InlineConversion	Boolean	Set/Get if unconfirmed character string is displayed in the IME as an insertion between confirmed character strings.
InsertedText Color	WdColor Index	Set/Get text color that is inserted while change tracking is enabled.
InsertedText Mark	WdInserted TextMark	Set/Get the text format that is returned while change tracking is enabled.
INSKeyFor Paste	Boolean	True if INS key can be used for pasting.

Table Continued on Following Page

Name	Returns	Description
Interpret HighAnsi	WdHigh AnsiText	Set/Get how to interpret text containing character codes (128 - 255 High-ANSI text).
MapPaper Size	Boolean	Set/Get if paper size is automatically adjusted for printing.
MatchFuzzyAY	Boolean	Set/Get if the distinction between Japanese row characters is ignoreds during a search.
MatchFuzzyBV	Boolean	Set/Get if the distinction between some Japanese characters is ignored.
MatchFuzzy Byte	Boolean	Set/Get if the distinction between full-width and half-width characters is ignored during a search.
MatchFuzzy Case	Boolean	Set/Get if the distinction between uppercase and lowercase letters is ignored during a search.
MatchFuzzy Dash	Boolean	Set/Get if the distinction between minus signs, long vowel sounds and dashes is ignored during a search.
MatchFuzzyDZ	Boolean	Set/Get if the distinction between some Japanese characters is ignored during a search.
MatchFuzzyHF	Boolean	Set/Get if the distinction between some Japanese characters is ignored during a search.
MatchFuzzy Hiragana	Boolean	Set/Get if the distinction between some Japanese characters is ignored during a search.
MatchFuzzy IterationMark	Boolean	Set/Get if the distinction between repetition marks is ignored during a search.
MatchFuzzy Kanji	Boolean	Set/Get if the distinction between some Japanese characters is ignored during a search.
MatchFuzzy KiKu	Boolean	Set/Get if the distinction between some Japanese characters is ignored during a search.
MatchFuzzyOld Kana	Boolean	Set/Get if the distinction between some Japanese characters is ignored during a search.

Name	Returns	Description
MatchFuzzyPro LongedSoundMark	Boolean	Set/Get if the distinction between short and long vowel sounds is ignored during a search.
MatchFuzzy Punctuation	Boolean	Set/Get if the distinction between types of punctuation marks is ignored during a search.
MatchFuzzySmall Kana	Boolean	Set/Get if the distinction between dipthongs and double constants is ignored during a search.
MatchFuzzy Space	Boolean	Set/Get if the distinction between space markers is ignored during a search.
MatchFuzzyTC	Boolean	Set/Get if the distinction between some Japanese characters is ignored during a search.
MatchFuzzyZJ	Boolean	Set/Get if the distinction between some Japanese characters is ignored during a search.
Measurement Unit	Wd Measurement Units	Set/Get the standard measurement unit for Word.
MonthNames	WdMonth Names	Set/Get how western month names are displayed in Arabic.
MultipleWord Conversions Mode	WdMultiple Word Conversions Mode	Set/Get direction for conversion between hangul and hanja.
OptimizeFor Word97byDefault	Boolean	Set/Get if all new documents are optimized for viewing in Word 97 by disabling any incompatible formatting.
Overtype	Boolean	Set/Get if overtype mode is active.
Pagination	Boolean	Set/Get if documents are repaginated in the background.
PictureEditor	String	Set/Get the name of the application used to edit pictures.
PrintBackground	Boolean	Set/Get if background is printed.

Table Continued on Following Page

Name	Returns	Description
PrintComments	Boolean	Set/Get if comments are printed on a new page at the end of a document.
PrintDraft	Boolean	Set/Get if printing with minimal formatting.
PrintDrawing Objects	Boolean	Set/Get if printing drawing objects.
PrintEvenPages InAscendingOrder	Boolean	Set/Get printing even pages in ascending order during manual duplex printing.
PrintFieldCodes	Boolean	Set/Get if field codes are printed instead of field results.
PrintHiddenText	Boolean	Set/Get if hidden text is printed.
PrintOddPages InAscendingOrder	Boolean	Set/Get if odd pages are printed in ascending order during manual duplex printing.
PrintProperties	Boolean	Set/Get if summary information is printed on a separate page.
PrintReverse	Boolean	Set/Get if printing is in reverse order.
ReplaceSelection	Boolean	Set/Get if typing or pasting replace the selection. False if the result of typing or pasting is added before the selection, leaving the selection in tact.
RevisedLines Color	WdColor Index	Set/Get the color of changed lines with tracked changes.
RevisedLines Mark	WdRevised LinesMark	Set/Get the placement of changed lines in a document with tracked changes.
Revised Properties Color	WdColor Index	Set/Get the color of formatting changes while change tracking is enabled.
Revised Properties Mark	WdRevised Properties Mark	Set/Get the mark used to show formatting changes while change tracking is enabled.
RTFInClipboard	Boolean	Macintosh Only. Set/Get if copied text retains its character and paragraph formatting.

Name	Returns	Description
SaveInterval	Long	Set/Get in minutes, time interval for saving AutoRecover information.
SaveNormalPrompt	Boolean	Set/Get if before quitting, Word prompts for confirmation when saving changes in the Normal template.
SaveProperties Prompt	Boolean	Set/Get when saving, prompts for document property information.
SendMailAttach	Boolean	Set/Get if the Send To on the File menu inserts the active document as an attachment to a mail message. False if the Send To command inserts the contents of the active document as text in a mail message.
ShortMenuNames	Boolean	Macintosh Only. True if Word displays abbreviated command names on menus
ShowControl Characters	Boolean	Set/Get if bi-directional characters are visible.
ShowDiacritics	Boolean	Set/Get if diacritics are visible in a right to left language document.
ShowReadability Statistics	Boolean	Set/get if a list of summary statistics are displayed after checking grammar.
SmartCutPaste	Boolean	Set/Get if Word automatically adjusts spacing between words and punctuation during cutting and pasting.
SnapToGrid	Boolean	Set/Get if AutoShapes or East Asian characters are automatically aligned when they are manipulated.
SnapToShapes	Boolean	Set/Get if Word automatically aligns all AutoShapes or East Asian characters in a new document.
StrictFinalYaa	Boolean	Set/Get if spell check uses special rules for Arabic words ending in 'yaa'.
StrictInitial AlefHamza	Boolean	Set/Get if spell check uses special rules for Arabic words beginning with an 'alef hamza'.

Table Continued on Following Page

Name	Returns	Description
SuggestFrom MainDictionary Only	Boolean	Set/Get if spelling suggestions come from the main dictionary only.
SuggestSpelling Corrections	Boolean	Set/Get if alternative spellings are always suggested when checking spelling.
TabIndentKey	Boolean	Set/Get if *Tab* and *Backspa* keys can increase and decrease left indents on paragraphs. If *Backspa* can change right aligned paragraphs to centered and vice versa.
UpdateFields AtPrint	Boolean	Set/Get if fields are automatically updated before printing.
UpdateLinks AtOpen	Boolean	Set/Get embedded OLE links are updated when a document is opened.
UpdateLinks AtPrint	Boolean	Set/Get if embedded links to other files are updated before printing.
UseCharacter Unit	Boolean	Set/Get if characters are the default unit of measurement.
UseDiffDiac Color	Boolean	Set/Get diacritics color.
UseGerman Spelling Reform	Boolean	Set/Get if new German post-reform rules are used when spell checking.
Visual Selection	WdVisual Selection	Set/Get the selection behavior based on visual cursor movements.
WPDocNavKeys	Boolean	Set/Get navigation keys for WordPerfect users.
WPHelp	Boolean	Set/Get key combinations for WordPerfect help dialog boxes.

Options Methods

Name	Returns	Parameters	Description
SetWP Help Options		[CommandKeyHelp], [DocNavigationKeys], [MouseSimulation], [DemoGuidance], [DemoSpeed], [HelpType]	Changes options for using the WordPerfect Help feature of Word.

Examples

Set up Word so that fractions typed as 1/2 do not change to ½:

```
Application.Options.AutoFormatAsYouTypeReplaceFractions = False
```

OtherCorrectionsException Object and the OtherCorrectionsExceptions Collection

The `OtherCorrectionsExceptions` collection holds the list of words, usually purposeful spelling mistakes, which you do not want AutoCorrect to correct. The `OtherCorrectionsException` object represents a single word AutoCorrect will not correct.

Besides the regular properties and methods associated with collections, the `OtherCorrectionsExceptions` has one additional method. The `Add` method of the `OtherCorrectionsExceptions` collection adds AutoCorrect entries using the `Name` parameter.

OtherCorrectionsException Common Properties

The `Application`, `Creator`, and `Parent` properties are defined at the beginning of this section.

OtherCorrectionsException Properties

Name	Returns	Description
Index	Long	Read Only. The position of the current object in the parent collection.
Name	String	Set/Get the name of the entry, e.g. "Plaese".

OtherCorrectionsException Methods

Name	Returns	Parameters	Description
Delete			Deletes the `AutoCorrectEntry` object.

Examples

Adding an entry to the `OtherCorrectionsExceptions` collection, display a message box with the value of the entry and then deleting it:

```
Dim OthEntry As OtherCorrectionsException

Set OthEntry = AutoCorrect.OtherCorrectionsExceptions.Add("Plaese")
MsgBox "Entry is " & OthEntry.Name
OthEntry.Delete
```

PageNumber Object and the PageNumbers Collection

The PageNumbers collection allows manipulation of the all the page numbers associated with a header or footer. The PageNumber object represents a single page number in an associated header or footer. The PageNumbers collection has a few properties and methods besides the typical collection properties and methods. The following table describes the collection's properties and methods:

PageNumbers Collection Special Properties and Methods

Name	Returns	Description
ChapterPage Separator	WdSeparator Type	Set/Get what character is used to separate a page number from a chapter number (e.g. dash).
DoubleQuote	Boolean	Set/Get whether double quotes are used.
HeadingLevel ForChapter	Long	Set/Get which heading style level to use for the chapter number.
IncludeChapter Number	Boolean	Set/Get whether chapter numbers are used with the page numbers.
NumberStyle	WdPageNumber Style	Set/Get the number style of the page number.
Restart NumberingAt Section	Boolean	Set/Get whether the page numbers restart with new sections.
ShowFirstPage Number	Boolean	Set/Get whether the first page has page numbering.
StartingNumber	Long	Set/Get what the starting number is for the page number.
Add	PageNumber	Method. [PageNumber Alignment], [FirstPage] parameters. Adds a page number to the current collection. Can specify the alignment of the first page and whether it appears on the first page.

PageNumber Common Properties

The Application, Creator, and Parent properties are defined at the beginning of this section.

PageNumber Properties

Name	Returns	Description
Alignment	WdPageNumber Alignment	Set/Get the alignment of the particular page number.
Index	Long	Read Only. The position of the current object in the parent collection.

PageNumber Methods

Name	Returns	Parameters	Description
Copy			Copies the PageNumber object to the clipboard.
Cut			Copies the PageNumber object to the clipboard and deletes the original from the document.
Delete			Deletes the current PageNumber object.
Select			Selects the PageNumber object in the document.

Examples

Create a page numbering in the primary footer of the first section of the active document. Then select the page number:

```
Dim pg As PageNumber

Set pg = ActiveDocument.Sections(1).Footers(wdHeaderFooterPrimary). _
    PageNumbers.Add(wdAlignPageNumberCenter)
pg.Select
```

PageSetup Object

The PageSetup object allows the manipulation of page properties for a document, range, section or selection.

> The equivalent to the Page Setup object is the **Page Setup** dialog box from the **File** menu.

PageSetup Common Properties

The Application, Creator, and Parent properties are defined at the beginning of this section.

PageSetup Properties

Name	Returns	Description
BottomMargin	Single	Set/Get the bottom margin of page.
CharsLine	Single	Set/Get the number of characters in the document grid.
DifferentFirstPageHeaderFooter	Long	Set/Get whether the header/footer on the first page is different from the documents header/footer.
FirstPageTray	WdPaperTray	Set/Get a different printer tray for the first page of the document.
FooterDistance	Single	Set/Get how far the footer bottom is from the bottom of the page.
Gutter	Single	Set/Get how much margin space is needed for binding.
GutterPos	WdGutterStyle	Set/Get what side of the page will have the gutter.
GutterStyle	WdGutterStyleOld	Set/Get what style is used for the gutter.
HeaderDistance	Single	Set/Get how far the header top is from the page top.
LayoutMode	WdLayoutMode	Set/Get the layout mode for the page.
LeftMargin	Single	Set/Get the left margin of page.
LineNumbering	LineNumbering	Set/Get an object that allows manipulation of line numbering.
LinesPage	Single	Set/Get how many lines are in a page.
MirrorMargins	Long	Set/Get whether margins on sequential pages should be mirrored, like a book.
OddAndEvenPagesHeaderFooter	Long	Set/Get whether odd and even pages have different header/footers.
Orientation	WdOrientation	Set/Get the page orientation.

Name	Returns	Description
OtherPages Tray	WdPaper Tray	Set/Get the printer tray for pages besides the first.
PageHeight	Single	Set/Get the height of the page.
PageWidth	Single	Set/Get the width of the page.
PaperSize	WdPaperSize	Set/Get the paper size such as letter.
RightMargin	Single	Set/Get the right margin of the page.
Section Direction	WdSection Direction	Set/Get the alignment and reading order.
SectionStart	WdSection Start	Set/Get where the section break occurs.
ShowGrid	Boolean	Set/Get whether the grid is shown.
Suppress Endnotes	Long	Set/Get whether endnotes are displayed at the end of the current section.
TextColumns	TextColumns	Set/Get an object allowing manipulation of the text columns.
TopMargin	Single	Set/Get the top margin of the page.
TwoPagesOnOne	Boolean	Set/Get whether two pages are printed on one piece of paper.
Vertical Alignment	WdVertical Alignment	Set/Get how the page text is aligned on the page.

PageSetup Methods

Name	Returns	Parameters	Description
SetAsTemplate Default			Saves the current page setup options to the active template.
Toggle Portrait			Switch between landscape and portrait orientation.

Examples

Change the page setup of the active document to a landscape orientation, a top margin of 5 centimeters, the first page to require manual feed of the printer, and the gutter to be on the left side of the page:

```
With ActiveDocument.PageSetup
    .Orientation = wdOrientLandscape
    .TopMargin = CentimetersToPoints(5)
    .FirstPageTray = wdPrinterManualFeed
    .OtherPagesTray = wdPrinterDefaultBin
    .GutterPos = wdGutterPosLeft
End With
```

Pane Object and the Panes Collection

The Panes collection allows manipulation of the different panes of a window. A Pane object is equivalent to single pane for a window. The parent object of the Panes collection is the Window object.

Besides the typical collection properties and methods the Panes collection has an Add method. The Add method is used to add a Pane object to the collection and add new panes to the current window.

Pane Common Properties

The Application, Creator, and Parent properties are defined at the beginning of this section.

Pane Properties

Name	Returns	Description
Browse Width	Long	Read Only. Returns the width of the pane in which text wraps in the Web layout view.
Display Rulers	Boolean	Set/Get whether to display rules in the pane.
Display Vertical Ruler	Boolean	Set/Get whether to display the vertical rules in a pane.
Document	Document	Read Only. Returns the document in the pane.
Frameset	Frameset	Read Only. Returns the collection of frames in the current pane.
Horizontal Percent Scrolled	Long	Set/Get where in the document the current pane is scrolled to.
Index	Long	Read Only. The position of the current object in the parent collection

Name	Returns	Description
MinimumFont Size	Long	Set/Get the smallest font used for the pane in an online layout view.
Next	Pane	Read Only. Returns the next pane in the parent collection
Previous	Pane	Read Only. Returns the previous pane in the parent collection.
Selection	Selection	Read Only. Returns the selected text in the current pane.
Vertical Percent Scrolled	Long	Set/Get where in the document the current pane is scrolled to.
View	View	Read Only. Allows manipulation of the current view in the pane.
Zooms	Zooms	Read Only. Allows manipulation of the current zoom settings.

Pane Methods

Name	Returns	Parameters	Description
Activate			Activates the pane.
AutoScroll		Velocity	Starts the document in the pane to scroll by itself until the user presses a mouse button or a key.
Close			Closes the pane.
Large Scroll		[Down], [Up], [ToRight], [ToLeft]	Causes the document to scroll a certain direction a screen at a time.
New Frameset			Creates a new Frameset in the current pane.
Page Scroll		[Down], [Up]	Causes the document to scroll a certain direction a document page at a time.
Small Scroll		[Down], [Up], [ToRight], [ToLeft]	Causes the document to scroll a certain direction a document line at a time.

Table Continued on Following Page

Name	Returns	Parameters	Description
TOCIn Frameset			Creates a table of contents based on the specified document and places it in a new frame on the left of the frames page.

Examples

Make the active pane scroll down by one line and turn off the ruler display:

```
Application.ActiveWindow.ActivePane.SmallScroll Down:=1
Application.ActiveWindow.ActivePane.DisplayRulers = False
```

Paragraph Object and the Paragraphs Collection

The Paragraphs collection represents the collection of paragraphs in the current selection, range or document. Each Paragraph object represents a single paragraph, with all the formatting options, in a selection, range or document.

The Paragraphs collection has many properties and methods besides the ordinary collection attributes. The following list describes the properties and methods:

Paragraphs Collection Special Properties

Name	Returns	Description
AddSpaceBetween FarEastAndAlpha	Long	Set/Get whether spacing is automatic between Japanese and English text.
AddSpaceBetween FarEastAndDigit	Long	Set/Get whether spacing is automatic between Japanese and numbers.
Alignment	WdParagraph Alignment	Set/Get the alignment of the paragraph.
AutoAdjustRight Indent	Long	Set/Get whether the settings for right indent is automatic.
BaseLineAlignment	WdBaseline Alignment	Set/Get alignment of the baseline font.
Borders	Borders	Set/Get the borders around the paragraphs.
CharacterUnit FirstLineIndent	Single	Set/Get distance in characters for use as a first line indent.

Name	Returns	Description
CharacterUnit LeftIndent	Single	Set/Get distance in characters for use as a left indent.
CharacterUnit RightIndent	Single	Set/Get distance in characters for use as a right indent.
DisableLine HeightGrid	Long	Set/Get whether characters are aligned to gridlines.
FarEastLine BreakControl	Long	Set/Get whether line break control options are on.
First	Paragraph	Read Only. Returns the first paragraph in the collection.
FirstLine Indent	Single	Set/Get how far the first line indent is.
Format	Paragraph Format	Set/Get the format of the paragraphs.
HalfWidth PunctuationOn TopOfLine	Long	Set/Get whether punctuation is half width at the start of a line.
Hanging Punctuation	Long	Set/Get whether hanging punctuation is active.
Hyphenation	Long	Set/Get whether hyphenation is automatic.
KeepTogether	Long	Set/Get whether all lines in a paragraph are kept together on a page.
KeepWithNext	Long	Set/Get whether a paragraph will be kept together with the next paragraph on the same page.
Last	Paragraph	Read Only. Returns the last paragraph in the collection.
LeftIndent	Single	Set/Get the left indent of the paragraphs.
LineSpacing	Single	Set/Get the line spacing for the paragraphs in relation to the LineSpacingRule.
LineSpacing Rule	WdLine Spacing	Set/Get how line spacing should be measured.

Table Continued on Following Page

Name	Returns	Description
LineUnitAfter	Single	Set/Get value (in number of lines) for space left after this paragraph.
LineUnitBefore	Single	Set/Get value (in number of lines) for space left before this paragraph.
NoLineNumber	Long	Set/Get whether line numbers are present for the paragraphs.
OutlineLevel	WdOutline Level	Set/Get the outline level.
PageBreak Before	Long	Set/Get whether a page break is before the paragraphs.
ReadingOrder	WdReading Order	Set/Get direction of reading, left-to-right or right-to-left.
RightIndent	Single	Set/Get the right indent.
Shading	Shading	Read Only. Modify the shading of the paragraphs.
SpaceAfter	Single	Set/Get the spacing after the paragraphs.
SpaceAfterAuto	Long	Set/Get whether automatic spacing is on.
SpaceBefore	Single	Set/Get the spacing before the paragraphs.
SpaceBefore Auto	Long	Set/Get whether automatic spacing is on.
Style	Variant	Set/Get the style associated with the paragraphs.
TabStops	TabStops	Set/Get the custom tab settings.
WidowControl	Long	Set/Get if the first and last lines of a paragraph stay on the same page as the rest of the paragraph.
WordWrap	Long	Set/Get whether Latin word-wrap is on.

Paragraphs Collection Methods

Name	Returns	Parameters	Description
Add	Paragraph	[Range]	Adds a paragraph to the collection.
CloseUp			Deletes spacing before the paragraphs.
Indent			Indents the paragraphs one level.
IndentChar Width		Count	Indents the paragraphs Count characters.
IndentFirstLine CharWidth		Count	Indents the first line of the paragraph Count characters.
OpenOrCloseUp			Toggles adding spaces or deleting spaces before the paragraphs.
OpenUp			Adds spaces before the paragraphs.
Outdent			Decrease the paragraphs one indent level.
OutlineDemote			Demotes the paragraphs by one heading level style.
OutlineDemote ToBody			Demotes the paragraphs to body text.
OutlinePromote			Promotes the paragraphs.
Reset			Removes any special formatting for the paragraphs.

Table Continued on Following Page

Name	Returns	Parameters	Description
Space1, Space2, Space15			Sets the line spacing for the paragraph to single, 1.5, or double.
TabHangingIndent		Count	Creates a hanging indent to a certain tab stop.
TabIndent		Count	Sets the tab stop for the indent.

Paragraph Common Properties

The Application, Creator, and Parent properties are defined at the beginning of this section.

Paragraph Properties

Name	Returns	Description
AddSpaceBetween FarEastAndAlpha	Long	Set/Get whether spacing is automatic between Japanese and English text.
AddSpaceBetween FarEastAndDigit	Long	Set/Get whether spacing is automatic between Japanese and numbers.
Alignment	WdParagraph Alignment	Set/Get the alignment of the paragraph.
AutoAdjustRight Indent	Long	Set/Get whether the right indent is automatic.
BaseLine Alignment	WdBaseline Alignment	Set/Get alignment of the baseline font.
Borders	Borders	Set/Get the borders around the paragraph.
CharacterUnit FirstLineIndent	Single	Set/Get distance in characters for use as a first line indent.
CharacterUnit LeftIndent	Single	Set/Get distance in characters for use as a left indent.
CharacterUnit RightIndent	Single	Set/Get distance in characters for use as a right indent.

Name	Returns	Description
DisableLine HeightGrid	Long	Set/Get whether characters are aligned to gridlines.
DropCap	DropCap	Read Only. Allows creation of a dropped capital letter as the first letter in the paragraph.
FarEastLine BreakControl	Long	Set/Get whether line break control options are on.
FirstLine Indent	Single	Set/Get how far the first line indent is.
Format	Paragraph Format	Set/Get the format of the paragraph.
HalfWidth Punctuation OnTopOfLine	Long	Set/Get whether punctuation is half width at the start of a line.
Hanging Punctuation	Long	Set/Get whether hanging punctuation is on.
Hyphenation	Long	Set/Get whether hyphenation is automatic.
ID	String	Set/Get the ID of the paragraph.
KeepTogether	Long	Set/Get whether all lines in a paragraph are kept together on a page.
KeepWithNext	Long	Set/Get whether a paragraph will be kept together with the next paragraph on the same page.
LeftIndent	Single	Set/Get the left indent of the paragraph.
LineSpacing	Single	Set/Get the line spacing for the paragraph in relation to the LineSpacingRule.
LineSpacing Rule	WdLine Spacing	Set/Get how line spacing should be measured.
LineUnitAfter	Single	Set/Get value (in number of lines) for space left after this paragraph.
LineUnitBefore	Single	Set/Get value (in number of lines) for space left before this paragraph.

Table Continued on Following Page

Name	Returns	Description
NoLineNumber	Long	Set/Get whether line numbers are present for the paragraph.
OutlineLevel	WdOutline Level	Set/Get the outline level.
PageBreak Before	Long	Set/Get whether a page break is before the paragraph.
Range	Range	Read Only. Returns the spot in the document where the paragraph is.
ReadingOrder	WdReading Order	Set/Get direction of reading, left-to-right or right-to-left.
RightIndent	Single	Set/Get the right indent.
Shading	Shading	Read Only. Modify the shading of the paragraph.
SpaceAfter	Single	Set/Get the spacing after the paragraph.
SpaceAfter Auto	Long	Set/Get whether automatic spacing is on.
SpaceBefore	Single	Set/Get the spacing before the paragraph.
SpaceBefore Auto	Long	Set/Get whether automatic spacing is on.
Style	Variant	Set/Get the style associated with the paragraph.
TabStops	TabStops	Set/Get the custom tab settings.
WidowControl	Long	Set/Get if the first and last lines of a paragraph stay on the same page as the rest of the paragraph.
WordWrap	Long	Set/Get whether Latin word-wrap is on.

Paragraph Methods

Name	Returns	Parameters	Description
CloseUp			Deletes spacing before the paragraph.
Indent			Indents the paragrap one level.

Name	Returns	Parameters	Description
IndentChar Width		Count	Indents the paragrap by Count characters from the page margin.
IndentFirst LineCharWidth		Count	Indents the first line of the paragraph by Count characters from the page margin.
Next	Paragraph	[Count]	Returns the next paragraph in the collection or moves forward by Count paragraphs.
OpenOrCloseUp			Toggles adding spaces or deleting spaces before the paragraph.
OpenUp			Adds spaces before the paragraph.
Outdent			Decrease the paragraph one indent level.
OutlineDemote			Demotes the paragraph.
OutlineDemote ToBody			Demotes the paragraph to body text.
Outline Promote			Promotes the paragraph.
Previous	Paragraph	[Count]	Returns the previous paragraph in the collection or moves backwards by Count paragraphs.
Reset			Removes any special formatting for the paragraph.
Space1			Sets single spacing for the paragraph.
Space15			Sets 1.5 line spacing for the paragraph.

Table Continued on Following Page

Name	Returns	Parameters	Description
Space2			Sets double spacing for the paragraph.
TabHanging Indent		Count	Creates a hanging indent to a certain tab stop.
TabIndent		Count	Sets the tab stop for the indent.

Examples

Set the left indent of the first paragraph of the active document to 0.5 centimetres, a 6 point space after the paragraph, line spacing to double, left alignment, a page break before the paragraph, and a 1 centimetre indent for the first line:

```
Dim prg As Paragraph

Set prg = ActiveDocument.Paragraphs.First
With prg
    .LeftIndent = CentimetersToPoints(0.5)
    .SpaceAfter = 6
    .LineSpacingRule = wdLineSpaceDouble
    .Alignment = wdAlignParagraphLeft
    .PageBreakBefore = True
    .FirstLineIndent = CentimetersToPoints(1)
End With
```

ParagraphFormat Object

The ParagraphFormat object provides formatting options for a specified paragraph. Possible parents of the ParagraphFormat object are the Find, Paragraph, Range, Replacement, Selection, and Style objects.

ParagraphFormat Common Properties

The Application, Creator, and Parent properties are defined at the beginning of this section.

ParagraphFormat Properties

Name	Returns	Description
AddSpaceBetween FarEastAndAlpha	Long	Set/Get whether spacing is automatic between Japanese and English text.
AddSpaceBetween FarEastAndDigit	Long	Set/Get whether spacing is automatic between Japanese and numbers.
Alignment	WdParagraph Alignment	Set/Get the alignment of the paragraph.

Name	Returns	Description
AutoAdjustRight Indent	Long	Set/Get whether the right indent is automatic.
BaseLineAlignment	WdBaseline Alignment	Set/Get alignment of the baseline font.
Borders	Borders	Set/Get the borders around the paragraph.
CharacterUnit FirstLineIndent	Single	Set/Get distance in characters for use as a first line indent.
CharacterUnitLeft Indent	Single	Set/Get distance in characters for use as a left indent.
CharacterUnit RightIndent	Single	Set/Get distance in characters for use as a right indent.
DisableLine HeightGrid	Long	Set/Get whether characters are aligned to gridlines.
Duplicate	Paragraph Format	Read Only. Duplicate the format settings into a new object.
FarEastLine BreakControl	Long	Set/Get whether line break control options are on.
FirstLineIndent	Single	Set/Get how far the first line indent is.
HalfWidth PunctuationOn TopOfLine	Long	Set/Get whether punctuation is half width at the start of a line
Hanging Punctuation	Long	Set/ Get whether hanging punctuation is enabled for the paragraph.
Hyphenation	Long	Set/Get whether hyphenation is automatic.
KeepTogether	Long	Set/Get whether all lines in a paragraph are kept together on a page.
KeepWithNext	Long	Set/Get whether a paragraph will be kept together with the next paragraph on the same page.
LeftIndent	Single	Set/Get the left indent of the paragraphs.

Table Continued on Following Page

Name	Returns	Description
LineSpacing	Single	Set/Get the line spacing for the paragraphs in relation to the LineSpacingRule.
LineSpacing Rule	WdLine Spacing	Set/Get how line spacing should be measured.
LineUnitAfter	Single	Set/Get value (in number of lines) for space left after this paragraph.
LineUnit Before	Single	Set/Get value (in number of lines) for space left before this paragraph.
NoLineNumber	Long	Set/Get whether line numbers are present for the paragraphs.
OutlineLevel	WdOutline Level	Set/Get the outline level.
PageBreak Before	Long	Set/Get whether a page break is before the paragraphs.
ReadingOrder	WdReading Order	Set/Get direction of reading, left-to-right or right-to-left.
RightIndent	Single	Set/Get the right indent.
Shading	Shading	Read Only. Modify the shading of the paragraphs.
SpaceAfter	Single	Set/Get the spacing after the paragraphs.
SpaceAfter Auto	Long	Set/Get whether automatic spacing is on.
SpaceBefore	Single	Set/Get the spacing before the paragraphs.
SpaceBefore Auto	Long	Set/Get whether automatic spacing is on.
Style	Variant	Set/Get the style associated with the paragraphs.
TabStops	TabStops	Set/Get the custom tab settings.
WidowControl	Long	Set/Get if the first and last lines of a paragraph stay on the same page as the rest of the paragraph.
WordWrap	Long	Set/Get whether Latin word-wrap is on.

ParagraphFormat Methods

Name	Returns	Parameters	Description
CloseUp			Deletes spacing before the paragraphs.
IndentChar Width		Count As Integer	Sets the number of characters to indent the paragraphs by.
IndentFirst LineCharWidth		Count As Integer	Sets the number of characters to indent the first line of a paragraph by.
OpenOrCloseUp			Toggles adding spaces or deleting spaces before the paragraphs.
OpenUp			Adds spaces before the paragraphs.
Reset			Removes any special formatting for the paragraphs.
Space1			Sets single spacing for the paragraph.
Space15			Sets 1.5 line spacing for the paragraph.
Space2			Sets double spacing for the paragraph.
TabHanging Indent		Count As Integer	Creates a hanging indent to a certain tab stop.
TabIndent		Count As Integer	Sets the tab stop for the indent.

Examples

See the Paragraph object. The example shown there would work the same way with the ParagraphFormat object.

PictureFormat Object

The PictureFormat object allows manipulation of the picture properties of the parent Shape object.

473

PictureFormat Common Properties

The `Application`, `Creator`, and `Parent` properties are defined at the beginning of this section.

PictureFormat Properties

Name	Returns	Description
Brightness	Single	Set/Get the brightness of the parent shape (0 to 1 where 1 is the brightest).
ColorType	MsoPicture ColorType	Set/Get the type of color setting of the parent shape.
Contrast	Single	Set/Get the contrast of the parent shape (0 to 1 where 1 is the greatest contrast).
CropBottom	Single	Set/Get how much is cropped off the bottom.
CropLeft	Single	Set/Get how much is cropped off the left.
CropRight	Single	Set/Get how much is cropped off the right.
CropTop	Single	Set/Get how much is cropped off the top.
Transparency Color	Long	Set/Get the color used for transparency.
Transparent Background	MsoTriState	Set/Get whether transparent colors appear transparent.

PictureFormat Methods

Name	Returns	Parameters	Description
Increment Brightness		Increment	Increases the brightness by the Increment value.
Increment Contrast		Increment	Increases the contrast by the Increment value.

Examples

Set the brightness and contrast of the first picture in the active document to as high as possible:

```
With ActiveDocument.Shapes(1).PictureFormat
    .Brightness = 1
    .Contrast = 1
End With
```

ProofreadingErrors Collection

The ProofreadingErrors collection holds the list of spelling and grammatical errors for the document or range. The ProofreadingErrors collection is made up of Range objects specifying the spot in the document for each error. The ProofreadingErrors collection can be accessed either through the SpellingErrors or GrammaticalErrors properties of the Document or Range object.

The ProofreadingErrors collection is like any regular collection except for one additional property. The Type property returns whether the ProofreadingErrors collection is a grammatical error collection or a spelling error collection.

Examples

Display all the spelling errors in the active document in message boxes:

```
Dim spError As Range
For Each spError In ActiveDocument.SpellingErrors
    MsgBox spError.Text
Next
```

Range Object

The Range object defines a specific point or area in a document. The Range object is one of the most used objects in the Word Object Model. The Range object is used to programmatically specify a spot in the document and then modify it. The area that the Range object specifies starts at the Start character and ends at the End character. Some examples of Range areas are bookmark locations, footnotes locations, comment locations, and Hyperlink locations.

Since the Range object specifies areas in a document, it is not surprising that most of the objects in the Word Object Model that describe parts of a document, such as the Footnote object, are possible parent objects of the Range object. The more important parent objects are Bookmark, Cell, Comment, Document, Endnote, Footnote, FormField, Frame, HeaderFooter, Hyperlink, Index, InlineShape, List, Paragraph, Revision, Row, Section, Selection, Subdocument, Table, TableOfAuthorities, TableOfContents, TableOfFigures, and TextFrame objects. The Range object is also a child object of the Characters, ProofreadingErrors, Sentences, and Words collection.

Range Common Properties

The Application, Creator, and Parent properties are defined at the beginning of this section.

Range Properties

Name	Returns	Description
Bold	Long	Set/Get whether the range text is bold.
BoldBi	Long	Set/Get if range is formatted as bold.
Bookmark ID	Long	Read Only. Returns the bookmark ID that includes the range, 0 if no range is part of a bookmark.
Bookmarks	Bookmarks	Read Only. Returns the bookmarks in the range.
Borders	Borders	Set/Get the borders around the range.
Case	Wd Character Case	Set/Get the text case of the range (e.g. uppercase).
Cells	Cells	Read Only. Returns the table cells in the range.
Characters	Characters	Read Only. Returns the characters in the range.
Character Width	Wd Character Width	Set/Get the character width of the characters in the range.
Columns	Columns	Read Only. Returns the table columns in the range.
Combine Characters	Boolean	Set/Get whether characters are combined.
Comments	Boolean	Read Only. Returns the comments in the range.
Disable Character SpaceGrid	Boolean	Set/Get whether the characters per line is set by the Page Setup dialog box.
Duplicate	Range	Read Only. Returns a range duplicating the current range.
Emphasis Mark	WdEmphasis Mark	Set/Get the emphasis mark for a character.
End	Long	Set/Get the ending character number of the range.
Endnotes	Endnotes	Read Only. Returns the endnotes in the range.
Fields	Fields	Read Only. Returns the fields in the range.

Name	Returns	Description
Find	Find	Read Only. Returns an object allowing the ability to find text in the range.
FitText Width	Single	Set/Get the width in which to fit the selected text.
Font	Font	Set/Get the font of the range.
Footnotes	Footnotes	Read Only. Returns the footnotes in the range.
Formatted Text	Range	Set/Get the formatted text that is part of the range.
FormFields	Form Fields	Read Only. Returns the form fields in the range.
Frames	Frames	Read Only. Returns the frames in the range.
Grammar Checked	**Boolean**	Set/Get whether the range has been grammar checked.
Grammatical Errors	Proofreading Errors	Read Only. Returns the list of grammatical errors in the range.
Highlight ColorIndex	WdColorIndex	Set/Get the color of the highlighted text in the range (e.g. yellow).
Horizontal InVertical	WdHorizontal InVertical Type	Set/Get formatting of horizontal text within vertical text.
Hyperlinks	Hyperlinks	Read Only. Returns the hyperlinks in the range.
ID	**String**	Set/Get the ID of the range.
Information	**Variant**	Read Only. Type parameter. Returns information specified by the Type parameter. Use the WdInformation constants.
InlineShapes	InlineShapes	Read Only. Returns the inline shapes in the range.
IsEndOfRow Mark	**Boolean**	Read Only. Returns whether the current range is the end-of-row marker in a table. Range has to be collapsed.
Italic	**Long**	Set/Get whether the range font is italic.

Table Continued on Following Page

Name	Returns	Description
ItalicBi	Long	Set/Get if text within a range is formatted as italic.
Kana	WdKana	Set/Get format of Kana text in the Range.
Language Detected	Boolean	Set/Get whether the language is detected.
LanguageID	WdLanguageID	Set/Get the language for the range.
LanguageID FarEast	WdLanguageID	Set/Get the language for the range.
Language IDOther	WdLanguageID	Set/Get the language for the range.
ListFormat	ListFormat	Read Only. Returns the formatting of the lists in the range.
List Paragraphs	List Paragraphs	Read Only. Returns the numbered paragraphs in the range.
NextStory Range	Range	Read Only. Returns a range containing the next story in the document.
NoProofing	Long	Set/Get whether proofing will be done for the range.
Orientation	WdText Orientation	Set/Get the text direction for the range (e.g. Vertical).
PageSetup	PageSetup	Set/Get an object manipulating the page characteristics.
Paragraph Format	Paragraph Format	Set/Get the paragraph formatting for the range.
Paragraphs	Paragraphs	Read Only. Returns the paragraphs in the range.
Previous BookmarkID	Long	Read Only. Returns the closest bookmark ID previous to, or in, the range.
Readability Statistics	Readability Statistics	Read Only. Returns the statistics for the range.
Revisions	Revisions	Read Only. Returns the revisions in the range.
Rows	Rows	Read Only. Returns the table rows in the range.

Name	Returns	Description
Scripts	Scripts	Read Only. Returns the HTML Scripts contained in the range.
Sections	Sections	Read Only. Returns the document sections in the range.
Sentences	Sentences	Read Only. Returns the sentences in the range.
Shading	Shading	Read Only. Modify the shading of the range.
Shape Range	ShapeRange	Read Only. Returns all the Shape objects in the range.
Spelling Checked	Boolean	Set/Get whether the range has been spell checked.
Spelling Errors	Proofreading Errors	Read Only. Returns the list of spelling errors in the range.
Start	Long	Set/Get the starting character of the range.
StoryLength	Long	Read Only. Returns the number of characters in the document story that the range is a part.
StoryType	WdStoryType	Read Only. Returns the type of document story that the range is a part.
Style	Variant	Set/Get the document style for the range.
Subdocuments	Subdocuments	Read Only. Returns the subdocuments in the range.
SynonymInfo	SynonymInfo	Read Only. Returns the thesaurus synonyms for the text in the range.
Tables	Tables	Read Only. Returns the tables in the range.
Text	String	Set/Get the text in the range.
Text Retrieval Mode	Text Retrieval Mode	Set/Get an object manipulating what is included in the range text.
TopLevel Tables	Tables	Read Only. Returns the top-level tables (non-nested tables) in the range.

Table Continued on Following Page

Name	Returns	Description
TwoLinesIn One	WdTwoLinesIn OneType	Set/Get this property to enable or disable the display of the selected text in one half of a regular line's height, allowing the display of two lines in the space of one. Takes one of several values for its parameter, controlling the appearance of the two-line text.
Underline	WdUnderline	Set/Get whether the font in the range is underlined.
Words	Words	Read Only. Returns the words in the range.

Range Methods

Name	Returns	Parameters	Description
AutoFormat			Formats a document as specified by the Kind property.
Calculate	Single		Calculates the math expression in the range text.
Check Grammar			Checks the grammar for the range.
Check Spelling		[Custom Dictionary], [Ignore Uppercase], [Always Suggest], [Custom Dictionary2], [Custom Dictionary3], ... [Custom Dictionary10]	Checks the spelling for the range.
Check Synonyms			Pop up the **Thesaurus** dialog box listing synonyms for the range.

Name	Returns	Parameters	Description
Collapse		[Direction]	Collapses the ranges to either the range start (default) or the range end (wdCollapseEnd direction).
Compute Statistics	Long	Statistic As WdStatistic	Calculates and returns the statistic set by the Statistic parameter.
Convert HangulAnd Hanja		[Conversions Mode], [Fast Conversion], [CheckHangul Ending], [EnableRecent Ordering], [Custom Dictionary]	Converts the specified range from hangul to hanja or vice versa
ConvertTo Table	Table	[Separator], [NumRows], [NumColumns], [InitialColumnWi dth], [Format], [ApplyBorders], [ApplyShading], [ApplyFont], [ApplyColor], [ApplyHeading Rows], [ApplyLastRow], [ApplyFirst Column], [Apply LastColumn], [AutoFit], [AutoFit Behavior], [DefaultTable Behavior]	Converts the range text to a table if possible. If default table settings are not appropriate, the parameters allow specifying table properties.
Copy			Copies the range to the clipboard.
CopyAsPict ure			Copies the range to the clipboard.

Table Continued on Following Page

Name	Returns	Parameters	Description
Create Publisher		[Edition], [Contains PICT], [Contains RTF], [Contains Text]	Macintosh Only. Publishes the selected text in an edition, which you can then subscribe to in other documents.
Cut			Copies the range to the clipboard and removes the original text.
Detect Languag			Determines the language of the specified text.
Delete	Long	[Unit], [Count]	Deletes Count number of Unit items. Use the WdUnits constants for Unit.
EndOf	Long	[Unit], [Extend]	Moves or extends the ending character of the range using a Unit type (WdUnits) and the type of movement with Extend.
Expand	Long	[Unit]	Expands the range by the specified Unit.

Name	Returns	Parameters	Description
Get Spelling Suggestions	Spelling Suggestions	[Custom Dictionary], [Ignore Uppercase], [Main Dictionary], [Suggestion Mode], [Custom Dictionary2], ... [Custom Dictionary10]	Get the spelling suggestions list for the current range.
GoTo	Range	[What], [Which], [Count], [Name]	Goes to a certain spot in a document returning a Range object specifying the start of the new spot. This method can be used to go to a certain type of thing (What), moving a specific way (Which) a number of times (Count) or to a certain named object (Name).
GoToNext	Range	What As WdGoToItem	Returns the range of the next What item.
GoToPrevious	Range	What As WdGoToItem	Returns the range of the previous What item.
InRange	**Variant**	Range As Range	Returns whether the Range parameter is part of the current range.

Table Continued on Following Page

Name	Returns	Parameters	Description
Insert After		`Text As String`	Inserts the `Text` parameter after the range and then includes it in the range.
InsertAuto Text			Uses the range text to search for an AutoText entry that matches it. The AutoText text then replaces the range text if a match is found.
Insert Before		`Text As String`	Inserts the `Text` parameter before the range and then includes it in the range.
InsertBreak		`[Type]`	Inserts a page break or a break specified by the `Type` parameter (`WdBreakType`).
Insert Caption		`Label, [Title], [TitleAuto Text], [Position]`	Inserts a caption label with the `Label` text either before or after the range.
InsertCross Reference		`Reference Type, ReferenceKind As WdReference Kind, ReferenceItem, [InsertAs Hyperlink], [Include Position]`	Inserts a cross-reference for an item in the range.

Name	Returns	Parameters	Description
Insert Database		[Format], [Style], [LinkTo Source], [Connection], [SQLStatement], [SQLStatement1], [Password Document], [Password Template], [WritePassword Document], [WritePassword Template], [DataSource], [From], [To], [IncludeFields]	Inserts data from a separate data source at the specified range.
Insert DateTime		[DateTimeFormat], [InsertAsField], [InsertAsFull Width], [DateLanguage], [CalendarType]	Inserts the date or time in the specified range.
Insert File		FileName As String, [Range], [Confirm Conversions], [Link], [Attachment]	Inserts the file specified by FileName replacing the range text.
Insert Paragraph			Replaces the current range as a new paragraph.
Insert Paragraph After			Inserts a paragraph at the end of the range.
Insert Paragraph Before			Inserts a paragraph at the start of the range.
Insert Symbol		CharacterNumber As Long, [Font], [Unicode], [Bias]	Inserts a symbol specified by the CharacterNumber as the range text.

Table Continued on Following Page

Name	Returns	Parameters	Description
InStory	Boolean	Range As Range	Returns whether the Range parameter is in the same story as the current range.
IsEqual	Boolean	Range As Range	Returns whether the Range parameter is the same as the current range.
Lookup Name Properties		Name As String	Does a lookup of the Name parameter in the global address book and displays the **Properties** dialog box.
Modify Enclosure			Adds, modifies, or removes an enclosure around the specified character or characters.
Move	Long	[Unit], [Count]	Collapses and moves the range.
MoveEnd	Long	[Unit], [Count]	Moves the end character of the range.
MoveEnd Until	Long	Cset, [Count]	Moves the end character of the range until the characters in Cset are found.
MoveEnd While	Long	Cset, [Count]	Moves the end character of the range while the characters in Cset are found.
MoveStart	Long	[Unit], [Count]	Moves the start character of the range.
MoveStart Until	Long	Cset, [Count]	Moves the start character of the range until the characters in Cset are found.
MoveStart While	Long	Cset, [Count]	Moves the start character of the range while the characters in Cset are found.

Table Continued on Following Page

Name	Returns	Parameters	Description
MoveUntil	Long	Cset, [Count]	Collapses and moves the range until the characters in Cset are found
MoveWhile	Long	Cset, [Count]	Collapses and moves the range while the characters in Cset are found
Next	Range	[Unit], [Count]	Moves the range to the next item specified by the Unit parameter and returns a Range object.
Next Subdocument			Moves the range to the next subdocument.
Paste			Pastes and replaces the clipboard contents into the range text.
PasteAsNeste dTable			Paste the clipboard contents as nested table if applicable.
PasteSpecial	Range	[IconIndex], [Link], [Placement], [DisplayAs Icon], [DataType], [IconFile Name], [IconLabel]	Past the clipboard contents in a special manner (e.g. as an OLE object).
Phonetic Guide		Text As String, Alignment As Long, Raise As Long, FontSize As Long, FontName As String	Add phonetic guides to the specified text. Alignment of the Phonetic text can be controlled by WdPhoneticGuideAl ignmentType constants

Table Continued on Following Page

Name	Returns	Parameters	Description
Previous	Range	[Unit], [Count]	Moves the range to the previous item specified by the Unit parameter and returns a Range object.
Previous Subdocument			Moves the range to the previous subdocument.
Relocate		Direction As Long	Moves the range before or after a visible paragraph in outline view.
Select			Selects the range text in the document.
SetRange		Start As Long, End As Long	Set the Start character and the End character of the range.
Sort		[Exclude Header], [Field Number], [SortFieldType], [SortOrder], [FieldNumber2], [SortField Type2], [SortOrder2], [FieldNumber3], [SortFieldType3], [SortOrder3], [SortColumn], [Separator], [CaseSensitive], [BidiSort], [IgnoreThe], [IgnoreKashida], [Ignore Diacritics], [IgnoreHe], [LanguageID]	Sort the items in the Range. Parameters equivalent to the Table | Sort menu item.

Name	Returns	Parameters	Description
Sort Ascending			Sort the range items ascending alphabetically.
Sort Descending			Sort the range items descending alphabetically.
StartOf	Long	[Unit], [Extend]	Changes the starting character of the range using a Unit type (WdUnits) and the type of movement with Extend.
Subscribe To		Edition As String, [Format]	Macintosh Only. Subscribes to published edition.
TCSC Converter		[WdTCSC Converter Direction], [Common Terms], [UseVariants]	Converts the range from Traditional Chinese to Simplified Chinese or vice versa. WdTCSCConverterDirection can be one of the WdTCSCConverterDirection constants. CommonTerms and UseVariants are optional parameters. CommonTerms specifies whether Word converts common expressions all together rather than by character by character. UseVariants specifies if Word uses Taiwan, Hong Kong or Macao character variants, only if translating from Simplified Chinese to Traditional Chinese.
WholeStory			Expands the range so that the whole story is included.

Examples

Go through all the paragraphs in the active document. If you the current paragraph is not in a table then make it bold. Make sure the current paragraph being checked is selected so that progress can be seen:

```
Dim prg As Paragraph
Dim rng As Range

For Each prg In ActiveDocument.Paragraphs
    Set rng = prg.Range
    rng.Select

    DoEvents 'Do this visually see the range being selected.  Will slow down
process.

    If Not rng.Information(wdWithInTable) Then
        rng.Bold = True
    End If
Next
```

ReadabilityStatistic Object and the ReadabilityStatistics Collection

The ReadabilityStatistics collection returns a list of statistics for the current range or document. Each ReadabilityStatistic object represents a single statistic for the current range or document. Valid items in the collection, in order, are Words, Characters, Paragraphs, Sentences, Sentences per Paragraph, Words per Sentence, Characters per Word, Passive Sentences, Flesch Reading Ease, and Flesch-Kincaid Grade Level.

ReadabilityStatistic Common Properties

The Application, Creator, and Parent properties are defined at the beginning of this section.

ReadabilityStatistic Properties

Name	Returns	Description
Name	String	Read Only. Returns the name of the statistic (e.g. Words).
Value	Single	Read Only. Returns the statistic count (e.g. number of words)

Examples

Display the number of words in the document:

```
MsgBox ActiveDocument.ReadabilityStatistics(1).Value
```

RecentFile Object and the RecentFiles Collection

The `RecentFiles` collection lists the files that have been recently opened and used in Word. Each `RecentFile` object represents one of the recently opened files in Word.

> **The items in the `RecentFiles` collection can be found at the bottom of the <u>F</u>ile menu.**

The `RecentFiles` collection has one method and one property besides the typically collection attributes. The `Add` method adds a document to the `RecentFiles` collection. The `Maximum` property sets how many documents are kept in the `RecentFiles` collection.

RecentFile Common Properties

The `Application, Creator,` and `Parent` properties are defined at the beginning of this section.

RecentFile Properties

Name	Returns	Description
Index	Long	Read Only. The position of the current object in the parent collection.
Name	String	Read Only. Returns the filename of the recent file.
Path	String	Read Only. Returns the path of the recent file.
ReadOnly	Boolean	Set/Get whether the document will be opened. Read Only.

RecentFile Methods

Name	Returns	Parameters	Description
Open	Document		Opens the recently opened document.
Delete			Deletes the object from the collection.

Examples

Open up the second most recently opened file as a read-only file:

```
Application.RecentFiles(2).ReadOnly = True
Application.RecentFiles(2).Open
```

Replacement Object

The `Replacement` object represents the properties and methods associated with the Replace part of the Find and Replace dialog box. The parent object of the `Replacement` object is always the `Find` object.

Replacement Common Properties

The `Application`, `Creator`, and `Parent` properties are defined at the beginning of this section.

Replacement Properties

Name	Returns	Description
Font	Font	Set/Get the font that will replace the found text.
Frame	Frame	Read Only. Returns an object allowing replace criteria for text in frames.
Highlight	Long	Set/Get whether highlighted text is part of the replacement.
LanguageID	WdLanguage ID	Set/Get the language to replace with.
LanguageID FarEast	WdLanguage ID	Set/Get the language to replace with.
NoProofing	Long	Set/Get if text ignored by the spell and grammar checker is replaced.
Paragraph Format	Paragraph Format	Set/Get the paragraph formatting to be part of the replacement.
Style	Variant	Set/Get the style to be part of the replacement.
Text	String	Set/Get the text to be part of the replacement.

Replacement Methods

Name	Returns	Parameters	Description
Clear Formatting			Clears all the formatting replacement settings previously made.

Examples

Find the text "Goto A" and replace it with the text "Goto B". Make sure that the replaced text is highlighted:

```
With Selection.Find
    .ClearFormatting
    .Replacement.ClearFormatting
    .Replacement.Highlight = True

    .Text = "Goto A"
    .Replacement.Text = "Goto B"
    .Forward = True
    .Wrap = wdFindContinue
End With
Selection.Find.Execute Replace:=wdReplaceAll
```

Revision Object and the Revisions Collection

The `Revisions` collection is a list of revisions made to a range or document. Each `Revision` object represents a single revision made to a document or range.

The `Revisions` collection has two methods besides the typical collection attributes. The `AcceptAll` method accepts all the revisions in the `Revisions` collection. The `RejectAll` method rejects all the revisions in the `Revisions` collection.

Revision Common Properties

The `Application`, `Creator`, and `Parent` properties are defined at the beginning of this section.

Revision Properties

Name	Returns	Description
Author	String	Read Only. Returns the name of the person who made the revision.
Date	Date	Read Only. Returns the date of the revision.
Index	Long	Read Only. The position of the current object in the parent collection.
Range	Range	Read Only. Returns the spot in the document containing the revision.
Type	WdRevision Type	Read Only. Returns what type of revision represents the current revision.

Revision Methods

Name	Returns	Parameters	Description
Accept			Accepts the revision.
Reject			Rejects the revision.

Examples

Accept all of the deletion revisions in the active document:

```
Dim rv As Revision
For Each rv In ActiveDocument.Revisions
    If rv.Type = wdRevisionDelete Then
        rv.Accept
    End If
Next
```

RoutingSlip Object

The RoutingSlip object represents the properties and methods of the routing slip of a document. The parent object of the RoutingSlip object is the Document object. The HasRoutingSlip property of the Document object has to be set to True before the RoutingSlip object can be manipulated.

RoutingSlip Common Properties

The Application, Creator, and Parent properties are defined at the beginning of this section.

RoutingSlip Properties

Name	Returns	Description
Delivery	WdRoutingSlip Delivery	Set/Get how the delivery process will proceed.
Message	String	Set/Get the body text of the routing slip message.
Protect	WdProtection Type	Set/Get what sort of modifications are allowed for the parent document.
Recipients	String	Read Only. [Index] parameter. Returns the list of recipient names to send the parent document to.
ReturnWhen Done	Boolean	Set/Get whether the message is returned to the original sender.
Status	WdRoutingSlip Status	Read Only. Returns the current status of the routing slip.
Subject	String	Set/Get the subject text for the routing slip message.
TrackStatus	Boolean	Set/Get whether the message is sent to the original sender each time the message is forwarded.

RoutingSlip Methods

Name	Returns	Parameters	Description
AddRecipient		Recipient As String	Add a recipient name to the recipients list.
Reset			Reset the routing slip.

Examples

Add a routing slip to the active document with a subject line of "Wrox Message" to Felipe Martins. Make sure the messages are delivered to the recipients one after another. Note that this example requires a "Felipe" and a "Duncan" in your address list.

```
With ActiveDocument
    .HasRoutingSlip = True
    .RoutingSlip.Subject = "Wrox Message"
    .RoutingSlip.AddRecipient "Felipe"
    .RoutingSlip.AddRecipient "Duncan"
    .RoutingSlip.Delivery = wdOneAfterAnother
    .Route
End With
```

Row Object and the Rows Collection

The Rows collection holds the list of table rows associated with the parent table, selection, or range. Each Row object represents a single row in a table, selection or range.

The Rows collection has many properties and methods besides the typical collection attributes. The following table lists and describes these extra properties and methods:

Rows Collection Special Methods and Properties

Name	Returns	Description
Alignment	WdRow Alignment	Set/Get the text alignment for the rows.
AllowBreak AcrossPages	Long	Set/Get whether row text in a row can be separated by page breaks.
Allow Overlap	Long	Set/Get if specified rows can overlap other rows. WdUndefined is returned if specified rows include overlapping and nonoverlapping rows.
Borders	Borders	Set/Get the borders around the rows.
Distance Bottom	Single	Set/Get the distance from bottom of the table and the text.

Table Continued on Following Page

Name	Returns	Description
Distance Left	Single	Set/Get the distance from left of the table and the text.
Distance Right	Single	Set/Get the distance from right of the table and the text.
Distance Top	Single	Set/Get the distance from top of the table and the text.
First	Row	Read Only. Returns the first row in the Rows collection.
Heading Format	Long	Set/Get whether rows are formatted as a header.
Height	Single	Set/Get the row height.
HeightRule	WdRow Height Rule	Set/Get how the row height is used to determine height.
Horizontal Position	Single	Set/Get the horizontal distance between the RelativeHorizontalPosition value and the rows edge.
Last	Row	Read Only. Returns the last row in the Rows collection.
LeftIndent	Single	Set/Get the distance between the row text and the page edge.
Nesting Level	Long	Read Only. Returns how deep the specified cell, column, row or table is nested within the respective collections.
Relative Horizontal Position	Long	Set/Get what the rows edge horizontal position is relative to.
Relative Vertical Position	Long	Set/Get what the rows edge vertical position is relative to.
Shading	Shading	Read Only. Returns the shading properties for the rows.
SpaceBetween Columns	Single	Set/Get the horizontal distance between column text in the rows.
Table Direction	WdTable Direction	Set/Get the direction that Word places cells in a table or row.

Name	Returns	Description
Vertical Position	Single	Set/Get the horizontal distance between the `RelativeVerticalPosition` value and the rows edge.
WrapAround Text	Long	Set/Get whether text in the row wraps to the next line.
Add	Row	Method. [`BeforeRow`] parameter. Adds a row to the `Rows` collection and a row to the table.
ConvertTo Text	Range	Method. [`Separator`], [`NestedTables`] parameters. Converts the rows into text.
Delete		Method. Deletes the rows.
Distribute Height		Method. Distributes all the rows' height equally.
Select		Method. Selects the rows in the document.
SetHeight		Method. `RowHeight As Single`, `HeightRule As WdRowHeightRule` parameters. Set the row height to `RowHeight` using the `HeightRule` rules.
SetLeft Indent		Method. `LeftIndent As Single`, `RulerStyle As WdRulerStyle` parameters. Sets the left indentation to `LeftIndent`.

Row Common Properties

The `Application`, `Creator`, and `Parent` properties are defined at the beginning of this section.

Row Properties

Name	Returns	Description
Alignment	WdRow Alignment	Set/Get the text alignment for the row.
AllowBreak AcrossPages	Long	Set/Get whether row text in the row can be separated by page breaks.
Borders	Borders	Set/Get the borders around the row.
Cells	Cells	Read Only. Returns the cells in the row.
Heading Format	Long	Set/Get whether a row is the formatted as a header.

Table Continued on Following Page

Name	Returns	Description
Height	Single	Set/Get the row height.
HeightRule	WdRowHeight Rule	Set/Get how the row height is used to determine height.
ID	String	Set/Get the ID for the row.
Index	Long	Read Only. Returns the position of the row in the collection.
IsFirst	Boolean	Read Only. Returns if the row is the first row in the parent table.
IsLast	Boolean	Read Only. Returns if the row is the last row in the parent table.
LeftIndent	Single	Set/Get the distance between the row text and the page edge.
NestingLevel	Long	Read Only. Returns how deep the current row's table is nested within other tables.
Next	Row	Read Only. Returns the next row in the parent collection.
Previous	Row	Read Only. Returns the previous row in the parent collection.
Range	Range	Read Only. Returns the spot in the document where the row is located.
Shading	Shading	Read Only. Returns the shading properties for the row.
SpaceBetween Columns	Single	Set/Get the horizontal distance between column text in the row.

Row Methods

Name	Returns	Parameters	Description
ConvertTo Text	Range	[Separator], [NestedTables]	Converts the row into text.
Delete			Deletes the row.
Select			Selects the row in the document.

Name	Returns	Parameters	Description
SetHeight		RowHeight As Single, HeightRule As WdRowHeightRule	Set the row height to RowHeight using the HeightRule rules.
SetLeft Indent		LeftIndent As Single, RulerStyle As WdRulerStyle	Sets the left indentation to LeftIndent.

Examples

Go through all the rows in all the tables in the active document. Highlight the rows in the document and deletes the rows that have "Old" as the first word in the first column:

```
Dim rw As Row
Dim celltext As String
Dim tbl As Table

For Each tbl In ActiveDocument.Tables
    For Each rw In tbl.Rows
        rw.Select
        celltext = rw.Cells(1).Range.Words.First.Text

        If celltext = "Old" Then
            rw.Delete
        End If
    Next
Next
```

Section Object and the Sections Collection

The Sections collection holds all of the sections in a document, selection, or range. Each Section object represents a single section in a document, selection, or range.

The Sections collection has a few properties and methods besides the typical collection attributes. The following table lists and describes these extra properties and methods:

Sections Collection Special Properties and Methods

Name	Returns	Description
First	Section	Read Only. Returns the first section in the collection.
Last	Section	Read Only. Returns the last section in the collection.

Table Continued on Following Page

Name	Returns	Description
PageSetup	PageSetu p	Read Only. Set/Get the page setup properties.
Add	Section	Method. [Range], [Start] parameters. Adds a Section to the parent object.

Section Common Properties

The Application, Creator, and Parent properties are defined at the beginning of this section.

Section Properties

Name	Returns	Description
Borders	Borders	Set/Get the borders around the section.
Footers	Headers Footers	Read Only. Returns the headers in the section.
Headers	Headers Footers	Read Only. Returns the footers in the section.
Index	Long	Read Only. Returns the position of the Section in the collection.
PageSetup	PageSetup	Set/Get the page setup properties.
ProtectedFor Forms	Boolean	Set/Get whether the section fields are the only modifiable part of the section.
Range	Range	Read Only. Returns the spot in the document where the section is.

Examples

Display the number of headers and footers in the first section of the active document:

```
With ActiveDocument.Sections(1)
    MsgBox .Footers.Count
    MsgBox .Headers.Count
End With
```

Selection Object

The `Selection` object represents a visibly selected part of a document or the current location of the insertion point in Word or in a window pane. Note that this object is similar to a `Range` object. There can, however, be many `Range` objects associated with a document but only one active `Selection` object for Word. Possible parents of the `Selection` object are the `Application`, `Pane` and `Window` objects.

Selection Common Properties

The `Application`, `Creator`, and `Parent` properties are defined at the beginning of this section.

Selection Properties

Name	Returns	Description
Active	Boolean	Read Only. Returns whether the selection is active or not.
BookmarkID	Long	Read Only. Returns the bookmark ID that includes the selection, 0 if no selection is part of a bookmark.
Bookmarks	Bookmarks	Read Only. Returns the bookmarks in the selection.
Borders	Borders	Set/Get the borders around the selection.
Cells	Cells	Read Only. Returns the table cells in the selection.
Characters	Characters	Read Only. Returns the characters in the selection.
Columns	Columns	Read Only. Returns the table columns in the selection.
ColumnSelect Mode	Boolean	Set/Get whether the column selection is active.
Comments	Comments	Read Only. Returns the comments in the selection.
Document	Document	Read Only. Returns the document that the current selection is in.
End	Long	Set/Get the ending character number of the selection.
Endnotes	Endnotes	Read Only. Returns the endnotes in the selection.

Table Continued on Following Page

501

Name	Returns	Description
ExtendMode	Boolean	Set/Get whether the current selection mode is the extend mode.
Fields	Fields	Read Only. Returns the fields in the range.
Find	Find	Read Only. Returns an object allowing the ability to find text in the range.
FitTextWidth	Single	Set/Get the width that Word fits the selected text into.
Flags	WdSelection Flags	Set/Get properties for the selection (e.g. Overtype).
Font	Font	Set/Get the font of the selection.
Footnotes	Footnotes	Read Only. Returns the footnotes in the selection.
Formatted Text	Range	Set/Get formatted text that is part of the selection.
FormFields	FormFields	Read Only. Returns the form fields in the selection.
Frames	Frames	Read Only. Returns the frames in the selection.
HeaderFooter	HeaderFooter	Read Only. Returns either a header or footer of the current selection.
Hyperlinks	Hyperlinks	Read Only. Returns the hyperlinks in the range.
Information	WdInformation	Read Only. Type parameter. Returns information specified by the Type parameter. Use the WdInformation constants.
InlineShapes	InlineShapes	Read Only. Returns the inline shapes in the selection.
IPAtEndOf Line	Boolean	Read Only. Returns whether the collapsed insertion point is at the end of a line but not an end of paragraph. False if not collapsed.
IsEndOfRow Mark	Boolean	Read Only. Returns whether the current selection is the end-of-row marker in a table. Selection has to be an insertion point (collapsed).

Name	Returns	Description
Language Detected	Boolean	Set/Get whether the language is automatically detected for the selection.
LanguageID	WdLanguageID	Set/Get the language for the selection.
LanguageID FarEast	WdLanguageID	Set/Get the language for the selection.
Language IDOther	WdLanguageID	Set/Get the language for the selection.
NoProofing	Long	Set/Get if text is replaced that the spell/grammar checker ignores.
Orientation	WdText Orientation	Set/Get the text direction for the selection (e.g. Vertical).
PageSetup	PageSetup	Set/Get an object manipulating the page characteristics.
Paragraph Format	Paragraph Format	Set/Get the paragraph formatting for the selection.
Paragraphs	Paragraphs	Read Only. Returns the paragraphs in the selection.
Previous BookmarkID	Long	Read Only. Returns the closest bookmark ID previous to, or in, the selection.
Range	Range	Read Only. Returns a range object equivalent to the selection object.
Rows	Rows	Read Only. Returns the table rows in the selection.
Sections	Sections	Read Only. Returns the document sections in the selection.
Sentences	Sentences	Read Only. Returns the sentences in the selection.
Shading	Shading	Read Only. Modify the shading of the selection.
ShapeRange	ShapeRange	Read Only. Returns all the Shape objects in the selection.
Start	Long	Set/Get the starting character of the selection.

Table Continued on Following Page

Name	Returns	Description
StartIs Active	Boolean	Set/Get whether the start of the selection has the active insertion point.
StoryLength	Long	Read Only. Returns the number of characters in the document story that the selection is part of.
StoryType	WdStoryType	Read Only. Returns the type of document story that the selection is part of.
Style	Variant	Set/Get the document style for the selection.
Tables	Tables	Read Only. Returns the tables in the selection.
Text	String	Set/Get the text in the selection.
TopLevel Tables	Tables	Read Only. Returns the top-level tables (non-nested tables) in the selection.
Type	WdSelection Type	Read Only. Returns what the current selection type is.
Words	Words	Read Only. Returns the words in the selection.

Selection Methods

Name	Returns	Parameters	Description
BoldRun			Sets the selection text to bold.
Calculate	Single		Calculates the math expression in the selection.
Collapse		[Direction]	Collapses the selection to either the selection start (default) or the selection end (WdCollapseEnd direction)

Name	Returns	Parameters	Description
ConvertTo Table	Table	[Separator], [NumRows], [NumColumns], [InitialColumn Width], [Format], [ApplyBorders], [ApplyShading], [ApplyFont], [ApplyColor], [ApplyHeading Rows], [ApplyLastRow], [ApplyFirst Column], [ApplyLast Column], [AutoFit], [AutoFit Behavior], [DefaultTable Behavior]	Converts the selection to a table if possible. If default table settings are not appropriate, the parameters allow specifying table properties.
Copy			Copies the selection to the clipboard.
CopyAs Picture			Copies the selection to the clipboard.
CopyFormat			Copies the format settings of the selection's first character. Use with PasteFormat.
CreateAuto TextEntry	AutoTe xtEntr y	Name As String, StyleName As String	Creates an AutoText entry for the selected text.
Create Textbox			Creates a textbox around the selection or sets the mouse to be able to draw a textbox (insertion point).
Cut			Cuts the selection to the clipboard.

Table Continued on Following Page

Name	Returns	Parameters	Description
Detect Language			Determines the language of the specified text.
Delete	Long	[Unit], [Count]	Deletes Count number of Unit items. Use the WdUnits constants for Unit.
EndKey	Long	[Unit], [Extend]	Equivalent to hitting the *End* key.
EndOf	Long	[Unit], [Extend]	Moves the ending character of the selection using a Unit type (WdUnits) and the type of movement with Extend.
EscapeKey			Equivalent to hitting the *Esc* key.
Expand	Long	[Unit]	Expands the selection by the specified Unit.
Extend		[Character]	Turns the extend mode on and then extends the selection to the next part of the current text.
GoTo	Range	[What], [Which], [Count], [Name]	Goes to a certain spot in a document returning a Range object specifying the start of the new spot. This method can be used to go to a certain type of thing (What), moving a specific way (Which) a number of times (Count) or a certain named object (Name).
GoToNext	Range	What As WdGoToItem	Returns the Range of the next What item.
GoTo Previous	Range	What As WdGoToItem	Returns the Range of the previous What item.
HomeKey	Long	[Unit], [Extend]	Equivalent to hitting the *Home* key.

Name	Returns	Parameters	Description
InRange	Boolean	Range As Range	Returns whether the Range parameter is part of the current selection.
Insert After		Text As String	Inserts the Text parameter after the selection and includes it in the selection.
Insert Before		Text As String	Inserts the Text parameter before the selection and includes it in the selection.
Insert Break		[Type]	Inserts a page break or a break specified by the Type parameter (WdBreakType).
Insert Caption		Label, [Title], [TitleAuto Text], [Position]	Inserts a caption label with the Label text either before or after the selection.
Insert Cells		[ShiftCells]	Inserts the same number of cells as is in the current selection. Use ShiftCells to define how to insert.
Insert Columns			Inserts to the left the same number of columns as is in the current selection.
Insert Columns Right			Inserts to the right the same number of columns as is in the current selection.

Table Continued on Following Page

Name	Returns	Parameters	Description
Insert Cross Reference		ReferenceType, ReferenceKind As WdReferenceKind, Reference Item, [InsertAs Hyperlink], [IncludePosition]	Inserts a cross-reference for an item in the selection.
Insert DateTime		[DateTimeFormat], [InsertAsField], [InsertAsFull Width], [DateLanguage], [CalendarType]	Inserts the date or time in the specified selection.
InsertFile		FileName As String, [Range], [Confirm Conversions], [Link], [Attachment]	Inserts the file specified by FileName replacing the range text.
Insert Formula		[Formula], [NumberFormat]	Inserts a formula and replaces the current selection.
Insert Paragraph			Sets the current selection as a new paragraph.
Insert Paragraph After			Inserts a paragraph at the end of the selection.
Insert Paragraph Before			Inserts a paragraph at the start of the selection.
InsertRows		[NumRows]	Inserts above the same number of rows as is in the current selection or specified by the parameter.
InsertRows Above		[NumRows]	Inserts above the same number of rows as is in the current selection or specified by the parameter.

Name	Returns	Parameters	Description
InsertRows Below		[NumRows]	Inserts below the same number of rows as is in the current selection or specified by the parameter.
Insert Symbol		Character Number As Long, [Font], [Unicode], [Bias]	Inserts a symbol specified by the CharacterNumber as the selection.
InStory	Boolean	Range As Range	Returns whether the Range parameter is in the same story as the current selection.
IsEqual	Boolean	Range As Range	Returns whether the Range parameter is the same of the current selection.
ItalicRun			Sets the selection to italic.
LtrPara			Sets text to a reading order of left-to-right.
LtrRun			Sets text to a reading order of left-to-right.
Move	Long	[Unit], [Count]	Collapses and moves the selection.
MoveDown	Long	[Unit], [Count], [Extend]	Moves the selection down by Count number of Unit items.
MoveEnd	Long	[Unit], [Count]	Moves the end character of the selection.
MoveEnd Until	Long	Cset, [Count]	Moves the end character of the selection until the characters in Cset are found.
MoveEnd While	Long	Cset, [Count]	Moves the end character of the selection while the characters in Cset are found.

Table Continued on Following Page

Name	Returns	Parameters	Description
MoveLeft	Long	[Unit], [Count], [Extend]	Read Only. Moves selection left by Count number of Units
MoveRight	Long	[Unit], [Count], [Extend]	Read Only. Moves selection right by Count number of Units.
MoveStart	Long	[Unit], [Count]	Moves the start character of the selection.
MoveStart Until	Long	Cset, [Count]	Moves the start character of the selection until the characters in Cset are found.
MoveStart While	Long	Cset, [Count]	Moves the start character of the selection while the characters in Cset are found.
MoveUntil	Long	Cset, [Count]	Collapses and moves the selection until the characters in Cset are found
MoveUp	Long	[Unit], [Count], [Extend]	Read Only. Moves the selection up by Count number of Units.
MoveWhile	Long	Cset, [Count]	Collapses and moves the selection while the characters in Cset are found
Next	Range	[Unit], [Count]	Moves the selection to the next item specified by the Unit parameter and returns a Range object.
NextField	Field		Makes the next Field selected in the selection.
Next Revision	Revision	[Wrap]	Returns the next revision in the selection.
Next Subdocument			Moves the selection to the next subdocument.

Name	Returns	Parameters	Description
Paste			Pastes and replaces the clipboard contents into the selection.
PasteAs NestedTable			Paste the clipboard contents as nested table if applicable.
Paste Format			Paste the clipboard contents with formatting.
Paste Special	Range	[IconIndex], [Link], [Placement], [DisplayAs Icon], [DataType], [IconFile Name], [IconLabel]	Pastes and replaces the clipboard contents into the selection in a special manner (e.g. as an OLE object).
Previous	Range	[Unit], [Count]	Moves the selection to the previous item specified by the Unit parameter and returns a Range object
Previous Field	Field		Makes the previous Field selected in the selection.
Previous Revision	Revision	[Wrap]	Returns the previous revision in the selection.
Previous Subdocument			Moves the selection to the previous subdocument.
RtlPara			Sets text to a reading order of right-to-left.
RtlRun			Sets text to a reading order of right-to-left.
Select			Selects all the text contained in the current selection.

Table Continued on Following Page

Name	Returns	Parameters	Description
Select Cell			Selects the whole of the cell that contains the current selection.
Select Column			Selects all columns that contain the selection.
Select Current Alignment			The selection is extended to the end of the current paragraph alignment.
Select CurrentColor			The selection is extended to the end of the current text color.
Select CurrentFont			The selection is extended to the end of the current font.
Select Current Indent			The selection is extended to the end of the current indentation type.
Select Current Spacing			The selection is extended to the end of the current line spacing.
Select CurrentTabs			The selection is extended to the end of the current stops.
SelectRow			Selects all the rows contained in the current selection.
SetRange		Start As Long, End As Long	Set the Start character and the End character of the new selection.
Shrink			Shrinks the selection by the next smallest unit.

Name	Returns	Parameters	Description
Sort		[ExcludeHeader], [FieldNumber], [SortFieldType], [SortOrder], [FieldNumber2], [SortFieldType2], [SortOrder2], [FieldNumber3], [SortFieldType3], [SortOrder3], [SortColumn], [Separator], [CaseSensitive], [BidiSort], [IgnoreThe], [IgnoreKashida], [IgnoreDiacritics], [IgnoreHe], [LanguageID]	Sort the items in the selection. Parameters equivalent to the Table|Sort menu item.
Sort Ascending			Sort the selection items ascending alphabetically.
Sort Descending			Sort the selection items descending alphabetically.
SplitTable			Splits the selected table by adding an empty paragraph above the current row.
StartOf	Long	[Unit], [Extend]	Moves or extends the starting point of the selection using a Unit type (WdUnits) and the type of movement with Extend.

Table Continued on Following Page

Name	Returns	Parameters	Description
Type Backspace			Equivalent to hitting the *Backspa* key.
Type Paragraph			Equivalent to hitting the *Enter* key
TypeText		Text As String	Inserts the Text parameter value before the current selection (or replace if ReplaceSelection is True.
WholeStory			Expands the selection so the whole story is included.

Examples

Add a table to the current selection point and type in the first three column titles as "Name", "Returns" and "Access":

```
ActiveDocument.Tables.Add Selection.Range, NumRows:=2, NumColumns:=3
With Selection
    .TypeText "Name"
    .MoveRight wdCell
    .TypeText "Returns"
    .MoveRight wdCell
    .TypeText "Access"
    .MoveRight wdCell
End With
```

Type the word "Document One" at the current selection point and then go to the next line:

```
Selection.TypeText Text:="Document One"
Selection.TypeParagraph
```

Sentences Collection

The Sentences collection returns a collection of Range objects representing all of the sentences in a selection, range, or document. The Sentences collection is like an ordinary collection except it has the following properties and it contains no Sentence object.

Sentences Collection Special Properties

Name	Returns	Description
First	Range	Read Only. Returns the first sentence in the collection.
Last	Range	Read Only. Returns the last sentence in the collection.

Examples

Delete any sentences in the active document that has less than two words:

```
Dim snt As Range
For Each snt In ActiveDocument.Sentences
    If snt.Words.Count < 2 Then
        snt.Delete
    End If
Next
```

Shading Object

The Shading object has the shading properties associated with the parent object. Possible parents of the Shading object are the Cell, Column, Font, Frame, Paragraph, ParagraphFormat, Range, Row, Selection, Style and Table objects and the Cells, Columns, Paragraphs, and Rows collections.

Shading Common Properties

The Application, Creator, and Parent properties are defined at the beginning of this section.

Shading Properties

Name	Returns	Description
BackgroundPattern Color	WdColor	Set/Get the background color.
BackgroundPattern ColorIndex	WdColor Index	Set/Get the background color.
ForegroundPattern Color	WdColor	Set/Get the foreground color.
ForegroundPattern ColorIndex	WdColor Index	Set/Get the foreground color.
Texture	WdTexture Index	Set/Get the shading texture.

Examples

Set the shading of the first paragraph of the active document to a cross texture:

```
ActiveDocument.Paragraphs(1).Range.Shading.Texture = wdTextureCross
```

ShadowFormat Object

The ShadowFormat object allows manipulation of the shadow formatting properties of a parent Shape object. Use the Shadow property of the Shape object to access the ShadowFormat object.

ShadowFormat Common Properties

The Application, Creator, and Parent properties are defined at the beginning of this section.

ShadowFormat Properties

Name	Returns	Description
ForeColor	ColorFormat	Read Only. Allows manipulation of the shadow fore color.
Obscured	MsoTriState	Set/Get whether the shape obscures the shadow or not.
OffsetX	Single	Set/Get what the horizontal shadow offset is.
OffsetY	Single	Set/Get what the vertical shadow offset is.
Transparency	Single	Set/Get how transparent the shadow is (0 to 1 where 1 is clear).
Type	MsoShadowType	Set/Get the shadow type.
Visible	MsoTriState	Set/Get whether the shadow is visible.

ShadowFormat Methods

Name	Returns	Parameters	Description
IncrementOffsetX		Increment As Single	Changes the horizontal shadow offset.
IncrementOffsetY		Increment As Single	Changes the vertical shadow offset.

ShadowFormat Examples

Set a shadow for the first shape on the active document. The color of the shadow should be red and totally opaque:

```
With ActiveDocument.Shapes(1).Shadow
    .Visible = msoCTrue
    .ForeColor.RGB = RGB(255, 0, 0)
    .Transparency = 0
End With
```

Shape Object and the Shapes Collection

The Shapes collection holds the list of shapes for a document, header, footer, or hyperlink. The Shape object represents a single shape such as an AutoShape, a freeform shape, an OLE object (like an image), an ActiveX control or a picture. Possible parent objects of the Subdocuments collection are the Document, HeaderFooter and Hyperlink object.

The Shapes collection has a few methods and properties besides the typical collection attributes. They are listed in the following table:

Shapes Collection Special Properties and Methods

Method Name	Returns	Description
AddCallout	Shape	Type As MsoCalloutType, Left As Single, Top As Single, Width As Single, Height As Single, [Anchor]. Adds a callout line shape.
AddCurve	Shape	SafeArrayOfPoints, [Anchor]. Adds a Bezier curve.
AddLabel	Shape	Orientation As MsoTextOrientation, Left As Single, Top As Single, Width As Single, Height As Single, [Anchor]. Adds a label.
AddLine	Shape	BeginX As Single, BeginY As Single, EndX As Single, EndY As Single, [Anchor]. Adds a line.
AddOLE Control	Shape	[ClassType], [Left], [Top], [Width], [Height], [Anchor]. Adds an OLE control.

Table Continued on Following Page

Method Name	Returns	Description
AddOLE Object	Shape	[ClassType], [FileName], [LinkToFile], [DisplayAsIcon], [IconFileName], [IconIndex], [IconLabel], [Left], [Top], [Width], [Height], [Anchor]. Adds an OLE object.
Add Picture	Shape	FileName As String, [LinkToFile], [SaveWithDocument], [Left], [Top], [Width], [Height], [Anchor]. Adds a picture.
Add Polyline	Shape	SafeArrayOfPoints, [Anchor]. Adds an open polyline or a closed polygon.
AddShape	Shape	Type As Long, Left As Single, Top As Single, Width As Single, Height As Single, [Anchor]. Adds a shape using the Type parameter.
Add Textbox	Shape	Orientation As MsoTextOrientation, Left As Single, Top As Single, Width As Single, Height As Single, [Anchor]. Adds a textbox.
AddText Effect	Shape	PresetTextEffect As MsoPresetTextEffect, Text As String, FontName As String, FontSize As Single, FontBold As MsoTriState, FontItalic As MsoTriState, Left As Single, Top As Single, [Anchor]. Adds a WordArt object.
Build Freeform	Freeform Builder	EditingType As MsoEditingType, X1 As Single, Y1 As Single. Accesses an object that allows creation of a new shape based on ShapeNode objects.
Range	Shape Range	Index parameter. Returns the subset of shapes as defined by the Index parameter.
SelectAll		Selects all the shapes in the collection.

Shape Common Properties

The Application, Creator, and Parent properties are defined at the beginning of this section.

Shape Properties

Name	Returns	Description
Adjustments	Adjustments	Read Only. An object accessing the adjustments for a shape.
Alternative Text	String	Set/Get the alternate text to appear if the image is not loaded. Used with a web page.
Anchor	Range	Read Only. Returns the spot in the document that points to the origin of the shape (not its current location on the page).
AutoShape Type	MsoAutoShape Type	Set/Get the type of AutoShape used.
Callout	CalloutFormat	Read Only. An object accessing the callout properties of the shape.
Fill	FillFormat	Read Only. An object accessing the fill properties of the shape.
GroupItems	GroupShapes	Read Only. Returns the shapes that make up the current shape.
Height	Single	Set/Get the height of the shape.
Horizontal Flip	MsoTriState	Read Only. Returns whether the shape has been flipped.
Hyperlink	Hyperlink	Read Only. Returns the hyperlink of the shape, if any.
Left	Single	Set/Get the horizontal position of the shape.
Line	LineFormat	Read Only. An object accessing the line formatting of the shape.
LinkFormat	LinkFormat	Read Only. An object accessing the OLE linking properties.
LockAnchor	Long	Set/Get whether the shape's anchor does not move when the shape moves.

Table Continued on Following Page

Name	Returns	Description
LockAspect Ratio	MsoTriState	Set/Get whether the dimensional proportions of the shape is kept when the shape is resized.
Name	String	Set/Get the name of the shape.
Nodes	ShapeNodes	Read Only. An object accessing the nodes of the freeform shape.
OLEFormat	OLEFormat	Read Only. An object accessing OLE object properties if applicable.
Picture Format	PictureFormat	Read Only. An object accessing the picture format options.
Relative Horizontal Position	Wd Relative Horizontal Position	Set/Get what the horizontal position is relative to.
Relative Vertical Position	Wd RelativeVertical Position	Set/Get what the vertical position is relative to.
Rotation	Single	Set/Get the degrees rotation of the shape.
Script	Script	Read Only. Returns the VBScript associated with the shape.
Shadow	ShadowFormat	Read Only. An object accessing the shadow properties.
TextEffect	TextEffectFormat	Read Only. An object accessing the text effect properties.
TextFrame	TextFrame	Read Only. An object accessing the text frame properties.
ThreeD	ThreeDFormat	Read Only. An object accessing the 3-D effect formatting properties.
Top	Single	Set/Get the vertical position of the shape.
Type	MsoShapeType	Read Only. Returns the type of shape.
Vertical Flip	MsoTriState	Read Only. Returns whether the shape has been vertically flipped.
Vertices	Variant	Read Only. Returns a series of coordinate pairs describing the freeform's vertices.

Name	Returns	Description
Visible	MsoTriState	Set/Get whether the shape is visible.
Width	Single	Set/Get the width of the shape
WrapFormat	WrapFormat	Read Only. An object accessing the shape wrap formatting properties.
ZOrder Position	Long	Read Only. Returns where the shape is in the z-order of the collection (e.g. front, back)

Shape Methods

Name	Returns	Parameters	Description
Activate			Activates the shape.
Apply			Applies the formatting that was set by the PickUp method.
ConvertTo Frame	Frame		Converts the shape to a frame shape.
ConvertTo InlineShape	Inline Shape		Converts the shape to an inline shape.
Delete			Deletes the shape.
Duplicate	Shape		Duplicates the shape and returns a new shape.
Flip		FlipCmd As MsoFlipCmd	Flips the shape using the FlipCmd parameter.
IncrementLeft		Increment As Single	Moves the shape horizontally.
Increment Rotation		Increment As Single	Rotates the shape using the Increment parameter as degrees.
IncrementTop		Increment As Single	Moves the shape vertically.

Table Continued on Following Page

Name	Returns	Parameters	Description
`PickUp`			Copies the format of the current shape so another shape can then `Apply` the formats.
`ScaleHeight`		`Factor As Single, RelativeTo OriginalSize As MsoTriState, [Scale As MsoScaleFrom]`	Scales the height of the shape by the `Factor` parameter.
`ScaleWidth`		`Factor As Single, RelativeToOrig inalSize As MsoTriState, [Scale As MsoScaleFrom]`	Scales the width of the shape by the `Factor` parameter.
`Select`		`[Replace]`	Selects the shape in the document.
`SetShapes Default Properties`			Sets the formatting of the current shape as a default shape in Word.
`Ungroup`	`Shape Range`		Breaks apart the shapes that make up the `Shape` object.
`ZOrder`		`ZOrderCmd`	Changes the order of the shape object in the collection.

Examples

Set the first shape in the active document to have a solid white fill, set the outside lines' colors, make the shape aspect ratio locked, set the top and left to 5 centimeters and set the zOrder of the shape to 1:

```
With ActiveDocument.Shapes(1)
    .Fill.Visible = msoTrue
    .Fill.Solid
    .Fill.ForeColor.RGB = RGB(255, 255, 255)
    .Line.Visible = msoTrue
    .Line.ForeColor.RGB = RGB(0, 0, 0)
    .Line.BackColor.RGB = RGB(255, 255, 255)
    .LockAspectRatio = msoTrue
```

```
      .Height = 95.55
      .Width = 95.55
      .Left = CentimetersToPoints(5)
      .Top = CentimetersToPoints(5)
      .ZOrder 1
End With
```

ShapeNode Object and the ShapeNodes Collection

The ShapeNodes collection has the list of nodes and curved segments that make up a freeform shape. The ShapeNode object specifies a single node or curved segment that makes up a freeform shape. The Nodes property of the Shape object is used to access the ShapeNodes collection.

The ShapeNodes collection has a few methods besides the typical collection attributes listed in the following table.

ShapeNodes Collection Special Methods

Name	Returns	Parameter	Description
Delete		Index as Long.	Deletes the node specified by the Index
Insert	Shape Node	Index As Long, SegmentType As MsoSegment Type, Editing Type As MsoEditing Type, X1 As Single, Y1 As Single, [X2 As Single], [Y2 As Single], [X3 As Single], [Y3 As Single]	Inserts a node or curved segment in the nodes collection.
Set Editing Type	Shape Node	Index As Long, EditingType As MsoEditingType	Sets the editing type for a node.
Set Position	Shape Node	Index As Long, X1 As Single, Y1 As Single	Moves the specified node.
Set Segment Type	Shape Node	Index As Long, SegmentType As MsoSegmentType.	Changes the segment type following the node.

ShapeNode Common Properties

The Application, Creator, and Parent properties are defined at the beginning of this section.

ShapeNode Properties

Name	Returns	Description
EditingType	MsoEditing Type	Read Only. Returns the editing type for the node.
Points	Variant	Read Only. Returns the positional coordinate pair.
SegmentType	MsoSegment Type	Read Only. Returns the type of segment following the node.

Examples

Create a triangle using the free form builder:

```
With ActiveDocument.Shapes.BuildFreeform(msoEditingAuto, 500, 60)
    .AddNodes msoSegmentLine, msoEditingAuto, 550, 160
    .AddNodes msoSegmentLine, msoEditingAuto, 350, 180
    .AddNodes msoSegmentLine, msoEditingAuto, 500, 60
    .ConvertToShape.Select
End With
```

ShapeRange Collection

The ShapeRange collection holds a collection of Shape objects for a certain range or selection in a document. Possible parent items are the Range and the Selection object. The ShapeRange collection has many properties and methods besides the typical collection attributes. These items are listed below.However, some operations will cause an error if performed on a ShapeRange collection with multiple shapes.

Common Properties

The Application, Creator, and Parent properties are defined at the beginning of this section.

Properties

Name	Returns	Description
Adjustments	Adjustments	Read Only. An object accessing the adjustments for a shape.
Alternative Text	String	Set/Get the alternate text to appear if the image is not loaded. Used with a web page.

Name	Returns	Description
Anchor	Range	Read Only. Returns the spot in the document that points to the origin of the shape (not its current location on the page).
AutoShape Type	MsoAuto ShapeType	Set/Get the type of AutoShape used.
Callout	Callout Format	Read Only. An object accessing the callout properties of the shape.
Count	Long	Read Only. Returns the number of shapes in the collection.
Fill	Fill Format	Read Only. An object accessing the fill properties of the shape.
GroupItems	Group Shapes	Read Only. Returns the shapes that make up the current shape.
Height	Single	Set/Get the height of the shape.
Horizontal Flip	MsoTri State	Read Only. Returns whether the shape has been flipped.
Hyperlink	Hyperlink	Read Only. Returns the hyperlink of the shape, if any.
Left	Single	Set/Get the horizontal position of the shape.
Line	Line Format	Read Only. An object accessing the line formatting of the shape.
LockAnchor	Long	Set/Get whether the shape's anchor does not move when the shape moves.
LockAspect Ratio	MsoTri State	Set/Get whether the dimensional proportions of the shape is kept when the shape is resized.
Name	String	Set/Get the name of the shape.
Nodes	ShapeNodes	Read Only. Returns the nodes associated with the shape.
Picture Format	Picture Format	Read Only. An object accessing the picture format options.
Relative Horizontal Position	WdRelative Horizontal Position	Set/Get what the horizontal position is relative to.

Table Continued on Following Page

Name	Returns	Description
Relative Vertical Position	WdRelative Vertical Position	Set/Get what the vertical position is relative to.
Rotation	Single	Set/Get the degrees rotation of the shape.
Shadow	Shadow Format	Read Only. An object accessing the shadow properties.
TextEffect	TextEffect Format	Read Only. An object accessing the text effect properties.
TextFrame	Text Frame	Read Only. An object accessing the text frame properties.
ThreeD	ThreeD Format	Read Only. An object accessing the 3-D effect formatting properties.
Top	Single	Set/Get the vertical position of the shape.
Type	MsoShape Type	Read Only. Returns the type of shape.
Vertical Flip	MsoTri State	Read Only. Returns whether the shape has been vertically flipped.
Vertices	Variant	Read Only. Returns a series of coordinate pairs describing the freeform's vertices.
Visible	MsoTri State	Set/Get whether the shape is visible.
Width	Single	Set/Get the width of the shape.
WrapFormat	WrapFormat	Read Only. An object accessing the shape wrap formatting properties.
ZOrderPosi tion	Long	Read Only. Changes the order of the object in the collection.

ShapeRange Methods

Name	Returns	Parameters	Description
Activate			Activates the shape.
Align		Align As MsoAlignCmd, RelativeTo As Long	Aligns the shapes in the collection to the alignment properties set by the parameters.

Name	Returns	Parameters	Description
Apply			Applies the formatting that was set by the PickUp method.
ConvertTo Frame	Frame		Converts the shape to a frame shape.
ConvertTo Inline Shape	Inline Shape		Converts the shape to an inline shape.
Delete			Deletes the shape.
Distribute		Distribute As MsoDistribute Cmd, RelativeTo As Long	Distributes the shapes in the collection either evenly either horizontally or vertically.
Duplicate	Shape Range		Duplicates the shape and returns a new ShapeRange.
Flip		FlipCmd As MsoFlipCmd	Flips the shape using the FlipCmd parameter.
Group	Shape		Groups the shapes in the collection.
Increment Left		Increment As Single	Moves the shape horizontally.
Increment Rotation		Increment As Single	Rotates the shape using the Increment parameter as degrees.
Increment Top		Increment As Single	Moves the shape vertically.
PickUp			Copies the format of the current shape so another shape can then Apply the formats.
Regroup	Shape		Regroup any previously grouped shapes.

Table Continued on Following Page

Name	Returns	Parameters	Description
Scale Height		Factor As Single, RelativeTo OriginalSize As MsoTriState, [Scale As MsoScaleFrom]	Scales the height of the shape by the Factor parameter.
ScaleWidth		Factor As Single, RelativeToOrigin alSize As MsoTriState, [Scale As MsoScaleFrom]	Scales the width of the shape by the Factor parameter.
Select		[Replace]	Selects the shape in the document.
SetShapes Default Properties			Sets the formatting of the current shape as a default shape in Word.
Ungroup	Shape Range		Breaks apart the shapes that make up the Shape object.
ZOrder		ZOrderCmd As MsoZOrderCmd	Changes the order of the shape object in the collection.

Examples

Select the first shape in the active document. Then, treating it like a shape range, set a solid white fill, set the outside lines' colors, make the shape aspect ratio locked, set the top and left to 5 centimeters and set the zOrder of the shape to 1:

```
ActiveDocument.Shapes(1).Select
With Selection.ShapeRange
    .Fill.Visible = msoTrue
    .Fill.Solid
    .Fill.ForeColor.RGB = RGB(255, 255, 255)
    .Line.Visible = msoTrue
    .Line.ForeColor.RGB = RGB(0, 0, 0)
    .Line.BackColor.RGB = RGB(255, 255, 255)
    .LockAspectRatio = msoTrue
    .Height = 95.55
    .Width = 95.55
    .Left = CentimetersToPoints(5)
    .Top = CentimetersToPoints(5)
    .ZOrder 1
End With
```

SpellingSuggestion Object and the SpellingSuggestion Collection

The SpellingSuggestion Object is a spelling suggestion for an incorrectly spelled word. It is a member of the SpellingSuggestions collection, which includes all the suggestions for a particular word or the first word in a specified range. In addition to the usual properties and methods the SpellingSuggestions collection object has an extra property. The SpellingErrorType property returns one of the SpellingErrorTypes constants: wdSpellinCapitalization, wdSpellingCorrect and wdSpellingNotInDictionary as read only Long.

SpellingSuggestion Object Common Properties

The Application, Creator, and Parent properties are defined at the beginning of this section.

SpellingSuggestion Object Properties

Name	Returns	Description
Name	String	Read Only. Returns the spelling suggestion

Example

Get the spelling suggestions for the first spelling mistake in the active document, and display a message box for each spelling suggestion:

```
Dim suggs As SpellingSuggestions
Set suggs = ActiveDocument.SpellingErrors.Item(1). _
        Get SpellingSuggestions

If suggs.Count > 1 then
     For Each spellsugg In suggs
            MsgBox spellsugg
     Next spellsugg
End If
```

StoryRanges Collection

The StoryRanges collection is a collection of all the stories in a document. The collection holds Range objects. To access a particular story Range, use one of the WdStoryType constants as the Index of the Item method.

Examples

Display the number of words in the main story of the document:

```
MsgBox ActiveDocument.StoryRanges(wdMainTextStory).Words.Count
```

Style Object and the Styles Collection

The Styles collection holds the list of both the built-in and user-defined styles in a document. The parent object of the Styles collection is always the Document object. Use the WdBuiltinStyle constants to access the built-in styles from the Styles collection.

Besides the typical collection attributes, the Styles collection has one additional method. The Add method takes a style name parameter and adds a style to the Styles collection. In the actual document, the Add method adds a style to the parent document.

Style Common Properties

The Application, Creator, and Parent properties are defined at the beginning of this section.

Style Properties

Name	Returns	Description
Automatically Update	Boolean	Set/Get if the style is changed for the current selection automatically when manual changes are made to the style.
BaseStyle	Variant	Set/Get what the name, WdBuiltinStyle constant or style object is the base style of the current object.
Borders	Borders	Set/Get the borders around the style.
BuiltIn	Boolean	Read Only. Returns whether the style is built into Word.
Description	String	Read Only. Returns the description of the style.
Font	Font	Set/Get the Font object associated with the style.
Frame	Frame	Read Only. An object allowing modification of the frame settings.
InUse	Boolean	Read Only. Returns whether the style is in use or has been modified/created in the current document.
LanguageID	WdLanguage ID	Set/Get the language associated with the style.
LanguageIDFar East	WdLanguage ID	Set/Get the language associated with the style.

Name	Returns	Description
ListLevel Number	Long	Read Only. Returns the list level number associated with the style.
ListTemplate	List Template	Read Only. An object holding the list formatting properties of the style.
NameLocal	String	Set/Get the local language name of the style.
NextParagraph Style	Variant	Set/Get what style will be associated when a new paragraph is created after the current paragraph is formatted with the style.
NoProofing	Long	Set/Get if spell/grammar checker ignores text formatted with this style.
Paragraph Format	Paragraph Format	Set/Get the paragraph formatting options for the style
Shading	Shading	Read Only. Returns the shading properties for the style.
Type	WdStyle Type	Read Only. Returns the type of style.

Style Methods

Name	Returns	Parameters	Description
Delete			Deletes the style.
LinkToList Template		ListTemplate As ListTemplate, [ListLevel Number]	Link the style to a list template specified by the parameters.

Examples

Loop through all the styles in the active document and list all of the styles in use to the Immediate window:

```
Dim mnStyle As Style
For Each mnStyle In ActiveDocument.Styles
    If mnStyle.InUse Then
        Debug.Print mnStyle.NameLocal
    End If
Next
```

Subdocument Object and the Subdocuments Collection

The Subdocuments collection holds the list of subdocuments for a master document or range. The Subdocument object represents a single subdocument in a master document or range. Possible parent objects of the Subdocuments collection are the Document and Range object.

The Subdocuments collection has a few methods and properties besides the typical collection attributes. They are listed in the following table:

Subdocuments Collection Special Properties and Methods

Name	Returns	Description
AddFromFile	Subdocument	Name, [ConfirmConversions], [ReadOnly], [PasswordDocument], [PasswordTemplate], [Revert], [WritePasswordDocument], [WritePasswordTemplate]
		Adds a subdocument from the specified file to the parent master document.
AddFromRange	Subdocument	Range As Range
		Adds a subdocument from the specified range to the parent master document.
Delete		Deletes the subdocuments.
Expanded	Boolean	Set/Get whether the subdocuments are expanded.
Merge	Subdocument	[FirstSubdocument], [LastSubdocument]
		Merges the subdocuments into one subdocument.
Select		Selects the subdocument in Word.

Subdocument Object Common Properties

The Application, Creator, and Parent properties are defined at the beginning of this section.

Subdocument Object Properties

Name	Returns	Description
HasFile	Boolean	Read Only. Returns whether the subdocument has been saved to a file.
Level	Long	Read Only. Returns which heading level is equivalent to a subdocument.
Locked	Boolean	Set/Get whether the subdocument is protected.
Name	String	Read Only. Returns the file name of the subdocument.
Path	String	Read Only. Returns the directory path of the subdocument.
Range	Range	Read Only. Returns the spot in the master document where the subdocument is located.

Subdocument Object Methods

Name	Returns	Parameters	Description
Delete			Deletes the subdocument.
Open	Document		Opens the subdocument and returns the document.
Split		Range	Splits the subdocument at the beginning of the Range parameter into two subdocuments. An error occurs if the active document isn't in the master document or outline view or if the range isn't at the beginning of a paragraph in a subdocument.

Examples

Lock all the subdocuments associated with the active document:

```
Dim subdoc As Subdocument
For Each subdoc In ActiveDocument.Subdocuments
    subdoc.Locked = True
Next
```

SynonymInfo Object

The `SynonymInfo` object returns the synonyms, antonyms and related words found for a word or phrase. Possible parents of the `SynonymInfo` object are the `Application` object and the `Range` object. The `Application` object's `SynonymInfo` property requires a string parameter. The first word in the `Range` object's text is used as the key word. Word's thesaurus is used to find the synonyms, antonyms and related words.

SynonymInfo Common Properties

The `Application`, `Creator`, and `Parent` properties are defined at the beginning of this section.

SynonymInfo Properties

Name	Returns	Description
AntonymList	Variant	Read Only. Returns an array of strings containing antonyms for the passed word or phrase.
Found	Boolean	Read Only. Returns whether any the thesaurus information was found for the word or phrase.
MeaningCount	Long	Read Only. Returns how many different general meanings are found for the word or phrase.
MeaningList	Variant	Read Only. Returns an array of strings containing the different types of meanings for the word or phrase.
PartOfSpeech List	Variant	Read Only. Returns an array of integers. These integers correspond to the `WdPartOfSpeech` constants that in turn relate to the meanings of speech (words or phrases) looked up in the thesaurus.
Related Expression List	Variant	Read Only. Returns an array of strings containing the expressions that are related to the synonym word or phrase.
RelatedWord List	Variant	Read Only. Returns an array of strings containing the words that are related to the synonym word or phrase.
SynonymList	Variant	`Meaning` parameter. Read Only. Returns an array of strings holding the list of synonyms for the word or phrase with the `Meaning` parameter.

Name	Returns	Description
Word	String	Read Only. Returns the word or phrase that is being looked up.

Examples

Find the different meanings associated with the first word of "Document3". Display the different meanings to the Immediate window:

```
Dim syn As SynonymInfo
Dim mList As Variant
Set syn = Documents("Document3").Words(1).SynonymInfo
If syn.MeaningCount <> 0 Then
    mList = syn.MeaningList
    For i = 1 To UBound(mList)
        Debug.Print mList(i)
    Next i
Else
    Debug.Print "There were no meanings found."
End If
```

System Object

The System object contains information about the Word user's computer system.

System Common Properties

The Application, Creator and Parent properties are defined at the beginning of this section.

System Properties

Name	Returns	Description
ComputerType	String	Read Only. Returns the Macintosh model being used (eg. "Power Macintosh 6100". Returns an error if not a Macintosh.
Country	WdCountry	Read Only. Returns the country set for the computer.
Cursor	WdCursorType	Set/Get the mouse pointer cursor.
FreeDiskSpace	Long	Read Only. Returns the free disk space for the current drive.
Horizontal Resolution	Long	Read Only. Returns the horizontal screen resolution.
Language Designation	String	Read Only. Returns the language used in the system.

Table Continued on Following Page

535

Name	Returns	Description
MacintoshName	String	Read Only. Returns the Macintosh name as set in the **Sharing Setup** control panel. Not applicable in Windows.
MathCoprocessor Installed	Boolean	Read Only. Returns whether a math coprocessor is installed on the computer.
Operating System	String	Read Only. Returns the Operating System name.
PrivateProfile String	String	`FileName As String`, `Section As String`, `Key As String` Set/Get a registry setting.
ProcessorType	String	Read Only. Returns the processor name on the system.
ProfileString	String	`Section As String`, `Key As String` Set/Get registry settings.
QuickDraw Installed	Boolean	Read Only. Returns whether Quick Draw is installed.
Version	String	Read Only. Returns the operating system version number.
Vertical Resolution	Long	Read Only. Returns the vertical screen resolution.

Methods

Name	Returns	Parameters	Description
Connect		`Path As String`, `[Drive]`, `[Password]`	Maps to a network drive. Cannot be used on a Macintosh.
MSInfo			Starts the Microsoft System Information application.

Examples

Display the free disk drive space for the current drive:

```
MsgBox Application.System.FreeDiskSpace & " Bytes free"
```

Table Object and the Tables Collection

The `Tables` collection holds the list of tables in a selection, range or document. Each `Table` object represents a single table in a selection, range or document.

The `Tables` collection has one additional property and method besides the typical collection attribute. The `Add` method uses `Range`, `NumRows` and `NumColumns` parameters to add tables to the `Tables` collection. The `NestingLevel` property returns the nesting level number.

Table Common Properties

The `Application`, `Creator`, and `Parent` properties are defined at the beginning of this section.

Table Properties

Name	Returns	Description
AllowAuto Fit	Boolean	Set/Get whether the table columns will automatically adjust depending on the text.
AllowPage Breaks	Boolean	Set/Get whether page breaks are allowed in a table.
AutoFormat Type	Long	Read Only. Returns what type of `WdTableFormat` formatting has been set for the table.
Borders	Borders	Set/Get the borders around the table cells.
BottomPadding	Single	Set/Get the bottom margin in a cell.
Columns	Columns	Read Only. Returns the columns in the table.
ID	String	Set/Get the ID of the table.
LeftPadding	Single	Set/Get the left margin in a cell/all cells in a table.
NestingLevel	Long	Read Only. Returns how deep the current table is nested within other tables.
Preferred Width	Single	Set/Get the preferred width of the table in the measure set by `PreferredWidthType`.
Preferred WidthType	WdPreferred WidthType	Set/Get the measure used by `PreferredWidth`.

Table Continued on Following Page

Name	Returns	Description
Range	Range	Read Only. Returns the spot in the document that contains the table.
RightPadding	Single	Set/Get the right margin in a cell.
Rows	Rows	Read Only. Returns the rows in a table.
Shading	Shading	Read Only. Returns the shading properties for the table.
Spacing	Single	Set/Get the spacing between cells.
Table Direction	WdTable Direction	Set/Get the order in which cells are placed in a table.
Tables	Tables	Read Only. Returns the tables in the current table.
TopPadding	Single	Set/Get the top margin in a cell.
Uniform	Boolean	Read Only. Returns whether every row has the same number of columns.

Table Methods

Name	Returns	Parameters	Description
AutoFit Behavior		Behavior As WdAutoFit Behaviour	Sets how the table reacts when new text is added through the AutoFit feature. The AutoFit feature can also be turned off to fix the table size.
Auto Format		[Format], [ApplyBorders], [ApplyShading], [ApplyFont], [ApplyColor], [ApplyHeadingRows], [ApplyLastRow], [ApplyFirst Column], [ApplyLast Column], [AutoFit]	Formats the table using the parameters.

Name	Returns	Parameters	Description
Cell	Cell	Row As Long, Column As Long	Returns the cell in the table using the Row and Column parameters.
Convert ToText	Range	[Separator], [NestedTables]	Converts the table to text.
Delete			Deletes the table.
Select			Selects the table in the document.
Sort		[ExcludeHeader], [FieldNumber], [SortFieldType], [SortOrder], [FieldNumber2], [SortFieldType2], [SortOrder2], [FieldNumber3], [SortFieldType3], [SortOrder3], [CaseSensitive], [BidiSort], [IgnoreThe], [IgnoreKashida], [Ignore Diacritics], [IgnoreHe], [LanguageID]	Sorts the table with the parameters provided.
Sort Ascending			Sorts the table data alphabetically ascending using the first column.
Sort Descending			Sorts the table data alphabetically descending using the first column.
Split	Table	BeforeRow	Splits the table before the BeforeRow row and returns the new split table.

Name	Returns	Parameters	Description
`UpdateAuto Format`			Changes the format of the table to match the `AutoFormatTyp` e property.

Examples

Add a new table the current selection point. Make the first row the heading row:

```
ActiveDocument.Tables.Add Range:=Selection.Range, _
        NumRows:=2, NumColumns:=2, _
        DefaultTableBehavior:=wdWord9TableBehavior, _
        AutoFitBehavior:=wdAutoFitFixed
ActiveDocument.Tables(1).Rows(1).HeadingFormat = True
```

TableOfAuthorities Object and the TablesOfAuthorities Collection

The TablesOfAuthorities collection holds the list of tables of authorities in a document. The TableOfAuthorities object represents a single table of authorities in a document.

The TablesOfAuthorities collection has a few methods and properties besides the typical collection attributes, as outlined in the following table:

TablesOfAuthorities Collection Special Properties and Methods

Name	Returns	Description
`Format`	`WdToaFormat`	Property. Set/Get the format of the `TableOfAuthorities` to the specified format.
`Add`	`TableOf Authorities`	`Range As Range, [Category], [Bookmark], [Passim], [KeepEntryFormatting], [Separator], [IncludeSequenceName], [EntrySeparator], [PageRangeSeparator], [IncludeCategoryHeader], [PageNumberSeparator]` Adds a `TableOfAuthorities` object to the collection at the specified range.

Name	Returns	Description
MarkAll Citations	ShortCitation As String, [LongCitation], [LongCitation AutoText], [Category].	Creates a Table of Authorities entry for all instances of the ShortCitation text.
Mark Citation	Field	Range As Range, ShortCitation As String, [LongCitation], [LongCitationAutoText], [Category] Creates a Table of Authorities entry for the ShortCitation text at the Range spot.
Next Citation		ShortCitation As String. Selects the next Table of Authorities entry with the ShortCitation text.

TableOfAuthorities Common Properties

The Application, Creator, and Parent properties are defined at the beginning of this section.

TableOfAuthorities Properties

Name	Returns	Description
Bookmark	String	Set/Get the bookmark that contains the table of authorities entries.
Category	Long	Set/Get the type of entries included in the table of authorities.
EntrySeparator	String	Set/Get the text separating the entry from the page number.
IncludeCategory Header	Boolean	Set/Get whether the category name appears as part of the table of authorities.
IncludeSequence Name	String	Set/Get the sequence field identifier.
KeepEntry Formatting	Boolean	Set/Get whether the formatting of specific entries are kept in the table of authorities.

Table Continued on Following Page

Name	Returns	Description
PageNumber Separator	String	Set/Get the page number separator.
PageRange Separator	String	Set/Get the page range separator.
Passim	Boolean	Set/Get whether many page references to the same authority is replaced with "Passim".
Range	Range	Read Only. Returns the spot in the document containing the table of authorities.
Separator	String	Set/Get the separator between the sequence number and the page number.
TabLeader	WdTab Leader	Set/Get what sort of leading tabs are used between entries and the page numbers.

TableOfAuthorities Methods

Name	Returns	Parameters	Description
Delete			Deletes the TableOfAuthorities object.
Update			Updates the table of authorities with the table of authorities entries.

Examples

See the TableOfContents object and the TablesOfContents collection for examples.

TableOfAuthoritiesCategory Object and the TablesOfAuthoritiesCategories Collection

The TablesOfAuthoritiesCategories collection holds all of the possible categories associated with tables of authorities. The TableOfAuthoritiesCategory object represents a single category of table of authorities. The TableOfAuthoritiesCategory objects are accessed by using a category name or number as the Index property of the TablesOfAuthoritiesCategories collection.

TableOfAuthoritiesCategory Common Properties

The Application, Creator, and Parent properties are defined at the beginning of this section.

TableOfAuthoritiesCategory Properties

Name	Returns	Description
Index	Long	Read Only. Returns the position of the TableOfAuthoritiesCategory in the collection.
Name	String	Set/Get the name of the table of authorities category.

Examples

Display all the table of authorities category names in message boxes:

```
Dim TOACat As TableOfAuthoritiesCategory
For Each TOACat In ActiveDocument.TablesOfAuthoritiesCategories
    MsgBox TOACat.Name
Next
```

TableOfContents Object and the TablesOfContents Collection

The TablesOfContents collection holds the list of tables of contents in a document. The TableOfContents object represents a single table of contents in a document.

The TablesOfContents collection has a few methods and properties besides the typical collection attributes outlined in the following table.

TablesOfContents Collection Special Properties and Methods

Name	Returns	Description
Format	WdToc Format	Property. Set/Get the format of the TableOfContents to the specified format.
Add	TableOf Contents	Range As Range, [UseHeadingStyles], [UpperHeadingLevel], [LowerHeadingLevel], [UseFields], [TableID], [RightAlignPageNumbers], [IncludePageNumbers], [AddedStyles], [UseHyperlinks], [HidePageNumbersInWeb] Adds a TableOfContents object to the collection at the specified range.
MarkEntry	Field	Range As Range, [Entry], [EntryAutoText], [TableID], [Level] Creates a table of contents entry for the Range spot.

TableOfContents Common Properties

The `Application`, `Creator`, and `Parent` properties are defined at the beginning of this section.

TableOfContents Properties

Name	Returns	Description
HeadingStyles	Heading Styles	Read Only. An object accessing the additional styles associated with a table of contents.
HidePageNumbers InWeb	Boolean	Set /Get whether page numbers are hidden in a web page.
IncludePage Numbers	Boolean	Set/Get whether to include page numbers in the table of contents.
LowerHeading Level	Long	Set/Get the smallest level heading to be included in the table of contents.
Range	Range	Read Only. Returns the spot in the document containing the table of contents.
RightAlignPage Numbers	Boolean	Set/Get whether the page numbers are right aligned.
TabLeader	WdTab Leader	Set/Get what sort of leading tabs is used between entries and the page numbers.
TableID	String	Set/Get the table of contents identifier.
UpperHeading Level	Long	Set/Get the highest level heading to be included in the table of contents.
UseFields	Boolean	Set/Get whether fields are used to create a table of contents.
UseHeading Styles	Boolean	Set/Get whether heading styles are used to create a table of contents.
UseHyperlinks	Boolean	Set/Get whether entries in a table should be formatted as hyperlinks when publishing as a web page.

TableOfContents Methods

Name	Returns	Parameters	Description
Delete			Deletes the `TableOfContents` object.

Name	Returns	Parameters	Description
Update			Updates the table of contents with the table of contents entries.
Update Page Numbers			Update the table of contents with the current page numbers for the entries.

Examples

Add a table of contents at the current selection point. The heading levels used are from level 1 to 3, page numbers are included, hyperlinks are used, and the tab leaders are dots:

```
Dim toc As TableOfContents

Set toc = ActiveDocument.TablesOfContents.Add (Range:=Selection.Range, _
                         RightAlignPageNumbers:=True, _
                         UseHeadingStyles:=True, _
                         UpperHeadingLevel:=1, _
                         LowerHeadingLevel:=3, _
                         IncludePageNumbers:=True, _
                         AddedStyles:="", _
                         UseHyperlinks:=True)
    toc.TabLeader = wdTabLeaderDots
       toc.Delete
End With
```

TableOfFigures Object and the TablesOfFigures Collection

The TablesOfFigures collection holds the list of tables of figures in a document. The TableOfFigures object represents a single table of figures in a document.

The TablesOfFigures collection has a few methods and properties besides the typical collection attributes, as outlined in the following table:

TablesOfFigures Collection Special Properties and Methods

Name	Returns	Description
Format	WdTof Format	Property. Set/Get the format of the TableOfFigures to the specified format.

Table Continued on Following Page

545

Name	Returns	Description
Add	TableOf Figures	Range As Range, [Caption], [IncludeLabel], [UseHeadingStyles], [UpperHeadingLevel], [LowerHeadingLevel], [UseFields], [TableID], [RightAlignPageNumbers], [IncludePageNumbers], [AddedStyles], [UseHyperlinks], [HidePageNumbersInWeb] Adds a TableOfFigures object to the collection at the specified range.
Mark Entry	Field	Range As Range, [Entry], [EntryAutoText], [TableID], [Level] Creates a table of figures entry for the Range spot.

TableOfFigures Common Properties

The Application, Creator, and Parent properties are defined at the beginning of this section.

TableOfFigures Properties

Name	Returns	Description
Caption	String	Set/Get caption used for the table of figures.
HeadingStyles	Heading Styles	Read Only. An object accessing the additional styles associated with a table of figures.
HidePageNumber sInWeb	Boolean	Set/Get whether page numbers are hidden in a web page.
IncludeLabel	Boolean	Set/Get whether the label is included with the table of figures.
IncludePage Numbers	Boolean	Set/Get whether to include page numbers in the table of figures.
LowerHeading Level	Long	Set/Get the level heading that ends the table of contents.
Range	Range	Read Only. Returns the spot in the document containing the table of figures.

Name	Returns	Description
RightAlignPage Numbers	Boolean	Set/Get whether the page numbers are right aligned.
TabLeader	WdTabLeader	Set/Get what sort of leading tabs are used between entries and the page numbers.
TableID	String	Set/Get the table of figures identifier.
UpperHeading Level	Long	Set Set/Get the highest level heading to be included in the table of figures.
UseFields	Boolean	Set/Get whether fields are used to create a table of figures.
UseHeading Styles	Boolean	Set/Get whether heading styles are used to create a table of figures.
UseHyperlinks	Boolean	Set/Get whether contents of a table should be formatted as hyperlinks when publishing as a web page.

TableOfFigures Methods

Name	Returns	Parameters	Description
Delete			Deletes the TableOfFigures object.
Update			Updates the table of figures with the table of figures entries.
UpdatePage Numbers			Update the table of figures with the current page numbers for the entries.

Examples

Add a table of figures at the current selection point. The caption should be "Figure", the heading levels used are from level 1 to 3, page numbers are included, hyperlinks are used, and the tab leaders are dots:

```
Dim tof As TableOfFigures

    Set tof =ActiveDocument.TablesOfFigures.Add Range:=Selection.Range, _
                Caption:="Figure", _
                IncludeLabel:=True, _
                RightAlignPageNumbers:=True, _
                UseHeadingStyles:=False, _
                UpperHeadingLevel:=1, _
```

```
                          LowerHeadingLevel:=3, _
                          IncludePageNumbers:=True, _
                          AddedStyles:="", _
                          UseHyperlinks:=True, _
                          HidePageNumbersInWeb:=True
      tof.TabLeader = wdTabLeaderDots
End With
```

TabStop Object and the TabStops Collection

The TabStops collection holds the list of tab stops for a particular paragraph, a collection of paragraphs, or a ParagraphFormat object. The TabStop object represents a single tab setting for a particular paragraph or collection of paragraphs. Possible parents objects of the TabStops collection are the Paragraph object, the ParagraphFormat object, and the Paragraphs collection.

The TabStops collection has a few methods besides the typical collection attributes. These methods are listed in the following table:

TabStops Collection Special Methods

Name	Returns	Description
Add	TabStop	Position As Single, [Alignment], [Leader] Adds a tab stop to the paragraph or paragraphs.
After	TabStop	Position As Single. Returns the next tab stop after the Position parameter.
Before	TabStop	Position As Single. Returns the previous tab stop before the Position parameter.
ClearAll		Deletes all the custom tab stop settings.

TabStop Common Properties

The Application, Creator, and Parent properties are defined at the beginning of this section.

TabStop Properties

Name	Returns	Description
Alignment	WdTabAlignment	Set/Get the type of tab alignment (e.g. center, decimal align).
CustomTab	Boolean	Read Only. Returns whether the current tab stop is custom.
Leader	WdTabLeader	Set/Get what the leading text is for the tab stop.

Name	Returns	Description
Next	TabStop	Read Only. Returns the next tab stop in the collection.
Position	Single	Set / Get the distance from the left margin for the tab stop.
Previous	TabStop	Read Only. Returns the previous tab stop in the collection.

TabStop Methods

Name	Returns	Parameters	Description
Clear			Deletes the custom tab stop.

Examples

Clear out all the custom tab stops for the active document:

```
ActiveDocument.Paragraphs.TabStops.ClearAll
```

Task Object and the Tasks Collection

The Tasks collection lists all of the currently running tasks on the system. Each Task object represents one of the running tasks on the system.

The Tasks collection has two methods besides the typical collection attributes that are listed in the following table:

Tasks Collection Special Methods

Name	Returns	Description
Exists	Boolean	Name As String parameter. Returns whether the task specified by the Name parameter is currently in the Tasks collection.
ExitWindows		Exits Windows. The changes made to Word documents are not saved.

Task Common Properties

The Application, Creator, and Parent properties are defined at the beginning of this section.

Task Properties

Name	Returns	Description
Height	Long	Set/Get the height of the task's window.
Left	Long	Set/Get the horizontal position of the task's window.
Name	String	Read Only. Returns the name of the task.
Top	Long	Set/Get the vertical position of the task's window.
Visible	Boolean	Set/Get whether the task is visible or not.
Width	Long	Set/Get the width of the task's window.
WindowState	WdWindowState	Set/Get what the window state is (e.g. minimized).

Task Methods

Name	Returns	Parameters	Description
Activate		[Wait]	Activates the task.
Close			Closes the task.
Move		Left As Long, Top As Long	Moves the task window.
Resize		Width As Long, Height As Long	Resizes the task window.
SendWindow Message		Message As Long, wParam As Long, lParam As Long	Sends the Message parameter with the parameters lParam and wParam to the task.

Examples

Check to see if Microsoft Visual Basic Help is open. If that task is open then close it:

```
Dim tsk As Task
For Each tsk In Application.Tasks
    If tsk.Name = "Microsoft Visual Basic Help" Then
        tsk.Close
    End If
Next
```

Template Object and the Templates Collection

The `Templates` collection holds the list of the open templates, attached templates, and global templates currently loaded. Each `Template` object represents a single open template, attached template, or global template currently loaded in the Word session. An index number or the template name can be used in the `Templates` collection to access a particular `Template` object. The `Application` object is the parent of this collection

Template Common Properties

The `Application`, `Creator`, and `Parent` properties are defined at the beginning of this section.

Template Properties

Name	Returns	Description
AutoText Entries	AutoText Entries	Read Only. Returns the AutoText entries associated with the template.
BuiltIn Document Properties	Object	Read Only. Returns a DocumentProperties collection representing all of the Word defined attributes of the template (e.g. Author).
CustomDocument Properties	Object	Read Only. Returns an object manipulating the custom document properties.
FarEastLine BreakLanguage	WdFarEastLine BreakLanguageID	Set/Get the line break language used.
FarEastLine BreakLevel	WdFarEastLine BreakLevel	Set/Get the line break control level.
FullName	String	Read Only. Returns the path and template filename.
Justification Mode	WdJustification Mode	Set/Get the amount of spacing used between letters.
KerningBy Algorithm	Boolean	Set/Get whether kerning of half width characters is executed.
LanguageID	WdLanguageID	Set/Get the language associated with the template.
LanguageID FarEast	WdLanguageID	Set/Get the language associated with the template.

Table Continued on Following Page

Name	Returns	Description
ListTemplates	ListTemplates	Read Only. Returns the collection of lists formatted with list templates in the parent template.
Name	String	Read Only. The template filename.
NoLineBreak After	String	Set/Get where to break a line when using kinosku language characters.
NoLineBreak Before	String	Set/Get where a line won't break when using kinosku language characters.
NoProofing	Long	Set/Get whether proofing is done for the template.
Path	String	Read Only. Returns the path of the document.
Saved	Boolean	Set/Get whether the document has been saved.
Type	WdTemplateType	Read Only. Returns the template type.
VBProject	VBProject	Returns an object allowing access to the VB project associated with the template.

Template Methods

Name	Returns	Parameters	Description
OpenAs Document	Document		Opens up the template as a document.
Save			Saves the current template.

Examples

Display the full name and path of the template attached to the current document:

```
Dim tmp As Template
Set tmp = ActiveDocument.AttachedTemplate
MsgBox tmp.FullName
```

TextColumn Object and the TextColumns Collection

The TextColumns collection holds all the columns in a document or a particular section of a document. Each TextColumn object represents a column of text in a document or section. The TextColumns property of the PageSetup object is used access the TextColumns collection. The PageSetup object is the parent of this collection.

The following table lists the few properties and methods that the TextColumns collection includes besides the typical collection attributes:

TextColumns Collection Special Properties and Methods

Name	Returns	Description
Evenly Spaced	Long	Set/Get whether the columns are evenly spaced between each other.
Flow Direction	WdFlow Direction	Set/Get whether columns flow from left-to-right or right-to-left.
Line Between	Long	Set/Get whether vertical lines are visible between columns.
Spacing	Single	Set/Get the spacing between columns.
Width	Single	Set/Get the column widths.
Add	TextColumn	Method. [Width], [Spacing], [EvenlySpaced] parameters. Adds a text column to the collection.
SetCount		Method. NumColumns As Long. Puts the current text into the NumColumns number of columns.

TextColumn Common Properties

The Application, Creator, and Parent properties are defined at the beginning of this section.

TextColumn Properties

Name	Returns	Description
SpaceAfter	Single	Set/Get the amount of space after the current column.
Width	Single	Set/Get the width of the text column.

Examples

Set the number of columns to two in the active document. The columns should be evenly spaced, a line must be located between columns, and the width must be 10 centimeters with a 1-centimeter space in between columns:

```
With ActiveDocument.PageSetup.TextColumns
    .SetCount NumColumns:=2
    .EvenlySpaced = True
    .LineBetween = True
    .Width = CentimetersToPoints(3)
    .Spacing = CentimetersToPoints(1)
End With
```

TextEffectFormat Object

The TextEffectFormat object contains all the properties and methods associated with WordArt objects. The parent object of the TextEffectFormat is always the Shape object.

TextEffectFormat Common Properties

The Application, Creator, and Parent properties are defined at the beginning of this section.

TextEffectFormat Properties

Name	Returns	Description
Alignment	MsoTextEffect Alignment	Set/Get the alignment of the WordArt.
FontBold	MsoTriState	Set/Get whether the WordArt is bold.
FontItalic	MsoTriState	Set/Get whether the WordArt is italic.
FontName	String	Set/Get the font used in the WordArt.
FontSize	Single	Set/Get the font size in the WordArt.
KernedPairs	MsoTriState	Set/Get whether the characters are kerned in the WordArt.
Normalized Height	MsoTriState	Set/Get whether both the uppercase and lowercase characters are the same height.
PresetShape	MsoPresetText EffectShape	Set/Get the shape of the WordArt.
PresetText Effect	MsoPresetText Effect	Set/Get the effect associated with the WordArt.

Name	Returns	Description
RotatedChars	MsoTriState	Set/Get whether the WordArt has been rotated by 90 degrees.
Text	String	Set/Get the text in the WordArt.
Tracking	Single	Set/Get the spacing ratio between characters.

TextEffectFormat Methods

Name	Returns	Parameters	Description
Toggle VerticalText			Toggles the text from vertical to horizontal and back.

Examples

The first shape in the active document is a WordArt object. Set the text to "Wrox", font size to 18, and make the text bold and italic:

```
With ActiveDocument.Shapes(1).TextEffect
    .Text = "Wrox"
    .FontSize = 18
    .FontBold = msoTrue
    .FontItalic = msoTrue
End With
```

TextFrame Object

The TextFrame object contains the properties and methods that can manipulate text frame shapes. Possible parent objects of the TextFrame object are the Shape and ShapeRange objects.

TextFrame Common Properties

The Application, Creator, and Parent properties are defined at the beginning of this section.

TextFrame Properties

Name	Returns	Description
Containing Range	Range	Read Only. Returns the text in the collection of linked text frames.
HasText	Long	Read Only. Returns whether text is inside the text frame.

Table Continued on Following Page

Name	Returns	Description
MarginBottom	Single	Set/Get the bottom spacing in a text frame.
MarginLeft	Single	Set/Get the left spacing in a text frame.
MarginRight	Single	Set/Get the right spacing in a text frame.
MarginTop	Single	Set/Get the top spacing in a text frame.
Next	TextFrame	Set/Get the next linked text frame.
Orientation	MsoText Orientation	Set/Get the orientation of the text in the text frame.
Overflowing	Boolean	Read Only. Returns whether the text fits in text frame.
Previous	TextFrame	Set/Get the previous linked text frame.
TextRange	Range	Read Only. Returns the range in the document containing the text inside a text frame.

TextFrame Methods

Name	Returns	Parameters	Description
BreakForward Link			Breaks the forward link in a collection of linked frames.
ValidLink Target	Boolean	TargetText Frame As TextFrame	Returns whether the TargetTextFrame is a valid text frame to link to.

Examples

If the text of the first text frame is overflowing then change all the margins to 5 points:

```
With ActiveDocument.Shapes(1).TextFrame
    If .Overflowing Then
        .MarginBottom = 5
        .MarginTop = 5
        .MarginLeft = 5
        .MarginRight = 5
    End If
End With
```

TextInput Object

The `TextInput` object contains the properties and methods associated with a single text form field. The `FormField` object is the parent of the `TextInput` object.

TextInput Common Properties

The `Application`, `Creator`, and `Parent` properties are defined at the beginning of this section.

TextInput Properties

Name	Returns	Description
Default	String	Set/Get the default contents of the text form field.
Format	String	Read Only. Returns the formatting associated with the text form field text.
Type	WdTextForm FieldType	Read Only. Returns the text form field type.
Valid	Boolean	Read Only. Returns whether the text form field is valid.
Width	Long	Set/Get the width of the text form field.

TextInput Methods

Name	Returns	Parameters	Description
Clear			Clears the text in the text form field.
EditType		Type As WdTextForm FieldType, [Default], [Format], [Enabled]	Sets some of the properties associated with the text form field.

Examples

Change the first form field name in the active document to "TxtName". Then set the default text to be "Normal", format it so that the first letter is capitalized, and make the form field a regular type:

```
With ActiveDocument.FormFields(1)
    .Name = "TxtMain"
    .Enabled = True
    With .TextInput
        .EditType Type:=wdRegularText, _
                  Default:="Normal", _
                  Format:="First capital"
        .Width = 0
    End With
End With
```

TextRetrievalMode Object

The TextRetrievalMode object contains properties associated with how text is accessed from a Range object. The TextRetrievalMode object is accessed through the Range object.

TextRetrievalMode Common Properties

The Application, Creator, and Parent properties are defined at the beginning of this section.

TextRetrievalMode Properties

Name	Returns	Description
Duplicate	Text Retrieval Mode	Read Only. Returns a new object containing all of the current text retrieval properties.
IncludeField Codes	Boolean	Set/Get whether field codes are included in Range text.
Include HiddenText	Boolean	Set/Get whether hidden text is included in Range text.
ViewType	WdViewType	Set/Get what type of characters are included in the Range text.

Examples

Set the range text retrieval to include hidden text for the current selection:

```
Selection.Range.TextRetrievalMode.IncludeHiddenText = True
```

ThreeDFormat Object

The ThreeDFormat object contains all of the three-dimensional formatting properties of the parent Shape object. The ThreeD property of the Shape object is used to access the ThreeDFormat object.

ThreeDFormat Common Properties

The `Application`, `Creator`, and `Parent` properties are defined at the beginning of this section.

ThreeDFormat Properties

Name	Returns	Description
Depth	Single	Set/Get the 'depth' of a 3D shape.
ExtrusionColor	ColorFormat	Read Only. An object manipulating the color of the extrusion.
ExtrusionColor Type	MsoExtrusion ColorType	Set/Get how the color for the extrusion is set.
Perspective	MsoTriState	Set/Get whether the shape's extrusion has perspective.
PresetExtrusion Direction	MsoPreset Extrusion Direction	Read Only. Returns the direction of the extrusion.
PresetLighting Direction	MsoPreset Lighting Direction	Set/Get the directional source of the light source.
PresetLighting Softness	MsoPreset Lighting Softness	Set/Get the softness of the light source.
PresetMaterial	MsoPreset Material	Set/Get the surface material of the extrusion.
PresetThreeD Format	MsoPreset ThreeDFormat	Read Only. Returns the preset extrusion format.
RotationX	Single	Set/Get how many degrees the extrusion is rotated.
RotationY	Single	Set/Get how many degrees the extrusion is rotated.
Visible	MsoTriState	Set/Get whether the 3D shape is visible.

ThreeDFormat Methods

Name	Returns	Parameters	Description
Increment RotationX		Increment As Single	Changes the RotationX property.

Table Continued on Following Page

Name	Returns	Parameters	Description
Increment RotationY		Increment As Single	Changes the RotationY property.
Reset Rotation			Resets the RotationX and RotationY to 0.
SetExtrusion Direction		PresetExt rusionDir ection As Long	Changes the extrusion direction.
SetThreeD Format		PresetThr eeDFormat As Long	Sets the preset extrusion format.

Examples

Change the currently selected three dimensional properties to decrement the y-rotation by 5, set the depth to 26 and set the lighting source to be the top left:

```
Selection.ShapeRange.ThreeD.Visible = msoTrue
Selection.ShapeRange.ThreeD.IncrementRotationY -5
Selection.ShapeRange.ThreeD.Depth = 36
Selection.ShapeRange.ThreeD.PresetLightingDirection = _
        msoLightingTopLeft
```

TwoInitialCapsException Object and the TwoInitialCapsExceptions Collection

The TwoInitialCapsExceptions collection represents the list of exceptions to the "Do correct two initial capital letters of a word" rule of the AutoCorrect object. Each TwoInitialCapsException object represents an abbreviation that is not included in the AutoCorrect object two caps rule. The TwoInitialCapsExceptions collection can only be accessed through the AutoCorrect object.

The TwoInitialCapsExceptions collection has an Add method in addition to the regular collection properties and methods. The Add method is used to add TwoInitialCapsException objects to the collection.

TwoInitialCapsException Common Properties

The Application, Creator, and Parent properties are defined at the beginning of this section.

TwoInitialCapsException Properties

Name	Returns	Description
Index	Long	Read Only. Returns the item number in the parent collection.
Name	String	Read Only. Returns the TwoInitialCapsException item name and the exception itself.

TwoInitialCapsException Methods

Name	Returns	Parameters	Description
Delete			Deletes the TwoInitialCapsException object.

Examples

Add an exception to the Two Initial Caps rule for the word "HEllo":

```
Application.AutoCorrect.TwoInitialCapExceptions.Add "HEllo."
```

Variable Object and the Variables Collection

The Variables collection holds the list of variables associated with a document or template. A Variable object represents a single variable stored with a document or template. The Variables collection allows settings to be saved between Word sessions. The Document object is the parent of the Variables collection.

The Variables collection has an Add method besides the typical collection attributes. The Add method takes a variable name and value and adds a Variable object to the Variables collection.

Variable Common Properties

The Application, Creator, and Parent properties are defined at the beginning of this section.

Variable Properties

Name	Returns	Description
Index	Long	Read Only. Returns the item number of the object in the collection.
Name	String	Read Only. Returns the variable name.
Value	String	Set/Get the data stored in the variable.

Variable Methods

Name	Returns	Parameters	Description
Delete			Deletes the variable.

Examples

Add a variable to the active document called `Name`. The value "Joe" should be stored in the variable:

```
ActiveDocument.Variables.Add "Name", "Joe"
```

Version Object and the Versions Collection

The `Versions` collection lists all of the versions of a document. Each `Version` object represents one version of a document. The `Versions` collection is accessed throughout the `Document` object.

The `Versions` collection has one property and one method besides the typical collection attributes. The `AutoVersion` property uses the `WdAutoVersions` constants to set whether versions of the current document are kept. Currently setting the AutoVersion property to `WdAutoVersionOff` will turn of versioning while `WdAutoVersionOnClose` turns versioning on. The `Save` method saves the document and adds the saved document as a new version in the `Versions` collection.

Version Common Properties

The `Application`, `Creator`, and `Parent` properties are defined at the beginning of this section.

Version Properties

Name	Returns	Description
Comment	String	Read Only. Returns the comment associated with the version.
Date	Date	Read Only. Returns the date the version was created.
Index	Long	Read Only. Returns the item number in the parent collection.
SavedBy	String	Read Only. Returns the name of the user who saved the version.

Version Methods

Name	Returns	Parameters	Description
Delete			Deletes the version.
Open	Document		Opens the document version in Word.

Examples

Delete all the versions of the active document created by the user 'Felipe':

```
Dim vrsn As Version

For Each vrsn In ActiveDocument.Versions
    If vrsn.SavedBy = "Felipe" Then
        vrsn.Delete
    End If
Next
```

View Object

The `View` object represents all of the view properties and methods associated with a window or a pane. Possible parents of the `View` object are the `Window` and `Pane` objects.

View Common Properties

The `Application`, `Creator`, and `Parent` properties are defined at the beginning of this section.

View Properties

Name	Returns	Description
BrowseTo Window	Long	Set/Get whether the text wraps at the window edge instead of the page margin edge.
Draft	Boolean	Set/Get whether the document is viewed in draft mode.
EnlargeFonts LessThan	Long	Set/Get what the minimum font size is that is displayed.
FieldShading	WdField Shading	Set/Get the displayed form field shading.
FullScreen	Boolean	Set/Get whether the window is viewed full screen.
Magnifier	Boolean	Set/Get whether the print preview view can be zoomed.

Table Continued on Following Page

563

Name	Returns	Description
MailMergeData View	Boolean	Set/Get whether the mail merge data is being viewed.
SeekView	WdSeekView	Set/Get what is displayed in the page layout view.
ShowAll	Boolean	Set/Get whether all characters are shown in the parent window.
ShowAnimation	Boolean	Set/Get whether animations are shown in the parent window.
ShowBookmarks	Boolean	Set/Get whether bookmarks are shown in the parent window.
ShowDrawings	Boolean	Set/Get whether drawings are shown in the parent window.
ShowField Codes	Boolean	Set/Get whether field codes are shown in the parent window.
ShowFirstLine Only	Boolean	Set/Get whether only the first line of text is shown in the parent window in outline view.
ShowFormat	Boolean	Set/Get whether text formatting is shown in the parent window.
ShowHidden Text	Boolean	Set/Get whether hidden text is shown in the parent window.
ShowHighlight	Boolean	Set/Get whether highlights are shown in the parent window.
ShowHyphens	Boolean	Set/Get whether hyphens are shown in the parent window.
ShowMain TextLayer	Boolean	Set/Get whether main text is shown in the parent window when a header/footer is displayed.
ShowObjectAnc hors	Boolean	Set/Get whether object anchors are shown in the parent window.
ShowOptional Breaks	Boolean	Set/Get whether optional line breaks are shown in the parent window.
Show Paragraphs	Boolean	Set/Get whether paragraph marks are shown in the parent window.
ShowPicture PlaceHolders	Boolean	Set/Get whether placeholders are shown in the parent window instead of the actual pictures.

Name	Returns	Description
ShowSpaces	Boolean	Set/Get whether space marks are shown in the parent window.
ShowTabs	Boolean	Set/Get whether tab marks are shown in the parent window.
ShowText Boundaries	Boolean	Set/Get whether dotted lines around page margins, text columns, objects and frames are shown in the page layout view of the parent window.
SplitSpecial	WdSpecial Pane	Set/Get the active pane in the current window.
Table Gridlines	Boolean	Set/Get whether table gridlines are shown in the parent window.
Type	WdView Type	Set/Get what the current view is for the parent window.
WrapToWindow	Boolean	Set/Get whether the document text wraps in the current window boundaries.
Zoom	Zoom	Read Only. An object manipulating the zoom properties.

View Methods

Name	Returns	Parameters	Description
Collapse Outline		[Range] As Range	Collapses the text in all the lower heading levels of the current selection or Range parameter.
Expand Outline		[Range] As Range	Expands the text in all the lower heading levels of the current selection or Range parameter.
NextHeader Footer			Moves the current selection point to the next header or footer.
Previous HeaderFooter			Moves the current selection point to the previous header or footer.

Table Continued on Following Page

Name	Returns	Parameters	Description
ShowAll Headings			Toggles between showing only headings and showing headings and body text.
ShowHeading		Level As Long	Expands all the text up to the Level parameter. All subordinate headings and text is hidden.

Examples

Change the view settings for the active window so that animations, bookmarks, spaces, hidden text, and highlights are shown. Change the view to the Normal view, making sure to take into consideration the panes involved in the active window:

```
With ActiveWindow
    With .View
        .ShowAnimation = True
        .ShowBookmarks = True
        .ShowSpaces = True
        .ShowHiddenText = True
        .ShowHighlight = True
    End With
End With
If ActiveWindow.View.SplitSpecial = wdPaneNone Then
    ActiveWindow.ActivePane.View.Type = wdNormalView
Else
    ActiveWindow.View.Type = wdNormalView
End If
```

WebOptions Object

Allows programmatic changes to items associated with the Web Options dialog for a particular document.

WebOptions Common Properties

The Application, Creator, and Parent properties are defined at the beginning of this section.

WebOptions Properties

Name	Returns	Description
AllowPNG	Boolean	Set/Get whether Portable Network Graphics Format is allowed as an output format. PNG is a file format for the lossless, portable, well-compressed storage of images.
Browser Level	WdBrowser Level	Set/Get what browser to target new web pages created in Word (e.g. IE5).

Name	Returns	Description
Encoding	MsoEncoding	Set/Get the type of encoding when viewing a saved document.
FolderSuffix	String	Read Only. Returns the folder suffix that Word will use to save a document as a Web page.
OptimizeFor Browser	Boolean	Set/Get whether the document should be optimized for the browser specified in the `BrowserLevel` property.
OrganizeIn Folder	Boolean	Set/Get whether Web page supporting files, like graphics, are organized in a separate folder from the Web page.
PixelsPer Inch	Long	Set/Get the density of pixels per inch for graphic images and table cells on a Web page.
RelyOnCSS	Boolean	Set/Get whether Cascading Style Sheets (CSS) is used for `font` formatting when viewing a saved Word document in an HTML browser.
RelyOnVML	Boolean	Set/Get whether Vector Markup Language (VML) is used to generate graphics from drawing objects. Setting this to `True` will not generate images. VML is an XML based format for high-quality vector graphics on the Web.
ScreenSize	MsoScreen Size	Set/Get the target monitor's ideal minimum screen size for viewing a saved Web page.
UseLongFile Names	Boolean	Set/Get whether long file names are used whenever possible.

WebOptions Methods

Name	Returns	Parameters	Description
UseDefault FolderSuffix			Tells Word to use its default-naming scheme (based on the document name) for creating supporting folders.

WebPageFont Object and the WebPageFonts Collection

The WebPageFonts collection object is a collection of WebPageFont objects that contain the font information that is used when documents are saved as web pages. For each character set you can specify the web page font properties. The WebPageFonts collection only has one property, the Item property.

WebPageFont Properties

Name	Returns	Description
FixedWidth Font	String	Set/Get fixed-width font setting in the host application.
FixedWidth FontSize	Single	Set/Get fixed-width font setting in the host application in points.
Proportional FontProperty	String	Set/Get proportional font setting in the host application.
Proportional FontSize	Single	Set/Get proportional font size setting in the host application.

Example

Set the proportional font and the proportional font size properties for a WebPageFont object called examplefont:

```
With examplefont
    ProportionalFont = Courier
    ProportionalFontSize = 16
```

Window Object and the Windows Collection

The Windows collection holds the list of open windows in the Word session or for a specific document. The Window object represents a single window associated with a document or the Word session. Possible parents of the Windows collection are the Application and Document objects.

The Windows collection has two methods besides the typical collection attributes. The Add method adds a window to the Windows collection. The Arrange method arranges the open windows using the method specified by the ArrangeStyle parameter.

Window Common Properties

The Application, Creator, and Parent properties are defined at the beginning of this section.

Window Properties

Name	Returns	Description
Active	Boolean	Read Only. Returns whether the window is the active window.
ActivePane	Pane	Read Only. Returns the active pane in the window.
Caption	String	Set/Get the caption of the window.
DisplayHorizontal ScrollBar	Boolean	Set/Get whether to display the horizontal scrollbar.
DisplayLeftScroll Bar	Boolean	Set/Get whether to display the left scrollbar.
DisplayRightRuler	Boolean	Set/Get whether to display the right ruler in print layout view.
DisplayRulers	Boolean	Set/Get whether to display the rules.
DisplayScreenTips	Boolean	Set/Get whether to display screen tips.
DisplayVertical Ruler	Boolean	Set/Get whether to display the vertical ruler.
DisplayVertical ScrollBar	Boolean	Set/Get whether to display the vertical scrollbar
Document	Document	Read Only. Returns the document contained by the window.
DocumentMap	Boolean	Set/Get whether the documents map is visible.
DocumentMap PercentWidth	Long	Set/Get what the percentage space is that the document map takes up in the window.
EnvelopeVisible	Boolean	Set/Get whether the envelope associated with the document is visible.
Height	Long	Set/Get the height of the window.
HorizontalPercent Scrolled	Long	Set/Get what the percentage of the document width has been scrolled.
IMEMode	WdIMEMode	Set/Get the default start-up mode for the Japanese input system.

Table Continued on Following Page

Name	Returns	Description
Index	Long	Read Only. Returns the item number in the current parent collection.
Left	Long	Set/Get the horizontal position of the window.
Next	Window	Read only. Returns the next window in the windows collection.
Panes	Panes	Read Only. Returns the panes in the window.
Previous	Window	Read only. Returns the previous Window in the Windows collection.
Selection	Selection	Read Only. Returns the current selection in the window.
Split	Boolean	Set/Get whether the window is split into panes.
SplitVertical	Long	Set/Get what percentage of the current window is split.
StyleAreaWidth	Single	Set/Get how big the style area is.
Top	Long	Set/Get the vertical position of the window.
Type	WdWindow Type	Read Only. Returns the type of window.
UsableHeight	Long	Read Only. Returns what is the current height available to use in the window.
UsableWidth	Long	Read Only. Returns what is the current width available to use in the window.
VerticalPercent Scrolled	Long	Set/Get what the percentage of the document height has been scrolled.
View	View	Read Only. An object allowing modification of the View properties.
Visible	Boolean	Set/Get whether the window is visible.
Width	Long	Set/Get the width of the window.

Name	Returns	Description
WindowNumber	Long	Read Only. Returns the window number of the window when multiple versions of the same document are open.
WindowState	WdWindowState	Set/Get the window state (e.g. minimized).

Window Methods

Name	Returns	Parameters	Description
Activate			Activates the window.
Close		[SaveChanges], [RouteDocument]	Closes the window.
GetPoint		ScreenPixelsLeft As Long, ScreenPixelsTop As Long, ScreenPixels Width As Long, ScreenPixels Height As Long, obj As Object	Returns the screen coordinates of the specified range or shape. An error occurs if the whole range or shape isn't visible on the screen.
Large Scroll		[Down], [Up], [ToRight], [ToLeft]	Causes the document to scroll a certain direction a screen at a time.
NewWindow	Window		Creates a new window with the same document as the current window.
PageScroll	Window	[Down], [Up]	Causes the document to scroll a certain direction a document page at a time.

Table Continued on Following Page

Name	Returns	Parameters	Description
PrintOut		[Background], [Append], [Range], [OutputFileName], [From], [To], [Item], [Copies], [Pages], [PageType], [PrintToFile], [Collate], [ActivePrinterMacGX], [ManualDuplexPrint], [PrintZoomColumn], [PrintZoomRow], [PrintZoomPaperWidth], [PrintZoomPaperHeight]	Prints out the document using the specified settings.
RangeFrom Point		x As Long, y As Long	Returns the portion of the document correspondi ng to the specified coordinates.
ScrollInto View		obj As Object, [Start]	Scrolls through a window so that the object specified by the obj parameter can be seen.
SetFocus			Sets focus of the window to an area of an e-mail message.
Small Scroll		[Down], [Up], [ToRight], [ToLeft]	Causes the document to scroll a certain direction a document line at a time.

Examples

Activate the window with the `Document1` document. Make sure that the document window is maximized and then turn off the rulers. After that, turn on the vertical scrollbar, change the caption to "The Main Document", and finally display the document map so that it only takes up 10 percent of the window:

```
Windows("Document1").Activate
Application.WindowState = wdWindowStateMaximize
ActiveWindow.DisplayRulers = False
ActiveWindow.DisplayVerticalScrollBar = True
ActiveWindow.Caption = "The Main Document"
ActiveWindow.DocumentMap = True
ActiveWindow.DocumentMapPercentWidth = 10
```

Words Collection

The `Words` collection contains the list of words in a selection, range, or document. Each item in the `Words` collection is a `Range` object. There is no Word object.

Words Common Properties

The `Application`, `Creator`, and `Parent` properties are defined at the beginning of this section.

Words Properties

Name	Returns	Description
First	Range	Read Only. Returns the first word in the collection.
Last	Range	Read Only. Returns the last word in the collection.

Examples

Delete all the sentences in the active document that have "Delete" as the first word of the sentence:

```
Dim snt As Range

For Each snt In ActiveDocument.Sentences
    If snt.Words.First.Text = "Delete " Then
        snt.Delete
    End If
Next
```

WrapFormat Object

The `WrapFormat` object contains properties and methods associated with how text wraps in a shape or shape range. Possible parents of the `WrapFormat` object are the `Shape` object and the `ShapeRange` collection.

WrapFormat Common Properties

The `Application`, `Creator`, and `Parent` properties are defined at the beginning of this section.

WrapFormat Properties

Name	Returns	Description
AllowOverlap	Long	Set/Get if a shape can overlap another shape.
Distance Bottom	Single	Set/Get the distance between the bottom of the shape and the top of the text below.
DistanceLeft	Single	Set/Get the distance between the text and the left edge of the text-free area around the shape.
Distance Right	Single	Set/Get the distance between the right of the shape and the left of the text.
DistanceTop	Single	Set/Get the distance between the top of the shape and the bottom of the text above.
Side	WdWrapSide Type	Set/Get how text should wrap on the sides of the shape (e.g. left).
Type	WdWrapType	Set/Get how the text will wrap around the frame.

Examples

Change the wrapping formatting for the currently selected shapes. The text can wrap on both sides of the shapes but it should be a square wrap. The left and right sides of the shape should have 0.5 centimeters of space:

```
Selection.ShapeRange.WrapFormat.Side = wdWrapBoth
Selection.ShapeRange.WrapFormat.DistanceTop = _
        CentimetersToPoints(0)
Selection.ShapeRange.WrapFormat.DistanceBottom = _
        CentimetersToPoints(0)
Selection.ShapeRange.WrapFormat.DistanceLeft = _
        CentimetersToPoints(0.5)
Selection.ShapeRange.WrapFormat.DistanceRight = _
        CentimetersToPoints(0.5)
Selection.ShapeRange.WrapFormat.Type = wdWrapSquare
```

Zoom Object and the Zooms Collection

The Zooms collection holds the different magnification options associated with the different document views in Word such as outline, normal and page layout views. Each Zoom object represents the magnification options for a specific window or pane. Each window or pane can only have one document view at a time. The WdViewType constants can be used as the index in the Zooms collection to access all the different Zoom objects associated with a document. A possible parent of the Zooms collection is the Pane object. The Zoom object can also be accessed throughout the View object.

Zoom Common Properties

The `Application`, `Creator,` and `Parent` properties are defined at the beginning of this section.

Zoom Properties

Name	Returns	Description
PageColumns	Long	Set/Get the number of pages to see in the current window side by side.
PageFit	WdPageFit	Set/Get how the much of the page should fit in the current window.
PageRows	Long	Set/Get how many pages are viewed in the current window one above the other.
Percentage	Long	Set/Get the zoom percentage of the magnification.

Examples

Change the current documents view to print layout view and zoom to 50 percent:

```
ActiveDocument.ActiveWindow.View.Type = wdPrintView
ActiveDocument.ActiveWindow.View.Zoom.Percentage = 50
```

Quick VBA Reference

Logical, Arithmetic and Comparison Operators

The following table lists all of the different operators that can be used in VBA expressions and statements. The **Operator** column specifies the operator syntax and the **Group** column specifies the type of operator.

Operator	Group	Description
^	Arithmetic	Raises the value on the left of the symbol to the exponent on the right of the symbol.
+	Arithmetic	Adds the expressions on the left and right of the symbols.
−	Arithmetic	Subtracts the expression on the right of the symbol from the expression on the left of the symbol.
/	Arithmetic	Divides the expression on the right of the symbol into the expression on the left of the symbols.
*	Arithmetic	Multiplies the expressions on the left and right of the symbol.
\	Arithmetic	Finds the whole number result when the expression on the left of the symbol is divided by the expression on the right of the symbol.
&	Arithmetic	Used to concatenate the expression on the left and right of the symbol into a string.
=	Arithmetic	Assigns the results of the right hand side of the equals sign to the variable or property on the left hand side of the equals sign.

Table Continued on Following Page

Operator	Group	Description
Mod	Arithmetic	Finds the division remainder when the expression on the left of the symbol is divided by the expression on the right of the symbol.
=	Comparison	If the left and right of the symbol are equal then the expression evaluates to TRUE.
<>	Comparison	If the left and right of the symbol are not equal then the expression evaluates to TRUE.
>	Comparison	If the left of the symbol is greater than the right side the expression evaluates to TRUE.
<	Comparison	If the left of the symbol is less than the right side the expression evaluates to TRUE.
>=	Comparison	If the left of the symbol is greater than or equal to the right side the expression evaluates to TRUE.
<=	Comparison	If the left of the symbol is less than or equal to the right side the expression evaluates to TRUE.
Is	Comparison	If the object reference on the left side is the same as the object reference on the right side then the expression evaluates to True.
Like	Comparison	If the string on the left side matches the pattern-matching string specified on the right side then the expression evaluates to TRUE.
And	Logical	Logical addition or conjunction.
Eqv	Logical	Logical equivalence.
Imp	Logical	Logical implication.
Not	Logical	Logical negation.
Or	Logical	Logical disjunction.
Xor	Logical	Logical exclusion.

Coding Structures

The following table lists the more common structures that can be used to control how a program executes in VBA.

Structure	Description

Select Case TestExpression
 	
   Case Expression1
 	
      Statement1
 	
...
 	
   Case ExpressionN
 	
      StatementN
 	
  [Case Else
 	
      ElseStatement]
 	
End Select
	Uses the TestExpression result to match it to one of the ExpressionN values. The StatementN statements will execute for the matching ExpressionN value where N is any number of expressions. Optionally, if no ExpressionN values match the results of the TestExpression, the ElseStatement statements are executed.

If Expression Then
 	
   Statements
 	
[ElseIf ElseIfExpressionN Then
 	
   ElseIfStatementsN]
 	
[Else
 	
   ElseStatements]
 	
End If
	Executes the statements if Expression evaluates to TRUE. Optionally evaluates the ElseIfExpressionN expressions until one of the expressions evaluates to TRUE. The corresponding ElseIfStatementsN is then executed. If no expression evaluates to TRUE then the ElseStatements executes.

With Object Properties and Methods End With	Executes all of the properties and methods associated with the object without having to specify the object name for all the properties and methods. Using the With ... End With makes a run of object calls more efficient then specifying the object name before all the object calls. With ... End With statements can be nested. However, after any With statement only the object specified in the With can be specified without the leading object name.

Table Continued on Following Page

Structure	Description
While Condition 　　　Statements Wend	Executes the statements while the condition evaluates to TRUE.
For Each Element In Group 　　　Statements Next [element]	Iterates through each element in a group of elements and executes the statements. The group can be a collection or an array. The element can be a single item in the collection or a single array item. The Exit For can be used somewhere in the statements to jump out of the For loop.
For Counter = Start To End [Step Step] 　　　Statements Next [Counter]	Executes the statements a certain number of times specified by the For line. The counter starts at the start value, increments or decrements a certain value specified by Step (Default +1), and finishes at the End value. The Exit For can be used anywhere in the statements to jump out of the For loop.
Do {While I Until} Condition 　　　Statements Loop or Do 　　　Statements Loop {While I Until} Condition	When using the While construct, the statements will execute and re-execute while the condition is TRUE. When using the Until construct, the statements will execute and re-execute until the condition is TRUE. The Exit Do can be used anywhere in the statements to jump out of the Do loop. The only difference between the two looping constructs is that the Do Loop condition structure will execute the statements once.
Stop	Suspends the currently running code. The Stop statement has the same effect as setting a breakpoint. When a program is compiled into an executable, the Stop statement acts the same way as an End statement.
End	Terminates the currently running code. The End statement is considered a sloppy way to end a program because no code cleanup is performed and no termination events (such as the Terminate event or the Form_Unload event) are triggered.

Table Continued on Following Page

Structure	Description
Exit Function	The Exit Function statement causes the execution to jump out of the current function to the statement following the call to the function.
Exit Property	The Exit Property statement causes the execution to jump out of the current property procedure to the statement following the call to the property procedure.
Exit Sub	The Exit Sub statement causes the execution to jump out of the current procedure to the statement following the call to the procedure.

Conversion

The following table lists all the different built-in functions and procedures associated with manipulating one data type to another data type.

Name	Returns	Parameters	Description
CBool	Boolean	Expression	Converts the Expression to a Boolean.
CByte	Byte	Expression	Converts the Expression to a Byte value.
CCur	Currency	Expression	Converts the Expression to a Currency.
CDate	Date	Expression	Converts the Expression to a Date value.
CDbl	Double	Expression	Converts the Expression to a Double value.
CDec	Variant	Expression	Converts the Expression to a Decimal value.
CInt	Integer	Expression	Converts the Expression to an Integer value.
CLng	Long	Expression	Converts the Expression to a Long value.

Table Continued on Following Page

Name	Returns	Parameters	Description
CSng	Single	Expression	Converts the Expression to a Single value.
CStr	String	Expression	Converts the Expression to a String value.
CVar	Variant	Expression	Converts the Expression to a Variant value.
CVDate	Variant	Expression	Converts the Expression to a Variant Date.
CVErr	Variant	Expression	Converts the Expression to a Variant error number.
Error	String	[ErrorNumber]	Returns the description of the ErrorNumber.
Fix	Variant	Number	Converts the Number to an Integer. Negative values are rounded down.
Hex	String	Number	Returns the hex value of the Number as a string.
Int	Variant	Number	Converts the Number to an Integer. Negative values are rounded up.
Oct	String	Number	Returns the octal value of the Number as a String.
Str	String	Number	Converts the Number to a String.
Val	Double	String As String	Converts the first numeric part of the String to a Double.

DateTime

The following table lists all the different built-in functions and procedures associated with date and time manipulation.

Name	Returns	Parameters	Description
Calendar	VbCalendar		Set/Get the type of calendar to use.
Date	Variant		Returns the system date.
DateAdd	Variant	Interval As String, Number As Double, Date	Returns the addition of the Number value to the Interval part of the Date. E.g. DateAdd("d", 5, "1/1/1999") adds 5 days to the date 1/1/1999, returning: 1/6/1999.
DateDiff	Variant	Interval As String, Date1, Date2, [FirstDayOfWeek] As VbDayOfWeek, [FirstWeekOfYear] As VbFirstWeekOfYear	Returns the subtraction of the Interval part of Date1 from Date2.
DatePart	Variant	Interval As String, Date, [FirstDayOfWeek] As VbDayOfWeek, [FirstWeekOfYear] As VbFirstWeekOfYear	Returns the Interval part of the Date.
DateSerial	Variant	Year As Integer, Month As Integer, Day As Integer	Returns a Variant of subtype Date for the Year, Month and Day parameters.
DateValue	Variant	Date As String	Returns a Variant of subtype Date for the Date string.

Table Continued on Following Page

Name	Returns	Parameters	Description
Day	Variant	Date	Returns the day part of the Date.
Hour	Variant	Time	Returns the hour part of the Time.
Minute	Variant	Time	Returns the minute part of the Time.
Month	Variant	Date	Returns the month part of the Date.
Now	Variant		Returns the system date and Time.
Second	Variant	Time	Returns the second part of the Time.
Time	Variant		Returns the current system Time.
Timer	Single		Returns the fraction number of seconds passed since midnight.
TimeSerial	Variant	Hour As Integer, Minute As Integer, Second As Integer	Returns a Variant of subtype Date for the Hour, Minute, and Second parameters.
TimeValue	Variant	Time As String	Returns a Variant of subtype Date for the Time string.
Weekday	Variant	Date, FirstDayOfWeek As VbDayOfWeek	Returns the weekday number from the Date.
Year	Variant	Date	Returns the year part of the Date.

FileSystem

The following table lists all the different built-in functions and procedures associated with manipulating files and directory structures.

Name	Returns	Parameters	Description
ChDir	N/A	Path As String	Changes the current directory to Path.
ChDrive	N/A	Drive As String	Changes the current drive to Drive.
CurDir	String	[Drive]	Returns the current path.
Dir	String	PathName, [Attributes] As VbFileAttribute	Returns the name of the file or directory that matches the wildcard or file attributes.
EOF	Boolean	FileNumber As Integer	Returns whether the end of file has been reached for the FileNumber file.
FileAttr	Long	FileNumber As Integer, ReturnType As Integer	Returns the file mode for the FileNumber file.
FileCopy	N/A	Source As String, Destination As String	Copies the source file to the destination file.
FileDateTime	Variant	PathName As String	Returns the last modified date for the file specified in the PathName.
FileLen	Long	PathName As String	Returns the byte file length for the file specified in the PathName.
FreeFile	Integer	[RangeNumber]	Returns the next available file number.

Table Continued on Following Page

585

Name	Returns	Parameters	Description
GetAttr	VbFileAttribute	PathName As String	Returns the file attributes for the file specified in the PathName.
Kill	N/A	PathName	Deletes the file specified in the PathName.
Loc	Long	FileNumber As Integer	Returns the current read/write position for the FileNumber file.
LOF	Long	FileNumber As Integer	Returns the byte size of the FileNumber file.
MkDir	N/A	Path As String	Creates the Path directory.
Reset	N/A		Closes all files opened with the Open statement.
RmDir	N/A	Path As String	Removes the Path directory.
Seek	Long	FileNumber As Integer	Returns the current read/write position.
SetAttr	N/A	PathName As String, Attributes As VbFileAttribute	Sets attribute information for the PathName file.
Open Filename For Mode [Access Access] [Lock] [#]Filenumber [Len=Reclength]	As		Opens up the Filename in a specified Mode (Append, Binary, Input, Output or Random). If the mode is OUTPUT or APPEND, and the file does not exist, a new file gets created. The type of write actions can be specified with Access (Read, Write, or Read Write). A certain type of external Lock can also be specified (Shared, Lock Read, Lock Write, or Lock Read Write). The Filenumber integer is then used to access the file.
Close [FilenumberList]			Closes the files associated with the file numbers in the FilenumberList.

Financial

The following table lists all the different built-in functions and procedures associated with finance.

Name	Returns	Parameters	Description
DDB	Double	Cost As Double, Salvage As Double, Life As Double, Period As Double, [Factor]	Returns the depreciation using the parameter values.
FV	Double	Rate As Double, NPer As Double, Pmt As Double, [PV], [Due]	Returns the future value of an annuity based on the parameters.
IPmt	Double	Rate As Double, Per As Double, NPer As Double, PV As Double, [FV], [Due]	Returns the interest payment for a given period of an annuity based on the parameters.
IRR	Double	ValueArray As Special, [Guess]	Returns the internal rate of return for a series of periodic cash flows.
MIRR	Double	ValueArray As Special, FinanceRate As Double, ReinvestRate As Double	Returns the modified internal rate of return using the parameter values.
NPer	Double	Rate As Double, Pmt As Double, PV As Double, [FV], [Due]	Returns the number of periods for an annuity using the parameter values.
NPV	Double	Rate As Double, ValueArray As Special	Returns the net present value of an investment using the parameter values.

Table Continued on Following Page

Name	Returns	Parameters	Description
Pmt	Double	Rate As Double, NPer As Double, PV As Double, [FV], [Due]	Returns the payment for an annuity using the parameter values.
PPmt	Double	Rate As Double, Per As Double, NPer As Double, PV As Double, [FV], [Due]	Returns the principal payment for a given period using the parameters.
PV	Double	Rate As Double, NPer As Double, Pmt As Double, [FV], [Due]	Returns the present value of an annuity using the parameters.
Rate	Double	NPer As Double, Pmt As Double, PV As Double, [FV], [Due], [Guess]	Returns the interest rate per period for an annuity using the parameters.
SLN	Double	Cost As Double, Salvage As Double, Life As Double	Returns the straight-line depreciation using the parameters.
SYD	Double	Cost As Double, Salvage As Double, Life As Double, Period As Double	Returns the sum-of-years digits depreciation for an asset for a specified period.

Information

The following table lists all the different built-in functions and procedures associated with general information retrieval.

Name	Returns	Parameters	Description
IsArray	Boolean	VarName	Returns whether VarName is an array.
IsDate	Boolean	Expression	Returns whether Expression is a date.
IsEmpty	Boolean	Expression	Returns whether Expression is empty.
IsError	Boolean	Expression	Returns whether setting Expression will result in an error value.
IsMissing	Boolean	ArgName	Returns whether the ArgName argument is missing from an optional parameter. Parameter must be of variant type.
IsNull	Boolean	Expression	Returns whether Expression is Null.
IsNumeric	Boolean	Expression	Returns whether Expression is numeric.
IsObject	Boolean	Expression	Returns whether Expression is an object.
QBColor	Long	Color As Integer	Returns the RGB color code for the specified Color that can be an integer value from 0 to 15 representing Black to Bright White.
RGB	Long	Red As Integer, Green As Integer, Blue As Integer	Returns the RGB color code for the Red, Green, and Blue parts passed. Each part is an integer which can accept values from 0 to 255 which result in colors going from Black (0,0) to White (255,255,255)
TypeName	String	VarName	Returns type information from the VarName.
VarType	Special	VarName	Returns the subtype of a variant VarName.

Interaction

The following table lists all the different built-in functions and procedures describing actions or interaction methods with an end user, the file system and the registry.

Name	Returns	Parameters	Description
AppActivate	N/A	Title, [Wait]	Activates the Title application.
Beep	N/A		Causes a beep through the computer speaker.
CallByName	Variant	Object As Object, ProcName As String, CallType As VbCallType, Args() As Variant	Calls the ProcName property or method of the Object object. CallType defines the ProcName type.
Choose	Variant	Index As Single, ParamArray Choice As Variant	Returns the Index item in the variant array.
Command	String		Returns the arguments passed to the Visual Basic application. Not available in Office applications.
CreateObject	Variant	Class As String, [ServerName] As String	Creates an object of type Class.

Table Continued on Following Page

Name	Returns	Parameters	Description
DeleteSetting	N/A	AppName As String, [Section], [Key]	Deletes the settings in the AppName registry settings.
DoEvents	Integer		Lets the operating system catch up queued tasks by yielding the execution of the current thread.
Environ	String	Expression	Returns the value in the Expression operating system variable.
GetAllSettings	Variant	AppName As String, Section As String	Gets all the registry settings located in the AppName/Section.
GetObject	Variant	[PathName], [Class]	Returns a reference to a running ActiveX component or loads a component from the PathName.
GetSetting	String	AppName As String, Section As String, Key As String, [Default]	Get specific registry settings located by the parameters.
IIf	Variant	Expression, TruePart, FalsePart	Returns TruePart if Expression is True, else the FalsePart is returned. Both parts are always evaluated first.
InputBox	String	Prompt, [Title], [Default], [XPos], [YPos], [HelpFile], [Context]	Creates an InputBox with the set Prompt.

Table Continued on Following Page

Name	Returns	Parameters	Description
MsgBox	vbMessageBoxResult	Prompt, Buttons As VbMsgBoxStyle, [Title], [HelpFile], [Context]	Creates a message box with the specified prompt and buttons.
Partition	Variant	Number, Start, Stop, Interval	Returns the string range that the Number falls from the Start to Stop range. For example, if Num = 5 then the function Partition (Num, 0, 100, 10) would return "0-10". If Num was 25 then that same function would return "20-30".
SaveSetting	N/A	AppName As String, Section As String, Key As String, Setting As String	Saves the settings Setting in the AppName, Section, and Key part of the registry.
SendKeys	N/A	String As String, [Wait]	Sends the String parameter to the current window.
Shell	Double	PathName, WindowStyle As VbAppWinStyle	Runs the program specified by PathName.
Switch	Variant	ParamArray VarExpr As Variant	Returns the first associated value for the first true expression.

Math

The following table lists all the different built-in functions and procedures associated with mathematical manipulation of values.

Name	Returns	Parameters	Description
Abs	Variant	Number	Returns the absolute value of the Number.
Atn	Double	Number As Double	Returns the arctangent of the Number.
Cos	Double	Number As Double	Returns the cosine of the Number.
Exp	Double	Number As Double	Returns the base of natural logarithms (e) raised to the Number.
Log	Double	Number As Double	Returns the natural logarithm of the Number.
Randomize	N/A	[Number]	Start the random-number generator.
Rnd	Single	[Number]	Returns a random number.
Round	Variant	Number, [NumDigitsAfter Decimal] As Long	Returns the Number rounded.
Sgn	Variant	Number	Returns a numeric description of the sign.
Sin	Double	Number As Double	Returns the sine of the Number.
Sqr	Double	Number As Double	Returns the square root of the Number.
Tan	Double	Number As Double	Returns the tangent of the Number.

Strings

The following table lists all the different built-in functions and procedures associated with string manipulation.

Name	Returns	Parameters	Description
Asc	Integer	String As String	Converts the String parameter to its ASCII equivalent.
AscB	Byte	String As String	Converts the String parameter to its Byte equivalent.
AscW	Integer	String As String	Converts the String parameter to its Unicode equivalent.
Chr	String	CharCode As Long	Converts the ASCII CharCode to the equivalent string.
ChrB	String	CharCode As Byte	Converts the first byte of the CharCode to the ASCII equivalent string.
ChrW	String	CharCode As Long	Converts the Unicode Charcode to the equivalent string.
Filter	Variant	SourceArray, Match As String, [Include] As Boolean, [Compare] As VbCompareMethod	Returns a subset of the SourceArray string array that matches the Match string.
Format	String	Expression, [Format], [FirstDayOfWeek] As VbDayOfWeek, [FirstWeekOfYear] As VbFirstWeekOfYear	Formats the Expression string using the Format parameter.

Table Continued on Following Page

Name	Returns	Parameters	Description
FormatCurrency	String	Expression, [NumDigitsAfterDecimal] As VbTriState, [IncludeLeadingDigit] As VbTriState, [UseParensForNegativeNumbe rs] As VbTriState, [GroupDigits] As VbTriState	Formats the Expression as a currency value using the rest of the parameters as formatting options.
FormatDateTime	String	Expression, [NamedFormat] As VbDateTimeFormat	Formats the Expression as a date or time.
FormatNumber	String	Expression, [NumDigitsAfterDecimal] As VbTriState, [IncludeLeadingDigit] As VbTriState, [UseParensForNegativeNumbe rs] As VbTriState, [GroupDigits] As VbTriState	Formats the Expression as a number using the rest of the parameters as formatting options.
FormatPercent	String	Expression, [NumDigitsAfterDecimal] As VbTriState, [IncludeLeadingDigit] As VbTriState, [UseParensForNegativeNumbe rs] As VbTriState, [GroupDigits] As VbTriState	Formats the Expression as a percentage using the rest of the parameters as formatting options.

Table Continued on Following Page

Name	Returns	Parameters	Description
InStr	Variant	[Start], String1, String2, [Compare] As VbCompareMethod	Returns the position number of when String2 first occurs in String1. VbCompareMethod determines whether case sensitivity should be used or if it should be binary. If it is omitted, the Option Compare setting determines what comparison method should be used.
InStrB	Variant	[Start], String1, String2, [Compare] As VbCompareMethod	Returns the byte position of when String2 first occurs in String1. VbCompareMethod determines whether case sensitivity should be used or if it should be binary. If it is omitted, the Option Compare setting determines what comparison method should be used.
InStrRev	Long	StringCheck As String, StringMatch As String, [Start] As Long, [Compare] As VbCompareMethod	Returns the position number of when StringMatch first occurs in StringCheck starting at the string end. VbCompareMethod determines whether case sensitivity should be used or if it should be binary. If it is omitted, the Option Compare setting determines what comparison method should be used.
Join	String	SourceArray, [Delimiter]	Returns a single string from the SourceArray string array.
LCase	String	String As String	Returns the lowercase of the String.
Left	String	String As String, Length As Long	Returns the left Length characters of the String.

Table Continued on Following Page

Name	Returns	Parameters	Description
LeftB	String	`String As String, Length As Long`	Returns the left Length bytes of the String.
Len	Variant	`Expression`	Returns the character length of the string or the bytes needed to store the variable.
LenB	Variant	`Expression`	Returns the number of bytes needed to store the string.
LTrim	String	`String As String`	Returns the String without leading spaces.
Mid	String	`String As String, Start As Long, [Length]`	Returns the part of the String starting at Start with a specified Length.
MidB	String	`String As String, Start As Long, [Length]`	Returns the part of the String starting at Start with a specified Length.
MonthName	String	`Month As Long, [Abbreviate] As Boolean`	Returns the month name for the numeric Month.
Replace	String	`Expression As String, Find As String, Replace As String, [Start] As Long, [Count] As Long, [Compare] As VbCompareMethod`	Replaces the Find sub string in the Expression string with the Replace sub string.
Right	String	`String As String, Length As Long`	Returns the right Length characters of the String.
RightB	String	`String As String, Length As Long`	Returns the right Length bytes of the String.

Table Continued on Following Page

Name	Returns	Parameters	Description
RTrim	String	String As String	Returns the String without spaces after the string.
Space	String	Number As Long	Returns a string with Number spaces.
Split	Variant	Expression As String, [Delimiter], [Limit] As Long, [Compare] As VbCompareMethod	Splits the Expression string using the Delimiter string into a string array.
StrComp	Variant	String1, String2, [Compare] As VbCompareMethod	Compares String1 with String2 and returns the comparison between them.
StrConv	Variant	String, Conversion As VbStrConv, [LocaleID As Long]	Returns the String converted as specified by the VbStrConv enumerated types. Some of the possible conversions include uppercase, lowercase, Unicode, and Katakana.
String	String	Number As Long, Character	Returns a string consisting of Number times of the Character.
StrReverse	String	Expression As String	Returns the reverse string of Expression.
Trim	String	String As String	Returns the String without leading and ending spaces.
UCase	String	String As String	Returns the uppercase of the String.
WeekdayName	String	Weekday As VbDayOfWeek, [Abbreviate] As Boolean, [FirstDayOfWeek] As VbDayOfWeek	Returns the weekday name for the numeric Weekday.

ADO Object Summary

For a detailed explanation of ADO, you should read ADO 2.0 Reference" book by Wrox Press. It is an excellent comprehensive reference for ADO.

Connection Object

The Connection object represents the connection to a data source. The Connection object can also be used to execute SQL statements, stored procedures, or queries against the data source.

Connection Properties

Name	Returns	Description
Attributes	Long	Set/Get characteristics of the Connection object.
CommandTimeout	Long	Set/Get how many seconds to wait for a command to finish processing before generating an error message.
ConnectionString	String	Set/Get the information used to establish a connection.
ConnectionTimeout	Long	Set/Get how many seconds to wait for a connection to establish before generating an error message.
CursorLocation	CursorLocationEnum	Set/Get where the cursor engine is located (e.g. client side).
DefaultDatabase	String	Set/Get the default database for the connection.

Table Continued on Following Page

Name	Returns	Description
Errors	Errors	Read Only. The collection of all the errors associated with a failure by the data source.
IsolationLevel	IsolationLevelEnum	Write Only. Set the transaction isolation level for the connection.
Mode	ConnectModeEnum	Set/Get the data modification permissions of the connection.
Properties	Properties	Read Only. Returns the collection of properties associated with the connection.
Provider	String	Set/Get the provider name of the connection.
State	Long	Read Only. Returns whether the connection is open or closed.
Version	String	Read Only. Returns the ADO version number.

Connection Methods

Name	Returns	Parameters	Description
BeginTrans	Long		Begins a new transaction.
Cancel	N/A		Cancels execution of any asynchronously running Execute or Open method that was invoked by a Connection object. Each Connection object can only cancel their own executions.
Close	N/A		Closes the connection and any dependent objects.
CommitTrans	N/A		Commits all the changes made since the BeginTrans.
Execute	Recordset	CommandText As String, [RecordsAffected], [Options] As Long	Executes the query, SQL statement, stored procedure or special provider text specified by the CommandText. Specifying a variable for can return the number of records affected.
Open	N/A	[ConnectionString] As String, [UserID] As String, [Password] As String, [Options] As Long	Opens a connection to a data provider. All the necessary information to connect can be set with the parameters or through the corresponding connection properties.
OpenSchema	Recordset	Schema As SchemaEnum, [Restrictions], [SchemaID]	Returns a recordset containing database schema associated with the connection's data source.
RollbackTrans	N/A		Cancels all the changes made since the BeginTrans.

Connection Events

Name	Parameters	Description
BeginTransComplete	TransactionLevel As Long, pError As Error, adStatus As EventStatusEnum, pConnection As Connection	Triggered after a BeginTrans operation finishes executing.
CommitTransComplete	pError As Error, adStatus As EventStatusEnum, pConnection As Connection	Triggered after a CommitTrans operation finishes executing.
ConnectComplete	pError As Error, adStatus As EventStatusEnum, pConnection As Connection	Triggered after a connection has begun (Open method).
Disconnect	adStatus As EventStatusEnum, pConnection As Connection	Triggered after a connection has ended (Close method).
ExecuteComplete	RecordsAffected As Long, pError As Error, adStatus As EventStatusEnum, pCommand As Command, pRecordset As Recordset, pConnection As Connection	Triggered after a command has finished executing (Execute method).
InfoMessage	pError As Error, adStatus As EventStatusEnum, pConnection As Connection	Triggered whenever a connection event completes successfully or unsuccessfully. The information comes from the data source.
RollbackTransComplete	pError As Error, adStatus As EventStatusEnum, pConnection As Connection	Triggered after a RollbackTrans operation finishes executing.

Table Continued on Following Page

Name	Parameters	Description
WillConnect	ConnectionString As String, UserID As String, Password As String, Options As Long, adStatus As EventStatusEnum, pConnection As Connection	Triggered just before a connection opens. (Open method).
WillExecute	Source As String, CursorType As CursorTypeEnum, LockType As LockTypeEnum, Options As Long, adStatus As EventStatusEnum, pCommand As Command, pRecordset As Recordset, pConnection As Connection	Triggered just before a command is executed (Execute method).

Command Object

The Command object represents a specific query, SQL statement, or stored procedure you intend to execute against a data source.

Command Properties

Name	Returns	Description
ActiveConnection	Variant	Set/Get the Connection associated with the command.
CommandText	String	Set/Get the query, SQL statement, or stored procedure to be issued against the data provider.
CommandTimeout	Long	Set/Get how many seconds to wait for a command to finish processing before generating an error message.
CommandType	CommandTypeEnum	Set/Get the type of Command object.

Table Continued on Following Page

Name	Returns	Description
Name	String	Set/Get the name of the Command object.
Parameters	Parameters	Read Only. Returns the list of parameters associated with the Command object.
Prepared	Boolean	Set/Get whether a compiled version of the Command is saved before execution. This can be useful if you are going to reuse a Command.
Properties	Properties	Read Only. Returns the collection of properties associated with the command.
State	Long	Read Only. Returns if the Command is open (AdStateOpen) or closed (AdStateClosed).

Command Methods

Name	Returns	Parameters	Description
Cancel	N/A		Cancels the execution of a pending Execute call for the same Command object.
CreateParameter	Parameter	[Name] As String, [Type] As DataTypeEnum, [Direction] As ParameterDirectionEnum, [Size] As Long, [Value]	Creates a new parameter to be associated with the Command object.
Execute	Recordset	RecordsAffected, Parameters, Options As Long	Executes the query, SQL statement, or stored procedure set in the CommandText property.

Recordset Object

The Recordset object represents all the records associated with a table or SQL query as specified by the Source property. As well the Recordset object can be the results of an executed command. The Recordset object can be used to add, edit, and delete recordset associated with an underlying data source.

Recordset Properties

Name	Returns	Description
AbsolutePage	PositionEnum	Set/Get the page that the current record resides in.
AbsolutePosition	PositionEnum	Set/Get the ordinal position of the current record in the recordset.
ActiveCommand	Object	Read Only. Returns the Command object that is associated with the recordset.
ActiveConnection	Variant	Set/Get the Connection object or the connection string associated with the recordset.
BOF	Boolean	Read Only. Returns whether the recordset pointer is before the first record of the recordset.
Bookmark	Variant	Set/Get a bookmark uniquely identifying a record in the recordset.
CacheSize	Long	Set/Get the number of records that are cached in local memory for the recordset.
CursorLocation	CursorLocationEnum	Set/Get the location of the cursor engine.
CursorType	CursorTypeEnum	Set/Get the type of cursor that is used in the cursor engine.
DataMember	String	Sets the data member name used to retrieve data from the data source.

Table Continued on Following Page

Name	Returns	Description
DataSource	Variant	Sets the data source used by the recordset.
EditMode	EditModeEnum	Read Only. Returns the editing status of the current record.
EOF	Boolean	Read Only. Returns whether the recordset pointer is after the end of the recordset.
Fields	Fields	Read Only. Returns the collection of fields in the recordset.
Filter	Variant	Set/Get the criteria to filter out of the recordset.
Index	String	Set/Get the index of the current recordset, if supported.
LockType	LockTypeEnum	Set/Get the types of record locking used for the recordset.
MarshalOptions	MarshalOptionsEnum	Set/Get which records are to be marshaled back to the server (i.e. All records or only modified records).
MaxRecords	Long	Set/Get the maximum number of records returned in a recordset.
PageCount	Long	Read Only. Returns the number of pages of data a recordset contains.
PageSize	Long	Set/Get how many records are placed in a page.
Properties	Properties	Read Only. Returns an object that can manipulate properties of the recordset.
RecordCount	Long	Read Only. Returns the number of records in a recordset. Note that the value may not always be correct depending on property settings.
Sort	String	Set/Get which fields to sort by.
Source	Variant	Set/Get the source of the recordset data.

Table Continued on Following Page

Name	Returns	Description
State	Long	Read Only. Returns whether the recordset is open, closed, or executing something asynchronously.
Status	Long	Read Only. Returns the status of the current record in regards to updates and bulk operations.
StayInSync	Boolean	Read Only. Returns whether the parent row of a hierarchical recordset changes when the child recordset changes.

Recordset Methods

Name	Returns	Parameters	Description
AddNew	N/A	[FieldList], [Values]	Adds a new record to the currently updateable recordset.
Cancel	N/A		Cancels the execution of a pending asynchronous Open call.
CancelBatch	N/A	[AffectRecords] As AffectEnum	Cancels the pending batch update.
CancelUpdate	N/A		Cancels the changes or additions pending to a recordset.
Clone	Recordset	[LockType] As LockTypeEnum	Returns a duplicate recordset of the current recordset.
Close	N/A		Closes the recordset and any dependent objects
CompareBookmarks	CompareEnum	Bookmark1, Bookmark2	Compares Bookmark1 with Bookmark2 and returns the relative position comparisons.

Table Continued on Following Page

Name	Returns	Parameters	Description
Delete	N/A	[AffectRecords] As AffectEnum	Deletes the current record in the recordset.
Find	N/A	Criteria As String, [SkipRecords] As Long, [SearchDirection] As SearchDirectionEnum, [Start]	Moves to the first or last record (depending on SearchDirection) that matches the Criteria parameter in the recordset.
GetRows	Variant	[Rows] As Long, [Start], [Fields]	Returns a multidimensional array holding a certain number of records in the recordset.
GetString	String	[StringFormat] As StringFormatEnum, [NumRows] As Long, [ColumnDelimeter] As String, [RowDelimeter] As String, [NullExpr] As String	Returns the recordset or certain rows in the recordset as a delimited string.
Move	N/A	[NumRecords] As Long, [Start]	Moves the position of the current record by the NumRecords number of records.

Table Continued on Following Page

Name	Returns	Parameters	Description
MoveFirst	N/A		Moves the position of the current record to the first record in the recordset.
MoveLast	N/A		Moves the position of the current record to the last record in the recordset.
MoveNext	N/A		Moves the position of the current record to the next record in the recordset.
MovePrevious	N/A		Moves the position of the current record to the previous record in the recordset.
NextRecordset	Recordset	[RecordsAffected]	Returns the next Recordset where more than one recordsets have been specified by a command or through the Recordset's Open method.
Open	N/A	[Source], [ActiveConnection], [CursorType] As CursorTypeEnum, [LockType] As LockTypeEnum, [Options] As Long	Opens a recordset and optionally specifies the required parameters.
Requery	N/A	[Options] As Long	Re-executes the recordset query against the underlying data and updates the recordset.

Table Continued on Following Page

Name	Returns	Parameters	Description
Resync	N/A	[AffectRecords] As AffectEnum, [ResyncValues] As ResyncEnum	Refreshes the recordset data with the data from the underlying data.
Save	N/A	[FileName] As String, [PersistFormat] As PersistFormatEnum	Saves the recordset to a flat file.
Seek	N/A	KeyValues, [SeekOption] As SeekEnum	Seeks through the recordset using the KeyValues parameter to find specific records. The Index property must be set first.
Supports	Boolean	CursorOptions As CursorOptionEnum	Returns whether the recordset supports one of the CursorOptions parameter.
Update	N/A	[Fields], [Values]	Saves any changes made to the current record in a recordset.
UpdateBatch	N/A	AffectRecords As AffectEnum	Writes all the pending changes to the underlying data source.

Recordset Events

Name	Parameters	Description
EndOfRecordset	fMoreData As Boolean, adStatus As EventStatusEnum, pRecordset As Recordset	Triggered when trying to move past the last record of the recordset.
FetchComplete	pError As Error, adStatus As EventStatusEnum, pRecordset As Recordset	Triggered when all the records have been retrieved in asynchronous recordset retrieval.
FetchProgress	Progress As Long, MaxProgress As Long, adStatus As EventStatusEnum, pRecordset As Recordset	Triggered periodically while records are retrieved asynchronously from a recordset.
FieldChangeComplete	cFields As Long, Fields, pError As Error, adStatus As EventStatusEnum, pRecordset As Recordset	Triggered when a field value in a recordset has been changed.
MoveComplete	adReason As EventReasonEnum, pError As Error, adStatus As EventStatusEnum, pRecordset As Recordset	Triggered when the current record in the recordset changes.
RecordChangeComplete	adReason As EventReasonEnum, cRecords As Long, pError As Error, adStatus As EventStatusEnum, pRecordset As Recordset	Triggered when one or more records change in the recordset.

Table Continued on Following Page

Name	Parameters	Description
RecordsetChangeComplete	adReason As EventReasonEnum, pError As Error, adStatus As EventStatusEnum, pRecordset As Recordset	Triggered when the Recordset changes.
WillChangeField	cFields As Long, Fields, adStatus As EventStatusEnum, pRecordset As Recordset	Triggered before a field's value is about to be changed.
WillChangeRecord	adReason As EventReasonEnum, cRecords As Long, adStatus As EventStatusEnum, pRecordset As Recordset	Triggered before one or more records is about to change in the recordset.
WillChangeRecordset	adReason As EventReasonEnum, adStatus As EventStatusEnum, pRecordset As Recordset	Triggered before a recordset is about to change.
WillMove	adReason As EventReasonEnum, adStatus As EventStatusEnum, pRecordset As Recordset	Triggered before the current record position changes in the recordset.

Error Object and the Errors Collection

The Errors collection contains the list of errors associated with a single failure in a data provider. Each Error object contains the details of a specific error associated with a single failure in a data provider.

Properties and Methods of the Errors Collection

Name	Returns	Description
Count	Long	Read-Only. Returns the number of Error objects in the collection.
Item	Error	Index parameter. Returns the Error object from the spot in the collection specified by the Index parameter.
Clear		Method. Removes all the Error objects from the Errors collection.
Refresh		Method. Updates the Error objects with the error information from the data provider.

Error Properties

Name	Returns	Description
Description	String	Read Only. Returns the description of the error associated with the error number
HelpContext	Integer	Read Only. Returns the ContextID in the help file associated with the error.
HelpFile	String	Read Only. Returns the name of the help file.
NativeError	Long	Read Only. Returns the provider-specific error code associated with the error.
Number	Long	Read Only. Returns the error number representing the unique error that occurred from the source.
Source	String	Read Only. Returns the object or application name that created the Error.
SQLState	String	Read Only. Returns the ANSI SQL standard SQL state for the Error object. This is a 6-character string value.

615

Field Object and the Fields Collection

The Fields collection holds the list of fields associated with a specific recordset. Each Field object represents a single column or field associated with a recordset.

Properties and Methods of the Fields Collection

Name	Returns	Description
Count	Long	Read-Only. Returns the number of Field objects in the collection.
Item	Field	Index parameter. Returns the Field object from the spot in the collection specified by the Index parameter.
Append		Name As String, Type As DataTypeEnum, [DefinedSize As Long], [Attrib As FieldAttributeEnum = adFldDefault] parameters. Adds a field to the collection with the specified Name and data type.
Delete		Method. Index parameter. Deletes the Field object from the Fields collection specified by the Index parameter.
Refresh		Method. Updates the Fields collection with the field information from the field.

Field Properties

Name	Returns	Description
ActualSize	Long	Read Only. Returns the actual length of the field value.
Attributes	Long	Set/Get different characteristics associated with the field such as whether the field is updateable.
DataFormat	Variant	Set/Get the formatting characteristics associated with the field (from the DataFormat object).
DefinedSize	Long	Set/Get the size defined by the field definition.
Name	String	Read Only. Returns the name of the field.
NumericScale	Byte	Set/Get the number of decimal places used for the field.
OriginalValue	Variant	Read Only. Returns the value of the field before any changes have been.
Precision	Byte	Set/Get the numeric precision of the field.
Properties	Properties	Read Only. Returns an object allowing manipulation of all the properties associated with the field.
Type	DataTypeEnum	Set/Get the data type associated with the field (e.g. adBoolean).
UnderlyingValue	Variant	Read Only. Returns the database value associated with the field.
Value	Variant	Set/Get the current value of the field.

Methods

Name	Returns	Parameters	Description
AppendChunk		Data	Appends the Data parameter to a binary or large character data field.
GetChunk	Variant	Length As Long	Returns the contents of a binary or large character data field. The amount returned is specified by the Length parameter.

Parameter Object and the Parameters Collection

The Parameters collection contains the list of parameters associated with a particular Command object. Each Parameter object represents a parameter or argument associated with a Command object based on a parameterized query or stored procedure.

Properties and Methods of the Parameters Collection

Name	Returns	Description
Count	Long	Read-Only. Returns the number of Parameter objects in the collection.
Item	Parameter	Index parameter. Returns the Parameter object from the spot in the collection specified by the Index parameter.
Append		Object As Object parameter. Adds the Object parameter to the collection.
Delete		Method. Index parameter. Deletes the Parameter object from the Parameters collection specified by the Index parameter.
Refresh		Method. Updates the Parameter objects with the parameter information from the provider.

Parameter Properties

Name	Returns	Description
Attributes	Long	Set/Get different characteristics associated with the parameter such as whether the parameter accepts nulls.
Direction	ParameterDirectionEnum	Set/Get whether the parameter is an input, output, or two-way parameter.
Name	String	Set/Get the name of the parameter.
NumericScale	Byte	Set/Get the number of decimal places used for the parameter.
Precision	Byte	Set/Get the numeric precision of the parameter.
Properties	Properties	Read Only. Returns an object allowing manipulation of all the properties associated with the parameter.
Size	Long	Set/Get the maximum size (bytes or characters) of the parameter.
Type	DataTypeEnum	Set/Get the data type of the parameter.
Value	Variant	Set/Get the value of the parameter.

Methods

Name	Returns	Parameters	Description
AppendChunk		Val	Appends the Val parameter to a binary or character data parameter.

Property Object and the Properties Collection

The Properties collection holds the list of properties associated with the parent object. All the other objects in this section are possible parent objects of the Properties collection. The Property object represents a dynamic characteristic of a specific ADO object. The Properties collection includes both built-in properties and dynamic properties that are specific to a particular provider

Properties and Methods of the Properties Collection

Name	Returns	Description
Count	Long	Read-Only. Returns the number of Property objects in the collection.
Item	Property	Index parameter. Returns the Property object from the spot in the collection specified by the Index parameter.
Refresh		Method. Updates the Property objects with the parent property information.

Property Object Properties

Name	Returns	Description
Attributes	Long	Set/Get different characteristics associated with the Property object such as whether the property is required.
Name	String	Read Only. Returns the name of the property.
Type	DataTypeEnum	Read Only. Returns the data type of the property.
Value	Variant	Set/Get the value of the property.

Programming with the Office Assistant

Introduction

Office 97 introduced the Office Assistant, which by default was Clippit, an animated paperclip that generally annoyed and bothered most users while pretending to be helpful:

Office 2000 has evolved this concept into a new family of assistants that are more graphically appealing and useful. The latest version of Office Assistant appears to be based on the Microsoft Agent technology, as it is no longer contained within a small tool window, making it appear less intrusive:

Whether you like them or hate them, these assistants are available and can be used in your own development. This appendix will take you through the programming interface of the assistants and demonstrate how you can use them in your own programs. The specific topics that will be covered are:

- ❑ Determining if the assistant is available, and which assistant is currently in use

- ❑ Making the assistant animate and move on the screen

- ❑ Creating and displaying custom "balloons" as an alternative to dialogs

Determining the Assistant's Status

Before using the Office Assistant in your programs it is important to determine if the assistant is currently visible. This can easily be accomplished through the properties of the `Assistant` object. The `Assistant` object is available as a property of the `Application` object, and can be retrieved with the following code:

```
Dim objAssistant As Office.Assistant

Set objAssistant = Application.Assistant
```

Once you have the `Assistant` you can use the following properties related to determine (and set) its options and status.

Property	Description
On	This property allows you to get or set the current state of the `Assistant`. `True` if the `Assistant` is available, `False` if it is not.
Visible	Used to control whether or not the `Assistant` is `Visible`. Not the same as `On`, the `Assistant` can be `On` and not `Visible`.
Top, Left	Sets or returns the current vertical and horizontal position of the `Assistant`. Can be used to move the `Assistant` to a new location. With objAssistant .Top = 100 .Left = 100 End With
Name	Returns which character is in use. Read Only.

AssistWithAlerts, AssistWithHelp, AssistWithWizards, FeatureTips, GuessHelp, HighPriorityTips, KeyboardShortcutTips, MouseTips, MoveWhenInTheWay, SearchWhen Programming, Sounds, TipOfDay	Represents all the settings from the Office Assistant dialog box, shown below this table Although these values are not Read Only, they should be treated as such (in most cases). It isn't good programming practice to change application settings from the values chosen by the user. If you use these properties at all it should be to determine the actions of your own program:
	
	 If objAssistant.AssistWithAlerts Then
	
	 UseAssistant = True
	
	 Else
	
	 UseAssistant = False
	
	 End If

Property	Description
FileName	Can be used to set the current Assistant character. Covered in detail below, under "Selecting the Office Assistant".

Many of the properties listed above correspond to settings from the Office Assistant dialog box:

Resetting the user's tips can be done with the ResetTips method of the Assistant object.

Selecting the Office Assistant

There is more than one Office Assistant available (9 assistants are shipped with Office 2000), and it is possible to use code to find out which assistant is currently selected through the Assistant object's Name property. This property will return the "friendly name" of the current Office Assistant, such as Rocky, or Links. The Name property is Read-Only though, and cannot be used to specify which assistant is selected, that has to be done through the FileName property.

All the graphics and sounds that define an Office Assistant are stored into .acs files, which are installed onto your computer. The FileName property returns the current .acs file that is in use, and can be set to point to different .acs file to change to a different assistant. You have to specify the correct path along with the name of the .acs file, which is usually the same path as the WinWord.exe file (the actual program file for Microsoft Word) and is available through the DefaultFilePath collection of the Application.Options object. The code below demonstrates selecting "Rocky" as the assistant:

```
Dim objAssistant As Office.Assistant

Set objAssistant = Application.Assistant

objAssistant.FileName = Application.Options.DefaultFilePath _
    (wdProgramPath) & "\rocky.acs"
```

If you attempt to set `FileName` to an assistant that is available but not installed, you will receive an alert asking if you wish to install it, selecting <u>No</u> will cause an error. Setting it to a filename that is not present or available through the Office installation will cause an error:

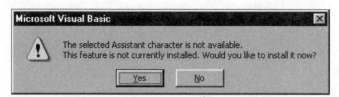

The assistants available with the shipping version of Office include the following:

Friendly Name	Filename	Appearance
Clippit	`Clippit.acs`	
Dot	`Dot.acs`	
F1	`F1.acs`	
Genius	`Genius.acs`	
Links	`Offcat.acs`	
Mother Nature	`Mnature.acs`	
Office Logo (Animated)	`Logo.acs`	
Office Logo (No Animation)	`Stillogo.acs`	
Rocky	`Rocky.acs`	

For each assistant, their name and associated filename is shown, you will need the filename if you want to programmatically determine which assistant is used. More assistants may be available from the Office web site, through other Office software, or from third parties, but the assistants shown above should be available without any additional software.

> As with the Assistant Options, it would not be good programming practice to change a user's Office Assistant. All of the assistants are capable of the same basic functionality and if the user has chosen one, that choice should be respected. If the user has chosen the Office logo that does not animate, for instance, and you want to change it so that the user sees the animations you are performing, you are overriding that user's decision to turn off a feature that they do not like. If you must change the Assistant, always change it back to exactly what it was before.

Moving and Animating the Office Assistant

The `Assistant` object has the ability to be moved through two different means: the `Move` method which moves the `Assistant` to the x, y co-ordinates passed to the method, or through the manipulation of the `Top` and `Left` property values:

```
objAssistant.Move 350, 200

objAssistant.Top = 200
objAssistant.Left = 350
```

Animation is a little bit more complicated, but is completely controlled through a single location, the `Assistant's Animation` property. The Office Assistant is capable of the following animation states, although a single animation may be used for more than one state:

State	Description of Usage/Appearance
`msoAnimationAppear`	The arrival of the character, usually coming through a door or other opening.
`msoAnimationBeginSpeaking`	Varies widely between characters, but used to signify that the character is not idle.
`msoAnimationCharacterSuccess_Major`	The character has done something good, and is being rewarded.
`msoAnimationCheckingSomething`	Looking up a value or performing calculations.
`msoAnimationDisappear`	Character going away.
`msoAnimationEmptyTrash`	Used to signify the deletion or destruction of a document or value.

Table Continued on Following Page

State	Description of Usage/Appearance
msoAnimationGestureDown msoAnimationGestureLeft msoAnimationGestureRight msoAnimationGestureUp	The Gesture animations are used to draw attention to a particular item or area of the page, and all involve the character pointing, looking or otherwise indicating a particular direction. Note that this is not the most precise method of indicating an item on the page.
msoAnimationGetArtsy	Used to indicate a graphical/image related operation, the character paints, or otherwise indicates an artistic theme.
msoAnimationGetAttention_ Major msoAnimationGetAttention_ Minor	Used to get the user's attention focused on the assistant, the Major version of the animation is more visible than the Minor one, and usually involves sound.
msoAnimationGetTechy	Indicates a technical operation is in progress. Some of the characters have more related animations for this state than others. For instance, Rocky lies down for this state, while Links turns into an image full of binary data.
msoAnimationGetWizardy	Indicates that a wizard or other helpful utility is being invoked.
msoAnimationGoodbye	The assistant is leaving.
msoAnimationGreeting	The character makes itself known, often involves sound.
msoAnimationIdle	The most common animation state, used to indicate that nothing is happening.
msoAnimationListensToComputer	Used to signify that the assistant is waiting for something.
msoAnimationLookDown msoAnimationLookDownLeft msoAnimationLookDownRight msoAnimationLookLeft msoAnimationLookRight msoAnimationLookUp msoAnimationLookUpLeft msoAnimationLookUpRight	The Look animations are similar to the Gesture animations, except that the character will only look in a specific direction, no pointing is done.

State	Description of Usage/Appearance
msoAnimationPrinting	Indicates a print operation is in progress, could also be used for a Fax or any other operation that produces paper documents.
msoAnimationRestPose	The default animation used as an intermediate state between other animations.
msoAnimationSaving	Indicates the saving of information to disk.
msoAnimationSearching	Indicates looking or searching for information.
msoAnimationSendingMail	Indicates the creation and sending of e-mail.
msoAnimationThinking	Indicates calculations are in progress.
msoAnimationWorkingAt Something	Indicates an operation (of some type) is in progress.
msoAnimationWritingNoting Something	Generally indicates an operation, but more specifically indicates that information is being recorded.

To make the Office Assistant perform any particular animation, you set the Animation property to one of the values listed above. The code below will make the current assistant perform the "Working At Something" animation, if it is currently active and visible:

```
Application.Assistant.Animation = msoAnimationWorkingAtSomething
```

Most animations run for a short period of time and then return the assistant to the idle state, but some are looping animations and will run until another animation is requested. If you need to ensure that an animation you start is ended by a certain time, you need to check the value of the Animation property and set it back to the Idle state if required. An example of this is shown below:

```
With Application.Assistant

    .Animation = msoAnimationSearching

    'Perform Long Operation
    '...

    If .Animation = msoAnimationSearching Then

        .Animation = msoAnimationIdle

    End If

End With
```

Which animations are continuous is different for each character, so it is important that you use code like that shown above to ensure that your animation is stopped when you have completed your operation.

Creating and Displaying Balloons

The Office Assistant has the ability to display alerts that provide the user with information, allow the user to make choices or change settings. These alerts are displayed as cartoon-style balloons and are a good alternative to the standard MsgBox function.

Balloon Features

These "balloons" can display lists of bullets, buttons, and even numbered items (as shown above), in addition to the usual selection of buttons along the bottom of the dialog. All of these options make these dialogs more flexible than the standard MsgBox function, and able to replace that function when available. Each balloon is capable of displaying the following elements:

- ❑ A heading (Newsgroups in the pictures above)

- ❑ Balloon text (There are three levels available: above)

- ❑ Any number of labels (Local, Regional, and Global above), which can be shown as a numbered list, a bullet list, or a list of buttons

- ❑ A variety of button types (an OK button, a set of Abort, Retry, and Ignore buttons, and the no buttons setting are all shown above)

- ❑ A variety of different icons, one of which (the question mark icon) is shown on the third dialog above

- ❑ Any number of checkboxes (as in the third dialog), each of which can be selectively checked or unchecked and display their own text label

Creating the Balloon

All of these various options are set through the Balloon object, which is obtained through the Assistant's NewBalloon function. The code below shows how to obtain a new, empty balloon object that you can then prepare and display:

```
Dim objBalloon As Balloon
Set objBalloon = Assistant.NewBalloon
```

Once this code has executed, you can work with the properties of the balloon object (objBalloon), to control its appearance and behavior.

Setting the Balloon Type

The balloon object's type is determined by its BalloonType property, which can be set to one of three values:

- ❑ Bullets (msoBalloonTypeBullets), which creates a balloon where the label items are a bulleted list

- ❑ Buttons (msoBalloonTypeButtons), which creates label items that are buttons and can be clicked on to close the balloon

- ❑ Numbers (msoBalloonTypeNumbers), which creates a numbered list representation of the label items

This property will control the appearance of the labels you place onto the balloon.

Adding Labels to the Balloon

Labels are the text items that appear as a numbered list, a bulleted list, or as buttons on the balloon, depending on the setting of the `BalloonType` property. The number of labels displayed on the balloon is controlled through the `Count` property of the balloon's `Labels` collection. The code below specifies that the balloon will have 4 labels:

```
Dim objBalloon As Balloon
Dim objLabels As BalloonLabels

Set objBalloon = Assistant.NewBalloon

    objBalloon.BalloonType = msoBalloonTypeNumbers

    Set objLabels = objBalloon.Labels

    objLabels.Count = 4
```

The text on each label is specified through the `Text` property of each individual label object. These objects, and their properties, can be accessed through the collection. An example of this, setting each label's text, is shown below:

```
Set objLabels = objBalloon.Labels
objLabels.Count = 4

objLabels(1).Text = "Accounting"
objLabels(2).Text = "Human Resources"
objLabels(3).Text = "Sales"
objLabels(4).Text = "Manufacturing"
```

Adding Checkboxes to the Balloon

Checkboxes are added in almost identical manner as labels - setting the `Count` property of the `Checkboxes` collection, then manipulating the individual checkboxes through that collection. The only difference is that the individual checkboxes have a property that labels do not have, a `Checked` property, which determines the state of the checkbox. The sample code below adds two checkboxes, sets their text values, and marks the first one as checked:

```
Set objBalloon = Assistant.NewBalloon

    objBalloon.Checkboxes.Count = 2

    objBalloon.Checkboxes(1).Text = "Set this department to be " & _
                                    "the default"
    objBalloon.Checkboxes(2).Text = "Do not ask for a department"

    objBalloon.Checkboxes(1).Checked = True
    objBalloon.Checkboxes(2).Checked = False
```

Setting the Balloon's Heading and Text

The two text strings displayed at the top of the balloon are controlled through the `Text` and `Heading` properties. These are regular string properties that can be set through code like the example below:

```
Set objBalloon = Assistant.NewBalloon

    objBalloon.Text = "Which one do you belong to?"
    objBalloon.Heading = "Choose Department"
```

Setting the Balloon's Icon

A balloon can have one of several icon settings, each of which is listed below with an image of the corresponding icon:

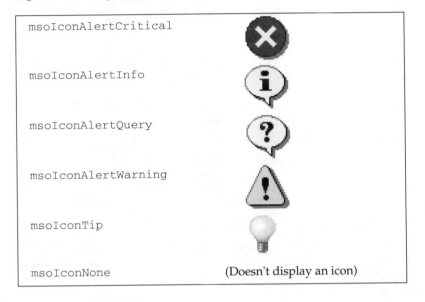

`msoIconAlertCritical`	
`msoIconAlertInfo`	
`msoIconAlertQuery`	
`msoIconAlertWarning`	
`msoIconTip`	
`msoIconNone`	(Doesn't display an icon)

Setting the Buttons

The balloon can have any one of several sets of buttons displayed, depending on the setting of its `Button` property. Each of the possible settings is listed below along with a description of the buttons it displays.

State	Description of Buttons Shown
`msoButtonSetAbortRetryIgnore`	Three buttons: Abort, Retry, and Ignore
`msoButtonSetBackClose`	Two buttons: Back and Close
`msoButtonSetBackNextClose`	Three buttons: Back, Next, and Close
`msoButtonSetBackNextSnooze`	Three buttons: Back, Next, and Snooze
`msoButtonSetCancel`	One button: Cancel
`msoButtonSetNextClose`	Two buttons: Next and Close
`msoButtonSetOK`	One button: OK
`msoButtonSetOkCancel`	Two buttons: OK and Cancel
`msoButtonSetRetryCancel`	Two buttons: Retry and Cancel

Table Continued on Following Page

State	Description of Buttons Shown
msoButtonSetYesAllNoCancel	Four buttons: Yes, Yes To All, No, and Cancel
msoButtonSetYesNo	Two buttons: Yes and No
msoButtonSetYesNoCancel	Three buttons: Yes, No, and Cancel
msoButtonSetSearchClose	Two buttons: Search and Close
msoButtonSetTipsOptionsClose	Three buttons: Tips, Options, and Close
msoButtonSetNone	No buttons are displayed, only valid if the BalloonType is msoBalloonTypeButtons (making the list items buttons).

Setting the Balloon's Animation

The Balloon object has an Animation property that can be set to any one of the Assistant's Animation values (described in the section above, "Moving and Animating the Office Assistant"). This controls which animation the assistant will perform when this balloon is visible.

Setting the Balloon's Mode

The Mode property of the balloon determines whether the balloon will be displayed as a modal or modeless dialog. A **modal** balloon will prevent the interaction with Word and the execution of the rest of your code until the user makes a choice of which button to click, and closes the balloon. **Modeless** balloons behave in the opposite manner, allowing the user to continue to interact with Word as desired, and the code that follows displaying the balloon will continue executing. More details will be given in the next section about the balloon's mode and the effect it has on your code.

Displaying the Balloon

The balloon object that you have created and prepared, as described in the sections above, has to be displayed before the user can interact with it. To display it, you use the balloon's Show method, which will cause it to become visible:

```
objBalloon.Show
```

Determining Which Button Was Pressed

The Show method returns a numeric value (for modal windows) to indicate which button was clicked. For the labels, the number returned is the label's index, and there are special values to indicate when a non-label button was pressed. Modeless balloons behave very differently and are covered separately below:

```
Public Function WhichDepartment() As String

Dim objBalloon As Balloon
Dim objLabels As BalloonLabels

    Assistant.On = True
    Assistant.Visible = True

    Set objBalloon = Assistant.NewBalloon

    objBalloon.Text = "Which one do you belong to?"
    objBalloon.Heading = "Choose Department"
    objBalloon.BalloonType = msoBalloonTypeButtons
    objBalloon.Mode = msoModeModal
    objBalloon.Button = msoButtonSetNone
    objBalloon.Animation = msoAnimationGetAttentionMajor
    objBalloon.Icon = msoIconAlertQuery

    Set objLabels = objBalloon.Labels

    objLabels.Count = 4

    objLabels(1).Text = "Accounting"
    objLabels(2).Text = "Human Resources"
    objLabels(3).Text = "Sales"
    objLabels(4).Text = "Manufacturing"

    Dim Result

    Result = objBalloon.Show

    Select Case Result

        Case 1 'Accounting

            WhichDepartment = "Accounting"

        Case 2 'HR

            WhichDepartment = "Human Resources"

        Case 3 'Sales

            WhichDepartment = "Sales"

        Case 4 'Manufacturing

            WhichDepartment = "Manufacturing"

    End Select

End Function
```

When the Button property of the balloon is set to anything other than
msoButtonSetNone (show no buttons), then the user may click any of those
displayed buttons in addition to one of the label buttons (if the BalloonType
property is set to msoBalloonTypeButtons). If one of the non-label buttons is
clicked, then a negative value is returned from the Show method, and that value
corresponds to one of the special constants used to identify which button it was:
msoBalloonButtonAbort, msoBalloonButtonYes, msoBalloonButtonOK,
msoBalloonButtonCancel, etc. These additional values can be checked for in the
same manner as the label buttons (using the Select Case statement, as shown
above) or inline like you would with the MsgBox statement:

```
If objBalloon.Show = msoBalloonButtonYes Then

    'Do it

End If
```

Checkbox Values

After a balloon has been closed, you will often want to know which checkboxes are checked and which are not. This can be accomplished in the same manner as their values were set, through the Checked property which is accessible through the Checkboxes collection. The code below demonstrates setting the value of two checkboxes, displaying the balloon, and then retrieving the value of the two boxes:

```
Public Sub WhichDepartments()

Dim objBalloon As Balloon
Dim objLabels As BalloonLabels

    Assistant.On = True
    Assistant.Visible = True

    Set objBalloon = Assistant.NewBalloon

    objBalloon.Text = "Which one(s) do you belong to?"
    objBalloon.Heading = "Choose Departments"
    objBalloon.BalloonType = msoBalloonTypeBullets
    objBalloon.Mode = msoModeModal
    objBalloon.Button = msoButtonSetOK
    objBalloon.Animation = msoAnimationGetAttentionMajor
    objBalloon.Icon = msoIconAlertQuery

    objBalloon.Checkboxes.Count = 2
    objBalloon.Checkboxes(1).Text = "Accounting"
    objBalloon.Checkboxes(2).Text = "Management"
    objBalloon.Checkboxes(1).Checked = False
    objBalloon.Checkboxes(2).Checked = False

    objBalloon.Show

    If objBalloon.Checkboxes(1).Checked = True Then

        'User is part of Accounting Department

    End If

    If objBalloon.Checkboxes(2).Checked = True Then

        'User is (also) part of Management Department

    End If

End Sub
```

Modeless Balloons

Modeless balloons are ones that do not force the user to deal with them before doing anything else. Code execution and other Word functions are all completely available when a modeless balloon is visible. The behavior of these balloons prevents the regular method of calling Show and retrieving the result from working. A special way of handling modeless balloons is available, using the Callback property of the balloon to specify a routine that should be called to handle anything that happens with the balloon. This routine has to have certain parameters, values that will be supplied when the balloon calls it, but can have any name you wish. An example of one of these routines is shown below:

```
Sub DepartmentCallback(objBalloon As Balloon, _
        lngButtonPressed As Long, lngBalloonID As Long)

    If lngButtonPressed = msoBalloonButtonOK Then

        'OK Pressed

    Else
```

```
        Select Case lngButtonPressed

            Case 1
                'Selected Label 1

            Case 2
                'Selected Label 2

            Case 3
                'Selected Label 3

        End Select
    End If

    objBalloon.Close

End Sub
```

It is important that you call `objBalloon.Close` in response to at least one type of button click, or else there will be no way for the balloon to be dismissed. With this particular routine, you would specify it as the `Callback` using code like the following:

```
Public Sub WhichDepartments()

Dim objBalloon As Balloon
Dim objLabels As BalloonLabels

    Assistant.On = True
    Assistant.Visible = True

    Set objBalloon = Assistant.NewBalloon

    objBalloon.Text = "Which one do you belong to?"
    objBalloon.Heading = "Choose Department"
    objBalloon.BalloonType = msoBalloonTypeButtons
    objBalloon.Mode = msoModeModeless
    objBalloon.Button = msoButtonSetOK
    objBalloon.Animation = msoAnimationGetAttentionMajor
    objBalloon.Icon = msoIconAlertQuery

    objBalloon.Callback = "DepartmentCallback"

    objBalloon.Labels.Count = 3
    objBalloon.Labels(1).Text = "Accounting"
    objBalloon.Labels(2).Text = "Management"
    objBalloon.Labels(3).Text = "Human Resources"

    objBalloon.Show

End Sub
```

When specifying the callback routine, remember that it is a string and requires quotes around it, and that if it is part of another module or project you need to specify the complete name of it (as in `"Normal.DepartmentCallback"`).

Summary

The Office Assistant is a powerful alternative to the standard `MsgBox` command and, as it available throughout the Office suite, can be used for all of your programs. The information above details everything you should need to use the Assistant's features, and all of the code is completely functional in the VBA environments of any of the Office applications. Go ahead, have some fun and try something different in your programs by using the Assistant.

Index

Outlook, 273
MAPIAvailable
Application object, properties, 108
Merge method
Document object, methods, 119
Messaging Application Programming Interface
see MAPI
Microsoft Data Link File
ADO, 213
connection strings
constructing, 213
Mid function, 144
module-level scope, 64
monetary values, 43
MouseAvailable
Application object, properties, 108
MouseDown event, 91
parameters, 91
MouseMove event, 92
care in using, 92
MouseUp event, 91
parameters, 91
MoveFirst method
Recordset object, methods, 219
MoveLast method
Recordset object, methods, 219
MoveNext method
record pointer, 221
Recordset object, methods, 219, 221
MovePrevious method
record pointer, 221
Recordset object, methods, 219, 221
MsgBox function, 39, 153, 225
named arguments, 158
multi-dimensional arrays, 50
multiple index sizes, 50
multi-page control, 96
multiple documents
summarising, 169
multiple macros
playing back macros, 24

N

Name
Document object, properties, 117, 143
FileConverter object, properties, 201
forms, properties, 87
Name parameter
GetAddress method, 159
named arguments, 158
NameSpace object
GetDefaultFolder method, 275

GetFolderFromID method, 275
Outlook, 272
PickFolder method, 275
New event
Connection object, creating, 226
Document object, events, 224
Recordset object, creating, 226
New keyword, 52, 211, 217, 262
Normal.dot template, 31

O

Object Browser
ADO, 211
COM objects, 261
Visual Basic Editor, 211, 261
object variables, 46
objects
events, 90
exposed objects, 105
forms, 86
instances, creating, 262
Excel, 268
Office 2000, 266
Outlook, 272
Word, 278
introduction, 38
methods, 38
object model, 105
properties, 38
ODBC, 212
Office 2000
Excel, 265
examples, 267
instances, of objects
creating, 268
macro recorder, 270
objects
instances, creating, 268
opening file, 268
printing file, 269
references, adding, 268
saving file, 268
instances, of objects
creating, 266
macro recorder, 270
objects
instances, creating, 266
Outlook, 265, 271
email, 271
folders, obtaining, 275
instances, of objects
creating, 272
mail messages, sending, 276

TestFindFiles procedure
InputBox function, 180
selecting folders, 180
Text
Range object, properties, 140, 234
text box control, 95
toggle button control, 96
TopLeft alignment, 88
TopRight alignment, 88
Trim function, 181

U

Unload statement, 90
Update method
Recordset object, methods, 220, 222
UpdateRecentAddresses parameter
GetAddress method, 162
UseAutoText parameter
GetAddress method, 159
UserAddress
Application object, properties, 109
UserForm1
default name, 87
UserInitials
Application object, properties, 109
UserName
Application object, properties, 109, 143

V

variable length strings, 44
variables
constants, 56
data types, 41
declaring, 40
definition, 40
procedures
  passing by reference, 61
  passing by value, 61
scope, 64
variable declarations, 65
variants, 47
VBA
constants, 47
data access layer, 209
  databases, 209
Dir function, 170
  parameters, 174
Format function, 253
GetAttr function, 175
InputBox function, 180
InStr function, 144

InStrRev function, 144
introduction, 37
Join function, 146
Left function, 143
Len function, 144
Mid function, 144
MsgBox function, 39, 153, 225
  named arguments, 158
Replace function, 145
Right function, 143
Split function, 146
Trim function, 181
Word, 101
  exposed objects, 105
VBA code
applications, 259
  COM objects, 259
DLLs, 261
  COM objects, 261
invoice, production, 247
macros, 8, 26
VBA development environment, 26
VBA intrinsic controls
check box, 95
combo box, 95
command button, 96
control events, 97
frame, 96
image, 96
label, 95
list box, 95
multi-page, 96
option button, 95
scroll bar, 96
setting properties, 97
spin button, 96
tab strip, 96
text box, 95
toggle button, 96
viruses
macros, 32
Visual Basic Editor, 26
Object Browser, 211, 261
  COM objects, 261
Project Explorer window, 27
Properties window, 28
References dialog, 210, 260
  COM objects, 260
Visual Basic toolbar
macros
  recording, 7
playing back macros, 21

WROX PRESS INC.

Wrox writes books for you. Any suggestions, or ideas
about how you want information given in your
ideal book will be studied by our team.
Your comments are always valued at Wrox.

Free phone in USA 800-USE-WROX
Fax (312) 397 8990

UK Tel. (0121) 687 4100   Fax   (0121) 687 4101

NB. If you post the bounce back card below in the UK, please send it to:
Wrox Press Ltd., Arden House, 1102 Warwick Road, Acocks Green, Birmingham. B27 6BH. UK.

Word 2000 Programmer's Reference

Name _____

Address _____

_____

City _____ State/Region _____

Country _____ Postcode/Zip _____

E-mail _____

Occupation _____

How did you hear about this book?

☐ Book review (name) _____

☐ Advertisement (name) _____

☐ Recommendation _____

☐ Catalog _____

☐ Other _____

Where did you buy this book?

☐ Bookstore (name) _____ City _____

☐ Computer Store (name) _____

☐ Mail Order _____

☐ Other _____

What influenced you in the
purchase of this book?

☐ Cover Design   ☐ Contents   ☐ Other (please specify)

How did you rate the overall
contents of this book?

☐ Excellent   ☐ Good
☐ Average   ☐ Poor

What did you find most useful about this book? _____

What did you find least useful about this book? _____

Please add any additional comments. _____

What other subjects will you buy a computer
book on soon? _____

What is the best computer book you have used this year? _____

*Note: This information will only be used to keep you updated
about new Wrox Press titles and will not be used for any other
purpose or passed to any other third party.*

Check here if you DO NOT want to receive further support for this book. ■

2556

2556

wrox

PROGRAMMER TO PROGRAMMER™

BUSINESS REPLY MAIL

FIRST CLASS MAIL   PERMIT#64   CHICAGO, IL

POSTAGE WILL BE PAID BY ADDRESSEE

WROX PRESS INC.
1512 NORTH FREMONT
SUITE 103
CHICAGO IL 60622-2567